TESTAMENT

TESTAMENT
The Bible and History

JOHN ROMER

MICHAEL O'MARA BOOKS LIMITED

First published in Great Britain by
Michael O'Mara Books Limited
20 Queen Anne Street
London W1N 9FB

Reprinted 1989

British Library Cataloguing in Publication Data

Romer, John
Testament: the Bible and history.
1. Middle East. Places associated with
Bible
I. Title
220.9'1

ISBN 0-948397-12-8 hardback
ISBN 1-85479-005-6 paperback

Design: Martin Bristow
Cartography: M.L. Design
Indexes: Diana LeCore

Typeset by Florencetype Ltd, Kewstoke, Avon
Printed and bound in Spain
by Gráficas Estella, S.A. Navarra

This publication is based on the television series
TESTAMENT, produced for Channel Four
by Antelope Films Ltd

CONTENTS

CONTENTS

LIST OF COLOUR PLATES

LIST OF COLOUR PLATES

LIST OF ILLUSTRATIONS
AND MAPS

For full bibliographical details of the modern works cited below see the Select Bibliography, pages 351–55.

The drawing of the carp used throughout the book is an adaptation of a nineteenth-century Japanese stencil.

LIST OF ILLUSTRATIONS AND MAPS

FOREWORD

The Bible's history, the story of how it was made and how it has been used, is the story of how some of civilization's oldest ideas passed from the ancient East to the modern West. In the course of its journey, the Bible provided the West with a unique sense of universal order and its understanding of God. It also gave the West its particular ambitions, its sense of progress and tension, and something, too, of its discontents. To echo these extraordinary continuities I have used quotations from the King James' Bible of 1611 whose prose is itself deeply embedded inside the English language. When its beautiful language obscures an accurate understanding of the ancient words, however (though, given the state of biblical research in King James's time, this is far less frequent than one might imagine), I have used the plain English of the New English Bible and follow the citation with the letters NEB.

It has been a delight for me to apply methods imbibed in the study of ancient Egypt to the discipline of biblical history. Unlike the calm pastures of ancient Egypt, however, ancient Israel holds within it minefields of politics and prejudice. As a discipline that often seems isolated from the mainstream of historical research it has also developed its own criteria, its own consensus of opinions. Most biblical archaeologists, for example, employ biblical names to distinguish different historical periods, a habit which begs the question of whether or not the Bible can be so freely used as an accurate guide to ancient history.

Much of the Old Testament was compiled over a very wide span of time, and it is common to find in it the names of countries that existed in different periods of history, used side by side. Nowadays, such a liberal use of terminology for places in the Holy Land is fraught with religious and political significance. Some modern Israeli placenames, for example, employ biblical names whose real locations remain unknown to science. Others mask older Arabic names by which the site had long been known in the West. I have generally opted for the usages most familiar to Western readers.

I have also employed that splendid Jacobean abstraction 'Jehovah' to identify the god of the Old Testament Israelites rather than the word *Jahweh*, which is currently favoured by most biblical scholars. I trust that the term will not act as a vehicle by which modern pieties are projected back into ancient ages which never knew such things. My concern is not one of faith, to assert a belief or disbelief in God, but to recreate something of what ancient people themselves perceived; what they would have understood by the word. Similarly, my use of capitals and lower case for the term 'god' is not founded in disrespect. In the ancient world, Jehovah's world, the term god was a general one; there were many gods in the ancient East, as Jehovah himself is perfectly aware. It was Judaism and Christianity that awarded this particular god an upper case, and its accompanying titles; when I have used them, it is to identify the god whom those faiths have recognized and worshipped. Similarly, I use the term Christ (= 'the anointed one' = the *Messiah*) to identify a specific image of Jesus of Nazareth employed in faith and art. The West did not award this tremendous title to a carpenter who lived in Roman Palestine, but to someone who, Christendom affirmed, is the Son of God.

John Romer
Aiola, Tuscany, June 1988

Chapter One
GENESIS

Introduction: Visiting Abraham

Early in 1862, escaping a grey spring and the fresh grief of the Windsor Court after the death of his father Prince Albert, the Prince of Wales embarked upon a tour to Egypt and the Holy Land, 'the wish' his tutor recorded, 'of the lamented Prince Consort'. For many years, Prince Albert had worked hard, but with little effect, to transform his eldest son into his own likeness, but it was the Princess Royal who had inherited her father's cast of mind. 'Duty, duty, duty, dearest brother', she had cabled the Prince of Wales as his party journeyed its way through the East, advice that the Prince had long borne with the patience of a saint, if with a genuine air of puzzlement.

The Prince's party was a mixed bag gathered together by General Bruce, who died of exhaustion shortly after their return to England. It included the Prince's two hunting companions, Meade and Keppel (Keppel's wife later became the Prince's favourite mistress); assorted equerries and servants; a photographer to memorialize them, a taxidermist to stuff their game and an eminent divine, Dean Stanley, to tend to their souls. 'There is only one man in Oxford to whom I would entrust Bertie' Prince Albert had once declared, 'and that is Dean Stanley', and he it was who now organized the trip's itinerary. Like Abraham they went down into Egypt, like Joseph they left it and all the while the Dean sermonized them; at Nazareth on Good Friday; by Lake Tiberias on Easter Day and on the road to Damascus on the day of St Paul's conversion.

As the Prince, Meade and Keppel had blazed away at Nile crocodiles and game birds from the royal yacht, with the taxidermist 'up to his elbows in doves and partridges' and the photographer, Francis Bedford snapping away 'enduring gratefully every hint that was given him', Dean Stanley prepared his sermons. At Thebes in Upper Egypt, he held forth in the Great Hypostyle Hall of the Temple of Karnak, taking as his theme Psalm 80:8 'Thou hast brought a vine out of Egypt'; 'Another tumbledown old temple', the Prince had observed, 'like those theatres of somebody or other in Rome with only a stone or two left'. Bedford recorded the service in the Great Hypostyle Hall, the Dean, bird-like in white flannels, grey jacket and a pith helmet, the young Prince standing with Keppel and Meade, a little apart from the rest, his face lost in the heavy shadow of a column. Patiently his mentors had directed the young man's unsteady gaze toward the old stones of Egypt. 'What steadfast nobility', the Dean declared as he first caught sight of the Giza Pyramids 'almost as Abraham himself' and set off with the others to ascend steadfastly to their summit. The

Prince stayed behind, however, and they later found the young man 'sitting in front of his tent, smoking and reading *East Lynne*'.

Unlike the young Prince, Dean Stanley was enraptured by the landscapes of history, especially the sites of battles, murders and burials. At Westminster Abbey he had personally supervised the opening of the royal graves; now, on their ride through Palestine, a unique adventure loomed; a visit to the temple turned-synagogue turned-church turned-mosque at Hebron that held, according to traditional Jewish, Christian and Muslim beliefs, the sepulchres of the Bible's Patriarchs, of Abraham and all his family – and even, legend had it, of Adam and Eve whose flesh and bones God had squeezed from the red dust of the hill on which the Mosque of Hebron stands.

Monday 7 April 1862 saw Hebron occupied by regiments of Turkish infantry; the infidel Prince had come to visit a holy building where no Christian had trodden for 500 years, and the Pasha's officers were worried that an outraged Muslim would try and kill the Englishmen. Slowly the royal party filed down through lines of red-uniformed soldiers, then stepped up the polished steps of the mosque where the chief guardian and his attendants were waiting. 'The Prince of any other nation would have passed over my dead body rather than enter here', said the old Imam in courteous if reluctant welcome 'but to the eldest son of England's Queen we are willing to accord even this privilege'.

In their stockinged feet, breathing lightly in the shadowed air, the party moved silently into the mosque, down long decorated corridors into a modest white-washed room filled with two rows of low-domed sepulchres, each one the tomb of a biblical Patriarch or his wife. The guardians regretted that it was not possible for the foreigners to examine the sepulchres of the women who, in death, were still subject to the rules of the harem. Neither could they visit the sepulchre of Isaac, Abraham's son, for, as it was well known, he had a jealous and dangerous soul; why, even the terrible Ibrahim Pasha of Egypt, the conqueror of Palestine, had been driven speechless from his presence. After a minute, the Dean asked if he could walk inside the railing which, in the Turkish manner, shut off the tomb of Abraham. A great groan went up from the Muslims as the Englishman stepped over the tomb's threshold, which flashed with embroideries and Damascus silks as the gate squeaked open. 'O friend of God, forgive this intrusion', said the guardians to their saint.

At one end of the mosque there was a small circular aperture in the floor, the single opening to the burial vault beneath, which allowed the air, the very atmosphere that surrounded the dead Patriarchs, to rise and fill the room above with its holiness. Slowly, Dean Stanley fitted his arm down into the dark slot, his fingers poised to touch the people of the Book of Genesis. Below him, perhaps, in the darkness lay Abraham, who, the Book of Genesis relates, bought this Cave of Machpelah for 400 shekels, from Ephron the Hittite

(Genesis 23:8–16); and Abraham's descendents too, Joseph and Jacob, still wrapped in their Egyptian burial linens. The churchman's hand moved gently in the cool air, his grey-jacketed arm reaching out toward the fathers of his faith. Dean Stanley's generation was perhaps the last whose hands and minds could reach out toward the ancient Patriarchs in such a simple and uncomplicated gesture of belief.

Bible Beginning

In the beginning God created the heaven and the earth. And the earth was without form, and void; and darkness was upon the face of the deep. And the Spirit of God moved upon the face of the waters. And God said, Let there be light . . .

(Genesis 1:1–3)

As you read the Bible's opening lines you stand alone with God as he builds the world; the great stage on which all the stories of the Bible will be set. Where and when did Genesis have its beginnings? There is no record of its writing but there are many clues inside the book itself. The Bible tells us that Adam and Eve, the first people, had lived in a walled garden, that their children were herdsmen and hunters and founded the first cities, that their descendants founded the nations of the earth. Their story fills the first ten chapters of the Book of Genesis providing a pedigree for Abraham and his family, the Patriarchs of ancient Israel whose kingdoms are the subject, indeed, the hero of the Old Testament. Abraham and his family are the first biblical characters whose lives, whose manners and customs are described in any detail in the Bible; the first people of the Bible whose culture is described sufficiently to place it into profane history. Abraham first appears living in a city called 'Ur of the Chaldees' and there, it is said, he lived in his own country and among his own kinsmen (Genesis 12:1). Chaldea is a biblical term for Mesopotamia, that most ancient region that lay between two rivers, the Tigris and the Euphrates, and ran from the foothills of eastern Turkey and north Iraq right down to the Persian Gulf. This biblical identification of Abraham's home is confirmed by the landscapes in the first stories of the Book of Genesis which are set in the Near East amid deserts, pastures, rivers and dusty roads.

And Genesis' people too, nomads and town dwellers alike, are those of the ancient east. Nowadays, as you read the Book of Genesis it may seem to be set in a strange and mythic world, but in its day it was real enough and, in the straightforward manner of ancient scribes, Genesis itself tells us its geography. Abraham, it tells us, was born in Chaldea and travelled to Egypt, a route that describes the entire arc of the ancient Near East. If we are to understand the Book of Genesis, its motives and its authors, it is a route that we too must follow. It is a world, indeed, that archaeology has already described for us in great detail; a world of tents, temples and dark cities, of olives and corn, brick, bronze and gold. In ancient times when the barriers between things human and those divine seemed lower than they do today, these lands held gardens like Eden and Towers of Babel, princes, pharaohs and stone temples which in their darkness held gods with many of the manners of Abraham's God, Jehovah. Find Abraham in ancient history and you will have found the beginnings of the Bible and a large part of the root of Western civilization. And you will also have found the world of the people who *made* the Bible's stories of Creation, of the Flood and Noah's Ark and all the rest of Genesis. But where does one begin?

For the scribes who wrote the Book of Genesis, time was counted not in years but in generations, in lists of ancestors; a common ancient system that traces paternity, inheritance and alliances back to a single patriarch, a single beginning. So the genealogies of the Book of Genesis are the first links in a chain that stretches right through the Old Testament, from Adam to the kings of Israel. Biblical historians, however, require more than these amiable demonstrations of bloodline and inheritance for an account of history; they want dates. And many of these Bible scholars have specific aims in their work. Some, for example, are looking for Abraham to demonstrate the 'truth' of their Bible and their faith. Many begin from the assumption that the Abraham of the Bible once lived, that the Book of Genesis is a sort of ethnic history book and that archaeological discoveries can be fitted into its tales willy-nilly. Often, you feel that, in all innocence, the 'evidence' is being heavily manipulated. To hold conviction then, the search for Abraham must begin in a less literal-minded manner; by trying to locate not Abraham but his way of life inside the ancient world. Where then might we appropriately begin?

The inhabitants of the Turkish city of Urfa, in ancient times a part of northern Mesopotamia, believe that their city is the Bible's 'Ur of the Chaldees' from which Abraham began his wanderings. Muslims believe that the biblical Abraham was a prophet, the first man to recognize that one God alone had made the universe. At Urfa, local tradition holds that Abraham was thrown into a fiery furnace by wicked Nimrud, King of Chaldea after he had attacked the idols of the gods of the sun and the moon. Abraham's trial, it is said, had taken place in Nimrud's palace, the wicked king ordering him to be tied between two huge pillars in the central hall. The modern city of Urfa holds in it a sacred landscape; a cave where Abraham was born; two pillars standing silhouetted on the ancient citadel above the town; and two springs that feed two pools filled with fine fat fish; Nimrud's firebrands which, tradition tells us, were turned to gleaming carp when his executioners tried to burn the prophet. Today, no one dares to catch or eat the sacred fish.

So it has been for many years. A hundred years ago an English missionary saw some of Urfa's Christian community fishing the sacred streams at dead of night and cooking their catch, discreetly, in a white wine sauce. Fifteen hundred years earlier, a Christian pilgrim, the Lady Egeria, had written that she had never seen fish of 'such size, so gleaming and succulent'. While Egeria stayed at Urfa, the Bishop had also shown her Abraham's house and the very well where, she was told, Abraham's grandson Jacob had first met Rachel. The Christians of Urfa were a most ancient community. They counted themselves the subjects of the first Christian Kingdom in the world; Jesus himself, they believed, had corresponded with their king. Egeria tell us that Jesus' letter to King Abgar V was still to be seen at the Bishop's Palace.

But the succulent carp of Urfa had been swimming in their sacred pools for thousands of years before the rise of either Christianity or Islam. Most ancient, pagan, Mesopotamian Urfa had worshipped gods of the sun and moon and stars, a faith that survived in the surrounding countryside until the Middle Ages, when the Crusaders found a remnant priesthood still at their rituals in ancient ruined temples. The cult had come to Urfa and its neighbouring cities from southern Mesopotamia. In those days several cities had sacred pools like those at Urfa; some of them with stone altars that stood out of the water and the priests who would swim to their daily devotions were surrounded, it is said, by leaping fish, by sacred fish, so tame that they would come to you if you called their names. One especially celebrated carp, an ancient author says, carried a golden jewel upon its upper fin.

Nowadays, Abraham's carp are a local delight, their green pools the focus for the city's evening promenade. Legends have attached themselves to the fish as they have done to the ravens of the Tower of London. Urfa's city council bears the heavy cost of the weekly cleansing of the pools; licensed street vendors sell bags of crumbs and lentils with which to feed the fish. No one in Urfa would dream of killing the carp for it is said that they are filled with an instant, deadly, paralysing poison, and, anyway, a local law forbids it. Here then, we move inside a world where belief is part of a continuum and where different faiths are merely its decoration. And there is much of this in the Book of Genesis, in the world of Abraham. For that too was a world where sacredness was hard reality and pragmatism had nothing like such credibility. And this is a world largely lost to us; a world that was neither stupid nor especially gullible; a world with no science or morality outside of faith, a world where everyone could sense the power of holiness that underlaid the universe. A world in which the problem was not whether or not the gods existed, for everyone could see quite clearly that they did, but what their personalities and names were. Along with the production of food, such investigations took all the effort of the ancient world; priests at their rituals; the poets with their hymns and poetry; the artists and architects in their sculptures, paintings and temples. The Bible is simply a literary continuation of these same researches; a further definition of sacredness and deity.

Swimming on, through faith after faith, Urfa's sacred fish show how difficult it is to fix a single date in the continuum of sacredness. And the Book of Genesis, with its lively faith and family stories, is exactly the same. Nonetheless, today, both Urfa's carp and Adam and Eve require a pedigree: we want to know where they came from: 'that it has always been so' is simply not sufficient for us any more. Unlike the Book of Genesis, we move in modern time. The time of the Book of Genesis and its story of Creation, the time of Abraham and his family is to be found inside the written records of the ancient world.

Abraham in his Time

It is a depressing, if perhaps inevitable, fact that the first words that men ever wrote were entries in a ledger: lists of goods stored in a Mesopotamian temple recorded in pictographic abstractions impressed onto shiny pillows of clay with a wedge-shaped stick. This system of writing called cuneiform was invented, so archaeologists have found, about 3300 BC in southern Mesopotamia, then spread quickly through the merchant cities of the ancient East. And with it went many of the sophistications of the southern cities. For, as well as recording accounts, receipts and contracts these little tablets also carried with them notions of civil law, the systems and order of Mesopotamian science and literature – a scale of time in years and minutes, numbering systems in units of sixty, which provided a 360 degree circle and the twelve divisions of the zodiac. And the Mesopotamian gods also travelled with these tablets; their names and their stories, their rites and rituals permeated the East. Like Abraham, all this came from ancient Mesopotamia. Only Egypt, set in its quiet warm valley, went complacently upon its own way, transforming the Mesopotamian invention of writing into its own laboriously heraldic hieroglyphic script. Though Egypt's dignified skills always impressed the rest of the ancient world they usually prompted only lumpish imitations. Mesopotamian culture, on the other hand, was closer to the daily experience of most other ancient eastern peoples and its culture had a correspondingly greater impact on them. It is fitting, then, that Abraham begins his biblical journeyings in ancient Mesopotamia.

The Bible tells us that Abraham travelled from Ur of the Chaldees to a city called Haran, and Haran, the cuneiform tablets tell us, stood close by ancient Urfa. Nowadays it is a field of ruins, a huge bare mound standing by a river ford in the centre of a red-earth plain; this is the biblical 'Padan-Aram', the fields of Haran (see Plate 1) (Genesis 25:20). The city of Haran – its very name means 'crossroads' – guarded ancient trade routes. Five hundred miles to the south and east down the Tigris and Euphrates rivers was the ancient Mesopotamian heartland, the Land of Sumer, from where cuneiform writing had come. Sumer's most powerful city states are listed in the Book of Genesis; 'Babel, Erech and Accad in the Land of Shinar' (Genesis 10:10): the cities of Babylon, Uruk and Akkad, in the Land of Sumer. These southern cities not only traded north to Haran and beyond but south and east as well, maintaining colonies on islands in the Persian Gulf and trading, too, along the roads that ran to India and China. So ivories and lapis lazuli, precious stones, exotic perfumes and woods were all traded through the southern cities to Haran and beyond. And in return Sumer imported scarce metals and building stone. Massive cedar logs from the Lebanon were floated down to Sumer on the two great rivers, as an ancient scribe wrote, 'like snakes upon the stream'. Riverside cities had vast wharves and well-organized police and customs authorities. And there were fortified hostels for the merchant caravans, too, and military patrols guarding the rivers and the trade routes. Northern Mesopotamian cities like Mari, Nuzi and Haran were as rich as Sumer and traded in an enormous range of goods; in vintage wines, in honey and rare oils, in exotic cloths, dyed, perhaps, in Cypriot or Syrian *teinteries*. And there was a constant demand from Sumer for fine foods, for pickled locusts, truffles and smoked fish roe. In the winter, game from the northern mountains was packed in ice and snow and sent to the southern cities.

North of Haran over the mountains, high on the cold plain, lay the city states of Anatolia, the trading link between Mesopotamia and Europe. South and west of Haran, along the roads that led down into Egypt, lay the trading cities of Syria and Canaan. By 2600 BC, one of these cities, Ebla, was raiding down the Euphrates deep into southern Mesopotamia; in their turn most of these more northerly cities were sacked by southern armies. Stacks of Cretan jars excavated in a Syrian warehouse show one of the many routes between Mesopotamia and the Mediterranean: Mesopotamian and Greek myths, and Bible stories too, passed back and forth down these ancient trading routes; the same routes down which Abraham and his herds travel in the Book of Genesis: Ur, Haran, Canaan and into Egypt.

This great arc of trade, the huge highway from Sumer through Syria and Canaan into Egypt, was the only practical route for both merchants and nomads like Abraham, whose donkeys and sheep could not cross the central deserts of Syria and Arabia. Camel caravans which travel for long distances without water were not widely used in the ancient world until a few centuries before Jesus' time and as soon as they were introduced these most ancient trade routes that skirted the desert went out of use and brand new cities like Palmyra and Petra grew up at the oases of the new desert highways. Straight away, these changing patterns of ancient trade tell us something interesting about the Book of Genesis. For unless we assume that Abraham and his family actually lived in this later period of ancient history when camels were in common use – and the ancient trade routes that Abraham follows in the Book of Genesis strongly suggest otherwise – then the common biblical descriptions of their expert use and herding of camels must have been added to a body of older stories at a later date, like so much else in the Book of Genesis: 'Ur of the Chaldees', for example, is another of these later interpolations, for the term Chaldea was only introduced in this later period of ancient history.

Of the more ancient East however, the East of Abraham's journeyings, of Mesopotamia and Canaan and Egypt and the great arc of trade that went along the rivers and around the deserts' edges, there is an embarrassment of information: hundreds upon hundreds of thousands of contemporary documents, cuneiform texts dug by archaeologists from the ruins of the ancient cities. And large numbers of them hold names and customs that we also know of from the Book of Genesis, as this text, written in the city of Mari some nineteen centuries before Christ, clearly shows: 'To my Lord; so says Bannum your servant; Yesterday I left Mari and spent the night at Zuruban. All the Benjaminites of the Terka district raised fire signals in response and so far I have not understood the meaning of these signals ... let the guard of the city of Mari be strengthened ...'

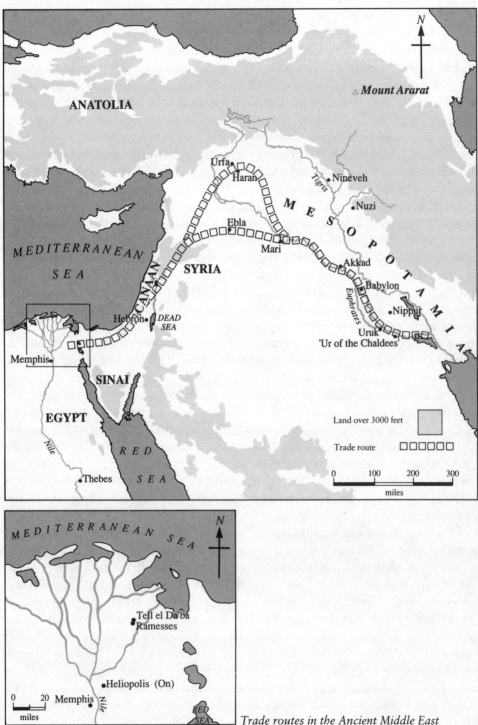

Trade routes in the Ancient Middle East

This tribe that was causing Bannum such apprehension, the Benjaminites – the name literally means 'the sons of the right hand' or 'of the south' – echoes the name of the Israelite tribe of Benjamin, the descendants of Abraham's great-grandson. And along with these Benjaminites, the cuneiform texts hold a great number of other biblical names, both of the Patriarchs themselves and of the people whom they meet in the Book of Genesis. The names of Abraham, of Isaac, of Jacob and even Israel are all present in these ancient texts; but then, such names were as common then as they are upon the headstones in a Quaker churchyard – and they will supply us with similarly misleading evidence as to the ethnic origins of their owners, for these Old Testament names were used right through the ancient world.

Many of the ancient texts call nomads like the Benjaminites the *Habiru*, a term often employed as 'peasant' or 'gipsy' is sometimes used today; as much in abuse as in description. Not surprisingly, a scholarly battle has long raged around this word *Habiru* which, linguistically, is the same as the biblical word *Hebrew*. Like so many Old Testament names, the term was used throughout the ancient east: in a text dating to about 1500 BC, for example, a Syrian prince tells us that he spent six years living rough with the *Habiru* when he was a young man. Usually references to the *Habiru* imply that they were considered to be a perennial menace that roamed the trade routes from Sumer down to Egypt. A popular question then is were these *Habiru* the Bible's ancient Hebrews, the 'sons of Abraham'? In short, it must seem that they were not. Indeed, the very question, confusing as it does race and culture, is part of a peculiarly modern obsession. The ancient use of the word *Habiru* describes a culture, a social group. As the ancient texts make quite clear, these *Habiru* were people who moved back and forth down the trade routes between the ancient cities, sometimes settling, sometimes moving. In *this* sense, then, Abraham and his family as they appear in the Book of Genesis may certainly claim the title *Habiru*, though neither they nor their descendants would have been the exclusive bearers of it.

At all events, during the lifetime of Bannum of Mari, at least, it seems that it was the Benjaminites who were considered threatening enough to be carefully watched on their journey south. At the city of Haran, a text tells us that 'Asditakim and the Kings of Zalmakum on the one hand, and the Sakaku and the elders of the Benjaminites on the other, have made a treaty in the Temple of the Moon'. Here, like Genesis' Patriarchs, the Benjaminites move by treaty rather than the sword. Quite often, so the tablets tell us, the relationship between the city dwellers and the nomads was based upon respect and friendship rather than suspicion. Texts tell of markets where the nomads exchanged their produce; skins, cheeses and meat and the like for the products of city craftsmen. Fragments of the nomad vocabulary, words for hills and valleys, for example, entered the language of the cities while some of the city's gods, like Dagon, a god of grain, and Ada, a god of storm were adopted by the nomads and travelled with them from Sumer into Canaan and even into Egypt. The texts also tell us, that many city dwellers took to the road, just like Abraham in Genesis, and sometimes they re-settled in other towns, farming or herding on nearby pastures like Abraham in Canaan. With a vivacity and an intimacy that no cuneiform text possesses, Genesis (23:3–17) gives a description of Abraham the traveller engaged in an activity commonly described in cuneiform legal texts; bargaining for a plot of land 'at the town gate', the usual place for such negotiations on market day. It is tempting to see the scribes sitting there with their fresh clay tablets waiting to draw up the records of such dealings, just as their modern successors sit with their typewriters outside eastern courthouses today. Many of the ancient archives that held these legal contracts have been found in storerooms by the city gates (see Plate 2). (Genesis' story of Abraham's purchase of his Hebron burial cave holds accuracy in its detail. Similarly, the moving story of Jacob, Abraham's grandson, stealing Esau's blessing (Genesis 27ff.), is partly paralleled and given a formal legal context in a cuneiform text written about 1500 BC at the city of Nuzi east of Haran. 'My father Huya was ill and lay in bed: then my father seized my hand and said to me, that my other son being older has acquired wives but you have not acquired a wife, so I give you Sululi-Ishtar as your wife . . .' The text goes on to tell how the wishes of the dying man were contested but ends by asserting that, just as the biblical Patriarch's family believed, the words spoken by the head of a family on his deathbed were considered to be the legal equivalent of a written testament. (Another text, also from Nuzi, even refers to a man selling his birthright, as Esau does in the Book of Genesis, though Tupkitilla of Nuzi sold *his* inheritance, an orchard, not for Esau's biblical 'mess of pottage' (Genesis 25:29ff.), but for three sheep.)

This correspondence, this common framework of law and custom in the Book of Genesis and the cuneiform texts is very deep. The Old Testament's commandments and covenants, their structures and their very subject matter, are often close to the great legal codes of Sumer, the oldest surviving written law codes in the world. And just as Moses received his Law from Jehovah, his God, at the top of a mountain, so King Hammurabi of Babylon is shown upon his famous law stela of the eighteenth century BC, receiving his laws from his god at the top of a ziggurat, the man-made temple-mountains of the Mesopotamian plains.

The evidence, then, is overwhelming: a great part of the world in which the Book of Genesis is set is that same world which is documented in such careful detail in the texts of ancient Mesopotamia. You might imagine, then, that once this link had been so thoroughly established, it would be very simple to place Abraham and all his family into history and then to find the age in which the oldest Bible stories received their inspiration. But this is very difficult. The parameters of these ways of life are very broad. The ancient trade routes along which Abraham travels in the Book of Genesis are at least 10,000 years old and at the other end of this timescale many of the names and customs described in the Book of Genesis and in the ancient cuneiform texts survive in the East down until today.

More precisely, however, most of these cuneiform texts that parallel these biblical names and stories can be dated within the period of 1850–500 BC. However, the discovery in the 1960s of many more texts, in the archives of the Syrian city of Ebla, showing many further correspondences with the Book of Genesis, has pushed back these commonly accepted dates some seven hundred years and has also served to remind us that these cuneiform concordances depend not only upon what chance has preserved for us from the past but also upon what archaeologists have so far chanced to find. Presently the best that may be said of Abraham and his family is that, if, as the Book of Genesis asserts, the Patriarchs once had real existence on this earth, then they must have lived before the first-known record of Israel in Canaan – and presently, that is before 1207 BC, according to the ancient Egyptian record. Abraham *may* have lived somewhere in the 1000-year period before that date, though no trace of him or his family has ever been found.

In most other religions, of course, the Patriarchs, the forefathers, the walkers with God, are themselves gods or, at least, demi-gods. But Abraham's Jehovah was a jealous God who allows 'no other God but me' and generations of ancient editors have worked upon the text to ensure that Genesis' heroes never appear to be more than mortal. So these biblical Patriarchs have come down to us as vigorous flesh and blood. And this insistence upon mortality, upon humanity, has given Genesis a priceless dividend. Of all the world's creation stories only the Bible's first people have this quality, an eerie hovering between the myth and reality that has given the Bible its ambiguity, its unique tension. There is a very great deal in these stories of Abraham and his family that rings true; their journeys through the ancient world, with their tents, their donkeys and their herds. Amid all the angels and miracles there is an ordinariness, a banality, an overwhelming sense of archaeological and anthropological reality. Yet like the sacred fish in Urfa's pools, Abraham is truly part of that continuum of faith and custom. And if you try to pin these Patriarchs down more precisely in time the whole family will quietly pack their tents and set off along the old trade routes, over horizons that stretch back thousands upon thousands of years.

Archaeology as Myth

In spite of Abraham's elusiveness, there is still a general belief that archaeology has 'proved' many of Genesis' sacred stories. Christians especially have powerful precedent to try to place the Patriarchs inside Western time: our very calendar begins its counting from the year that Christ the Son of God came down to earth and lived in time inside the ancient East. Unlike Jesus, however, Abraham and his family appear to have been authenticated by new, scientific, myths: has not great 'Ur of the Chaldees', Abraham's native city, been mapped by modern archaeologists, were not the very silts of Noah's Flood recovered in scientific excavations in that same place? Today, no Christian pilgrims visit Turkish Urfa in the belief that they will tread upon the ground on which Abraham once walked. Haran, they have sensibly pointed out, is only a Sunday walk away, and Abraham's heroic emigration was surely longer than that! But, then, opinion about the location of Abraham's city has been divided for a very long time. Some people, for example, held that the ancient Sumerian city of Ur-uk was Abraham's Ur; others favoured another Mesopotamian mound called *Tell el Mukkayer*, the 'Hill of Pitch', so named because of the quantities of bitumen once used as cement, that sparkled on its slopes. Alternatively it has also been suggested that the word 'Ur' is simply an ancient Mesopotamian term for 'town'. Yet in the 1930s virtually all this discussion was stopped: for *Tell el Mukkayer*, science announced to the world, was indeed Abraham's Ur; Leonard Woolley, the brilliant archaeologist had excavated the site and produced groundplans of a city of temples and houses which, he said, were 'of the time of Abraham'. At this same time, Woolley fixed his 'Ur of the Chaldees' in the public mind by excavating a golden treasure: for a while *Tell el Mukkayer* was as famous as Tutankhamun's tomb. And that is how this myth of Ur was made.

Archaeology in Mesopotamia is usually a dull and thankless task and not one often accompanied by the discovery of such buried treasures. Early in his career, Woolley had noted the 'want of pence that vexes public institutions' and consequently developed a grand style of publicizing his excavations with a stream of telegrams, newspaper articles and books that maintained popular interest and financial support for his expeditions throughout his life. Woolley also believed that it was part of his work to 'bring the Bible to life', and he had an imagination that easily peopled the dust of his excavations with its ancient inhabitants. Like many archaeologists of his generation, Woolley had first studied theology. The son of a Surrey clergyman, he was fond of quoting passages of the Old Testament to his fellow workers. Right from the first days at *Tell el Mukkayer* he never doubted that it had been Abraham's city, and nothing he found there challenged his opinion. He published the result of the excavations in splendid volumes entitled *Ur of the Chaldees*, though he well knew that the term Chaldea had no meaning for the Mesopotamians who had built the succession of ancient cities that he had excavated.

Woolley had designated one of these cities as being 'of the time of Abraham' by linking the most up-to-date estimates of the dates of Abraham's lifetime (in the 1920s this was thought to be about 1800 BC) with his own estimates of the age of the archaeological material from *Tell el Mukkayer*. Both these dates still lack proof. But simply by labelling some of his archaeological plans 'houses from the time of Abraham' Woolley had unwittingly created a circular system of proof: Abraham lived around 1800 BC because the city in which he had lived (which had been scientifically excavated!) dated from this same period. Thus science creates its own myths.

Abraham's city or not – indeed there are many indications that *Tell el Mukkayer* was once called Ur – Woolley had certainly excavated one of the most vital centres of Sumerian civilization, a succession of cities built like the rings of a tree around a sacred compound established at the same time as the great pyramids of Egypt. Woolley also excavated the better part of this central enclosure, uncovering a beautifully preserved Mesopotamian pyramid called a ziggurat, and the sensational cemetery that was filled with golden tombs. Here lay princes and princesses; all buried with their musicians, servants and concubines lying where poison had felled them some 5000 years before. These burials were not like Tutankhamun's tomb in Egypt, rock rooms all neatly stacked with treasure. At *Tell el Mukkayer* everything, corpses and treasures alike, were squashed flat under the weight of earth. Only gold and stone remained intact; bone, wood, leather, silver, all the perishable goods, were in deep decay. With amazing ingenuity and method Woolley excavated nearly 2000 burials and resurrected their fragile contents. Not only did he recover one of archaeology's greatest treasures but in his books he placed these images of neglected Mesopotamia firmly in the public mind. Archaeologists have a lot to thank Woolley for, indeed, he was knighted for his services to the profession. Today when archaeologists talk of 'Ur', they refer to Woolley's cities at *Tell el Mukkayer*; but the ghost of Abraham haunts them still.

Yet even as Woolley announced the uncovering of the gold tombs, the discovery was upstaged by another. In a huge trench that he had excavated under the 'Deathpit', as he cannily dubbed the largest of the gold tombs, deep down amid the strata of more ancient cities, he found a great blank band of natural river silt; the debris of a vast destroying flood. And from the very first, Woolley believed that this was the Flood in the Book of Genesis. These ancient silts, Woolley now telegraphed to the world's press, had been dropped by the very waters on which Noah's Ark had sailed! And so it was that all the gold of Ur, the jewels, the harps and helmets all glistening amid the powdered bones of ancient princes, were yet submerged by that most common of all archaeological sensations; proving the Bible to be 'true'. And, indeed, it seems true that the Bible's story of the flood had had its origins in the terrible ancient floods of Mesopotamia when the Tigris and Euphrates rivers overflowed their banks. Silty strata of many different dates have become a fairly common archaeological find in Mesopotamia since Woolley's day. Such all-enveloping deluges never occurred in Abraham's other countries, certainly not in the hills of Canaan nor in the quiet valley of Egypt where the annual inundation was the means of life. But it is not the mere fact of a flood that gives Genesis' tale of Noah and his Ark its fascination; the significance lies in the story that has been cast around it.

Nowadays, the attraction of such tales is sometimes said to lie in the 'collective unconscious', a hypothetical memory bank of shared human experience. Linking Genesis' Flood to such memories, some anthropologists have proposed that this image of a universal inundation begins in the amniotic waters that surround a foetus in its mother's womb, or the sensations of a baby's involuntary urination. But ancient stories like that of the Flood were not written as literature designed to recapture such 'elemental experiences' but as a practical method of giving order and meaning to lives lived at the mercy of a capricious environment. It was a kind of natural science. By turning random catastrophes into an ordered story, into a dialogue between gods and people (between Jehovah and Noah, for example), a sort of environmental history was established that gave some purpose and even a humanity to apparently random happenings that seemed to mock man and his works.

Retold compulsively, in words and pictures, century after century, such ancient tales still hold their fascination, even in the modern West. And so successful in its day, was this south Mesopotamian story of a world-destroying flood and a hero riding its waves, that it became well-known throughout the ancient world. Presently, the oldest-known version of the tale is on a cuneiform tablet excavated from the ruins of the south Mesopotamian city of Nippur, and this dates from about 1600 BC. But the story is far more ancient than that, for this flood story is but a single episode of the long poem known as 'The Epic of Gilgamesh' and other fragments of the poem that exist are at least a thousand years older. Certainly in the second millennium BC this ancient epic was to be found in many libraries of the East. Fragments of it have been found in the ruins of the city states of Syria and Turkey, the archives of an Egyptian palace and, of a slightly later date, in the city fortress of Megiddo in Canaan.

This story of the Flood and its hero travelled further afield with the merchant ships and trading caravans of Mesopotamia. Just as at *Tell el Mukkayer* Woolley found stone brooches cut in the shape of a peacock imported from Persian Baluchistan, so in Persia, at the other end of this trade route, there is an ancient story telling of a hero named Yima who built a great fortress to protect the world's animals against a dreadful flood. And just as small polished gem-stones traded from northern India have been found in several Mesopotamian cities, so there is an Indian hero, too, who builds an ark against the flood which is towed through the waves by a gigantic fish! From India and Persia this same story went out further, even to China and the Far East.

A little later in history the West too had its flood stories, brought along those same ancient trade routes. In ancient Greece, great Zeus plays the god who sends the flood, Deukalion, the son of Prometheus is the hero, Parnassus the mountain on which the hero's boat comes to rest. Echoing a Persian priest, the classical historian Flavius Josephus in his *History of the Jews* gave the West its first taste of that still-flourishing tale of a ruined boat lying upon Mount Ararat; 'it is said that there is still a part of this ship in Armenia . . . and that some people carry off pieces of the bitumin which they take away and use chiefly as amulets for the averting of mischiefs'.

That all of these flood stories had a common origin in Mesopotamia and were not derived from the commonly shared experiences, conscious or un-conscious, of people who live by dangerous rivers, is shown by the fact that outside these ancient cultures that were connected by trade, other riverside societies made quite different flood stories, never once repeating *this* particular tale of a flood and a man and a boat. Now, unless Genesis' Flood story is older yet than all of these other stories from the ancient world, then its beginnings, like Abraham's, are to be found in Mesopotamia. Indeed, the exact regional version that the compilers of the Book of Genesis used for their story of Noah has been found written in Hurrian, the language of a tribe which travelled into the ancient East from north India around 1600 BC. For the Hurrian version of the flood story holds the very roots of Noah's name in it, its hero called

Nahmizuli bears the Hebrew word for Noah, *Nhm*, in its first three letters. And the geography of the Hurrian Flood story is also that of the Book of Genesis; just like Noah's, Nahmizuli's ark comes to rest on Mount Ararat, and this lay in the heartland of the ancient Hurrian Empire.

Like the sacred carp of Urfa, the story of the Flood survives the ancient faith that bore it, but it swims on still with its ancient *purposes* intact; an ancient natural science that the Bible has taken over from Mesopotamia along with many other stories. Just as there are ten generations between Genesis' Adam and Noah, so there were also ten generations of kings who ruled before the most ancient Mesopotamian flood – a pattern the Bible again repeats in its lists of the ten generations of Patriarchs between Noah and Abraham. But beyond these simple, inherited patterns of history, even beyond the sense of form the story promises to give to random misadventure, there is another purpose in the tale and this lies at its heart. For at the end of Noah's story there is a compact made between him and Jehovah that guarantees man's continued existence upon the earth; a covenant that shows that humankind is not helpless, that it will survive. This is the straw for mankind that the scribes of Genesis clutch to their bosom, the notion of a contract that states that man also has rights alongside the infinite power of God.

And this is a part of a carefully weighed-out balance between man and God, a balance which many of the Book of Genesis first stories carefully ponder and define. The astonishing tale of the giants and the daughters of men, (Genesis 6: 1–4) for example, hints of ages when deity and mankind were on more familiar terms. And Genesis' story of the Tower of Babel which never mentions, as do so many Christian explanations of it, the sin of man's presumption, describes Jehovah's mounting apprehension as the great Tower rises into the sky; 'behold the people' he says 'how nothing will be restrained from them, from what they have imagined to do' (Genesis 11:6). (An ancient Jewish commentary on the tale tells how the builders shot off arrows from the top of the Tower and how angels, after dipping them in blood, sent them down to earth again.) Faced with such intelligent, such belligerent, creatures it is hardly any wonder that, in common with many other ancient gods, Jehovah felt threatened by mankind. At Babel, he makes a confusing babble of language; the Flood, of course, is a more vigorous gesture. And it is fascinating to see how the Book of Genesis bends this ancient tale to its own purposes, while keeping some of the smallest details of the Mesopotamian original. And it is also fascinating to see how the gods of Mesopotamia are reduced by Genesis' scribes to a single omnipotent deity. In the Mesopotamian flood story, it is the god Enlil who, like Jehovah, angrily brings down the deluge and afterwards is still angry that life on earth survives for he had intended to destroy it all; 'What, has any of the mortals escaped?' he exclaims, 'No-one was to have survived the destruction' and he is only calmed by a speech of the goddess Ishtar. Then, all the Mesopotamian gods gathered around the sacrifice that their Mesopotamian Noah has made to them (his first act upon reaching dry land, just as it will later be Noah's in the Book of Genesis). The gods had sorely missed their offerings since the flood began, 'the sweet savour . . . of the wood and cane, the cedar and the myrrh . . . all the smoking meats of sacrifice'; and they 'buzzed' over the offerings, the ancient scribes tell us, 'like flies'. Afterwards, just as Jehovah will do with Noah, the goddess Ishtar makes the contract with humankind, pledging to save it from Enlil's wrath for evermore, vowing never to desert it again. She dedicates a marvellous necklace, that the god of the Sky has made for her in memory of the deep-drowned world. With what genius is that image of the goddess Ishtar holding up the 'Jewels of Heaven' transformed into the vision of a rainbow, in the Book of Genesis; where it becomes the sign of Jehovah's covenant with man:

> I do set my bow in the cloud, and it shall be for a token of a covenant between me and the earth.
> And it shall come to pass, when I bring a cloud over the earth, that the bow shall be seen in the cloud:
> And I will remember my covenant, which is between me and you and every living creature of all flesh; and the water shall no more become a flood to destroy all flesh.
>
> (Genesis 9:13–15)

Sarah and the Mandrakes

When Noah sails upon the Flood, or Jehovah transforms Ishtar's necklace into a rainbow to make a covenant with man, pragmatists quickly take a step back. What is 'reasonable' has greatly changed since ancient times. Modern attempts to fit Abraham into history begin, almost unconsciously, by separating the 'reasonable' from the fabulous. All of the statements in the Book of Genesis that can be sensibly fitted into modern histories of the ancient world are extracted from its stories like plums from a pie. All of its wonders, its visiting angels, universal floods, the miraculous fertility of the Patriarch's wives are either ignored or blandly explained away, while the 'reasonable' adventures of Abraham and his family are placed firmly inside the ethnic security of images of real ancient people herding real ancient sheep! Yet 1500 years ago a rabbi writing a commentary on the Book of Genesis suggests a different sort of reason for the extraordinary fertility of Sarah, Abraham's wife; and one much closer to the world of ancient people like Abraham. It was due, he asserted, to eating a mandrake, a plant whose dark purple flowers ripened into magic apples every autumn and whose roots grew like clustered penises. Mandrakes held fertility inside them. But, warns the rabbi, if the plant is not doused with menstrual blood before it is plucked, it will surely kill its harvester, unless he faces west with the wind behind him while describing three circles round the plant with the point of a sword. As a mandrake was pulled from the ground, it was said that the plant's scream would send you mad.

Clearly we have travelled a long way from modern history, and we have arrived in quite another world and one with its own logic and its own wisdom; it is the world of myth, and there is much of this, too, in the Book of Genesis. Myth, that is, in the proper sense of the word, not, as in the common modern misusage a falsehood, but a sacred tale. A tale whose purposes are passed with the story's telling as precisely and as unconsciously as babies learn the grammar of their mother-tongue. Myths differ from history, that mere continuum of events, in that they are carefully designed: and it is these designs that hold the myth's real meanings. And these are seldom simple moral stories, but deal with the deepest issues of the day.

Such antique stories in the Book of Genesis had a silent re-assurance for the nation of ancient Israel, the descendants of Abraham and Sarah. For example, by the Laws of Jehovah, Abraham had committed incest by marrying his half-sister, Sarah, 'the mother of nations' (Genesis 17). But here, there are other overriding considerations at work. A close family member must bear Abraham's legitimate offspring so that his descendants, the children of Israel, will be of pure lineage. Just as the incest of Adam and Eve fathers the nations of the earth, so Abraham and Sarah's engenders Israel. This is a common ideal of many ancient and tribal societies; ancestral purity held inside a single family. So there are always strong tensions inside such family trees; the unresolved contradiction between incest and purity. And this contradiction is not only seen in the story of Abraham and Sarah but in other Bible stories too, and indeed, in the myths of many other ancient cultures. Frequently the contradictions between incest and ancestral purity are spelled out in the telling of the story; sterility, for example, is a common punishment for incestuous couplings. Just as in Greek myth, the marriage of Oedipus and his mother Jocasta was barren, so Abraham's Sarah, too, was 'stopped up' until she was ninety. Genesis also shows that Abraham was aware of his sin in marrying his half-sister. Twice, we are told, he tries to give Sarah in concubinage to foreign kings, but in the interests of ancestral purity, Jehovah does not let this happen. Similar stories of loaned wives are repeated in the following generation with Isaac and Rebecca. 'Like father, like son' it is commonly suggested; an 'ancient custom' is another explanation, but such crude comments do little justice to the careful tales, which, even if they were literally true, would still not explain the deliberate selection of such mundane and repetitive stories in the great family history of Genesis. But then, these stories differ greatly from a documentary history, a simple continuum of events, in that they are so carefully constructed. Such repetitions are also the very stuff of oral story-telling which, like soap operas, are required by their audiences to operate inside a continuously familiar framework, making minor variations on constantly stated themes. And through them all, all possible propriety is observed, the essential sinfulness of incest shrouded, in Sarah's case, by picturesque encounters with lascivious kings, by a prolonged barrenness and finally, a heaven-ordained pregnancy (Genesis 12:10–20). Similarly, the scandalous seduction of Abraham's nephew Lot by his two daughters (Genesis 19) is preceded by a story that includes two visiting angels, Sodom and Gomorrah, a volcanic smokescreen of fire and brimstone of atomic proportions and two young women who think that their father is the last male alive on earth! Ultimately, though, in both these tales, the contradictions between incest and the imperatives of ancestral purity are clearly identified and firmly resolved: Abraham and Sarah engender Isaac, the father of Jacob/Israel and Lot and his daughters who were the ancestors of ancient Israel's Eastern neighbours.

Obviously if such subtle stories are attacked with the blunt instruments of 'rational' explanation – 'Scientist says conception possible at ninety' or 'Dead

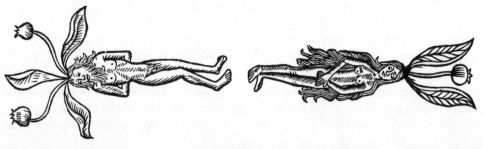

Sea volcanic eruption dated to 1234 BC' – the true purposes of the ancient stories will run through our fingers like sand. Read sympathetically, however, they will tell us about a part of Abraham's world that archaeologists can never hope to find.

Genesis

> In the beginning God created the heaven and the earth. And the earth was without form, and void; and darkness was upon the face of the deep. And the Spirit of God moved upon the face of the waters. And God said, Let there be light: and there was light. And God saw the light, that it was good: and God divided the light from the darkness. And God called the light Day, and the darkness he called Night. And the evening and the morning were the first day.
>
> (Genesis 1:1–5)

God's grand division of light and darkness marks out all the later events of his Creation: God has made himself a clock and with it he will measure out the making of his world in seven units; seven days.

'Man may mock at Moses and Sabbaths', a seventeenth-century New England puritan pithily observed, 'but neither doctors nor infidels can make a typhoid fever turn except upon the seventh day'. The preacher had seen that the entire Bible was haunted by sevens: the pull of the number runs through the Old and New Testaments. The world, created in seven days, was revived, he knew, by the Seven Last Words of Jesus on the cross; it will be undone with the Seven Seals of the Book of Revelations and returned to the keeping of Almighty God, at its ending, at the blast of seven trumpets. Nor was Jehovah the first creator to base his universe upon a system of sevens. The *Enuma Elish*, the story of the creation of Mesopotamia and man, which was recited in the temples of Ur and Haran as in every Mesopotamian temple every year for some 4000 years and more, also ordered its story in seven units, in seven generations of a family of gods.

And the convergence runs far beyond this magic number. Just as in the first three days of Genesis' Creation, Jehovah makes the elements of the world, so, in the *Enuma Elish*, the first three generations of gods are the gods of water, silt, and sky, the elements of the Mesopotamian world. And just as in the fourth, fifth and sixth days of Genesis' Creation, God makes the animate world, so, in the *Enuma Elish*, the fourth, fifth and sixth generation of gods are gods of moving things. Jehovah makes the sun, moon and stars of the calendar on the fourth day; so the male deity of the fourth generation of *Enuma Elish* is Anu, the god of heaven. Just as Jehovah rests after these six days and then makes man, so the god Marduk too of the sixth generation of *Enuma Elish*, creates man so that the Mesopotamian gods might rest. The two stories, the two universes are built of the same bricks. And both of them build the same environment: not Iceland, nor New England nor even ancient Israel, but a south Mesopotamian landscape where the sweet waters of the Tigris and Euphrates empty into the salt waters of the Persian Gulf, where there are cloudless dawns with no horizon to be seen in the morning haze. And slowly, the dark rivers drop their silty islands in the delta, and the sun, rising, burns through the cloud and then, in the blue-hazed sky, the earth and heavens both suddenly appear. At different times, in many different cities, the Gods of *Enuma Elish* have changed their names, as does the hero of the flood story. But nonetheless, it is always the same Mesopotamian landscapes that these gods make, the same story that they act out. And their great saga clearly holds priority over Genesis. For the god Jehovah of the hardy tribes of hilly Israel orders a Mesopotamian creation, a distant memory of that wide, well-watered plain.

Like Adam's world outside Eden, Mesopotamia gave its people a hard uncertain life. Eden, indeed, was typical of thousands of walled gardens that sheltered kitchen crops and orchards from the sweeping rains, violent storms and the driven sand that constantly encroached from the deserts of the west to smother the ancient fields. Not only was Mesopotamia erratically devastated by this harsh climate but it was also raided and sacked periodically by nomads sweeping down from the surrounding mountains. And this violence, this continual tragedy, is movingly reflected in the cuneiform literature of the ancient cities, in tragic myths that alone survived their empires and their mud cities now dissolved away. How strange it is to watch as Genesis' scribes re-cast the violent saga of *Enuma Elish* to hold the solitary majesty of Jehovah, this ancient poem that the priests of the ancient cities chanted from the doorways of their temples each New Year's Day.

Enuma Elish la nabu shamanu, they began, 'When, on high, the heavens were not yet named', then, the story tells, there were only the gods Tiamat and Apsu, the deities of the sweet rivers and the salt seas. And the mixing of these waters with Mammu, the god of form, made the gods of the silt banks, Lahmu and Lahamu. In their turn they generated the gods of the horizons, Kinshar and Anshar, and they engendered the god of heaven, Anu, whose son was Ea, the god of the earth. Ea is the fifth generation; his son Marduk will make man and Mesopotamia itself.

Just as in the story of Abraham and Sarah, the story of *Enuma Elish* also grapples with the contradiction of ancestral purity and unlawful incest. The entire saga is a serpentine and claustrophobic tale of seven generations of family passions. It begins with Apsu, the great patriarch resolving to kill all his descendants for making so much noise. But Ea, his great-grandson kills him first, rousing Tiamat, Apsu's wife, to fury. Leading a host of demons, she and a new husband declare war upon the rest of the family, and so paralysed with fear are they all, that even crafty Ea cannot think of a ruse to save them. Then Marduk, the youngest of them all, offers to be their champion if they will accept him as their king, and this they gladly do. So Marduk goes off to war, routs the demon army and, catching Tiamat in a net, drives a tempest into her open mouth;

> the fierce wind filled her belly,
> her inside conjested and retching
> she opened wide her mouth.
> He let fly an arrow, it split her belly,
> cut through her inward parts
> and gashed her heart.
> He held her fast, extinguished her life.

Then Marduk smashes Tiamat's skull and orders the wind to return her spilled blood which blows in across the Mesopotamian plain like the rains of a storm. Marduk then splits her carcass in half to make heaven and earth and, from the arch of her legs, a vault to support the sky. Tiamat's head he buries under a mountain, piercing her eyes so that the Tigris and Euphrates can flow from them. Marduk has made Mesopotamia his royal estate. And he has set the stage for man. Kingu, Tiamat's second husband is brought before the other gods and slaughtered. 'Arteries' says Marduk 'I will knot . . . I will create *lullu* and man will be his name . . .' The slave is put to work to finish a ziggurat which the gods were labouring to build for King Marduk; and which, the saga states, is the Tower of Babel at Babylon.

At first glance it seems highly improbable that such unholy mayhem could underpin the magisterial Creation of Jehovah in the Book of Genesis. Yet it does. Not only are the six building blocks of these two worlds the same, but the problems of emotion and intellect that are dealt with in Genesis and in *Enuma Elish* are also very similar. The differences are largely those of structure: Genesis separates the intense dramas of *Enuma Elish* into two halves. In the first, the abstract creation of Jehovah is played out alone; all the forces that drive *Enuma Elish*, jealousy, rage, all the underlying conflicts of incest and purity are quite absent. In Genesis they will appear in the stories of the first generations of man. An essential difference, however, is that *Enuma Elish* not only describes the creation of the human race, but gives the ancestry of its creator too. And that Genesis cannot do, for Jehovah alone is the fount of all things.

With this solitary universal Creation, all the passions that the Mesopotamians thought were omnipresent, as natural as the winds, must be carefully invented and introduced inside the Book of Genesis. So Adam is first made innocent and unknowing, a blank slate. Then the subtle serpent faces Eve with two choices; sin and wisdom or the lack of them. After their liberative bite of the apple, Jehovah expels his first two people, now properly human, from their timeless Eden into the hard Mesopotamian plain. Unlike Abraham, Adam and Eve are not nomads, but farmers. (One ancient rabbi commented that the angels must have helped Adam in his first year away from Paradise 'so that he did not fall behind with his ploughing'.) The subsequent founding of the race (Genesis 4:1) is part of the consequence of their fall, the knowledge of the Tree of Good and Evil. So the conundrum of incest that must always accompany stories of the first family is resolved, as it is again with Abraham and his family, by showing it as the lesser of two evils when faced with the necessity of procreation.

Enuma Elish takes another route in its resolution of incest. It separates Marduk, man's creator, from his partner Tiamat, by several generations and then obscures their passion in the smoke of battle. Marduk tears into his partner with the ferocity of a psychopath, his arrows pierce her womb; Tiamat is a defeated enemy, not a lover. She is butchered to make Mesopotamia; her second husband, dispatched with all the resentment of an abandoned child, is also butchered; 'blood is massed and bones are caused to be'. And man is made mechanically.

Cultured Mesopotamians saw their civilization as descending from a wild natural force that was changed into a sacred, civilizing order by the mediation of Marduk. When he goes off to do battle with Tiamat, Marduk's grandfather, the god of heaven, gives him the four winds that will later stop up Tiamat's mouth and, in exchange, he gives his grandfather a quiver full of arrows: works of civilization borne on the natural winds. Gross and terrifying as he is, though, he raids the corpses of his family to make Mesopotamia and man, it is Marduk that mediates between wild nature and the culture of mankind.

This subtle dialectic of natural force and civilization appears in Genesis in the stories of Adam's family. Eve's two children are the founders of pastoral and urban society; Abel, the herdsman and hunter, lives in the West; Cain, the farmer, to the East of Eden with the sunrise and renewal. And both of them live in the Mesopotamian landscape of Tiamat. Cain, the first man to live apart from God, has his offerings rejected by Jehovah. But it is Cain who builds the first city and, when he murders his blameless brother, Jehovah does not punish him but marks him so that all will see that he is divinely protected. Cain's killing of Abel is a sacrifice that Jehovah accepts. Cain the murderer, the founder of cities, is the founder of civilization.

In separating the moods of man from the manufacture of the universe in this way, the opening chapter of Genesis has put the ancient gods on trial. In Genesis, man in all his wisdom, takes responsibility. Just as Genesis' first people generate sin and anger and separation from God, so they also generate freedom. In the Book of Genesis, mankind is not God's slave – 'let him be burdened with the toil of the gods' Marduk says – nor does emotion run as free, as natural as the winds; it is all accounted for in the world of man. And Jehovah, without beginning or end, the creator of everything, has become a lonely figure replacing an entire pantheon. But still the grand story is conducted inside the Mesopotamian order of the universe and on the Mesopotamian plain. And the tensions and pressures of that ancient fratricidal family of gods, bound and repelled inside relationships of love and hatred, have, through the Bible, given us a universe filled with the sense of a dynamic system of relationships. A model that scientists still use. And this whole process began when the sagas of Mesopotamia were carefully re-examined by the authors of Genesis and the thoughts and structures of that most ancient story were turned to the purposes of Israel and their most singular and solitary God.

The Tower of Babel and the Sphinx

About 450 BC, the Greek historian Herodotus visited the ancient city of Babylon in Mesopotamia and there he saw the Tower of Babel; 'the Gate of God'. The great brick ziggurat was still in use, still wafted by clouds of Arabian incense, still served by a large priesthood as it had been for thousands of years. And on the very top of Babel, Herodotus tells us, was a small shrine of blue-glazed brick and inside a 'well-covered couch and a golden table' where, the priests told their visitor, Marduk spent every New Year's night in the company of specially selected Babylonian maidens. This mystic union of earth and heaven was the spiritual centre of Mesopotamia's most important festival – perhaps the gold graves that Woolley found at Ur were the archaic tombs of Marduk's concubines and their retinues, killed when the rites had been played out.

The ziggurats, these huge stepped pyramids standing on the Mesopotamian flood plain were thought to hold the way to heaven, as the builders of the Tower of Babel in the Bible's story clearly understood (Genesis 11:1–9).

Herodotus tells us that the priests of Babylon were constantly ascending and descending the ziggurat's central staircase ministering to the topmost shrine that stood at heaven's gate. Jacob's Ladder, a biblical vision of 'the gates of heaven with angels going up and down it' (Genesis 28:12), was not originally a wooden stepladder; this, doubtless is a translator's error, but the brick stairway of a ziggurat. Once again the stories of the Book of Genesis are spun amid the scaffolding of Mesopotamian culture. But, at the same time, carefully and systematically, Genesis always rejects the Mesopotamian gods. At the top of the Bible's Tower of Babel, for instance, the builders do not discover Jehovah encouched with a beautiful maiden in a blue-tiled room, but confusion, mis-fortune and conflict. The Book of Genesis clearly tells us that Jehovah is not to be found inside this Mesopotamian faith, not in its buildings, nor its ritual; he is another kind of god.

Where, then, did Genesis' image of this deity come from, this slow, majestic, omnipotent god with his individual character? From whence came the manners of his worship and his cult, those essential decorations of religion that allow men to recognize and approach their gods? For many Westerners the special forms and rituals of this biblical Jehovah still hold the essential character of sacredness itself.

Genesis tells that Abraham and his family travelled from Mesopotamia to Egypt, and, quite clearly, the structures of Mesopotamian faith greatly influ-enced their religious life and their conception of the universe. Abraham's grandson, Jacob dreams of a Mesopotamian gateway to heaven. In Pharaoh's Egypt, similar experiences took on different forms and they too appear in the story of Jacob's dream. One famous Egyptian text describes the similar dream of a young prince as he lay sleeping in the noonday shadow of the Sphinx, during a rest in a desert hunting trip. 'I am your father' said the Egyptian god by way of introduction 'who will give you my kingdom'. 'I am the god of your father,' says Jehovah to the dreaming Jacob (Genesis 28:13 NEB) '. . . this land on which you are lying I will give to you and your descendants'. Years later when, just as his dream had promised, the prince had become Pharaoh (Tuthmosis IV, 1400–1390 BC), he recorded his vision upon a great granite stone which he set between the Sphinx's paws. And there, today, you may see a picture of Tuthmosis pouring out his offerings of oil onto an altar under pictures of the Sphinx; see the great doors, too, that are the Egyptian gates of heaven. Jacob also believed he had slept at Heaven's gate: he re-named the

PLATE 1 (*Opposite*): *Paddan-Aram; the plain of Haran seen from the mound of ancient Haran, the city from where, the Book of Genesis tells, Abraham travelled to Canaan and down into Egypt. The distant mounds in the plain are nameless ancient cities as yet unexcavated.*
PLATE 2 (*Overleaf*): *Cuneiform Tablets, the archives of the Syrian city of Ebla at about 2300 BC in the course of excavation, lying on the floor of an ancient storeroom by the city gate.*

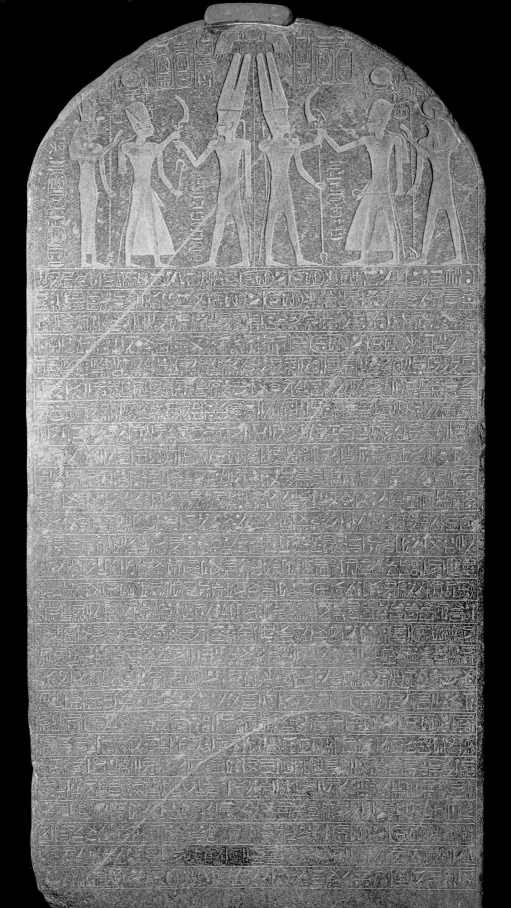

31408

Syrian sanctuary where he had his vision, *Beth-el*, the House of God. And just as Tuthmosis of Egypt had done, he set up a stone and poured oil upon it. Abraham's family may well have received their education in the great cities of Mesopotamia, but it was Egypt that would give the religion of Jehovah its earthly expression. And ancient Egypt held inside it a deep awareness of an underlying unity of holiness within the universe, quite separate from the ferociously divided gods of Mesopotamia.

Abraham's quiet departure from Ur is nicely balanced in the Book of Genesis by the royal welcome that Egypt affords his descendants Jacob and Joseph. '. . . take your father and your households and come to me,' says Pharaoh to these Patriarchs, 'I will give you the good of the land of Egypt, and ye shall eat the fat of the land' (Genesis 45:18). But as Joseph and his brothers prospered in the land of the Pharaohs so, Genesis tells us, the kings of Egypt became as apprehensive as Jehovah had been at the building of the Tower of Babel. 'Behold, the people of the children of Israel are more and mightier than we,' says Pharaoh in the Book of Exodus, 'Come on, let us deal wisely with them . . . Therefore they did set over them taskmasters to afflict them with their burdens. And they built for Pharaoh treasure cities, Pithom and Raamses' (Exodus 1:10–11). Thus speaks Pharaoh at the beginning of the great biblical saga that will end with the Exodus and the establishment of Israel. And what does it matter if no trace of the family of Abraham or any of the biblical Israelites has ever been found in the ruins of ancient Egypt; in the popular imagination they are condemned to bend under the Egyptian lash, make pyramids and palaces. But this vision, both of ancient Egypt and the foreigners who came to live there, is largely false, and serves only to distort our understanding of the Egyptian stories in the Old Testament.

In large part, this is due to the picture of the ancient Egyptians created by an earlier generation of historians. For just as the ancient Egyptians in their day had thought the rest of the world to be somewhat primitive, so many Western historians have similarly regarded the ancient Egyptians; a part of an old colonial dream of sensuous cruelty mixed with simpleness. It is certainly a world that neither the ancient Egyptians nor Abraham ever knew. 'Your ancient Egyptian' said Egyptologist Sir E.A. Wallis Budge in a popular British Museum handbook of the 1930s, 'was an *evviete effendi* – a Turkish phrase

PLATE 3 (Opposite): the Israel Stela from ancient Thebes. Its text celebrates, in the form of a long poem, Pharaoh Merneptah's campaign in Canaan. The second line of hieroglyphs from the bottom contains the first-known reference to Israel in history. Merneptah's raid into Canaan was in the fifth year of his rule, which by most modern estimates was the year 1207 BC. Black granite. Cairo Museum

for a "yes man", easy and simple, loving music, singing and dancing . . . attracted by displays of every kind.' Though Budge's Egyptians were 'bright and merry, loved wine, music and feasting', their religious outlook he dourly observed 'was deplorable'. Though they were 'keen ritualists' they did not believe like Budge that 'goodness on this earth was a passport to happiness in the life to come'. But goodness, as it has been observed in other circumstances, had very little to do with it. The practice of ancient Egyptian religion was not intended to provide the moral currency with which you bought your way to heaven, but was a method of attaining and maintaining cosmic harmony here on earth.

And it was extremely successful. With its flocks of priests, the state religion of ancient Egypt was the heart of one of the world's most successful cultures. As a rule, this state did not subject its citizens to great physical hardships, little more than a broad public morality was expected of them. Precise conceptions of sacredness, of kings, of gods, of life itself were all laid out in breathtaking arts and rituals that held a truly dynamic life in them for close on 3000 years.

Cosmic harmony, the fruitful balance of man and the gods, was achieved by correct public life and careful ritual observance. Disharmony, unbalance, led to falling out of sympathy with the gods and the cosmic order. Blindness might be due to blasphemy; an impious or incompetant pharaoh could provoke a drought or famine.

The Egyptian pantheon of gods was defined in much the same way that science has investigated the universe: by division and subdivision. So the world and human experience were both divided into ever smaller parts and every one of these was identified as a god; and each of these gods might change its identity, amalgamate with other gods, diminish or enlarge in its importance as man's perceptions of them changed. Behind this constant shifting and subdivision lay an awareness of a constant sacred force, a power not of these separate gods, but of sacredness, of deity itself, a calm power that ran through the natural order of the world, guaranteeing the life of Egypt. So self-assured was this belief, that even the most barbaric and violent of deities, the gods of war, confusion, plague and foreignness, found a place inside the pantheon of Egypt. Temples were founded for them and priests ministered to their cults. At their roots, even these gods of disorder were but a part of the unchanging and deeply holy order of the world.

Egypt, who invented nationhood, had made its state a mirror image of heaven; with the divine Pharaoh joining these two sacred domains at a single point. All temple offerings and rituals were celebrated in Pharaoh's name. His cults were so gilded, so silvered, so charged with craftsmanship and cosmic significance, that the kings and their priests must have seemed to be part of heaven upon earth. Even urbane travellers like the Greek Herodotus, who saw Egypt only in her decline, were impressed. Though most visitors and Egyptians alike had little access to the huge temples – the better part of the theologies and the ritual of the state were always hidden from public view – they would have seen the vast public processions on land and water that were the public heart of the ancient faith. And at the centre of every town, inside the dark temples, mysterious rituals tied to the procession of the seasons continued over centuries. The success of the system, of course, was visible in the prosperity of the state, and at its centre stood the power of the gods. From them came prosperity, victories, goods, crops, national fecundity and the authority of the Pharaoh. Egypt, then, knew a deep universal order, an optimism too that the rest of Abraham's world completely lacked. It is in this sense, then, that Israel, as the Book of Exodus tells us, truly 'came out of Egypt'.

Foreigners in Ancient Egypt
In the popular consciousness, in fiction and in Technicolor, 'ancient Egypt' forms a single image. And this will be a convenience on the last leg of our journey with Abraham, for outside the pages of the Bible, archaeology only allows us to fit him, along with all his descendants, into this general continuum called 'ancient Egypt', and not into any specific period inside its vast and diverse history. Medieval legends might tell us that the pyramids were Joseph's granaries, but archaeology has proved this to be as erroneous as the belief that they were built by Israelite slaves. But when Genesis tells us that 'Abraham went down into Egypt to sojourn here, for the famine was grievous in the land' (Genesis 12:10) that is a true statement about ancient Egypt. In all the ancient East Egypt was generally the country where grain and gold were both said to

be as the sands of the sea, and many ancient records tell us of nomads going south into Egypt in time of famine.

Abraham could have taken two roads south from Canaan into Egypt across the Sinai Desert; one along the coast which was later called the *Via Maris*; and another, a more eastern track that ran down through Sinai and Suez, called the 'Way of Horus', the highway along which, over millennia, Egyptian armies marched with their pharaohs into Canaan and Syria. The ending of the 'Way of Horus' at the approaches of north-eastern Egypt was guarded by a line of pharaonic fortresses that also controlled a line of ancient wells that ran through the desert of northern Sinai. 'From the scribe Inena to his Lord, the scribe of the treasury Kagabu . . . we have finished letting the Bedouin tribes of Edom pass the fortress of Pharaoh Merneptah . . . to the pools of Per-Atum . . . to keep them alive through the spirit of Pharaoh, life! prosperity! health! . . . in the year 8, the 5th day of Seth!' [i.e. late June 1204 BC].

'Edom', *The Red Land*, from where the Bedouin had come, was hill country, now south-eastern Israel, whose desert scarps gave winter grazing to herds which during the hot summers were, traditionally, brought down to the marshy Nile Delta. In the summer, Pharaoh and his officers really did give these tribesmen life. Quite possibly, the 'pools of Per-Atum' that Inena mentions, is the same place as the biblical city of Pithom, one of the two cities, 'Pithom and Raamses' which, the Book of Exodus tells us, were built by enslaved Israelites. Though ancient buildings at the desert fringe that were excavated at the turn of the nineteenth and twentieth centuries and are sometimes claimed to be the very bricks laid by the Israelites are nothing but the cellars of a Roman fort.

Bedouin herdsmen had come into Egypt for their summer grazing for many millennia before the scribe Inena wrote his report and they would do so for long after his death. Per-Atum and its pools were but the gates by which they entered the Camargue-like marsh of the east Delta, where the pharaohs came to hunt the great wild bulls that lived among the reeds. Even before ancient Egypt was made into one nation, towns were built on the long-ridged sand-banks that stood above the soft marshes. The people of these archaic towns must have kept an eye on these nomad herdsmen, just as their Mesopotamian counterparts were doing.

During the first and greatest age of pyramid building, around 2600–2500 BC, these Delta cities, like so much of provincial Egypt, had been impoverished as the population, which numbered about a million, was drawn into the gigantic enterprise of building the pharaohs' tombs. Some 600 years later, when the Nile's flow slackened and its valley began to desiccate, the wetlands of the eastern Delta were settled again, nobles being sent directly from Pharaoh's court to supervise the new developments. Artists who accompanied these nobles have left records of some of the Delta's traditional visitors in their masters' tombs. The most celebrated of these pictures, painted about 1890 BC, is in the tomb of the provincial governor Khumhotep. It shows a family of nomads, the men, bearded, and dressed like Abraham's great grandson Joseph in 'coats of many colours' going down into Egypt. Some people have seen Abraham and Sarah in this painting: more realistically, it is true to say that if Abraham and Sarah had lived like ancient desert nomads, the continuity of nomad life was such that these pictures would make a realistic illustration of them. Such careful Egyptian records give a unique glimpse, in rich detail, of an ancient people that otherwise are completely lost to us. Here we can see something of the style of northern nomads coming to Egypt to trade; brown-skinned men, with short and powerful bows of laminated horn and wood; their wives and children and their donkeys too, those engines of the ancient trade routes loaded with the tribe's belongings, and the heavy hair tents that were their homes: a caravan forming a colourful and, to Egyptian eyes, a distinctly foreign band.

These nomads have come to trade the products of the desert in the kingdom long known as the richest place on earth; they have brought gazelle and ibex, hides and cheese. The Egyptians thought little of such visitors: 'Miserable Asiatics' writes an Egyptian scribe – such northerners were often lumped under the general term of 'Asiatic' – 'he dwells not in any single place, driven abroad by want, his feet are always on the move', conditions that were complete anathema to the home-loving Egyptians. When these same tribesmen on their wanderings caused trouble in the northern provinces of the Egyptian Empire, in Canaan or in Syria, these same scribes would carefully cover little

clay figurines with the names of these miserable Asiatics and with high ceremonial and deep malice, smash them to fragments.

What must the Egyptian nobles and scribes have thought as they sat high in
their Delta palaces watching these tribesmen arrive, strange men from the
desert with dusty beards and heavy cloaks, their guard against the desert sun.
Wanderers like Abraham, who, as the Book of Genesis tells us, would offer
their wives as concubines and, at the call of an obscure god, were prepared to
sacrifice their children on distant windy hillsides. To the Egyptians they must
have seemed hardly human and, in fact, they would not have been considered
to be properly so until they had conformed to the Egyptian way of life.
Unlike most modern people, the ancient Egyptians had little interest in dividing
populations into ethnic types. Blonde Lybians and black Nubians were all
Egyptians if they lived in the Egyptian way. The difference was not racial but
cultural; Egyptian artists differentiated between foreign tribes and nations by
describing their hats and haircuts, their tattoos and weapons.

As well as the nomads seeking pasture and trade, a great many other
foreigners came down the 'Way of Horus' to live and work in Egypt. Foreigners
found places in every stratum of Egyptian society; in the armies, at court, as
servants, as labourers and as taskmasters in the great households. They dressed
in Egyptian clothes, took Egyptian wives and names and became a part of
Egypt. Nefertiti, that most famous of Egyptian queens, is thought by many
historians to have been born of foreign parents. After the invasions of Canaan
and Syria, Egypt became a magnet for many of its subject peoples and as in
many empires, people also came from beyond the imperial frontiers. Pharaoh's
first charioteers came from Anatolia along with their war chariots and their
horses. And with them came the Anatolian vocabulary of their trade. Regiments of foreign mercenaries who had sometimes threatened Egypt itself
joined the Egyptian armies and introduced their foreign gods into the Nile
Valley along with new weapons, strange costumes and pottery. In this genuine
historical environment, the Egyptian careers of the Patriarchs, of Joseph, who
entered Egypt as a slave and rose to control the civil administration of the land;
or the biblical adventures of Moses, a foreign foundling raised in an Egyptian
court, are entirely plausible. Even Abraham's ephemeral brushes with Pharaoh
(Genesis 12:14–20) – this 'Pharaoh' however was probably Pharaoh's officer
at a frontier post of the 'Way of Horus' – could well refer to an incident similar
to that recorded by the scribe Inena at the pools of Per-Atum. Until quite
recently, however, this was all that could be said on the subject.

In the last few years, however, excavations at an ancient town in the heart of
the eastern Delta at the modern mound of Tell el Dab'a have uncovered
startling fresh evidence of the extent of the foreign settlement in ancient Egypt.
A century ago, translated Egyptian poems had already told us that, with a good
wind behind you, you could sail from Tell el Dab'a upstream to the capital at

Memphis in a day and they had also told us that cultured Memphites regarded this Delta city as the start of foreign lands. These new excavations have shown us why. They have also shown us the only foreign settlements in Egypt that correspond, in some measure, to the Bible's description of Israel in Egypt.

A town, a royal foundation, had been established at Tell el Dab'a from at least 2000 BC, part of the re-settlement of that region in which Governor Khnumhotep was involved. The town had fine stone temples, at least five noble palaces and rich trading contacts with Syria, Crete and Mycenae. Over the following centuries, northerners came to this town, not just to trade or water their herds like the bedouin, but to settle down and to live. And with this foreign population came many foreign innovations too. Most interestingly, careful analysis of the large quantities of imported pottery found at Tell el Dab'a shows that the normal Egyptian practice of occasional trading did not apply at Tell el Dab'a, rather there were strong and continuing links with the coastal towns of Lebanon and northern Canaan. Chariots and foreign weapons were made at Tell el Dab'a; moulds for long swords, tough little axes shaped like a duck's bill and shields of un-Egyptian type have been found still lying in the damp earth of the ancient city. Recent excavations at a site close to modern Haifa have recovered Egyptian scarabs (one bearing the name of a prince called Jacob) and other importations, and this would seem to be a part of the other end of this Canaanite connection. Similarly, many Tell el Dab'a houses were of a square design, that although typical of Syria and Canaan at this period, are otherwise unknown in Egypt. Canaanite temples, too, have been found at Tell el Dab'a close by some small traditional Egyptian temples. Here, then, deep inside the borders of Egypt was a remarkable foreign town; a part of Canaan in Egypt.

After some 300 years of existence this city was overrun by a wave of northern invaders; this at a time when Egyptian military power was at a low ebb and, one might guess, the frontier forts along the roads of Sinai were left unmanned. About 1640 BC, using the old city of Tell el Dab'a as their military base, these newcomers conquered all of northern Egypt, which they then ruled from the ancient capital of Memphis. About a century later, these so-called Hyksos kings, the 'shepherd' kings, were expelled from Egypt by a dynasty of southern Theban princes, but not before one of the southern pharaohs, Sekenenre, had been killed in battle. His mummy, found at Thebes, still bears the devastating head wounds made by a northern axe and the Pharaoh's face still registers the pain and horror of that assault. Theban royal texts tell of their final victories over the northerners in the 1530s BC; archaeological evidence shows that the city of Tell el Dab'a was again burned and its new fortress abandoned at this same time. Every one of the Canaanite temples was destroyed; the large cemetery where Canaanites lay buried with their horses, weapons, dogs and jewellery was heartily plundered. The victory inscriptions of these southern pharaohs tell us that they threw these foreigners out of Egypt, then pursued them into Canaan and beyond. And this is the only foreign mass-migration, an Exodus from ancient Egypt, for which there is any evidence at all in the archaeological records.

Inevitably, after the episode of the Hyksos, the centre of Egypt moved north from the Nile Valley to the Delta. Pharaoh needed a finger on the international pulse and the court moved, leaving the temples and tombs of Thebes behind. In the thirteenth century BC, King Ramesses II built a huge new palace near the ruins of Tell el Dab'a; a palace much celebrated in museum collections as the source of hundreds of superb faience tiles which have been excavated, more usually plundered, from its ruins. The city that grew up in a vast five-mile sprawl around the palace is the celebrated city Ramesses, sometimes confusingly called Raamses in the Book of the Exodus, the city from which, we are told, the Israelites began their Exodus. In Ramesses II's day it was truly vast; its quarters and districts, temples, villas, palaces, barracks, houses, wharves, warehouses and dockyards all linked by a network of canals and river tributaries. But shortly after the great King's death the Nile stream that gave the city its life silted up and it lapsed into quiet ruin. Later kings, building other Delta cities, dragged away all the statuary and the stone. And later still, armies of Assyrians, Persians and Greeks passed through the Delta on their way to plunder the ancient cities of the Nile. And all through these hard times, the nomads came down from Palestine into the Delta with their herds for summer grazing or sometimes, like Joseph, Mary and the Infant Jesus, taking refuge in the ancient land. This, then, is the extent of the relationship between Egypt and her northern neighbours. Although it holds in it all the circumstances of the Bible's stories, just like Abraham in Mesopotamia there is nothing that can tie any of those famous stories into specific periods of Egyptian history.

Ancient Egypt in the Bible

Pharaoh said to Joseph, 'I hereby give you authority over the whole land of Egypt'. He took off his signet-ring and put it on Joseph's finger, he had him dressed in fine linen, and hung a gold chain round his neck. He mounted him in his viceroy's chariot and men cried 'Make way!' before him.

(Genesis 41:41–43 NEB)

In the story of Joseph the Book of Genesis comes close to the reality of Egypt. Just as Joseph's servants cry 'Make way' before his chariot, so, the servants of the princes and merchants of Egypt have done for thousands of years. Some of the most celebrated paintings and reliefs in the ancient Egyptian tomb chapels show the same ceremony that Genesis describes so vividly in the passage above. Here are pictures of ancient nobles, their arms raised exultantly, necks encircled with collars of gold, elaborate linen gowns carefully ironed and fitted by their servants, standing before a pharaoh who with due ceremony invests them as viziers of Egypt. Frequently alongside such tomb paintings, written biographies record the details of the vizier's career; Genesis' story of Joseph's life in Egypt gives the strong impression that it is one of these biographies recast by scribes with little notion of the heavy formality of the ancient original. What Genesis describes, in its typical manner, as a spontaneous happening between two people was in reality a courtly ceremony; the inauguration of a vizier was a public ritual as old as the Kingdom of Egypt.

In most of its details, however, Genesis' account of Joseph's career, is set inside the genuine ancient environment; Joseph's ride with a Midianite caravan down the 'Way of Horus' into the Egyptian Delta rings true, as does his bondage into the house of the priest Potiphar. Potiphar, indeed, is a genuine

Egyptian name which means 'He who the [sun] god has given', and this is an especially appropriate name for a priest of the ancient city of On where, Genesis tells us, Potiphar lives. At On, now in the suburbs of Cairo, stood the largest temple of the sun god in all Egypt, one in which priests like Potiphar served for 2000 years and more.

Wisdom and foresight are the two attributes most frequently claimed by Egyptian bureaucrats in their tomb-chapel biographies, for a great part of their work, as it is of modern politicians', was the ability to look into the future and plan for national prosperity. Nowadays, of course, politicians usually employ statistical persuasions and moral and historical precedent to argue their visions and their remedies: ancient Egyptians used dreams, magic and a practical knowledge of their country with much the same results. Sonomancy, dream interpretation, which the Book of Genesis tells us was Joseph's special gift, was very common. Ancient Egyptians believed that during a dream the spirit left the body and returned to the unformed darkness at the edge of creation, and that this perilous outing to the place where all time and all people could meet would reveal unknown truths about the future. 'And Pharaoh said unto Joseph, I have dreamed a dream, and there is none that can interpret it: and I have heard say of thee, that thou canst understand a dream to interpret it' (Genesis 41:15). Joseph's dream analysis (Genesis 41:17ff.) which brings him such fame in biblical Egypt, is the simplest of all the many methods of interpretation described in ancient Egyptian dream books, a transposition where 'fat cows' mean good harvests and 'lean cows' mean bad ones; a truth, indeed, that any countryman would know! Other Egyptian dream interpretations could reverse this most obvious meaning, as when the Tarot card of the Hanged Man is said to bring good luck. But Joseph sticks to the simplest path, relying more upon his understanding of the dreamers than the dreams. That Joseph's prison companions (Genesis 40) were dreaming of their future is hardly surprising; for ancient Egyptian prisons were not places of punishment but *ad hoc* holding centres where people were kept while they were investigated. Verdict and sentencing stood at the end of imprisonment. So the imprisoned baker's dream of birds pecking at a loaf, the spoiling of his livelihood, was interpreted by Joseph as an augury of doom; similarly, when the imprisoned royal butler dreamed he was at court again, Joseph predicted, correctly, that his confident dream would come true. Perhaps Joseph's foreignness – the royal butler describes him to Pharaoh as a young Hebrew (Genesis 41:12) – lent a weighty and exotic air to his pronouncements, as it does to those of many modern fortune-tellers. Genesis (44) tells us that Joseph went in for other forms of divination as well as sonomancy; the cup that his servants put into his brothers' grain sacks which led to their arrest, 'Why have you stolen the silver goblet? It is the one from which my Lord drinks, and which he uses for divination' (Genesis 44:5 NEB), was a magic cup, a device much used in ancient Egypt where vessels, made of silver or gold, or sometimes faience as blue as the Egyptian sky, were filled with water and 'read'. Sometimes, too, words were written on these cups in ink designed to dissolve into the water, which was then drunk as a medicine. To this day, such remedies are a common folk medicine in Egypt, sick villagers usually drinking the appropriate verses of the Holy Koran.

When Joseph recommended to Pharaoh that he should stave off the lean times ahead by storing the surplus produce of bountiful harvests, we see a man recognizing and coping with royal anxieties; acting as much as political advisor as a magician, a common combination of roles at Pharaoh's court. And like modern politicians, Pharaoh's advisors were not only expected to look into the future, but occasionally, so some Egyptian stories tell us, to perform tricks to amuse their bored masters. So, of the ancient age in which the pyramids were built, it was later said that one celebrated sage had 'held up the waters of a pleasure lake', piling them 'high on either side' so that a royal concubine could recover an earring lost in a harem rowing competition. Pharaoh, it is said, was delighted at the trick, a modest dry run, after all, for the biblical parting of the Red Sea. And Moses, too, was a court magician, filled with the power to send 'tokens and wonders into the midst of thee, O Egypt' (Psalm 135:9).

Obviously there is a great deal in the biblical Egyptian tales that places them firmly into a genuinely Egyptian environment, just as there is with Genesis' Mesopotamian stories. But however strong such cultural concordances are, they can never supply the proof that such stories record genuine historical events or that characters in them ever lived – just as Tolstoy's careful descriptions of Napoleon's army in *War and Peace* does not prove that the novel's characters once had real existence. And there is nothing in Genesis' Egyptian tales that will allow them to be placed on a timechart of Egyptian history. Theories that attempt to link biblical details with ancient lifestyles rely more on our ignorance of the past than our knowledge of it; for there are few manners and customs that can be precisely charted throughout ancient Egyptian history. There is, however, one effective link between the Old Testament and ancient Egypt that provides a rough indication of the age of these Bible texts, and that is the very designs of the texts themselves. Just as some Old Testament texts have obvious Mesopotamian origin, so others are clearly Egyptian. Passages in the Books of Genesis and Exodus and the Book of Proverbs, and in some of the Psalms as well, show direct connection with well-known ancient Egyptian texts. One especially famous poem, the 'Hymn to Aten', reputedly written by the heretic Pharaoh Akhenaten about 1345 BC, shows clear and subtle parallel with Psalm 104.

Hymn to the Aten	*Psalm 104:20ff.*

When thou dost set in the western horizon
The earth in darkness, like to death.
Men sleep in a bed-chamber, their heads
    covered,
One eye unable to behold the other.
Were all their goods beneath their heads
    stolen,
They would be unaware of it.
Every lion has come forth from his lair;
All the reptiles bite.
Darkness prevails, and the earth is silence,
Since he who made them rests in his
    horizon.
	Thou makest darkness, and it is night:
	wherein all the beasts of the forest do
	    creep forth.
	The young lions roar after their prey,
	and seek their meat from God.

Hymn to the Aten	*Psalm 104:25ff.*

Ships sail up and down stream alike,
Since every route is open at thine
    appearing.
The fish in the river leap before thee,
For thy rays are in the midst of the sea.
	So is this great and wide sea,
	wherein are things creeping
	    innumerable,
	both small and great beasts.
	There go the ships:
	There is that leviathan, whom thou hast
	    made to play therein.

Hymn to the Aten	*Psalm 104:24*

How manifold is that which thou hast
    made, hidden from view,
Thou sole god, there is no other like thee!
Thou didst create the earth according to
    thy will, being alone.
	O Lord, how manifold are thy works!
	in wisdom hast thou made them all:
	the earth is full of thy riches.

Though this Egyptian hymn was composed for a brief and schismatic faith, echoes of it persist in later Egyptian writings. Its date, about 1345 BC, several centuries before the earliest evidence of ancient Israel's existence, serves as an indication of the earliest possible date for the composition of the biblical Psalm, nothing more. Most of the other parallels of Old Testament and Egyptian texts will yield us similarly elusive results. One unique concordance, however, allows us to narrow down one 'earliest possible' date by a century or so, for the biblical story of Joseph and Potiphar's wife was also a well-known Egyptian tale that first appears in the ancient literature about 1200 BC.

In the Egyptian story, known as the 'Tale of Two Brothers', there is an estate manager, like Joseph, (c.f. Genesis 39) called Bata. And Bata, like Joseph, is accused by his master's wife of her attempted seduction. In what must be literature's oldest surviving boudoir scene, the Egyptian tale describes the master's wife 'sitting braiding her hair', admiring Bata's muscles as he carries sacks of seed from the house to the fields. As Joseph does, Bata rejects the woman's advances and is unjustly denounced by her. Then, magically forewarned of her husband's intentions to kill him, Bata flees to the far side of a crocodile swamp from where he upbraids the husband (who is also Bata's brother in the Egyptian tale) standing on the other side. In his extreme indignation and after a very long speech, Bata cuts off his penis and throws it into the water where it is promptly eaten by a small fish.

Such overtly Freudian goings-on hardly ever happen in the pages of the Bible; at this point Genesis and the Egyptian tale swiftly diverge, Bata's story following the mythic combat of two brother gods, Osiris and Seth, in which Osiris' penis suffers the same fishy fate. By joining Bata's simple story to a great state myth, Bata is cast in a role that would have been immediately familiar to the Egyptian audience. Similarly, though Joseph's story takes quite a different turn, it remains, like Bata's, a moral tale that tells of an injustice that is eventually corrected. But clearly, the Book of Genesis could not hold such obvious connections with one of the greatest myths of the ancient world.

Such biblical borrowings from ancient pagan literature,the constant use in the Book of Genesis of ancient myth and language serves above all else to set these Bible stories into the ancient world and at the very beginnings of civilization. To believe that such concordances as the stories of Noah and the Babylonian Flood, or the Tale of Two Brothers and the story of Joseph and Potiphar's wife serve to cast doubt upon the authenticity of the Book of Genesis, is to misinterpret its true purposes. Genesis, in common with most of the Old Testament, is not vulgar history. When the Old Testament decorates itself in the details of local colour, be they Mesopotamian or Egyptian, when stories like that of Bata and the Flood are retold, they are always put at the service of an overriding theme: the slow-developing relationship of Israel and Jehovah and this is an unfolding revelation; the definition of a god. The stories of the Book of Genesis are but the first episode of this lengthy saga. Appropriately, they use some of civilization's oldest stories.

In this greater saga, in this long process of revelation, Joseph's story becomes a part of the longer story of the interaction between Jehovah and the Patriarchs; family stories that hold in them all the seeds of the later history of ancient Israel. So, with Jehovah's help, Joseph is taken down into Egypt and later he will bring his brothers into the thrall of that ancient nation. This is the prelude to the Exodus from Egypt and the establishment of the Kingdom of Israel. The enslavement of the Israelites in Egypt, the descendants of Joseph's brothers who had come as Pharaoh's guests, is a similar injustice, if writ much larger, as the imprisonment of the innocent Joseph at the hand of Potiphar. And just as Joseph's cause was just and with Jehovah's help he triumphed and prospered, so Israel is led from its enslavement towards the Land of Milk and Honey. Jehovah's history repeats itself with utter consistency. The Exodus from Egypt, then, is the vindication of Israel, a proof of its closeness to Jehovah, the all-powerful god. As Jehovah had sustained Joseph and his brothers, so he will sustain their descendants, the Israelites, during their enslavement and reward their piety with the gift of a kingdom of their own. But this was only after a long sojourn in the land of Egypt. And there it was that for the first time Jehovah was revealed to the people of Israel, where the solemn worship of the ancient gods gave them an awareness of a calm and universal holiness and their response of solemn and unending pieties.

The Exodus

The Book of Exodus, literally the Book of 'Going Out', is the Bible's second book. It tells the story of Moses leading his people out of Egypt and on to the very edge of nationhood. In a few sentences at the book's beginning the family saga of Genesis is transformed into a national history. Abraham and his family were wanderers, foreigners in a strange land. Moses, the central character of the Book of Exodus, is not; his life has direction and a goal. The Old Testament is beginning to deal in larger and larger numbers; the Book of Exodus describes the birth of a nation.

After Joseph's death, Exodus tells us, there 'arose up a new king over Egypt, which knew not Joseph' (Exodus 1:8) and the people of Israel were enslaved. The story, then, is of an escape from slavery through the waters of the Red Sea, of a forty-year wandering in the desert wilderness of Sinai and of the arrival of the children of Israel at the gates of the Promised Land. At the same time it also tells the story of the development of a new religion, the religion of Jehovah.

As it stands today, the text of the Book of Exodus, like the Book of Genesis, is a product of several different periods of history. It holds a marvellous mixture of motives, stories and aspirations, and has become an archetypal Western story, a symbol that signifies that the ultimate destiny of the oppressed is freedom, that right will inevitably triumph. The saga begins, quietly enough, in the manner of the Book of Genesis. The story of Moses' childhood has a mythic ring and is firmly in the Mesopotamian tradition. The most un-Egyptian story of Moses' exposure to the elements, a baby floating down the Nile in a reed basket, is a variant of a tale told of several ancient heroes. Precisely the same story is told of King Sargon who around 2500 BC founded a huge new empire based upon southern Mesopotamia. Like King Sargon, baby Moses drifts in a basket caulked with pitch, a common commodity in Mesopotamia but a rare importation in ancient Egypt. Moses' name, however, is Egyptian enough, and one he shares with many famous pharaohs; Ra-moses or Ramesses, Thoth-Moses or Tuthmosis: Ramesses means 'born of the god Ra', Tuthmosis 'born of the god Thoth'; Israel's Moses would oversee the birth of Israel.

Much of the story of Moses in Egypt is held inside the realities of that ancient land, and this especially in the descriptions of the plagues. As Moses confronts Pharaoh in the terrible contest that finally forces Egypt to let the people of Israel go, the storyteller accurately describes some of the ecological realities of the ancient Egyptian environment, that rainless land locked along the sides of a great river. Here, indeed, the Bible's eye is typically acute. As Moses' prophecies unfold one by one, they combine to give us a picture of a genuine ancient catastrophe. For most of Moses' plagues are but the disasters that attended a superabundant flood, that rare distortion of the springtime inundation that brought Egypt's fields their annual watering. With the very first of Moses' plagues, when the Nile flows red with blood, you can see the river running syrupy-thick with Ethiopian silts, a warning of the disaster already born amid the melting snows of the African highlands at the Nile's source. This silt was the first evidence of the tremendous quantities of water in the river's upper reaches; in Egypt, the flood that followed this raw flow would be grotesquely large and the red micro-organisms that invariably accompanied it would already be destroying the river's normal ecology. In the 1960s, as Lake Nasser slowly filled behind the Aswan Dam, the shrinking islands of the lake quickly became infested with scorpions, snakes and frogs, all swarming to the higher ground, and this too Moses prophesied and would have been the fate of Egypt during the early stages of a high flood. Ancient records tell us, too, that such disastrous flooding also broke the dykes that contained normal annual floods, destroying towns and temples and even the corn stores that held the next year's seed corn. And later, as the flood waters lay over Egypt, the flies and pestilence that accompany mass drownings and stagnant water would have become unbearable, another plague. Then, as the waters slowly subsided, the new year's crops, late-sown and scanty, would fall prey to the fungus and bacteria flourishing now in the damp earth. Such abnormal seasons also brought freak storms with them; dust storms in which locusts, frogs and even fish might be whisked up into the air, then dropped dead and cold upon the earth. And all this, Moses prophesied (Exodus: from 7–12).

In normal times, a generous annual flood would be counted as a blessing from the gods, the mark of an especially potent pharaoh. Such a violent super-abundance, however, would have devastated Egypt. In the eighteenth century BC, such a disaster, continuing over several years, brought down the government of a pharaoh; his subjects would probably have thought that he was quite unfit to rule. For Pharaoh, they believed, held the balance between men and gods, and ensured prosperity in Egypt. In this world, then, the plagues that Moses prophesies would never have been seen as a punishment for enslaving the Israelites, but as part of a contest between two deities, Pharaoh and Jehovah. And, when, as the Book of Exodus describes, the staff of Aaron, Moses' High Priest, is transformed into a serpent at Moses' command, all of ancient Egypt would have understood the challenge for the serpent was an emblem of pharaonic power; golden spitting cobras sat on the front of every one of pharaoh's crowns. In common Egyptian symbolism, Moses and his god joined battle with the king of Egypt.

With the tenth and final plague, Jehovah reaches right into ancient Egypt's heart. For the death of the first born is a specifically Egyptian curse that goes far beyond the limits of its more obvious tragedy. In traditional Egyptian society, a family's eldest son not only inherited his father's position in the world, but, by careful attention to the cult of the dead, ensured a continuity between this world and the next. The destruction of this link would have dropped ancient Egyptians into rootless, unstructured oblivion, a cosmic chaos. The expulsion of Moses, who seemed to be the author of the plagues, with all his followers, would have been viewed by the Egyptians as an act of national preservation. Jehovah displays a diabolical understanding of the Egyptian mind; in its way, the tale rings true.

And it came to pass, that at midnight the Lord smote all the first born in the land of Egypt, from the first born of Pharaoh that sat on his throne unto the first born of the captive that was in the dungeon . . . And Pharaoh rose up in the night . . . . And he called for Moses . . . and said, Rise up, and get you forth from among my people, both ye and the children of Israel; and go, serve the Lord, as ye have said.

(Exodus 12: from 29–31)

How then, should we take this story of the walk out of Egypt; as a story of a mythical prince leading an unborn nation through seas standing in the air or as the history of an ancient emigration, the material evidence of which science will one day recover to allow us to plot and place this epic march in history. With its combination of vivid realism and moral symbolism, it is hardly surprising that there have been many attempts to fit the Exodus, as a real event, into the history of the ancient world. Yet neither Moses, nor an enslaved Israel nor the event of this Exodus are recorded in any known ancient records outside the Bible. And with the sheer size of this biblical emigration – more than 600,000 people, it is said, left Egypt, something between a fifth and a quarter of the ancient population – that is quite extraordinary. The social and economic trauma of such a happening, the sudden surplus of food, the labour shortages and all the rest, would have left a mark in existing Egyptian records, which, though erratically preserved, are widely spread and highly detailed.

The Bible itself shows a deliberate intention to fix the date of the Exodus; 'the sojourning of the children of Israel, who dwelt in Egypt, was four hundred and thirty years' (Exodus 12:40). And this biblical number can quickly supply us with a hypothetical date for the Exodus, or at least, an 'earliest possible' date. For the oldest-known text that records the Israelites living in the Promised Land is dated to 1207 BC and if we add to that figure the forty years of biblical Wandering in Sinai and the 430 years of the sojourn in Egypt, we will arrive at the year 1677 BC as the earliest possible date of the Exodus. All that, however, is roundly contradicted by another biblical passage, 'And the children of Israel journeyed from Ramesses to Succoth, about six hundred thousand on foot' (Exodus 12:37), part of the description of the departure. Now this city, Ramesses, is the Delta city of Ramesses II (see page 48) and that king lived four centuries after the date that we have calculated above, when the City of Ramesses was not in existence! If we assume, then, that this figure of 430 is wrong in some way and that the Israelites really did pass by the city, and if we again use the benchmark of 1207 BC and add to that the forty years of the Wandering, we obtain another 'earliest possible' date of 1247 BC for the Exodus departure. And, as we know that Ramesses II ruled from 1279 to 1212 BC, we can further narrow this down to a time slot of thirty-two years, that is, between 1279 and 1247 BC! However, any number of editors could have added that phrase about the City of Ramesses to the text at a later date, in helpful explanation of Egyptian geography, just as the phrase 'of the Chaldees' was probably added to the Ur of the Book of Genesis (see page 22). Can we really trust the 'forty year Wandering' to be an accurate figure? To tease such precise dates from the Bible's texts requires faith and a selective eye.

Hard evidence of the Exodus event in the preserving deserts of the Sinai, where most of the biblical Wandering takes place, is similarly elusive. Although its climate has preserved the tiniest traces of ancient bedouin en-campments and the sparse 5000-year-old-villages of mine workers there is not a single trace of Moses or the Israelites; and they would have been by far the largest body of ancient people ever to have lived in this great wilderness. Neither is there any evidence that Sinai and its little natural springs could ever have supported such a multitude, even for a single week. Several nineteenth-century vicars realized this fact within a day or two of the start of numerous expeditions in search of Moses' footsteps. 'Escaping from the rigours of an English winter,' as one of them says, 'in a land of the flock and the tent to which our only guide was the Bible' they quickly realized that the biblical Exodus was logistically impossible and that the Bible was a most ambiguous guide to that desolate region. The biblical description of the Exodus, then, flies in the face of practical experience; indeed, the closer you examine it the further it seems removed from all of ancient history.

If then, you would still try to prove this tale, you must begin by extracting from the ancient text the little phrases that hold probability in them. And you must also dispose of errors of information. The improbable figure of 600,000 people may quite properly be shrugged off with the observation that ancient texts are often as cavalier with large numbers as are modern journalists. But shall we then discard all the fantastic elements of the story as it is written; Moses' plagues, the miraculous crossing of the Red Sea, Jehovah guiding his people in a pillar of fire? Then, the entire significance of the story disappears and you are left with a few 'primitives', people more credulous than our-selves, more god-ridden than god-fearing, undertaking puny and haphazard adventures.

That, of course, was not the ancient way. Such carefully made stories as that of the Exodus were designed for other purposes than a mere record of events. In the second century AD, when the Jewish population of Egyptian Alexandria was large and influential, a new version of the Exodus story was in common circulation. It told not of Moses, but of a Mesopotamian priest called Osarseph, the leader of a band of 80,000 lepers whom Pharaoh had first enslaved then sent to live in a deserted Hyksos fortress close by Ramesses City. From there Osarseph sent a message to the Hyksos, who were then living in Jerusalem, calling them to return to Egypt. And this they did, joining forces with Osarseph's lepers, 'ravaging Egypt together, committing all kinds of blasphemies'. Then, the Egyptian kings, who had first retreated south, took the field and attacked the lepers and the Hyksos 'killing many, and pursuing the others even to the frontiers of Syria'. Now, this is hardly the grand saga of the Exodus; in fact it is a travesty, an anti-Jewish tract born of a city celebrated for intercommunal prejudice.

A contemporary Jewish historian, Josephus, said it was the result of historians following 'certain prejudiced informants'. And yet the excavations at Tell el Dab'a close by Ramesses City have indeed uncovered two separate eras of occupation, just as the story of Osarseph describes. Indeed, the scurrilous tale is as much confirmed by modern science as is the Book of Exodus and shows how misleading it will be to try to fit the biblical Exodus into history with such small scraps of information that the Bible gives us. It reminds us, too, that the real purpose of such ancient stories was not mere record making. For the Book of Exodus is the story of a nation's birth. The Alexandrian version recognizes that fact, then reverses the Bible's story to provide an *ignoble* ancestry for the Jews. To deny that more than half-a-million people walked unprepared into a savage desert and survived for forty years does not deny the extraordinary significance of the story. For there is real history in the tale, a vital part of Western history, too. Yet in this ancient book, this history is told in the language of the ancient world: the language, so common in the Book of Genesis, is taken up once more.

It is a language, too, that is used throughout the books of the Old Testament. The legendary struggle between Pharaoh and Moses is occasionally mentioned in odd phrases that tell of Moses fighting not Pharaoh, but the great dragons that, the Book of Job (e.g. 26:12) tells us, Jehovah had fought at the time of the Creation. Some of the Psalms (e.g. 89:10) and the Prophets describe these same combats. Suitably enough, they re-appear in the Bible's last Book where these same beasts that were at the world's beginning also attend its ending. Today it is sometimes said that these sophisticated monsters were merely hippopotami or crocodiles beheld by simple people. But it is difficult to imagine that such celebrated monsters as Leviathan, Rehab and Behemoth were quite that suburban, these terrifying things that breathed smoke and fire, stood ten feet high and, it was reported by an ancient rabbi, had even frightened the angels. These were the things that went bump in the ancient night and they were much better known at that time than their brief Bible appearances might suggest.

As an image of wicked Egypt, the demon Rehab is an especial favourite (e.g. Isaiah 30:7 NEB; Psalm 87:4). A Mesopotamian goddess of chaos and salt water, another of Rehab's names was Tiamat the mother-goddess that Marduk slaughters in the *Enuma Elish*. Here, then, in the Book of Exodus, these ancient stories have come full circle. Just as they were once used to build and underpin the Bible's story of Creation, so here they have been used again to describe the creation of a nation, ancient Israel. In this second creation Tiamat is the Red Sea and Marduk has become Moses the divider of the waters; a rare direct allusion to the Mesopotamian imagery that underlies so much of Genesis and

Exodus. Neither had the rabbis of the Roman period forgotten these most ancient images that underpinned their sacred stories. So, continuing to row in the waters of these most ancient tales, one such rabbi suggested that the waters of the Red Sea were the same ones that had flooded Noah's world, the same too that Jehovah had parted at Creation. And Moses had been allowed to stand them on their head as a punishment for their initial refusal to part from their embrace at the time of the Creation.

'And Moses stretched out his hand over the sea; and the Lord caused the sea to go back by a strong east wind all that night, and made the sea dry land, and the waters were divided' (Exodus 14:21). The new world born as Israel walks across the wet sand at the bottom of the sea is precisely described as a new creation. And this miraculous event, the climax of the Exodus story, stands between the old world and a new one.

A recent scientific theory has linked Moses' parting of the waters of the Red Sea with a volcanic eruption, which about 1450 BC destroyed the Mediterranean island of Thera; a cataclysm that not only damaged the Minoan cities of nearby Crete but sent tidal waves and a heavy fallout of ash over the coasts of Egypt, Canaan and Anatolia. It was these tidal waves, it is suggested, that destroyed Pharaoh's pursuing army, leaving the Israelites encamped that night upon higher ground, wondering at the power of their god. The Plagues of Egypt are explained as a description of the fallout of volcanic dust and a real plague that was virulent in the Near East at this time. The Pillar of Fire that held Jehovah as he led his Israelites into the desert was the red glow of the volcano reflected on the black clouds, and the Israelites' miraculous escape amid this shower of miracles suggested a divine intervention on their behalf which not only validated their national religion but gave them a special sense of destiny.

Yet all the other cultures of the eastern Mediterranean had thought so little of this eruption that until modern scientists found its traces in the earth there was not the slightest inkling that it had ever taken place. There is no mention of it in any of the known records. Ancient scribes had simply not bothered to record it. And that is hardly surprising, for in all of ancient history there are no records of a god making such a dramatic use of a natural event to intervene in human affairs. Ancient gods did not work in that way. How was it then that these ancient Israelites had seen the hand of god in this smoke and fire? If such unique understanding had been given to them in 1450 BC, this would truly represent a more thunderous happening than any exploding volcano. For this is nothing less than a new perception of deity, a new kind of god.

So many gods were there in the ancient world that Jehovah had had to introduce himself to Moses carefully when they had met at the Burning Bush. 'I am the God of thy Father,' he says 'the God of Abraham, the God of Isaac, and the God of Jacob' (Exodus 3:6). Of all the people of the ancient world perhaps only Moses would have had an openness of mind – by normal ancient standards the gullibility – that led him to believe this desert deity when it claimed to be the unique and universal god. To most people such words could only have been uttered by a dangerous megalomaniacal spirit. Yet Moses followed this god who, the Book of Exodus tells us, led the people of Israel for forty years from Egypt to the Promised Land. This vision of a rootless historical god, a god moving through time and space was a genuinely revolutionary perception; a notion, too, that the ancient world could hardly have understood. It is also, of course, a new vision of man's potential. No longer would his imagination be bounded by the holy rhythms of the ancient gods, the rivers' rise and fall, the sprouting of the wheat. This god, Jehovah, gave men the notion that they could walk with their god as Moses had done in Sinai, directly affecting their own lives by their own actions.

As Jehovah and his people wandered in Sinai, he still had to be *understood* by his chosen people; the Israelites had to discover the personality of this strange new god. Sometimes, as in his trick with the Burning Bush, he shows the same inclination to magic as some of the more ancient gods. And Jehovah also inherits some of their trappings too; the Israelites made him a carrying chair, the Ark, adapted from the designs of the chairs that carried Egyptian gods and pharaohs. Sometimes, too, Jehovah was as ruthless and erratic as a Mesopotamian god, angrily killing those who did not uphold his law. But in his calmer aspects, the Jehovah of the Book of Exodus also holds something of that awesome nimbus of power that was held inside the sacred pomp of Egypt.

What was completely new about Jehovah, however, is that unlike the gods of Egypt or Mesopotamia, he had not been perceived and made by artists and poets, nor was he a god of a single place that could be carried about and married off to father children and new alliances. Jehovah insists upon the unity of all holiness inside him alone; he is an all-inclusive abstraction, a theological and moral god. And no island explosion could have contained that. The real story of the Exodus then is not about volcanoes nor seas that stand on end, it is about a new vision of the world.

As the Israelites left the orbit of ancient Egypt, as they walked between the standing seas, they left the ancient world behind them. Even though the ancient gods appear to survive in their various ways, such a revolutionary perception of deity would have changed man's expectations and relationships with the gods, forever. And, like these Israelites, we too have been irrevocably severed from this ancient world. But Exodus still tells its story of this brand-new god in the most ancient language of the East, that magical universe of Arks and Edens, of ziggurats and pyramids. Genesis and Exodus take up these ancient tales again and spin them into a beautiful spiral of story-telling, enlarging them to hold the power and majesty of a new vision. A vision, indeed, that the Old Testament itself only slowly comprehends, book by book; a vision of a slow-revealed God.

The real crux of the Book of Exodus is not the date of a desert journey then; even if Moses were dug out of the desert sands tomorrow we would be no nearer to a better understanding of him and his god than we would be of the theories of Freud if King Oedipus' bones were excavated in Greece. What is crucial is the date when men first apprehended this new potential of god, for this has remained a vital part of the West until today. Fortunately it is easier to discover the age of the *Book* of Exodus than the route of an Exodus journey – and all the indications are that this was a very long time after Ramesses City had descended into ruin. For running alongside the ancient theme of creation and re-creation is the no-less powerful theme of a liberation from slavery and of Jehovah's revenge upon the slave masters. And it is in this account of Israel's enslavement that the Exodus story departs from the reality of the world of Genesis and Exodus. Slavery on such a scale and of the type described in the Book of Exodus did not exist in ancient Egypt nor anywhere in that ancient world, where mankind was set inside a holy order in which everyone from a pharaoh to a bonded peasant was at the disposal of the gods and the state. In such a world modern conceptions of slavery and freedom, even of ownership and buying and selling, have little meaning. Furthermore, explicit documentary evidence from ancient Egypt shows that foreigners who lived in that country, either as prisoners of war or as peaceful immigrants, were carefully and quickly integrated into the general mass of the population. (In this sense, the city of Tell el Dab'a was an exception, indeed, the Egyptians themselves regarded it as a foreign place). Ancient notions of race and culture were very different and Exodus' theme of liberation from oppression is entirely inappropriate to ancient reality. To periods, that is, before the times of the Greeks and Romans.

But the long age between the Israelite Exile in Babylon, in the fifth to sixth century BC, and the terror that accompanied the Roman presence in Judaea in the first to second century AD was an age in which ghetto life and slavery were hard realities for many Jews. Then the people of Israel had frequent cause to pray for a new Moses, a Messiah to lead them to a land of milk and honey. And in these later periods of ancient history, we will also find several cultures with conceptions of deity similar to those of Jehovah in Sinai, the same awareness of space and time and the belief that man can directly influence his own destiny. The Book of Exodus, then, is a document which joins the most ancient creation stories of civilization with the bones of a national saga and a later powerful theme of national liberation. Ancient stories of the national Patriarchs have been re-cast with a new conception of god at their centre, a god that holds within him all these national aspirations. It is this out-of-time god that gives the ancient tales their eerie and ambiguous air, an air of simultaneous reality and unreality. In this later age, the ancient openness and wonder and curiosity were all joined to a contemporary anguish and a powerful anger in an incredible fusion that produced a document of unfathomable antiquity and extraordinary significance.

Chapter Two
CHRONICLES AND KINGS

Introduction: Digging for God

In the spring of 1889 an Englishman with an Arab servant and a donkey, two loaded camels and a driver, arrived at a lonely mound – the *tell* – of Tell el-Hesi in the rolling hills of biblical Judaea some sixty miles southwest of Jerusalem. After ten seasons of excavation in Egypt, the archaeologist Flinders Petrie had come to dig in the Holy Land. Petrie had examined many sites before he fixed on Tell el-Hesi but most of them, his Egyptian experience had told him, were but Roman and Arab remains and he was after more ancient earth – earth that might hold in it the dust of the Kingdom of Israel.

The wide-open plain that Petrie saw from the top of the *tell* was burned brown and deserted but for a few black tents and some nomads taking sheep to the brackish stream that ran past the side of the mound. So ferocious, so poor were these people that the Turkish governors had long since left them to their own devices. Travellers were often attacked, sometimes even killed. On his way to Tell el-Hesi, Petrie was robbed and half-throttled, suffering a broken windpipe that left him slightly hoarse for the rest of his life. Petrie's camps were never places for the fainthearted. Tell el-Hesi, he later recalled, had swarmed with black scorpions and one night he had killed a tarantula in his bed. 'The course of an excavator' Petrie once observed, 'is not of the easiest'.

Part of Tell el-Hesi's slope had been eroded by the stream and here Petrie could see the archaeological strata, the successive layers of ancient cities one upon another, exposed in the sunlight. He spent the first few days of work climbing up and down this cliff face, digging out fragments of its ancient pottery with his penknife. Egypt had taught Petrie the importance of the strata of which many archaeological sites were composed; successive layers of dust and sand, brick and stone, the black ash of burning, the levelled walls of buildings cut through by the foundations of later ones, all piled high one upon the other. And sprinkled through all of it were the innumerable fragments of pots, plates, dishes, jars and all the rest of the paraphernalia of pre-industrial households. Ever since the 1860s, German archaeologists working in Greece had used some of their excavated pottery fragments, those that were painted in well-known styles, to date the strata from which they had come. In Egypt, Petrie had begun to extend this simple technique to include these humbler and more common domestic wares. Petrie's special talent was his phenomenal ability to remember an immense assortment of shapes and styles of pottery and to sort them, with all the crushing logic of a computer, into a linked pattern which, with a variety of other information, formed a picture of the history of his site. His genius lay in the ability to analyse this instinctual process and to produce a scientific method by which any archaeological site could be similarly analysed by those without his special talents. In six weeks' work at Tell el-Hesi, with only a handful of local labourers, 'thirty thirsty muslims, each with a woman or girl to carry their baskets' he says, Petrie had established the outlines of Palestinian archaeology, and that necessarily included the age of the kingdoms of Israel.

Right at the bottom of the mound, closest to the virgin soil and therefore in the oldest levels of the site, Petrie found a type of pottery he had never seen before, and this he called 'Amorite' after the biblical inhabitants of the land of Canaan whom the Book of Genesis told him had made a treaty with the Patriarch Abraham. This Petrie dated to a time before 2000 BC, because in the strata above he had found some rare fragments of Mycenaean pottery of a type which he had already found in his excavations in Egypt. Higher up, above these deep strata, were great bands of cities, all holding pottery of unknown type and dates. Above all this, again, were strata holding yet more fragments of Greek pottery, this of a well-known type easily dated to the fifth century BC. Accordingly, all the local wares in the strata that held the datable foreign fragments were dated to the same periods, while the mass of pottery from the mysterious strata which lay in the levels between 2000 and 500 BC were labelled 'Jewish'. These bands, Petrie concluded, were of the time of that ancient people. In the lower parts of this, he surmised, must be the very dust of the Kingdom founded by David, enriched by Solomon and finally defeated by the Babylonian invasions, just as the Books of Kings and Chronicles described.

After his work at Tell el-Hesi, Petrie took a two-week walk searching for more sites, travelling north to Jaffa on the coast, then back a 100 miles or so across the hills to Jerusalem. As he later said, his trip had 'determined the history of pottery in Palestine'. What it had also done, of course, was to lay out in scientific order the visible history of an ancient land which had been previously known only from the pages of the Bible. In the 1970s, another expedition came to work at Tell el-Hesi, which by this time was completely encompassed by the orange groves and wheat fields of Israeli farmers. Nearly fifty specialists took part in this work, geologists, archaeologists, anatomists, paleobotanists, photographers, artists and surveyors; the expedition prospectus alone was a larger document than Petrie's final report. Certainly, archaeological method has been greatly refined since those first wild days, and many of Petrie's conclusions on his lonely survey have been challenged and corrected. But Petrie's was the first, and by far the largest, step. For he had shown how scientific method could bring the dust of ancient Israel into the light. The strata of Tell el-Hesi had been opened up like the pages of a Bible and the hunt for the remains of the earthly kingdom of the Children of God was on.

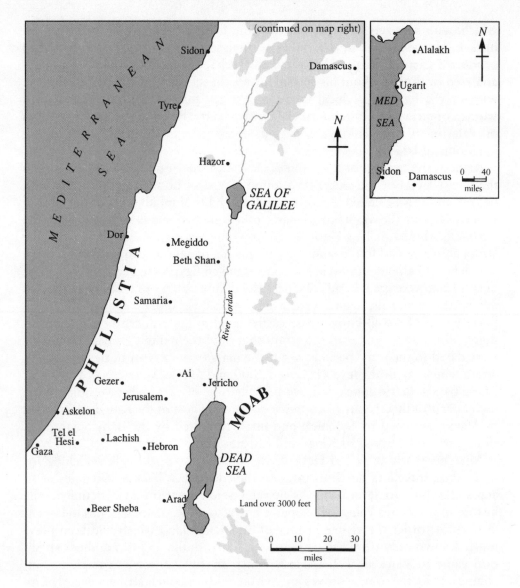

Ancient Israel with sites referred to in the text

Israelites and Archaeologists

Ten thousand years ago, long before men made pottery, farmers lived by the spring of Jericho in the wilderness of Judaea, a community of some 3000 people who built the famous stone tower 'the world's oldest building at the lowest point on earth'. Their great tower stands upon bedrock from which the spring still flows down to the River Jordan on its way to the Dead Sea, the last fresh water that travellers would have found before setting out on the desert road that climbs some twenty miles to Jerusalem – the last until the springs upon the Mount of Olives. Jericho stood at the edge of a broad oasis with palm groves so beautiful, so fecund that Mark Antony had once given them to Cleopatra as a wedding present. This most ancient of all cities, the Bible tells us, soft and beautiful on its low warm plain, was the first place in Canaan to fall as the Israelites entered the Promised Land.

Today, the grassless *tell* of Jericho, Tell es-Sultan, lies oddly at the edge of the oasis (see Plate 4). Once round and smooth, the brown hill is now a torn-up dust heap, a straggle of tips and trenches. The dust is the residue of the ancient city; the famous tower, now deep in dirt and ash, once stood twenty feet high upon a level plain. Walk westwards in the great trench in which the tower now sits and you walk through the largest slice of human history on earth. The first steps take you past walls as ancient as the tower, then past walls built at the time of the pyramids of Egypt, through spare strata of ancient Israel, where the letters JDH – Judah – have been found upon the handle of a jug. If, then, the Bible's description of the destruction of Jericho is anything more than a myth, evidence of Joshua's sack of the city should be here somewhere in these dusty strata. But which one of the many bands of ash and broken brick was made by the biblical Israelites?

Until the First World War every archaeological expedition that worked in Palestine followed Flinders Petrie in labelling their excavated strata with vague names like 'Amorite', 'Semitic' and the like – names that reflected the excavators' own interpretations of ancient history – and this had led to many confusions in biblical archaeology. In 1922, however, at a meeting in the offices of the Department of Antiquities of the British Mandate in Palestine, four scholars – one French, one American, and two British (both of them Petrie's pupils) – agreed upon the use of a single system of classification invented by a Danish museum curator in the early nineteenth century: the Stone, the Bronze and the Iron ages.

Much revised, divided and sub-divided into ever smaller phases, these three grand abstractions which began theoretically as these three materials were first introduced, have lasted until today. In the 1920s the precise dates of the three ages in Palestine were still unsure; the categories, however, were clearly discernible in all excavations. Now the biblical archaeologists might begin to trace the conquest of the land of Canaan by Joshua and his army.

It was clear to historians that the period between the end of the Bronze Age and the beginning of the Iron Age was of special importance for ancient history and for biblical archaeology as well. This period (presently estimated to have been around 1300–1200 BC) had been an era of destruction and invasion. Though the Old Testament supplies no date for the Israelites' invasion of their Promised Land, later ancient texts and the dramatic archaeological evidence suggested that this was the only possible period in which Joshua and the Israelites could have arrived in Canaan. Joshua's Jericho (Joshua 6), then, lay buried in the *tell* close to the point where the Bronze Age strata stopped and the Iron Age strata began. This marked the dividing period between the Canaanites and the Israelites. And between these two, of course, should have been a black band, the ash and the tumbled bricks of the city's fallen walls.

The same man who had chaired the Jerusalem meeting of 1922, John Garstang, was also the first to excavate Jericho's *tell* using modern archaeological method. Now he could date the various city walls which ran around the *tell* in concentric circles like the rings in a tree trunk. Parts of these walls, built in fine rich brown mud brick, that still stuck out of the dirt close to the top of the mound, Garstang attributed to the Early Bronze Age, while another, outer wall he ascribed to the Middle Bronze. As well as these walls, however, there were also elaborate ramparts and ditches, some of them still with their slippery slopes covered in shiny plaster, all a part of elaborate defensive systems designed to stop the rush of attacking chariots and troops. These were typical Bronze Age fortifications, known from Egypt to Syria. In a nearby grave Garstang had found Egyptian jewellery bearing the name of a pharaoh who had ruled at about 1350 BC. Clearly, here he was close to Joshua and the Israelites. Then, close by, Garstang found another wall. This he dated to the Late Bronze Age. It was a rough affair of loose stone and brick and it had been built on top of an earlier wall, showing the clear signs of haste that suggested the preparation for a siege. It showed, too, frequent signs of disastrous collapse, bricks lying sprinkled at its foot. And there, too, all around the bottom of the wall was a broad band of ash speckled like a butterfly's wing, gaudy dust, brick and plaster, all burned in a fire so fierce that the sun-dried bricks had been fired as if they were in a kiln. Garstang could see that the wall's attackers had placed brushwood against it to burn it down, the first phase of a general attack upon the city just as the Bible tells us the Israelites had done. 'And they burnt the city with fire and all that was therein' (Joshua 6:24). The wall seemed to be of precisely the right period and to have suffered a suitably biblical fate. Garstang also observed that the collapse of the wall could well have been provoked by one of the numerous earthquakes in the area, rather than by seven blasts of seven trumpets. Though Jehovah may have been deprived of a miracle by the common sense of archaeologists, at least the Bible story now seemed to have a rational foundation based on archaeological evidence.

Yet before long, Garstang's dating of Joshua's attack upon Jericho which he had estimated from the evidence at the burned wall to have been about 1500 BC, began to worry many Bible scholars. For one thing, they pointed out, the Book of Exodus says that the Israelites had begun their journey to the Promised Land from a city called Ramesses, and no town of Egypt would have borne that name before 1212 BC, when Ramesses II had come to the throne. Then over the years, as the classification of Palestinian pottery became further refined it also became clear that there was a serious error in Garstang's dating of the burned wall. In 1952 the English archaeologist Kathleen Kenyon began seven years of further excavations at Jericho in an attempt to clarify these problems, an excavation that proved to be as fundamental to Middle Eastern archaeology as Petrie's work at Tell el-Hesi. Kenyon's excavations showed that most of Garstang's dates were wrong – the oldest strata proved, with the aid of carbon dating, to have been some 4000 years older than Garstang had thought. Furthermore, Garstang's celebrated burned wall proved to be merely another wall of the Middle Bronze Age: the battle that Garstang had excavated had taken place a 1000 years before the Iron Age; Joshua and his Israelites retreated into the pages of the Bible from whence they had come.

Nor was this all. Kenyon had also found that during the Early Iron Age, the period which was the only possible time for the first Israelite settlements in Canaan, the city of Jericho had been largely deserted, having been in a state of ruin ever since the destruction of the last Bronze Age city 300 years before. Joshua and his Israelites would have found little more than a poor village atop an ancient hill when they arrived at Jericho, a state of affairs that has since been confirmed in excavations at other cities which, the Bible tells us, were also visited by Joshua and his army. All this was a serious blow to the biblical historians who had long been carefully gathering up archaeological evidence of a systematic invasion and destruction of all the cities of Canaan, and keying their evidence in with biblical accounts of the Israelite invasion. Now it appeared that the destruction of these cities had been earlier and more random than had previously been imagined. Several attempts have been made to salvage their theory by what might best be described as moving the goal posts; the archaeology was re-dated so that Joshua and the Israelites would find someone to fight on their arrival. But most scholars were agreed that the known archaeological facts called for a fresh look at our understanding of these Bible stories.

And this was not long in coming. By the 1960s, Joshua's Israelites had been transformed from a historic to a symbolic army, from an invading infant nation to disparate tribes of desert nomads grabbing up the lands of a weak country, Canaan, enfeebled after centuries of war. It was suggested that the writers of the Old Testament had united these separate tribes into a single Israelite army.

This hypothesis at least had the advantage of providing an explanation of the situation described in the Book of Judges before David became King of Israel, when the Twelve Tribes are united only in military coalition and by their worship of Jehovah. A major problem, however, is that the nomadic life style that had been wished onto these new-fangled Israelites had been drawn more from romantic nineteenth-century visions of desert Arabs than from ancient reality. The notion of desert tribes appearing land-hungry from the so-called 'semitic heartlands', the yellow deserts of Syria and Arabia, was simply not an ancient reality.

There were also growing objections to the very notion of a foreign invasion of Bronze Age Canaan. It had become clear to many archaeologists that the cultures of early Iron Age Palestine – the first 'Israelite' period – were in fact based firmly upon the older cultures of the area. The Bronze Age pottery forms had continued to develop through the Iron Age rather than suffer the complete break that the bloody biblical conquest might lead one to expect. And even the Hebrew language, the language of the Old Testament, was now seen to be a part of a local family of languages that also included the language spoken by the Canaanites, the very nation which Joshua, the Old Testament tells us, conquered and destroyed! Once again, fresh interpretations were needed if the Bible and history were to stay in step. So, once again the invading Israelites were transformed, this time into indigenous revolutionaries grouped together after the demise of the Canaanite cities whose end they had helped to hasten. Now, the parade of Joshua's army around the walls of Jericho became a symbolic gesture, a sign of the victory of an indigenous proletariat over the tyranny of the great city states. At this point, Joshua began to look more like Kirk Douglas' Spartacus than an Old Testament Israelite.

One thing that all these theories about Joshua and his invasion have in common is the conviction that in some way, behind all the miracles and fabulous stories, the Bible's story of Joshua's invasion of Canaan holds in its pages reflections of real events, garbled perhaps by time and telling, but nonetheless real for all that. One thing is, indeed, certain. In common with the Book of Exodus – indeed with most other ancient histories – the Old Testament gives us an un-modern view of the past. Though it is a carefully made history it has been made from an ancient viewpoint.

Consider just one fragment of Old Testament history, from a period known both from the Bible records and verified and dated in other ancient sources: the reign of King Ahab. In non-biblical texts Ahab's claim to fame is in his participation in a great battle with an invading Assyrian army on the plain of Qarqar in 853 BC. But of this the Bible mentions not a single word. Yet so weakened were the terrifying Assyrian armies by this battle that they did not take the field again in the west for three whole years. Assyrian records of the battle tell us only of a hard-won victory bringing honour to their gods. The

Bible's account of Ahab's reign tells us that he was a wicked king who did not walk in the ways of the Lord; it describes only his defeats and his bloody death. For both these ancient records, then, the Bible and the Assyrian Annals, significant history is not an all-inclusive documentary description of events but a careful selection of happenings that show the relationship of a nation to its god or gods. Traditionally, of course, both Christians and Jews have viewed Joshua's miraculous destruction of Jericho in exactly this way: as evidence of God's relationship with his chosen people. Similarly, the first archaeologists to dig in the Holy Land were Christians looking for the remains of the stage on which these sacred dramas had been acted out. Today, though techniques have been greatly sharpened, the inspiration has not greatly changed.

Ultimately, archaeology can neither 'prove' nor 'disprove' the Old Testament, only modern theories about what it might mean. What archaeology *can* do, however, is to give a fresh vision of this ancient literary world. The story of Joshua's battle for Jericho, for example, broadly reflects the archaeological realities of the destruction of Bronze Age Canaan. But like most Old Testament history, the story has been written, re-written, edited and collated over many centuries, by priestly members of a caste intent upon showing that the nation they ruled had been uniquely created by the single, universal god. The process of comparing biblical history with the mainstream of ancient history becomes extremely valuable. First, then, let us fix the dates of those few occasions described by both the Old Testament and the chronicles of other ancient nations. These, as we shall find, are all from the period of the Bible's own histories of the Kingdoms of Israel, the Books of Joshua and Judges, of Chronicles and Kings.

The First Israelites

Nowhere in the world is there more ancient history preserved than in Egypt, and when the ancient Kings of Israel ruled and fought, the sacred capital of that kingdom was the city of Thebes. No neat mound like Jericho, Thebes today is a ten-mile sprawl of stony ruins where excavations progress not only by the trowel and brush but with cranes, hawsers and massive scaffolding.

Six years after his work at Tell el-Hesi, Flinders Petrie was digging at Thebes, sifting his way through ton upon ton of sharp stone fragments, the pitiful debris of royal temples. It was, he recalled later, disastrously dull labour, and he was tempted to leave it. Then, all at once, objects that had been buried for millenia among the rubble started to turn up. A fine portrait sculpture of the king who had built one of the temples was found, the first ever discovered of the Pharaoh Merneptah, that son of Ramesses II who in those days was widely believed to have been the 'Pharaoh of the Exodus'. Then his men came across a huge rectangular granite block lying face down in the rubble, a great grey stela covered in small lines of hieroglyphic (see Plate 3). The block was massive and Petrie did not have the equipment to move it; but what a fascination! A huge new monument, well preserved and covered in history. Petrie had his men clear some of the rubble out from under the stone so that, as he says, 'one could crawl in and lie on one's back, reading a few inches from one's nose'. Then he asked a visiting scholar, who specialized in inscriptions, to examine the lengthy text. 'There are the names of various Syrian towns', he reported after a miserable afternoon on his back in Petrie's trench, 'and one which I do not know, *Isirir*'. 'Why,' said Petrie, 'That is Israel'. 'So it is,' his friend replied, 'and won't the reverends be pleased'. And so they were and have been ever since, for the Israel Stela as the great block is now called, holds upon it the most ancient mention of Israel yet discovered. During almost eighty years of field work in archaeology, Petrie wrote more than a 1000 books and articles. He excavated royal tombs, opened pyramids and discovered golden treasures but, as he himself said at dinner on the evening of the day the great grey stone was first deciphered, 'This stela will be better known in the world than anything else I have found'. Such was, and such remains, the allure of the Bible in archaeology.

Now the mention of Israel upon the stela was brief enough, part of a poem, a list of peoples conquered by Merneptah in a campaign in the thirteenth century BC.

Canaan has been plundered
and every sort of woe,
Askelon has been overcome,
Gezer has been captured,
Yano'am made non-existant,
Israel laid waste, his seed is not.

It was soon observed that the names of the three towns listed before the name of Israel, Askelon, Gezer and Yano'am, were each followed by the circular hieroglyph that signifies 'city', but that the sign which followed the phonetic hieroglyphs of the word Israel was different, a sign that signified a nomadic community, a tribe. To biblical archaeologists this suggested that in Merneptah's time the Israelites had yet to settle down in farms or towns and this fitted perfectly with Merneptah's reputation as 'Pharaoh of the Exodus'. Yet so formulaic, so commonplace was the stela's text that many scholars doubted that it had any basis in fact at all. After all, many of these Egyptian victory hymns were merely copies of older ones made to decorate the reign of a new pharaoh. If this was true, of course, Merneptah's lists of conquered towns and tribes were but distant echoes of other ancient wars. And there, for almost a century, the argument and speculation came to a full stop.

Then, in the 1970s, a young student working in the Temples of Karnak at Thebes noticed that a modest group of texts and pictures long assumed to have been a minor memorial of Ramesses II was, in fact, made for his son and successor Pharaoh Merneptah. Four badly damaged scenes accompanied four brief texts on a wall of one of the temple's many courtyards, and all of them were of a type so commonplace that no one had studied them carefully before. Now, three of these scenes showed foreign fortresses being attacked by Pharaoh and his army, and one scene still preserved the name of the city under attack: Askelon. Here the Canaanites are shown fighting for their lives, falling before Pharaoh's arrows. Egyptian infantry scale the city ramparts; a soldier chops at the wooden gates; fathers lower their children from the walls of the doomed city, while Askelon's elders beg Pharaoh for mercy.

In short, the scenes are regular run-of-the-mill ancient Egyptian battle scenes, common enough at Thebes. The fourth picture of this group, however, though badly damaged is somewhat different. For here there is no fortress, merely a mêlée of corpses lying on a plain, abandoned before Pharaoh's army. In this group of pictures the student recognized a direct parallel between these four scenes of battle and the poem on Merneptah's stela; in both the wall-scenes and the poem three Canaanite towns appear and one of them is called Askelon. So in the fourth picture, the one that has no city wall, the bodies that lie upon the plain should represent the army of Israel. This, then, would appear to be the oldest-known picture of Israelites made while they yet roamed Canaan. Though they still lived outside the great cities of the region, they were of sufficient strength to be remembered and memorialized by Pharaoh's artists. If nothing else, this second account of Merneptah's campaign confirmed the Israel Stela's status as a record of genuine historical events. Now, so accurate are the records of ancient Egyptian history that labels such as 'Bronze Age' and 'Iron Age' have long been as redundant as a flint axe. At ancient Thebes, historians often talk in individual years, sometimes even months and days. And

Merneptah's campaign in Canaan, most modern historians would agree, took place about 1207 BC. Here, then is the earliest evidence of ancient Israel, a date in its history to which all other events can be related.

The Land of Canaan

Ancient Canaan was full of those tough little fortresses that Pharaoh attacks so heartily on the Egyptian temple walls. There are hundred upon hundred of *tells* in Syria and Israel, usually lonely steep-sided hills as smooth as burned-out volcanoes set close by perennial springs that feed wild fennel and cyclamens as well as the ancient city wells and the crops of the surrounding plains. These *tells* hold the residences and warehouses of the princes that once ruled the area. There is a lively drawing of one of these courts cut onto a slip of Syrian ivory;

the local ruler sits proudly upon an Egyptianesque throne; all around him is his little court, musicians, scribes, soldiers, priests, ostlers and servants; there is a bustling air about it all, a lively intelligence. Tablets of Mesopotamian cuneiform, even of fragments of the great myth *Enuma Elish*, have been found in these *tells*; Egyptian seals and statuary, jewellery and weapons show the other major influences in these ancient lives. This Canaanite culture was so heterodox, so lacking in distinctiveness that if the fragments of the little ivory drawing had been excavated a 1000 miles from its modern findspot, no one would think it the least bit out of place. Only the local architecture and pottery, that invariable index of ancient cultures, give the land its own distinctive style. Yet, through the Books of the Old Testament the people of these cities have influenced all the West.

Canaan's miscellaneous landscape, framed by sea and desert, by Egypt and Anatolia, part bad lands, part green plains, never lent itself to the notion of nationhood. In the mountains it was hard enough to survive, let alone indulge in the luxury of court politics. And in the plains, the cities of central and southern Canaan were all on the ancient highways, on the roads to somewhere else, sometime vital links in the Egyptian empire. Many of these cities were also fat enough to encourage many Pharaohs to plunder their treasures and their harvests; cities like Megiddo, Hazor, Gezer and Beth Shan: black bands of ash in these cities' strata tell of numerous sackings.

Megiddo is the most famous of these Canaanite towns. This is the biblical city of Armageddon that stands above the plain where, at the end of the world, the final battle between the armies of the Lord and the kings of the earth will be fought out, as the Book of Revelations tells (Revelations 16:16). Armageddon is 'Ha-megiddo' – the hill of Megiddo. Unlike Jericho, where archaeologists cut trenches down into the strata like the slices of a cake, the *tell* of Megiddo has been shaved off horizontally, strata by strata, city by city. The depression of the 1930s put a stop to the whole expensive enterprise but by that time, American archaeologists had exposed the Iron Age city, the period of the biblical Israelite kingdom. At one end of the mound, however, in the area that overlooks the fatal plain, they continued their work cutting down vertically right to bedrock, through the strata of much older cities. There, standing straight upon the limestone hill, they found temples that were some 5000 years old; ancient temples of gods that the Bible's prophets had so reviled. Yet these most ancient temples of Megiddo shared something of their design with the Tabernacles and Temples of Jehovah: courts with water basins and altars for incense and animal sacrifices. A great circular altar made of undressed stone, just as the Book of Leviticus commands, stands in the oldest levels of the *tell*. When it was first excavated, it was found to be scattered with burned bones, ritual offerings of a type that would later be made to Jehovah and which the Bible calls *olah* – from which the word 'holocaust' is derived by way of the Greek. As both archaeology and the Bible tell, carved stones that held the presences of gods were often set up upon these altars. Though the books of the Old Testament often record the destruction of these shrines by pious prophets and righteous kings, Israel was never rid of these sacred forms and ancient gods which must have seemed as old as the land itself.

Contrary to the biblical story that a savage Israelite army destroyed Canaan's wicked old cities and established a new faith and a new nation in their place, archaeology shows that the reality of change between Bronze and Iron Age

Palestine was a gradual transformation in which the traditional forms of worship were maintained, as powerful expressions of men's relationship to the sacred, whether to biblical Jehovah or to the ancient gods of Canaan.

And, of course, without such basic continuities few would have recognized the divinity of Israel's new god. So, although the Bible stresses the novelty, the uniqueness of Jehovah, archaeology shows that the differences between the biblical ritual of his faith and the old cult of Canaan was slight – and this indeed was doubtless why the prophets so vigorously attacked the ancient gods for century after century, so that their new faith was not absorbed into the ancient ways. Were it not for the Bible's violent repudiation of the Canaanites, it would be hard for archaeologists to recognize that the ruins of Iron Age cities sitting atop the Bronze Age cities of Canaan were anything other than their natural successors. Ironically, this vehement opposition to Canaanite culture and faith, which the Bible often expresses in sacred rules and prohibitions that cover every aspect of daily life has left an inadvertent Canaanite legacy: that sort of negative of piety so innocently embraced by necromancers and followers of the occult!

The remains of *tells* like Megiddo seem like gnarled old trees, their walls hard-pruned by ancient armies. The ruins of more northern cities, however, seem more serene, the remains of small cosmopolitan buffer-states on rich red alluvial plains, princely fiefdoms, controlling satellite towns and hamlets. A prince who epitomizes the life of these cities, a lifestyle that disappeared completely at the ending of the Bronze Age, was a certain Idrimi, Prince of the city of Alalakh, now a small and lonely *tell* ridged with dark green firs in the extreme southwest of Turkey. Idrimi's statue is a perky little figure, limestone white on a black stone throne, huge eyes staring apprehensively into the world

just as the Mesopotamian ancestors of these temple statues had done for thousands of years. Idrimi ordered his biography to be written by one of his five scribes, a man called Shurrana, and it was carved with the first prayerful line 'May the gods of heaven and the unknown keep me' coming out of the statue's mouth, with the rest of the tale running down over the statue to cover both Idrimi and his life. 'I was king for thirty years, I wrote my achievement on my statue so that people will read it and bless me . . .' Idrimi, the inscription tells us, was the second son of a Prince of Alalakh who had been forced from his throne, probably by a revolt. Dissatisfied with life in exile in a foreign city, Idrimi left his family and, taking a horse, a chariot and a squire, roamed south into central Canaan, living with the *Habiru*, those infamous nomadic tribes, all the while watching the sacrifices on the temple altars to discover an auspicious moment to return to Alalakh. After six years it paid off. Idrimi returned in triumph with his family to his house, signed treaties with his neighbours and sat upon the city throne. He built a new palace at Alalakh in the local manner, with dignified grey stone walls and a wooden superstructure filled with brick. The entrance up a broad staircase lay between two huge pillars, a favourite Canaanite decoration for the doors of palaces and temples, and one that the biblical Temple of Solomon would also use. Behind the palace the excavator Leonard Woolley found a real treasure, for there one of Idrimi's successors had built the palace archives which still held the state's tablets, all written in Mesopotamian cuneiform in the local dialect. The decrees of Alalakh used exactly the same opening formula as the Israelite laws of the Book of Deuteronomy (Deuteronomy 26:16), 'This day the Lord thy God hath commanded thee to do these statutes and judgements . . .'

Idrimi's palace was small. As you visited the public chamber you would have smelled the cooking from the servants' quarters – perhaps, then, Idrimi would have invited you to dinner, for in the little kingdom of some two to three thousand people he must have known most of its subjects personally. And here, too, is another similarity with the Bible – this small-scale courtly life. For Idrimi's biography is written in the same manner as many Old Testament stories; in the human language of the small state. Idrimi's adventures read like those of David, Absalom and Saul. In a world where most literature spoke either in grand abstractions that told us of mighty pharaohs and great victories, or in cold legal documents and bureaucratic biographies, such a strong affinity of style is hardly accidental. In fact, Idrimi's scribes and the Old Testament writers share the same literary tradition.

Unfortunately, the excavation of Alalakh yielded very few religious texts; but another town nearby, the rich coastal city of Ugarit, did. In Idrimi's day, Ugarit traded widely throughout the Fertile Crescent and across the Mediterranean. But, like Alalakh, it could not resist the implacable advances of the northerners who swept through northern Canaan in about 1200 BC destroying everything.

As at Megiddo, Ugarit's temples also show the same ritual arrangements as the biblical Temple of Solomon, three-roomed buildings with three shrines in the innermost chambers. And here, precisely the same constructional methods were used as at Solomon's Temple: a distinctive local mixture of wooden beams and stone walls as described in the Book of Kings (1 Kings 6:6 NEB): '[Solomon's builders] made rebates all round the outside of the main wall so that the bearer beams might not [sic] be set into the walls'. Solomon's Temple, the Bible tells (1 Kings 9:11), had been built by the workmen of the Prince of Tyre, another coastal city, a hundred miles south of Ugarit.

Unlike Alalakh, Ugarit had a huge bureaucracy working from a lavish scriptorium where the clay was prepared and the tablets were made. Hundreds of their texts have survived; here was a multilingual community, one educated by its trading. Ugarit's accountants used a twenty-six letter cuneiform alphabet, an invention that would take writing out of the atmosphere of the ancient temples, away from the sacred obscurities of pictographs into a secular, demotic script which people of many different nations could easily adapt. This was a direct forerunner of modern Western alphabets as well as biblical Hebrew.

Just as the faith of biblical Israel was housed inside the traditional architecture of Canaan so some of the Old Testament's oldest passages, its liturgy and Psalms are also rooted in Canaanite literature. Indeed, at first glance the connections of the Old Testament and some of Ugarit's literature are so obvious that it is easy to imagine that this city had special links with ancient Israel. This, however, was not so. Ugarit's texts are much older than Israel, since the city itself was destroyed at the ending of the Bronze Age. Its literature was Canaanite and it is the traditions of that society that influenced the Old Testament. Even so, the scribes of Ugarit well knew of the city Jerusalem and its nearby holy Mount Zion; for the hill was known by that same name, which in Ugaritic Canaanite means 'the seat of a god'. Many Old Testament characters, too, have typically Canaanite names: Absalom and Solomon even hold in them the name of the Canaanite god of the evening star, Solom, just as does the name of Jerusalem itself. That numerous biblical terms for the articles of daily life, for clothes, perfumes and furniture were also Ugaritic, emphasizes the fact that this influence was not only linguistic but extended into the paraphernalia of daily life.

The sacred texts of Ugarit have even been helpful in deciphering some biblical passages that have been scrambled through millennia of copying. David's lament for his son Jonathan (2 Samuel 1:21), for example, contains the famous, if enigmatic, lines 'let there be no dew, neither let there be rain upon you, nor fields of offerings': an Ugaritic lament has supplied its true meaning, '[let there be] no dew, no rain, no surging up of the lower depths'. Here the pagan god is ordering the three sources of fresh water, dew, rain and spring water, to stop their flow during rites of mourning, and David's beautiful refrain repeats the ancient lament. Similarly, the famous words of the exile in Psalm 137, 'If I forget thee, O Jerusalem, let my right hand forget her cunning' have long been recognized as a poetic resolution of an ambiguous Hebrew passage which according to an Ugaritic parallel, should read rather more prosaically: 'If I forget thee, O Jerusalem, let my right hand wither'. Similarly, those splendidly enigmatic notations which often accompany the Psalms (so enigmatic, unfortunately, that the New English Bible has dropped them altogether) also have direct parallels in Ugaritic psalms where similar words are placed like the directions on a musical score, setting pace and mood. At sites like Meggido and Ugarit, small figures of musicians, harpists, drummers, and luteplayers were daily common finds in the temples – energetic little people, full of life and gesture, but now making silent music. These notations on the Bible's Psalms hint at the strong musical tradition in Canaanite ritual, which biblical Israel took to with enthusiasm.

Most interesting of all, perhaps, is that these Ugaritic texts have not merely illuminated small details of the Old Testament but have shown us the origins of some of its style. Just as the informal character of the narrative of many Old Testament stories is also found in works like Idrimi's biography, so many of the Old Testament's other literary manners are to be found in Ugaritic literature. Both Ugarit's great God Baal and Jehovah 'mount to the clouds' in their respective chariots, both 'utter voice' in thunder and storm, and both stand 'at the head of the assembly of gods'. And that most striking of Old Testament devices, the list of robust contrasts piled one upon the other, was also used first by Canaanite scribes.

Elijah's famous confrontation with Jehovah at Mount Horeb (1 Kings 19:11), for example, has Canaanite overtones.

> And, behold, the Lord passed by, and a great and strong wind rent the mountains, and brake into pieces the rocks before the Lord; but the Lord was not in the wind: and after the wind an earthquake; but the Lord was not in the earthquake: And after the earthquake a fire; but the Lord was not in the fire: and after the fire a still small voice.

Eighty years ago, most Bible scholars believed that the greater part of the Old Testament had been composed long after the Kingdom of Israel had come to its end. The recent discovery of this Canaanite literature, however, shows how deep the indigenous roots of the Old Testament run. Here, then, in Bronze Age Canaan are the origins of ancient Israel's sacred liturgy, both of its architecture and of its written word. And memories, too, of the lively kingdoms whose burned ruins quite literally underpinned the cities of ancient Israel. At Alalakh, at the end of the Bronze Age, the northern invaders had destroyed Idrimi's palace and temple along with the rest of the town. Woolley found the black throne of Idrimi's statue lying in the courtyard of the temple that had held it for 200 years. The statue, in fragments, had been carefully buried in the temple's rubble – someone must have returned to the ruined city and piously buried the fragments, but no one ever returned to rebuild the city itself. It was not the biblical Israelites, then, that destroyed Canaan's prosperity but these ferocious northerners moving down, anonymously, from the Asian plain. They passed through Canaan, skirting the coast in ships, and marching across the plains, destroying city after city. And they did not stop until they reached the gates of Egypt.

Sackers of Cities

The Egyptians did battle with the northern invaders in 1176 BC, some twenty-five years after the destruction of Ugarit and Alalakh. So fierce was the fighting, so high the stakes, so successful the outcome, that scenes of these wars were chosen as the decoration for the walls of the Theban mortuary temple of the warrior pharaoh, Ramesses III. With a most careful eye, his artists have left us the only pictures of the northern invaders, a great mass of people welded into a single terrifying migration; soldiers, women and children travelling in ox-carts, such as are still used by their descendants in Cyprus and Anatolia. Men of a dozen tribes, all the warriors in their distinguishing regalia, each group with its own headdresses and ornaments, cloak-pins, earrings, tattoos and, above all, their fearsome weapons; huge straight swords for thrusting and chopping, and great rounded shields. The texts of the pictures name the invaders *Sherdan*, mercenaries from the Egyptian border forts; the *Peleset*, the biblical Philistines; the *Tjekker*; and a host of others all pitted against Pharaoh and his regiments. Ramesses III trapped their ships in the marches of the Delta at the very edge of Egypt. The Egyptians had oared ships with lion-headed prows designed for ramming and had copied the efficient rigging of the northern boats. The duck-headed prows of the northern boats were decorated with huge pointed eyes like those that still can be seen on the prows of small Mediterranean craft to this day. The Egyptian archers caused carnage and huge numbers of the

northerners were slain and captured; the temple scenes show heaps of hands and uncircumsized penises all being carefully counted up by swarms of Egyptian scribes.

Millennia before this invasion of Egypt, more northern tribes had already dislodged neighbouring populations, sending them southwards, spilling into the ancient Near East in a series of rippling migrations. In the century before the destruction of Canaan, that is between 1300–1200 BC, there had been an enormous movement of disparate peoples: tribes, nomad nations, dispossessed bands of free-ranging, heavily armed men, travelling around the eastern Mediterranean, moving into Greece and Italy and into northern and western Europe. The invaders were buried where they fell, with their long swords, wearing jewellery, cloak pins and belt buckles of a type that has been found in lands from Sweden to Egypt. Such a widespread distribution of objects, even in the old days of the great trading networks, is quite unique.

Both Homer and the Old Testament, in their elliptical way, tell of the disorders of these days. Stories of wild bands of men, often of different races – 'sackers of cities' Homer calls them – travelling in boats, riding along the coasts not to conquer and rule but to plunder. At Troy, so Homer tells us, women, honour and gold were Achilles' spur, as they were for Nestor, Odysseus and Paris too. The last letter written in the city of Ugarit describes seven black boats coming close down the coast, boats that had already attacked and burned several smaller towns along their way. In the thirteenth century BC however, there was a breakdown and, as the walls of Troy and Ugarit fell away, an entire way of living fell with them. Only in Egypt and in southern Mesopotamia did the old cultures survive. This, then, is the age of the biblical Exodus, a savage age; an age of endings and beginnings.

Almost a century after the reign of Ramesses III, an Egyptian priest named Wen-amun pulled into the harbour of Dor on the coast of Canaan in a cargo boat, on his way to the Lebanon to buy cedarwood for the renewal of the Temple of Amun at Thebes. The town was ruled by the descendants of one of the tribes, the Tjekker, whom Ramesses had repulsed from Egypt. 'I embarked upon the great Syrian sea,' Wen-amun says in his official report. 'Within a month I reached Dor, a harbour of the Tjekker. Berer, its chieftain brought us fifty loaves . . .'

Dor was an important port, one of the very few on the long and featureless coastline. A small promontory of petrified sand-dunes had been sliced up by the people of Dor to make harbours, quays, docks and slipways. The Tjekker, a sister tribe to the Philistines, had a large fleet and close links with many other ports in the eastern Mediterranean. After their Egyptian defeat, many of the sea-going tribes had settled around the Mediterranean, the ancestors perhaps of the Achaian Greeks, the Sardinians, the Cypriots, the Sicilians (and even perhaps, the Etruscans). New trading networks and alliances had been established. By Wen-amun's day, Dor was a manufacturing town too, exporting a celebrated purple cloth; the freshwater springs along the shoreline providing the source for extensive dye works. Here there was also an international trade in copper, pottery, oils, glass, a whole range of Mediterranean goods. Wen-amun, then, visited a busy and successful city built by the Tjekker on the ashes of an old Canaanite town. Shortly after Wen-amun left Dor, however, the port was absorbed, so archaeology seems to show, into the growing orbit of the Philistines, who, after their defeat by Egypt, had settled closer to the Egyptian border and served the pharaohs as mercenary troops as their forefathers had done.

This then, was the new culture of the coast and its plain; an international culture, one that was barely literate but one especially blessed, so archaeologists have discovered, with a splendidly distinctive painted pottery in a rich tradition quite alien to that of the old Canaanite cities. At the height of their power, the Bible tells us, the Philistines controlled most of the seaboard and coastal plain of Canaan. But never did they enter the mountain areas above the coast and there, the Bible tells us, in the east were the ancient Israelites.

David, Goliath and Samson

As the tribes came into Canaan and settled along its coast, archaeology tells us, there were also waves of new settlements, poor farms and houses inland to the east along the Jordan valley, and to the north.

At about the same time the Israelites, according to the Bible, were establishing themselves in the highlands on the west bank of the Jordan. The Books of Judges and of Samuel also tell us that here in the hills the Israelites fought not only with each other but with their neighbours in the hills around them; the Edomites, the Moabites, the Ammonites, the Syrians.

Such mountainous terrain tends to produce small, isolated communities, as the archaeology of these hills confirms. The Bible describes the twelve tribes growing up in semi-isolation, each with their own distinctive customs, gathered together only to wage war against common enemies. Just as the country is rough, so early Israelite life there in biblical times was hard; sheep farming and smallholdings, with wine and olives a common crop on the poor limestone hillsides and wheat grown on tiny terraces and on the valley floors. It is difficult to see more comfortably-off plain dwellers, such as the Philistines, ever coveting anything in the hills. But the Bible has many tales of battles, and they, of course, provide some of the Old Testament's more famous heroes. And it is in these stories that the biblical Israelites and their Promised Land first begin to fit into a specific period of ancient history. David's fight with Goliath, for example, is set in the landscape between the Philistine plain and the Israelite uplands, a natural borderland later to be fortified by Arabs and Crusaders and, more recently, by Israelis and Jordanians. David's fight was a duel of champions; Goliath's speech a knightly challenge in an ancient manner. Another similar challenge is buried in the story of Abner, the commander of King Saul's army, who also fights a duel to settle a war between neighbours. 'Let the young men now arise, and play before us' he suggests (2 Samuel 2:14), an early example of youth fighting the wars of its fathers.

David, an Israelite shepherd boy, fights with a simple sling, a traditional weapon in Canaan. His stones, water-smoothed pebbles, he takes from a brook at the centre of a valley such as you may see today; where the aromatic scrub of the limestone uplands gives way to the sticky red alluvium of the plain. Goliath, the Philistine champion, has all the armour and weaponry of a professional soldier, a technology foreign to more ancient Canaan, the arms of the northern invaders. In fact, he wears armour similar to that of Homer's Achilles: a bronze helmet, hardly traditional in these hot southlands, an armoured vest and greaves on his shins – these were unknown during earlier periods in the Near East. But what most impressed the Israelites was Goliath's javelin (1 Samuel 17:7), 'And the staff of his spear was like a weaver's beam; and his spear's head weighed six hundred shekels of iron'. Iron was very little used in Palestine during the twelfth century BC – indeed it has been suggested that its initial development in the lands to the north was due to the breakdown of the traditional supplies of bronze from the Middle East. Smelted iron had first come into the region from Anatolia. Its strange cold hardness made an especial impression in Egypt where it was thought to have religious restorative properties and was buried close to the mummies of the pharaohs.

Traditionally, Goliath's javelin with its shaft 'like a weaver's beam' has been interpreted as an exaggeration, implying that the javelin was a specially huge weapon suitable for a giant. But later drawings of the javelins of Greek warriors show a binding around their shaft resembling the loops upon the leash-rod – the 'beam' – of an ancient weaver's loom. Inserting his finger into a loop of wool the thrower could use the loop to spin the javelin as it left his hand, producing an effect like that of the rifling of a gunbarrel which makes the bullets spin straight and true. Goliath, the Philistine champion, was armed, then, in the traditional manner of the northerners, the 'sackers of cities'. As he fell to David's slingshot, 'the men of Israel and of Judah at once raised the war-cry and hotly pursued them [the Philistines] all the way to Gath and even to the gates of Ekron' (1 Samuel 17:52 NEB) – two of the five main Philistine cities.

It is interesting to notice other similarities with archaic Greek stories in these Old Testament tales about fighting the Philistines. Samson, for example, the biblical Hercules, is like his Greek counterpart in many respects. Both are brave strong men destroyed by women, and Samson's career, as in the Greek myths, is also built of symmetries, even indeed in its numbers: he slays thirty men at his wedding feast; sets 300 foxes in the Philistine fields and requires 3000 Judaeans to take him captive. (As Samson's name derives from the word *shemish* – 'sun' – his burning of the Philistine corn is an apt gesture in a land of fierce summers!) Whether Samson ever lived or not is hardly relevant to the significance of the stories; they certainly describe real historical circumstance; that the scribes of the Books of Samuel order his tales in the classic manners of myth aids their deeper purposes. This, in part, is a definition of the precise limits of lawful Israelite contact with their pagan neighbours, people who when they were as wealthy and as cosmopolitan as the Philistines, must have posed real problems to the poor Israelite farmers. Samson is seduced by the alien delights of Delilah. Should one marry these pagans? And what of feasting with them? Samson's downfall tells us of the result of violating Jehovah's Law. As to the children of such mixed marriages, the Book of Ruth tells quite clearly who may be accepted as legitimate children of Israel. In all these stories of heroism and fortitude, the precise rules of inheritance and legitimacy are laid out once more, as they were in the histories of Abraham and his family. But here those general principles are amplified to cover the specific circumstances of biblical Israel. The stories teach by an almost unconscious absorption of what is 'natural' or 'unnatural', sacred or defiled, right or wrong. Beautiful Delilah, the instrument of Samson's downfall, is one of a large number of foreign biblical seductresses that includes Jezebel and the Queen of Sheba. And all of these women introduce foreign cults into holy Israel, seduce the populace with their charms, exciting sin and leading to inevitable damnation.

Unlike these mythic figures, however, the Philistines, as archaeology has shown, were real enough in twelfth century BC Canaan, and, in the following hundred years, they were moving northwards. The Bible tells us that it was the Israelites in the mountains that stopped their progress. Archaeology tells us that by about 100 BC the Philistines were again confined to the coastal plain in the area of their five cities. The wars that the Israelites fought, so the Bible tells us, brought them to nationhood. The biblical battle between Sisera and Barak and Deborah in the Vale of Jezreel, and the great Song of Victory that followed (Judges 5:2–31), considered by many authorities to be among the most ancient Bible passages, tell of the emerging federation and of the diversity of the tribes that followed Jehovah's Law.

The Vale of Jezreel, the wide plain in front of Megiddo on which the last battles of the world will be fought, is the biblical location where the Twelve-tribe confederation of Israel was blooded. On Mount Gilboa to the east, biblical King Saul and his sons were killed, then exposed, in the manner of a Canaanite harvest ritual, on the walls of the huge old city of Beth Shan. Israel, the Bible tells us, had begun to come down from the mountains into the rich plains, to capture the old cities and with them imbibe their ancient notions of kings and courts that the Bible's prophets so despise. This growing tension between the demands of the state and the rights of the individuals in it is one of the Old Testament's most precious legacies. Where, then, could the ideas of these single-minded biblical mountain folk have come from, this perception of God and government? The answer is to be found in the mountains in which the Bible says the Twelve Tribes were nurtured.

Israel's Beginning

Ai, the Book of Joshua tells us, was the first town that the Israelites took as they advanced into their Promised Land after their destruction of Jericho. 'Stretch out the spear that is in thy hand toward Ai; for I will give it into thine hand' says Jehovah to Joshua (Joshua 8:18). First Joshua tricked the militia into leaving their ramparts, then he turned upon the defenceless city, slaughtering its population of 12,000 people. The army was then destroyed, the king of Ai captured and hung for a day upon a tree before being cut down and buried in front of the ruined city gates. 'And Joshua burnt Ai, and made it an heap for ever, even a desolation unto this day' (Joshua 8:28). Archaeologists have dug up the gates of Ai but they did not find a hanged king in a stony grave. They did discover, however, that the huge city had been deserted for more than a thousand years before the beginning of the Iron Age: that is, a thousand years before the biblical Israelites appear in Canaan. If, then, you believe that the Old Testament tells us literal, modern truths, you must find another site for biblical Ai; alternatively, you may observe that the Bible is something other than a modern history book. Either way, Ai must seem a contentious place from which to start a history of Israel. Yet both that ancient kingdom and its god have much of their beginnings in places like it.

Today, the site of Ai, a lovely hill top some fifteen miles west of Jericho, presents its visitors with a summation of the archaeology of Canaan. Here are Bronze Age city walls, built at a time when these states were rich, literate and successful. Here is a fine temple with a wide hall and, outside, the standard courtyard that Israel would later adapt to its own purposes and here after a thousand-year gap in habitation are the scanty ruins of a settlement of the early Iron Age, built in and over the ancient city (see Plate 5).

Careful analysis of the pottery excavated in these Iron Age houses shows that most of it was made for storing food and water. On this mountain top among the ruins life was very hard, yet these settlers were not beginners at either farming or building. Their houses had unusual stone columns and well-laid out rooms based upon sensible designs with two or three cisterns cut into the rock beneath each one. The old Bronze Age cities all had communal water arrangements; these Iron Age houses collected their rainwater individually in cisterns which were arranged so that the water syphoned slowly from one tank to another allowing the impurities to settle to the bottom of the collection tanks.

The settlers employed a dual economy of animals – sheep and goats – and grain crops which they cultivated in small fields on the valley bottom and on terraces around the hill top that they made themselves, carrying the red earth up from the valleys to make small strip fields. Terrace cultivation is very hard work and here olives and grapes are an easier and more usual crop than wheat. This change of crop speaks of the customs of more fertile lands and the settlement's poverty – but it also shows an intelligent use of imported methods. Indeed, the organization of the settlement at Ai shows that these were people, like the settlers of nineteenth-century America, who while living hard lives in poor conditions were also adapting knowledge and skills gained on richer pastures.

In fact, the settlement at Ai is but one of hundreds, if not thousands, of similar settlements sprinkled throughout the hills of eastern Palestine. Ai is unusual only in that it was not built on virgin ground. Are these little hill-top farms on the edge of Canaan's plain, the houses of biblical Israel? So far, archaeological circumstance seems to fit the Bible's words. Archaeology also tells us where these settlers had come from and why they settled in such harsh land. These people had moved up into the hills to escape the troubled world below. This scanty hill-top culture, the style of pottery and houses and all the materials of their lives are not foreign to Canaan but a continuation, upon a small scale, of the life of Bronze Age cities. Even the underground cisterns have precedents in the city of Ugarit and other coastal towns where most houses had their own water supply held in similarly plastered water tanks. It seems likely, then, that these settlements were a refuge from the breakdown of Bronze Age Canaan, and that many of these people were city people escaping, initially, from the path of the migration of the northern tribes and later from the states that these invaders established in Canaan after their defeat at the borders of Egypt. Here in the mountains you could live safely, if by constant labour. Rare evidence of direct connection with the ancient cities is sometimes discovered in these hill-top settlements – small fragments of a Canaanite cuneiform text, a Bronze Age plough-share and the like.

Flight into the empty hills was a solution to the crisis of the ending of the Bronze Age, and one adopted by many differing people. Settlements with similar pottery and houses, even with similar methods of farming and water conservation, have been found running right along the edges of the Canaanite plains – and also in regions outside those areas of the biblical settlement of the tribes of Israel. Until quite recently these poor farms have promised very little in archaeological terms and it is only since biblical scholars pointed to their importance for biblical history that some of them have been surveyed and excavated. In all probability there are thousands more of them to be found stretching from south-eastern Turkey, through Syria, Israel and Jordan, down to the borders of Saudi Arabia, a great fringe of refugee communities, all fleeing from the uncertainties in the rich plains to the west.

As far as the Bible is concerned, of course, there is a major difference between these settlements inside the territory described in the Bible as being the lands inhabited by the early Israelites and those outside this area. For although the latter are archaeologically similar to the 'Israelite' settlements those outside were not built, so the Bible tells us, by the worshippers of Jehovah. But then no evidence of the religion of any of these settlers has ever been found by archaeologists; the remains merely indicate groups of farms and barns clustered together without even a wall to protect them. Where, then, was Israel and its god born? In Sinai with Moses and the people of the Exodus? If so archaeology is either mistaken or incomplete. Or here, in these small defenceless settlements, set in a hard harsh mountain landscape?

It was their rapacious warrior neighbours, the Bible tells us, that welded the Israelite farmers into warrior coalitions even, so many of its stories say, between families and tribes with little love for each other. Now archaeology can indeed supply us with evidence of this hill culture moving slowly down into the plains and valleys, to cities like Megiddo and Jerusalem. And this accords with the Bible's stories of tribes joining together in covenant under a common god to establish eventually the Kingdom of Israel and its capital, the city of covenant, the holy city of Jerusalem. Time and time again the Bible tells us that Jehovah was the god of this coalition, the cement that held the Israelite tribes together as, first, they held off invading neighbours, then later established cities and kings. Many of Jehovah's biblical laws show a practical basis for such success; covenants, treaties of peace and coalition, and a joint identity all based upon the worship of a single, unifying god. Naturally there was a distrust of the past, a hatred of the old city states and their cults that had so ruinously and obviously failed. And to those poor farmers, kings too were unnecessary, being merely in distant memory taxing overlords. And this the Prophet Samuel clearly spells out:

> This will be the manner of the king that shall reign over you; . . . He will take your sons . . . he will appoint him captains . . . and will set them to ear his ground, and to reap his harvest, and to make his instruments of war . . . And he will take your daughters . . . your fields, and your vineyards, . . . the tenth of your seed, your menservants, and your maidservants . . . your sheep . . . And ye shall cry out in that day because of your king.
>
> (1 Samuel 8:from 11–18)

In its first, pure form, the confederation of Israel did not require kings, only prophets to guide the holy vision of the confederation. The later history of Israel, in the Books of Kings and Chronicles, is a slow account of disaster, the slipping away from the ideal, a retreat from ritual purity and from Jehovah.

PLATE 4 (Opposite): The mounds of ancient Jericho, Tell es-Sultan, at the edge of the broad oasis that holds the River Jordan.
PLATE 5 (Overleaf above): Tell Ai, part of the early Iron Age settlement. Twelfth–thirteenth century BC.
PLATE 6 (Overleaf below): Tell es-Seba', the excavated gateway of a typical Iron Age city, of the tenth century BC. *This is often identified, though without good reason, as the gateway of ancient Beersheba whose well Abraham contested with Abimelech (Genesis 21:24 ff.).*

The biblical covenants impose a binding faith; Jehovah is a jealous god: these embattled farmers required all the links in their chain of coalition to be strong. There could be no mixed marriages like Samson's, no muddling of inheritance, no treaties with godless foreigners and no worship of foreign gods. And judges and prophets oversaw the rules of the faith. And this faith was not simply a political convenience: in the ancient world the gods filled all areas of life. Jehovah supplied all Israel's notions of the world and its order – infertility and illness, for example, were seen as the natural consequences of sin, just as was defeat in battle. It was Jehovah alone, the god of the covenant, who gave the covenanted hill tribes victory: divided they fell. This was a practical faith. What many today would think of as 'religion' was only the central mystery of their faith, the unknowable, ineffable centre. Forged in the violent perceptions of a hard new world, these biblical farmers had embraced a faith that explained the age and their route for survival. Adherence to the rules of Jehovah's biblical covenant promised security, peace, riches and a perfect world, and these were also the earthly rewards of coalition.

Today the ancient covenants and rules all carefully listed in the Old Testament have been organized and edited again and again by generations of scholars and theologians. Many stories far older than the history of ancient Israel have been shaped to fit the truths of these small hilltop communities. But it was there that the circumstances, the necessity to form a coalition arose and there perhaps that, in the ancient manner, a god of covenant, the embodiment of unity, was identified. The Bible knew this landscape intimately; great areas

PLATE 7 (Previous page above): The Iron Age fortifications of the so-called City of David at Jerusalem. Evidence of sixth–seventh-century BC Israelite occupation at this site, though not earlier has been confirmed by the discovery of some clay seal impressions bearing Hebrew inscriptions. On the eastern slope of the Kidron valley, the modern Arab village of Silwan maintains something of the appearance of an ancient hillside town.

PLATE 8 (Previous page below): Landscape around Bethlehem in December

PLATE 9 (Opposite above): Samaria; the excavated remains of the hilltop capital of the biblical Northern Kingdom, is still set among the traditional olive and almond trees of the region.

PLATE 10 (Opposite below left): The oldest-known Bible text: one of two scrolled silver amulets excavated in 1980 in an Israelite cemetery at Jerusalem. The text approximates the Priestly Benediction of the Book of Numbers, 6:24–26, beginning 'The Lord bless thee and keep thee. . . .' Judging by the style of its writing, the leaf of silver which was about ⅞ of an inch wide before it was unrolled, was inscribed in about the seventh century BC. Israel Museum.

PLATE 11 (Opposite below right): Jehu the King of Israel, or his ambassador, prostrates himself before Shalmanasser III: the only known contemporary picture of an Israelite king. The inscription above tells that the tribute offered to the Assyrian monarch included silver and gold, 'a staff for the royal hand' and some puruhati fruit. Dating from about 840 BC, it records an event that is not to be found in the Books of the Old Testament. Detail of the Black Obelisk from the city of Nimrud in Iraq. British Museum of these uplands are described in cool and knowing detail, small features of that landscape, even individual trees, are named and known. This is the biblical land of the early Israelites, the theatre of the Books of Judges, Ruth and Samuel. From these hills, the Bible tells us, the coalition of the tribes of Israel came down to the plains to fight Philistines and Canaanites. On such slopes Saul and his sons were slain, but David and his men came down and, with Jehovah's help, conquered the city of Jerusalem.

A Mighty Fortress is our God

Arad, high on the southern edge of ancient Israel facing the sands of the Negev, is a perfect place from which to view the meeting of archaeology and the Israelites. For here, on a hilltop inside an Israelite fortress, is an Israelite temple where Jehovah was worshipped when he was still a new and national god. The temple's design shares common origins with Megiddo's: the courtyard with a basin for ritual washing before worship, an altar of sacrifice and beyond, the hidden sanctuary of the god. Texts written in archaic Hebrew have been found in the fortress, letters written by professional scribes dealing mostly with military matters, one mentioning a 'House of the Lord'. These are some of the few texts to have survived from the time of the biblical Kingdom of Israel and they enable us to identify the fortress as Israelite and its temple as Jehovah's.

> To Eliashib [probably the commander of the fort, and a common enough Old Testament name] . . . give the mercenaries three baths of wine . . . and from what is left of the old wheat, grind up one measure to make bread for them. Serve the wine in punchbowls.

This Israelite fortress had about ten housing units inside the stout walls, rooms for officers and soldiers. Israelite Arad was destroyed several times, but the fortress was so strategically situated that it was maintained in continuous use down to the times of the early Arab invasions some 1500 years later. A cistern underlies the temple courtyard and, doubtless, the ritual basin there was once filled from it. The altar of sacrifice also stands in this courtyard, built of unhewn stone as the Law required (Exodus 20:25), and it had precisely the same measurements, $5 \times 5 \times 3$ cubits, as the desert altar of Moses' Tabernacle (Exodus 27:1).

While Arad's temple satisfies the biblical requirements of Israelite religion it also fits easily into ancient Canaanite traditions. But the god whose house this was, was new, and this not simply because this was the Old Testament's God. Nowadays an enormous distinction is drawn between Jehovah and the old Canaanite gods – the former having become the God of Jesus, the latter having been largely abandoned to the more salacious imaginings of the pious. But both these attitudes are distortions of ancient notions of divinity. Here at Arad, for example, ancient Israel's god, just like Luther's famous hymn, was indeed a fortress and salvation, but here this is not merely a metaphor of faith but part of the practical issue of defence. Arad's fort depends upon the temple's walls, just as ancient Israel was dependent upon the covenant of Jehovah. And just as in the Old Testament, Jehovah slowly reveals himself in stages which allow for a gradual dawning of awareness so this stony temple at Arad shows a similar process of refinement.

It is estimated that the first Israelite temple of Arad was built, along with its stone fort, in the tenth century BC, that is in the biblical age of King Solomon. Though, the Bible tells us, Solomon built the first great temple at Jerusalem, he did not prevent the establishment of other temples in Israel. The prophets, of course, were always opposed to such fragmentations of faith, preaching of a single centre for the Covenant at Jerusalem, and they encouraged the destruction of other shrines and temples inside Israel. Temples such as Arad's split the state by attacking the integrity of Jehovah. So, down through successive ages Arad's temple was successively diminished in its status. First the open court-yard was cut down in its size, its sacrificial altars closed. Only in Jerusalem could offerings be made to Jehovah. Later on, even the little sanctuary with its neatly cut incense altars and the tiny shrine at its back was bricked up. Similar reforms are described in the Books of Judges, Kings and Chronicles, at times when the state was threatened by invasion, and national unity was to be encouraged.

The identification of nationhood with the power of a god was not un-common in the ancient world and in this aspect Jehovah was not new. What is novel, however, is the removal of this state god from the rhythms and order of the natural world, from the rising sun and flooding rivers, from the ancient rituals of the kings and priests that marked the annual adventures of the gods that brought fertility into the world. Old Testament Jehovah makes his presence felt through the actions of individuals. The hard lives of the mountain farmers had led them to a conception of people, of families responsible for their own destinies. You will not find, for example, in these mountain settle-ments the thousand upon thousand of receipts and inventories that so clutter the archives of Bronze Age states, the 'scribal kingdoms' as they have been called. Biblical nationhood was born of covenant, not kingship. In places like Ai and Arad you may glimpse some of the earthly reality of that literary kingdom. Israel's perfection died at Jerusalem. There the Bible says the covenant broke down. As the prophets had prophesied, the sacred rules were broken and Jehovah extracted his penalty for this lapse through the medium of state history. The Old Testament historians clearly describe Israel's dilemma; the rule of kings is antipathetic to individual responsibility, yet the people feel the need of them. The splitting of the kingdom into two parts, Israel and Judah, is the tragedy; these monarchs were damned from their accession, their reigns are inevitable tragedies and the people of Israel stumble ever deeper into darkness and, eventually, into exile. King David's rule, however, was always seen as a golden age; a time when the covenant was strong, when the mountain farmers were not yet city scribes, soldiers or courtiers, when royal sins did not affect the destiny of Israel.

That city which, the Bible tells us, David took from its indigenous population the Jebusites, must be the Iron Age ruin beneath the Temple Mount in the south-east of the present city, excavated, in large measure, during the past fifty years (see Plate 7). But here, it must be admitted, there is still no hard evidence that this really is David's city. Neither, indeed, is there a shred of contemporary archaeological evidence to show that David or Solomon had existence outside the pages of the Bible. Once again, the question of the Bible's accuracy arises: how much of this book can be taken as an historical record in the modern sense of those words? Is it an historical document in the same sense as Eliashib's dispatches at Arad or the thousands of cuneiform tablets that are straightforward fragments of ancient daily life? Any scholar will say that the Bible is not at all like that; certainly there is a vast amount of genuine ancient material in its books, but this has been collected, collated and edited, checked time and time again. In other words, it is not simply a history book.

Yet Arad's temple and its changes, along with multitudes of other examples, show correspondences between archaeology and Bible text. And in Iron Age Jerusalem you will find many similarly circumstantial verifications. From his palace on top of the hill, for example, David would really have had a good view into most of his subjects' houses. Just as the Bible describes, he could have easily seen women like Bathsheba taking their baths. But it should also be said that if this Iron Age city at Jerusalem had been excavated in Jordan or Syria or even in another part of modern Israel, it would have gathered no more celebrity to itself than the numerous excavations of this type of city that are currently in progress. This City of David takes its name and its fame from the Bible. A few inscriptions from the site, odd lines inscribed in empty tombs, tiny impressions of seals that once fastened papyri, are written in Hebrew and therefore testify to a genuine Israelite presence in the Iron Age city; but these are all from ages later than the time of David and Solomon. Such a paucity of inscriptions and monuments, however, is quite normal and should not excite suspicions. The ancient Israelites were not given to memorials that would last.

Certainly, this ancient town beneath the Temple platform was a part of an ancient Jerusalem; David's city perhaps, just as it was Jesus' too. But long before Jesus' day it had grown up over the higher hills to the north overlooking the site of Solomon's biblical Temple of which, like the king who made it, not one trace has survived. Its presence, though, still seems to hang in the city's air, the golden dome on the Temple platform holds the once and future world of Judaism, Christianity and Islam alike. And the walls of the Iron Age town are easily enlivened by the numerous Bible stories about David's royal city. The extraordinary underground cistern cut under the entire length of its rocky spur which diverts the flow of a natural spring would have supplied the entire city with fresh water at time of siege, and such cisterns were tunnelled under other fortresses in Iron Age Israel as well. Perhaps sections of this tunnel were used by David's men to capture the city before the tunnel was enlarged by King Hezekiah at the time of an Assyrian advance upon Jerusalem in 701 BC. An inscription found on its walls in the nineteenth century is the longest composition in ancient Hebrew outside the Bible, and its lively style, uncommon in the ancient world, has a genuinely biblical ring to it. Building inscriptions in other ancient countries praise gods and kings in the language of the state scribes; here the text in the Siloam Tunnel is a friendly and enthusiastic affair, proud of the work and its achievement. It is probably to be identified with the work of King Hezekiah (2 Kings 20:20) and tells of the two teams of quarrymen who began at opposite ends of the hill breaking through to each other's tunnel deep in the rock beneath their city:

> ... and this is the story of the piercing through. Whilst the stone cutters were swinging their axes each towards his fellow, whilst there were yet three cubits to be cut, a man's voice [was heard] calling to his fellow, for there was a crack on the right ... and on the day of piercing, the stone cutters struck through to meet his fellow, axe against axe. Then the water from the spring to the pool ran for twelve hundred cubits, and a hundred cubits was the height of the rock above the stone-cutters' heads.

Close by the pool – the Siloam Pool – that this tunnel now feeds, right at the southern end of the Iron Age city, Roman quarrymen have cut down through the ancient city, taking stone for their fortresses and barracks; and there they have cut into three long vaulted chambers which, though there is no evidence of their age or purpose outside their architecture, conform with biblical descriptions of the locations and ritual requirements of royal tombs. These, then, might be the tombs of Israel's ancient kings. Unique in their architecture, as would befit royal tombs, but with traditional funerary shelves inside them, well cut with Iron Age chisels, these neglected chambers standing half in sunlight might conceivably be the tombs of Solomon and David – if, that is, those legendary kings are ever proved to have walked upon the earth.

That 'if', of course is the essence, the very heart of the Old Testament dilemma, the mystery of ancient Israel. For were it not for some minor concordances with biblical texts, all the remains of Iron Age Canaan could simply be interpreted, just as the similar remains in the surrounding lands are, as the modest dwellings of the region's unknown indigenous inhabitants. The Bible alone, that labyrinth of ambiguities, of myth and history, allows ancient Israel its rich and colourful existence. Strong in faith and convinced of biblical truth, many people use the Bible as an archaeological guidebook to Israel. Sceptics, however, may equally well use the results of this same archaeology to attack the biblical account. The standards adopted by historians working in areas outside the maze of biblical archaeology would seem to be the criteria to use. Using these standards, then, it should be said that, despite the numerous blank ruins of what, the Bible indicates, were once the cities of ancient Israel, only the hard evidence of the written word – a few hundred brief notes like the Arad letters, a few dozen tiny seals engraved with their owners' names and titles and a number of impressions from other long-vanished seals – really asserts the earthly existence of biblical Israel, so diffuse in its style and manner are the unlettered remains of Canaan's Iron Age.

Unexpectedly, however, in 1980 a small excavation in an Iron Age cemetery outside the city of Jerusalem recovered two small sheets of silver (see Plate 10) with texts faintly engraved upon them which, after the most delicate labours of conservation and decipherment, proved to be passages similar to two famous verses of the Book of Numbers, Chapter 6:24–26.

> The Lord bless thee, and keep thee: The Lord make his face shine upon thee, and be gracious unto thee: The Lord lift up his countenance upon thee, and give thee peace.

Not only did these small slips of silver have the oldest fragments of the Bible text yet discovered engraved upon them, but they also contained the earliest-known mention of Jehovah in his city of Jerusalem! And how appropriate that this text is the prayer known as the Priestly Benediction, that blessing repeated by rabbis at the ending of Sabbath prayers, by priests, too, on virtually every day of their calendar. If it is not a central text of biblical theology, it is certainly one of the most fundamental lines of its ritual and prayer, and that, of course, is where religion begins.

The graveyard where these two texts were found is to the west of the city almost at the head of a *wadi* that runs south, then eastwards along the city walls in an area now known as Ketef Hinnom. Here, there were extensive Israelite cemeteries, their graves cut into the limestone in accordance with biblical law, hinting that the Iron Age city may have been far larger than had previously been imagined. Inside these tombs, the dead were laid on shelves to rot until, after a suitable time, they were gathered up with all their grave goods and pushed into a family charnel house excavated in the rock behind the tomb chamber – quite literally a 'gathering up with the forefathers', just as the Bible says. The charnel house, in which the silver plaques were found, held the jumbled remains of a large family buried over a long period of time. Presently, the earliest estimate of the date of the script scratched on the silver sheets, and written, probably as the Prophet Jeremiah describes with a pen of iron, is of the seventh century BC, in the time of biblical kings. Other objects in the charnel house show that it was still in use a century later, after Jerusalem had been attacked and sacked by the Babylonians in 587 BC.

The two silver sheets had been carefully rolled up, probably around two strings, and tied around the necks of two dead children, amulets to protect them on their dark journey. Along with these two silver sheets was a mass of jewellery: fine golden earrings shaped like small pillows and as bright as buttons; elaborate pendants of silver which before their corrosion in the tomb had sparkled with small drops of silver laid out upon their surfaces in delicate ancient patterns; splendid beads of glass and stone, one shaped into a face like Mr Punch, a product of the several coastal cities which, by that time, were called Phoenecia. All in all, a small heap of treasures; but one so ordinary that if it had been found in half a dozen other countries of the Middle East no one would have raised an eyebrow. Egyptian, Assyrian, Phoenician; all the ancient Levantine traditions of design were in the little tomb. But the two small slips of silver and the dimensions of the tomb identify the cache as Israelite. Here, then, is a small part of the mixed culture of the people who are the subject of the Books of Chronicles and Kings. And immediately you see that Israel, like its neighbours, was but a modest collection of cities at the crossroads of the ancient world.

This, then, is the reality of the Old Testament. The glorious kingdom, whose rulers had the ear of the creator of the world, had a modest enough reality inside an indistinct and mixed material culture. The written word it was that transformed and modified this earthly existence and we appreciate the genius of those who first saw and described the vision; the men who celebrated and described the faith of this undistinguished culture with such power.

The Kingdoms

Egypt is at its coolest in January. Then, when there is little work to be done on the land, is the best time to build. So a workmanlike inscription in a stone quarry, dated to January 924 BC, by the Chiefs of Works of Pharaoh Sheshonk – whom the Bible calls Shishak – records that 'His Majesty gave orders for building a double door of innumerable cubits to make a festival court for the temple of his father, Amun-re, King of the Gods, and to surround all this with a colonnade'. And Sheshonk's huge colonnade and its gateway is still there today in the 'First Courtyard' of the Temple of Karnak. Its double doors of wood and bronze have long since gone, but the texts recalling Sheshonk's northern wars remain, cut deep into the stone. Sheshonk was the first pharaoh of Egypt to build on such a scale since the days of Ramesses III some centuries before; the first king too, for many years, to take an Egyptian army abroad. The Old Testament tells us that he also played host in Egypt to Jeroboam, one of Solomon's embattled successors. Perhaps this campaign recorded on his gateway reflects in some way the biblical story; but of this the Egyptian records tell us nothing; they mention neither Jeroboam nor any other foreign kings.

But what victories Sheshonk won in the land of Solomon! Here on his great gateway, though rather faint now, the figure of Sheshonk smites his northern enemies while Theban Amun-re, King of the Gods, holds the captive cities roped together, 130 of them, each a personification of a conquered town: bearded northern heads are fixed heraldically above the oval plans of fortresses, each with their names inside them, spelled out in hieroglyphs.

Once more in their history the cities of Megiddo, Gaza and Beth Shan are listed as besieged and captured, along with most of the towns that guarded routes through the Jordan Valley and the towns at the edge of the Negev – even Arad and its satellite forts. Still today archaeologists commonly find the dark wide bands of the ashes of Sheshonk's sackings in their excavations, showing that this fearsome list is a real reporting of events and not a ceremonial recital of more ancient victories. The country must have been fractured: the Bible tells us that it had already split into two Kingdoms – Israel and Judah, north and south. The Pharaoh seems to have made good progress through the land, taking cities large and small, and extracting such enormous tribute from Jerusalem that the Book of Kings calls it a looting. Jerusalem must have bought Sheshonk off, however, for there is no mention of the city in Sheshonk's great roll call of victories as there would have been if he had taken it by main force. But one thing *is* certain: ancient Israel always appears like this in the records of other nations; a collection of cities struggling to survive on the crossroads of an increasingly embattled ancient East that finally is defeated and loses everything. It is a sorry tale and the Old Testament makes the most of it, using the slow deaths of the Kingdoms of Israel and Judah as the instruments of divine retribution – the fate of hapless kings who had not kept Jehovah's Law. In the course of the relentless saga the plucky kings of Samaria, the capital of the northern kingdom, do especially badly. Although contemporary records show that they were active and intelligent rulers, such things were of little interest to the compilers of the Books of Kings and Chronicles who were out to demonstrate the mechanisms of divine retribution.

The biblical account of the career of King Ahab of Israel, the husband of Jezebel, one of the victors of the battle of Qarqar, serves as a good example of this method of writing history. At ancient Samaria, among olive groves and almond trees, you will find the ruins of his substantial palace, now part-wedged under the foundations of a Roman temple (see Plate 9). By all accounts Ahab was a sensible king and a brave man too. When he was wounded during his last battle with the King of Damascus, the Old Testament tells us that he did not retire from the fight but stayed propped upright in his chariot, a living icon at his army's head, bleeding to death so that his troops would not flee the field. The pool where the palace servants would have washed his bloody chariot now lies under the broad steps of the Roman temple. Close by, archaeologists have found fragments of the beautiful ivories that once decorated the walls of a celebrated palace room, decorations so lavish that Amos the Prophet (Amos 3:15; 6:4–5) was still denouncing their opulence a hundred years later.

These kings of Damascus were vigorous neighbours. According to Assyrian records, they fought in alliance with King Ahab at the Battle of Qarqar in 853 BC. But the Old Testament never mentions that great victory (see pages 70–71), telling only of Ahab's sinfulness, his defeats and his lonely death at the hands of the Damascus army. Extra-biblical records are always fascinating, supplying fragments of Israel's lost history. A round-topped stela from Moab, for example, a small state to the south of Damascus, boasts of an otherwise unknown uprising against Israelite overlords, an uprising that apparently defeated the armies of both Ahab and his father Omri and which led to an ancient altar of King David being taken from Jerusalem back to Moab as booty, along with many Israelite prisoners who were put to work to build a road and a palace. Other rare inscriptions even hint that these neighbouring kingdoms, like Damascus and Moab, also worshipped a god named Jehovah along with other gods; and for these kingdoms, too, this god Jehovah might also have been a god of covenant and nationhood.

In the eighth century BC, all these warring petty kingdoms were shattered by the conquests of the Assyrian armies. Both Israel and Judah quickly felt the blow. The geographic position of Palestine had always meant that it was a land controlled by outside events; and now Assyria was on the move. The Old Testament records the tribute-taking and the eventual destruction of the Kingdoms of Israel. A small black Assyrian stela, covered with lively scenes of tribute and notices of victory, shows an emissary of Jehu, Ahab's successor, prostrating himself before the kings who would prove to be his country's nemesis: 'I marched . . . to a headland by the sea . . .' the Assyrian king tells his gods, 'and put upon it a representation of my royal person. And at that time I received the tribute from Tyre, Sidon, and of Jehu, son of Omri' (see Plate 11).

As Pharaoh Sheshonk had done at Jerusalem, so now the raiding Assyrians made the Israelites of Samaria pay for their freedom with their harvests, their women and their treasures. Fragments of looted Phoenician ivories, like those in Ahab's palace, have been excavated in many Assyrian palaces.

The Assyrians' love of good order and hard battle made them a force that no one could match for centuries; their kingdom on the northern Euphrates was subsidized by the booty of conquest, brutal taxes collected over long years.

'In my eighteenth year as King, I crossed the Euphrates for the sixteenth time . . . Hazael of Aram [a small state to the north of Damascus] put his faith in the numbers of his soldiers . . . he made Mount Sanar, a mountain peak that stands out in front of Lebanon, his strong position. I fought with him and defeated him, killing 16,000 of his best troops. I snatched away from him 1,121 of his chariots and 470 of his cavalry horses and the baggage train. I cut down his plantations, I destroyed, tore down and burned with fire numberless villages, carrying away innumerable spoils . . .' The Assyrian records of the annual *razzia* became ever more violent as the years pass and all accompanied by terrible pictures of war. The Assyrian army – charioteers, well-armed infantry, bowmen, sappers – all advance neatly in regimental lines against the little kingdoms to their south and east, extracting heavy tribute, killing and enslaving all opposition. Finally, in these Assyrian annals biblical Israel enters unambiguously into ancient history. They tell that Israel, the northern Kingdom, was devoured by the Assyrian armies in 722 BC, when Sargon II entered Samaria, its capital, put the king and the nobles to death and transported the remaining citizens to cities far away in the east. The icy Assyrian record gives us the details of the campaign:

> . . . a commoner without claim to the throne, a cursed Hittite, schemed to become King of Hamath, and persuaded the cities of Arvad, Simirra, Damascus and Samaria to desert me . . . I called up the masses of the solders of Assur and besieged him . . . I conquered and burnt his city. He, I flayed, the rebels, I killed in their own cities . . . I besieged and conquered Samaria, led away as booty 27,000 inhabitants, forming from among them a regiment of fifty chariots . . . I crushed the tribes of the *hai-apa*, the Arabs who live far away in the desert and who knew neither overseers nor officials and who had not brought tribute before to any king, and I deported their survivors and settled them in Samaria.

So run the Assyrian accounts of the fate of the Kingdom of Israel. And in the vivid pictures that so often accompany these written histories you may see the defeated survivors. In the eighth century BC, when the Assyrian empire was at its height, Mesopotamia and Syria were filled with thousands of these displaced peoples, tribes and families all marching east to settle again amid the ruined cities of earlier Assyrian conquests. Never before was an ancient nation so universally feared and hated as were these Assyrians from north Iraq. But just as their records credit their victories to their gods, to the 'terror-inspiring glamour of Assur my Lord' so too the Old Testament similarly attributes victory and defeat to its god, Jehovah. The Book of Kings describes the catastrophe at Samaria so: 'In the ninth year of Hoshea the king of Assyria took Samaria, and carried Israel away into Assyria . . . For so it was, that the children of Israel had sinned against the Lord their God, which had brought them out of the land of Egypt . . . [there follows a long list of these sins] . . . Therefore the Lord was very angry with Israel, and removed them out of his sight.' (2 Kings 17:6–7, 18). These became the ten lost tribes of Israel. Now only Judah and its little ally Benjamin remained in the southern kingdom, though the Kingdom of Judah, with its capital in Jerusalem, had long been subject to Assyrian control, as contemporary records show.

Eighty years after Samaria fell when Assyria was occupied with revolts close to home, the Bible tells us that Josiah, King of Judah, tried to break out of its awful orbit. The Books of Kings and Chronicles tell us that Josiah did 'that which was right in the sight of the Lord, and walked in all the way of David' (2 Kings 22:2). They also tell us of his restorations in the Jerusalem temple, implying that Josiah had understood that the misfortune of his subjects was due to their forgetfulness of Jehovah and his laws. At Jerusalem, for example, the Bible says that there were temples for the gods of the Moabites, the Ammonites and several Phoenician deities too, including a shrine to Moloch in the Vale of Hinnom where human sacrifices were made – 'passed through the fire', as the Bible says. Some of Josiah's predecessors are described as having thus sacrificed their children to gain a victory. Josiah's religious reforms began, according to 2 Kings 22–23, after ancient holy books had been discovered in Solomon's Temple which was in the process of restoration. The Book of Chronicles records the event: 'Hilkiah the priest found a book of the law of the Lord given by Moses . . . [Hilkiah] said to Shaphan the scribe, I have found the book of the law in the house of the Lord . . . And Shaphan read it before the king. And it came to pass, when the king had heard the words of the law, that he rent his clothes . . . great is the wrath of the Lord that is poured out upon us, because our fathers have not kept the word of the Lord, to do after all that is written in this book' (2 Chronicles 34, taken from 14–21). This is the first biblical reference to the 'Books of Moses' – presumably the first five Bible books or parts of them. Whatever they may have been, the Book of Chronicles tells the story of the recovery of these holy texts as if it were a reward for King Josiah's pious restoration of Jehovah's dilapidated temple.

The story, however, should not be taken literally. How, for example, could Jehovah's High Priests have ever lost their essential guidebook or ever forgotten the words of their covenant with Jehovah? Probably this tale is a graphic way of describing the re-birth of religious observance under Josiah, a revival of Jehovah's cult that the Book of Chronicles describes as taking place at that time, an event to which modifications in the temple at Arad apparently bear witness. And all this under the mounting pressure of Assyrian attack. Whatever the circumstances, the story of the finding of the Law is a precious reference to the Bible's own ancient history.

As Assyrian power declined during the sixth century BC, so the Egyptian pharaohs, sensing the rise of yet more threatening empires further east, sent armies to help the Assyrian forces. The Old Testament tells us that at Megiddo Josiah attempted to block the progress of the Egyptian army in the hope, perhaps, that if this diabolical coalition could be stopped, his kingdom would retain its independence. 'What do you want with me, King of Judah?' shouts Pharaoh to Josiah, in the Book of Chronicles (2 Chronicles 35:21 NEB). 'I have no quarrel with you today, only with those with whom I am at war. God has purposed to speed me on my way, and God is on my side; do not stand in his way, or he will destroy you.' But King Josiah would not be deflected from his purpose but insisted on fighting the Egyptians. And so 'The archers shot at him:

he was severely wounded and told his bodyguard to carry him off. They lifted him out of his chariot and carried him in his viceroy's chariot to Jerusalem. There he died and was buried amongst the tombs of his ancestors, and all Judah and Jerusalem mourned for him ... The other events of Josiah's reign ... his acts, from first to last, are recorded in the annals of the Kings of Israel and Judah' (2 Chronicles 35: from 23–27). From such ancient annals, now lost, but which are often mentioned in the Bible, almost as footnotes, the Old Testament's history of Israel would be eventually compiled. Though most of the southern kingdom of Judah had escaped the Assyrian armies by paying heavy tribute, Lachish, a dignified ancient fortress-city to the south-west of Jerusalem did not. Its solemn mound, lying in the low Judaean hills, still bears the marks of the Assyrian assault upon it – of the ramp their sappers built against the outer side of the huge main gate and the tremendous band of ashes in the excavations of the city. Up this Assyrian ramp, all carefully laid with wooden beams to act as rails for their siege engines, came the mass of infantry while the city's defenders rained down fire and stones. Assyrian relief sculptures show the final assault; the implacable regiments of Assur are all in their regulation armour and the desperate defenders awaiting them on the walls. Other reliefs show the sad line of defeated Judaeans – the world's first images of refugees – directed by the victors, their possessions loaded onto camels and heaped into chariots, women and children in carts, men in front, one with his son across his shoulders, starting the journey across thousands of miles of sand and track to the east. And as they pass the tent of the Assyrian king, two of the soldiers carefully flay the leading citizens of Lachish lying pegged out upon the ground. As these artists cut the grey impassive stone, they had a terrible Old Testament compassion in them, seeking out the most awful moment, the dreadful gesture. In such vision is real pity and it would be mistaken to think the Assyrians were mere brutes. If that was the case, you could not now still feel the agonies of these ancient conquests.

The excavators of Lachish found extraordinary witness to its ancient torments, something of the reality of these ancient records. In a drain by the gateway, they found an Assyrian helmet identical to those the infantry are wearing in the reliefs, bronze arrow heads, heaps of catapult stones and spear tips buried deep in ash and cinders. Inside the town, atop the platform that had earlier held the palace of a Judaean prince, an Assyrian governor later built his residence; two fine square-cut stones that once held the pillars of his public hall of audience stand there still today.

At Lachish, too, archaeologists found a unique record of a second wave of invaders from the east who first destroyed Assyria herself and then the province of Judah. Letters excavated in a guard post by the city gate held the scanty records of some of the outposts of the Kingdom of Judaea in the years after the Assyrians, preoccupied with matters nearer home, had withdrawn. Written about 590 BC, these texts on simple potsherds are the last contemporary records of the Kingdom of Judah, that rump of the ancient confederation which claimed descent from Moses' Twelve Tribes. Written in Hebrew, in a style identical to that of the Old Testament, they are concerned, for the most part, with the minutiae of army administration, but, occasionally, they display a vivid flash of life.

> May Jehovah bring my Lord this very day, good tidings; in accordance with all that my Lord has written, so has your servant done . . . With regard to what my Lord has said about Beth Haraphid, there is no-one there . . . And [my Lord] will know that we are watching for the signals of Lachish, according to all the signs that my Lord has given, for we cannot see Azekiah.

This seems to refer to the advance of the Babylonian armies that brought Judah to its end in 586 BC. Both Beth Haraphid and Azekiah seem to have been military outposts – the latter is mentioned as a fortified city in Jeremiah 34:7. That one was deserted and the other was no longer sending (smoke?) signals may well have resulted from the inexorable advance of Judah's new foe, Nebuchadrezzar and his armies, the leaders of the confederation that had destroyed Assyria two decades before. If anything, the Babylonians were more cruel than the Assyrians. First they took Lachish, then they went on to Jerusalem, plundering the Temple treasury, exiling the king and installing a client prince named Zedekiah in his place. After some ill-judged politicking, so the Book of Kings tell us in its very last lines, Zedekiah rebelled and was defeated finally in a battle fought on the plain by Jericho, where biblical Israel had begun. Babylon's revenge was absolute. The Priests, the army commanders and the city's scribes were all killed. Solomon's fabled Temple was destroyed, its precious fitments plundered. As for Judah's last king, 2 Kings 25:7 tells us that 'they slew the sons of Zedekiah before his eyes, and put out the eyes of Zedekiah, and bound him with fetters of brass, and carried him to Babylon'. The remainder of the court, priests, scribes and noblemen were led off into exile with their blinded king.

Remembering Zion

The city stands on a broad plain and is an exact square, a hundred and twenty furlongs in length each way . . . Whilst such is its size, in magnificence there is no other city that approaches to it. It is surrounded, in the first place, by a broad and deep moat, full of water, behind which rises a wall fifty royal cubits in width and two hundred in height . . . On the top along the edges of the wall, they constructed buildings of a single chamber facing one another, leaving between them room for a four horse chariot to turn. In the centre of the wall are a hundred gates, all of brass and brazen lintels and side-posts . . . The city is divided into two portions by the river . . . The houses are mostly three and four stories high: the streets all run in straight lines . . . At the river end of these cross streets are low gates in the fence that skirts the stream, which are, like the great gates in the outer wall, of brass, and open on the water.

With great wonder, the Greek historian Herodotus recorded his impressions of Babylon in about 460 BC, when many Israelites were still living there in exile. When their forefathers had been brought to the city 130 years earlier, after the sack of Jerusalem, its great gates (of bronze plate, of course, not 'brass') must have seemed like the mouth of hell. Babylon the Great Whore, Israel's prophets would call her, but her ancient gods, venerable and venerated, made of tons of gold, standing in temples as old, it seemed, as the world itself, must have awed the courtiers of Jerusalem. Even as they had come into Babylon, walking past the seamless brand-new elegance of the blue glazed walls of the eerie processional way, they saw the gods and demons sculpted on the glassy bricks that had been the familiars of the Babylonians for millennia. In the Psalms, Jehovah himself fights some of these same terrifying gods at the Creation. The exiled Judaeans had entered an awful and seductive city where Jehovah's laws were quite unknown and where each day of their exile they would be forced into compromise with a pagan world.

The Babylonians had seen many such strange and dusty nobles arriving in their city: defeated kings with their courtiers, their gods with their attendant priests, city craftsmen and scribes, all brought as booty; Babylon's tax upon the world. In truth, if you were a foreign king brought here with your gods, life did not have to be so very bad; better indeed than their lives in many of their own cities and certainly far less dangerous. So, Jehoiachin, King of Judah, in the biblical accounts of him, was said to have gone to Babylon as a hostage years before Zedekiah's revolt. And there he lived in some style, in the company of eight of his courtiers and five of his sons, all provisioned from the royal magazines. A Babylonian cuneiform receipt excavated in a storeroom by the city gate tells:

To Ya'u-kinu [Jehoiachin] king of the land of Yahudu [Judah]
26 pints [of oil] for Ya'u-kinu, king of the land of Yahudu

3¾ pints, for the five sons of the king of the land of Yahudu
6 pints for eight men, Yahuduʻans – for each one ¾ of a pint.
by the hand of Kanama [scribe]

After thirty-seven years of captivity, the Book of Kings tells us (2 Kings 25:27–30), Jehoiachin found favour and promotion at the Babylonian court; he had become one of the great number of foreign princes sucked into the culture of the ancient cosmopolitan city.

The Kingdoms of Israel and Judah had finally been swallowed by Babylon after a Mesopotamian mastication of some two centuries. The towns and the fortresses, Solomon's Temple and its legendary treasure, all the substance of the kingdom had gone. Even the ancient Hebrew language had been replaced by Aramaic, the contemporary *lingua franca* of the dispossessed. Israel had come to an ending. Whatever literature the Israelite exiles possessed – scrolls of law, books of history, memories of temple ritual, folk stories, psalms and poems – must have taken on bitter new significance. At Babylon such things must have held the pith of their culture and they must have been recalled and recited with something of the character of a meditation. For what Jehovah had promised Israel in covenant, both as reward and as punishment, could now be seen, in the light of the catastrophe of the exile, to be perfectly true. Clearly their kingdom *had* been given to them as a gift, as a contingent gift, in covenant with Jehovah, just as the prophets say.

The Israelites had not lived in their homeland since the beginning of time, their histories told them; thus the covenants with Jehovah that had granted them their country now seemed almost as important as the act of Creation itself. And as their land had been granted by Jehovah upon specific conditions, it was obviously necessary to have accurate copies of these laws and to take special care of the 'Book of the Law given to Moses'. It was necessary, too, to record Israel's relationship with Jehovah through history, for this showed the operation of the covenant. To record as well, the genealogies of Israel's royal families and all the deeds and purchases by which they had gained their land-contracts such as Abraham's purchase of Machpelah at Hebron for the Patriarch's burial cave (Genesis 23:8–16), and David's dealings with Ornan the Jebusite, who had owned the land on which the Jerusalem Temple was later built (1 Chronicles 21, 18ff.)

What the Babylonian exile gave to the Old Testament was a full stop: a chance to look at Israel as a single entity, a finished thing. From behind the bars of their prison the past seemed quite different from circumstances remembered in more happy times.

But Babylon was not just a place of reflection for Israel. Under the pressure of exile, the very identity of their culture was attacked. In Babylon, Israel lived side by side with other captive peoples. Inevitably there was distrust and disgust; but also there were fresh insights to be gained from such cross-cultural concepts; new ways of thinking, new ways of seeing time and history, new ways of understanding and approaching god. In this competitive and often hostile city the Lost Kingdom took on the dimension of a dream, a simplicity, an age of purity, an age that though often harsh had been free from the brutal pressures of exile. Now visions of a perfect world were built from the images of such a past. Biblical histories that were also visions of the future, of an Eden that could be re-gained by following the laws that the Israelites had flouted. All this would be loaded into the ancient texts, the editors filling them with fresh insights and emotions.

September 1, 1939

I sit in one of the dives
On Fifty-Second Street
Uncertain and afraid
As the clever hopes expire
Of a low dishonest decade:

Auden's poem describes the emotions of a modern exile as the Second World War begins. Three thousand years hence what chance would we have of understanding the poet's feeling or even the precise power of the images that he has so carefully arranged? Future scholars might offer explanations of the curious use of words like 'dive', even perhaps suggest its theological under-tones. We might be shown a map of New York, the fruits of patient excavation, marked with a scientific reconstruction that showed precisely where the diving board had stood. Vicars could compile endless lists of parallel texts, archaeo-logists supply accurate accounts of the contemporary material culture. But despite all this no one could begin to understand the powerful resonances that Auden's poem had set up in the minds of people of his own time. What then of the words of another exile in the sixth century BC.

By the rivers of Babylon,
there we sat down, yea, we wept,
when we remembered Zion.

We hanged our harps upon the willows in the midst thereof.
For there they that carried us away captive required of us a song;
and they that wasted us required of us mirth, saying,
Sing us one of the songs of Zion.

How shall we sing the Lord's song in a strange land?
If I forget thee, O Jerusalem,
let my right hand forget her cunning.
If I do not remember thee, let my tonge cleave to the roof of my mouth . . .

The famous phrases of Psalm 137 have been transmuted endlessly into everything from moral parables to disco music. In Babylon, however, such Psalms did not just bring a tear to the collective Israelite eye. There are specific memories and allusions here; places, trees, brooks, tunes, all filled with precise significances whose specific connotations are lost to us. Archaeology, Bible study, even modern piety can take us only a tiny part of the way back to ancient Israel.

One universal quality that both these poems share, however, is nostalgia; looking back with the mind's eye. In the Old Testament you will find names of every village, every mountain and every stream of the Lost Kingdom; the scribes are walking there as they write. And the Bible's description of Israel's history, that fall from grace, is painted with a poignant and romantic glow, with images of fabled kings like Solomon, wise, rich and virile, of the greatest temple in the world, of huge heroes and beautiful young men, of women sanctified and sinful. And through it all there runs a sense of loss and guilt; an awareness of the fall from grace; a displacement from God and past perfections. And that still has profound effect upon the West.

Chapter Three
THE MAKING OF THE OLD TESTAMENT

Exile

There is an old Jewish story about a gathering of rabbis who were debating a point of Holy Law. At the end of the meeting just one man stood out against the majority. But this rabbi knew that God was on his side and in exasperation called upon his divine ally to show his hand. 'If I am right,' said the rabbi, 'may the streams of Israel flow uphill.' And they did. But the majority was not impressed. 'If I am right,' said the rabbi again, 'may the trees bend to the ground.' And they did. Still the meeting was not impressed. 'If I am right,' he cried in frustration, 'may the voice of God sound in assent.' And a voice came from heaven in the rabbi's defence. But still the assembly was unmoved. 'We pay no attention to heavenly voices,' they said, 'because the correct determination of this point has long since been written down.' Moses in Sinai had revealed the sacred truth to their ancestors, and no voice in the universe could alter that. On the question of the sacred written word, even God might be in error.

Why, of all the cultures living around the edges of the ancient Mediterranean, did the Jews alone produce such a set of sacred books? Obviously, there was a need to record the laws governing the covenant with Jehovah so that the people could adhere to the sacred contract from generation to generation. But there were also more immediate, more dramatic reasons: two disasters, two dislocations of national life, some five hundred years apart; first, the Exile to Babylon that followed the sacking of Jerusalem in 587 BC, and the second, the complete destruction of Jerusalem following the Roman wars of AD 70–135. Both these events threatened the annihilation of Israel. Through all of this, the sacred writings became the heart of national identity, the ancient written law its shield. Sacred writings that were almost a swan song became the means of Israel's survival.

The vice-like pressure of these two national disasters forced into being the Hebrew Bible, which is also the Christian Old Testament. But these disasters also affected the very identity of the god that the ancient books defined. For ancient gods changed when they were uprooted. These gods, with their cults and rituals, were bound into the life and character of the cities and civilizations in which they were first worshipped. These gods were well known to the local people, they were present in the landscape in the seasons of the year, they were seen, in sculpture and in paintings, described in rituals, hymns and sacred stories. But take them away from their birthplaces, and the confident public faith that had surrounded them would disappear. And for the followers of these exiled deities now living in strange lands, worship of their gods now became a foreign wisdom in a strange country. Faith that had once been as natural as the harvest and the storm that had given victory and prosperity now required, in exile, a careful justification, a subtle theology. And this is part of the function of the books of the Old Testament. But if local myths and gods are expanded to embrace new landscapes, to fit more general truths, these myths and gods become something like a science. Local creation stories are elevated into a universal account of creation. And so the followers of these uprooted gods come to believe that they alone hold the secrets of the universe and hence, salvation. Prayers, rituals and the wisdom of a local faith, once a public, confident and happy thing, became an exclusive powerful foreign mystery known only to a few. Thus were old gods changed. And this happened twice to the god of ancient Israel; during the two exiles from Jerusalem. And the literature of the first exile – vivid, biting, sometimes introspective, sometimes angry – held a powerful truth for the generations of the second exile. In those eras of repression, faith became like a tight-coiled spring. And the power in the spring was the word of God set down in the sacred books. And the ancient words refined, corrected and amplified over generations became the centre of a new nation.

The word 'Jew' was born in the Babylonian Exile, where it was used to describe the people of the southern kingdom of Judah. After 539 BC, when Babylon fell to Cyrus the Great, Judah became a Persian province. The astute Cyrus was well aware that his rapid victory over the old Empire was partly helped by the intolerance of the Babylonian kings toward their captive peoples, a mistake he did not mean to repeat. Bent on world domination, Cyrus looked for a wiser system of government that would bind, not alienate, the conquered. So he returned the Babylonian exiles, gods, kings and courtiers alike, back to their own lands, 'to the places that make them happy' as the royal edict says. After more than fifty years' exile, the Judaeans were encouraged to return to Jerusalem, to rebuild Judaea and to revive their national life and faith.

Unlike other captive nations, the Jews, as they may now be called, had no statues of Jehovah: their Law forbade such graven images. But the Bible tells us (Ezra 1) that the Babylonians had stored their loot from the destruction of the first Temple, so when Cyrus gave specific orders for the rebuilding of the Temple at Jerusalem he also handed back all the surviving Temple furnishings. Zerubbabel, grandson of Judah's last king, Jehoiachin, led the exiles home again and began the restoration of the Temple. Eighty years later he was followed to Jerusalem by Ezra the Scribe, who re-established the ancient law in the Holy City. Then Nehemiah, a Jewish official of the Persian Court, rebuilt the city walls. First the Temple, then the Law, then the fortress – the biblical restoration seemed complete. Yet these inhabitants of the city were very different people from their pre-exilic forefathers.

The return of the first group of exiles to Jerusalem led to an Israelite revival among those who remained in Babylon. During the time of exile many Israelites had, according to contemporary records, taken pagan names. Zerubbabel, indeed, means 'seed of Babylon'. With the revival of Jewish nationalism, parents gave their children pure old Israelite names once again. No doubt the Persians encouraged this sentiment. For such orderly nationalism could cement an empire that eventually ran from Libya to the borders of India.

The Bible tells us that Nehemiah was King Cyrus' cupbearer, a court-chamberlain and hence, most probably, a eunuch. Certainly he was a man of position and influence. Like pious Jews, the Persians of the court were bound by rules of ritual cleanliness and sacred order. The world, they believed, was under continual assault from hostile powers who used death, corruption and disease as their weapons. Ritual purity helped to keep the forces of darkness at bay. We may expect Nehemiah to have been a careful and sympathetic over-seer of such customs. The Persians, like the Jews, also had a set of religious books which held the substance of their faith, though the writings of the *Zend Avesta* are now mostly lost. Perhaps the urge to restore the sacred books of ancient Israel was first felt during this close contact with the Persian court.

Such foreign influences on the Old Testament should not be rejected out of hand. The years of the Babylonian exile had brought the Jews into renewed contact with the ancient East's oldest myths including some of the same stories of creation and flood that are in the Old Testament. A renewed contact with a fount of ancient wisdom could well have produced fresh religious insights, even leading to changes in the Israelite texts. The biblical version of the story of Adam and Eve, for example, seems to be set in the Persian period.

But the influence went deeper than mere similarity of stories. The old Persian faith was an abstract and subtle religion, offering many new ways of looking at divinity and the idea of the holy. Its influence upon the minds of Jewish scribes and rulers, men like Nehemiah and Ezra, was probably greater than surviving evidence can show. There are, however, numerous hints of this influence in the Old Testament. The 'Spirit of God', for example, that moves on the face of the waters in the opening of Genesis is a most remarkable idea; only at this one place in the Old Testament is Jehovah said to possess a 'spirit'. Yet in surviving Persian writings the idea of a 'spirit of god' is a common one. Similarly, some of the optimistic Persian notions of the afterlife seem to have entered into the later Books of the Prophets in the Bible. A rare view of the traditional Israelite afterlife (the afterlife is not often mentioned in older biblical writings) is briefly glimpsed in the tale of Saul's meeting with the dead Prophet Samuel, who is 'called up' by the Witch of Endor (1 Samuel 28:7–21) from a kind of Hades;

it is a shadowy survival. But in the Book of Isaiah, which was certainly compiled after the Babylonian exile, a full-blown theory of death and resurrection is implicit throughout, a forerunner of one of the major themes of the New Testament.

And at the same time, after the period of exile, other major themes of both Judaism and Christianity also begin to appear in the Bible, not the least important of which is the idea of the Messiah – 'the Anointed One'. Cyrus the Great is the first biblical person to be given this title. Later, biblical scribes redefined the term so that it came to mean, quite specifically, a son of the House of David, a defender of the Children of Israel who will establish a new era on earth and a new kingdom with its capital in Jerusalem. Thus the influence of ideas that once filled the mysterious faith of ancient Persia runs throughout the Old Testament and continues well into the pages of the New Testament, an influence that leaves a trace even in the words of Jesus.

Return

The Temple that, the Bible tells us, Zerubbabel and his successors built at Jerusalem has vanished. Not a trace remains on the ancient Temple platform which stands now, like a wide altar, on the summit of Mount Moriah. One of mankind's holiest places, a place of terrible pride and longing as well as of faith, the rectangle of four high stone walls framing the Dome of the Rock is hardly a welcoming site for archaeologists. Here, denied the more certain knowledge of archaeology, we must fall back, as we must with the biblical texts of this same period, upon likelihoods and probabilities.

Such large stone platforms on the top of low hills are typically Persian; typical, too, of the period of Cyrus the Great who had just such a platform built at his palace at Parsagadae in southern Persia, by masons captured in the war with Croesus of Sardis. At Jerusalem 1200 miles from Parsagadae, the four walls of the Temple platform show precisely the same distinctive techniques of stone-cutting. Both at Parsagadae and Jerusalem, the masons slightly stepped the bottom three courses of stone, just as Cyrus stipulates in his edict for the rebuilding of the Temple in Jerusalem: 'Cyrus the king made a decree concerning the house of God at Jerusalem, Let the house be builded, the place where they offered sacrifices, and let the foundations thereof be strongly laid; the height thereof threescore cubits, and the breadth thereof threescore cubits; With three rows of great stones, and a row of new timber:' (Ezra 6: 3–4). Ezra's copy of this imperial edict is written out in the typical bureaucratic manner of the day, providing a token of the accuracy of biblical record. Beyond this, however, the evidence for the period of Persian domination at Jerusalem between 587 and 331 BC is slim indeed. It is represented, hypothetically, by some massive stone walls deep in the Temple platform, and has been scientifically authenticated only by some excavated pottery, a few small inscriptions, and a few loose stone walls. There is very little to hold in your hand. Yet this age was a vital one in the building of the Bible. For in this period, Israel's most ancient literature was not only put in order and edited but was also updated, even re-written, to conform to contemporary preoccupations. What, then, were the ancient writings that the returning exiles would have used as the basis for their work? And what were the contemporary pressures that would so clearly leave their mark on the Old Testament? Once more, for lack of detailed evidence, we can only proceed by likelihood and probability.

At the time of the return from Babylon, many of the Old Testament books had not yet been begun. The existing writings – the works of Exile and the records of the kingdoms of Israel and Judah – must have been a very mixed bag. At the heart of this mass of material lay the writings that would come to form the Book of Law: the books, the Bible tells us, that were written by Moses himself: Genesis, Exodus, Leviticus, Numbers and Deuteronomy – the Pentateuch, the 'Five Volumed'. In the Bible's own history of ancient Israel, in the Books of Chronicles and Kings – and these are our only sources of information on the subject – there is only one occasion when a 'book of law' is mentioned: when Josiah's High Priest finds a 'book of Law' inside the dilapidated Temple at Jerusalem (2 Kings 22, 8 and 2 Chronicles 34, 14ff.) But unfortunately neither of these texts tells us what the 'book of Law' actually contained. As well as this unknown 'book of Law', however, the Books of Chronicles and Kings also mention some written annals from the period of the ancient kingdoms. But this material – the Annals of the Kings of Judah and Israel, the Book of Assher, the Acts of Solomon – has also disappeared.

As well as these literary ghosts, there must also have been a vast mass of material, some of it very old, some written in exile: a huge range of literature, some, perhaps, part-taken from ancient oral traditions, poetry, prophecies and stories, genealogies and myths; the incunabula of two little ancient states now so carefully subsumed into the body of the Old Testament. Here, in general, the specific origins are lost under the hands of later scribes, but occasionally an archaic passage of particular poignancy or power stands out from the body of the text – the marvellous Song of Deborah in the Book of Judges (5:2–31), or the strange tale of the giants and the daughters of men in Genesis (6:4), for example, that seem to be quite self-contained. Short fragments like these seem genuine survivals from the first era of the confederation, when the Twelve Tribes who worshipped Jehovah were separated by mountains and rivers so that each developed its own stories and traditions. Gathered up and pressed into the Bible, such fragments preserve an extraordinary mixture of custom and belief. And because of this variety of material, many of the books of the Old Testament have a freshness that is very different from the stodgy literature of most antique kingdoms.

There is no evidence whatsoever that the courts of Israel and Judah had literary scholars capable of rationalizing and re-ordering such a huge amount of diverse material, nor, indeed, that they possessed the will or desire to do so. No one, so far as we can see from contemporary historical evidence, had even thought of such a thing. Indeed, the total lack of monumental inscriptions from ancient Israel itself betrays a complete lack of interest in the preservation and perpetuation of its national history. So the Old Testament texts in their present form must be the result of these later processes of adaption and preservation which took place at the time of the Babylonian Exile and during the Persian period of the return to Jerusalem. And this is borne out by the fact that much of this ancient Israelite writing has been filled with the aspirations and insights of this new age.

Other, brand new Bible Books were written at this time. The Bible's own history of this Persian period, for example, is in the Books of Ezra and Nehemiah, and the broad facts of their story are confirmed by surviving fragments from the Persian Imperial Archives. Other texts of the same period tell of the aspirations of individuals embarked upon this great adventure. Just as the old histories were carefully shaped to show the route by which Israel fell from Jehovah's grace and into exile, so, after the return to Jerusalem, the narrative of the Persian Period proposes a vision of the future. The lessons learned from the nightmare of exile provide a basis for future dreams.

The tremendous cruelties of the age were rejected in visions of a Second Coming leading to a new Heaven and new Earth. This vision, that had first been seen and recorded by prophets in Babylon, was now celebrated in the Book of Psalms, that wonderful collection of hymns ancient and modern designed for use in the new Temple that Zerubbabel built in Jerusalem. All illness, all wickedness will be banished from the earth, they tell us; Jehovah's Law will be written not on papyrus nor on scrolls of vellum but on men's hearts, so that they will grow in understanding of their God. It was a dream of paradise, a paradise prepared for the nation that kept Jehovah's Law.

Just below the Temple Mount, in the Kidron Valley facing the Mount of Olives, is ancient Jerusalem's most prolific spring. The spring of Gihon runs through King Hezekiah's elaborate tunnel, feeds the Pool of Siloam and waters a fine orchard of dark green fig trees. In ancient times, the spring was outside the city walls (hence Hezekiah's tunnel) and it was usually visited through the Water Gate. This, so the Book of Nehemiah tells us (7:73 to 8:12), was the place where Ezra the Scribe gathered all the people of the city, both the returned exiles and the 'people of the land' (as the Bible calls the indigenous inhabitants), and there Ezra read the 'Book of the Law of Moses' to the assembly.

Apart from the earlier obscure references to Josiah's 'book of Law', this story of re-affirmation of the Law is the first clear mention of its existence in the Bible. And though the account of these proceedings in the Book of Nehemiah is somewhat out of its place and time – Ezra is described as if he were an elder, ritually reciting a text in a synagogue, a building not then in existence – the passage graphically portrays the beginnings of a national preoccupation with precise ritual observance – the 'joyous observance' of the Law, a ritual part of the resurgent national faith that would be held with a passion unto death. This story of Ezra's public recitation of the Law can be seen as the symbolic beginning of Judaism.

But what exactly was this Book of the Law of Moses which Ezra read to the assembled people, and where had it come from? Clearly, the biblical assertion that Moses himself wrote the Pentateuch, the five biblical Books of the Law, cannot be taken at face value. Deuteronomy, for example, the last book of the Pentateuch is a first-hand report of Moses' words and actions, and the final verses even describe the great man's death and burial! A more basic objection, however, for such an early date for the Pentateuch is that these five books hold in them the precise beginnings of a much larger story; one that is carefully developed through the later books of the Old Testament, the history of ancient Israel. Few works of literature have a more awe-inspiring introduction. The story of the Creation proceeds by majestic steps to an examination of the solitary relationship between Jehovah and the Patriarch Abraham. Slowly the tale expands to bring into its powerful embrace the progeny of Abraham and the Twelve Tribes. The beginnings of the sacred drama of Israel are carefully elaborated, generation by generation, to the point where the real heroes of the Old Testament, the people of Israel, are themselves standing on the edge of maturity, poised to invade the Promised Land. Then gradually the story moves in the slow beat of an approaching doom, as the backslidings of the kings and bad faith of the people drag the children of Judah into the Babylonian captivity, from which their descendants, encouraged by Ezra and Nehemiah, return to Jerusalem and attempt to re-establish the pure faith of Moses.

This is a story composed with the benefit of hindsight. For Moses to have written such a story would have required supernatural foresight and the suspension of Israel's free will. In fact, many modern scholars believe that the opening of Genesis, with its reference to the Persian 'Spirit of God', was written when the ancient texts were being re-organized to make a suitable prologue for the new sense of national destiny that would fill the Old Testament. With what genius did these editors reconcile the archaic literature of Israel with the new-felt pomp of national destiny! They also made a heady cocktail of myth and nationalism still greatly to the taste of modern man.

Who, then, composed this brilliant, influential history? The traditional attribution of all the Pentateuch to Moses himself seems to be a device used by these later editors to personify a single human source of Jehovah's Law. But there are many hints of later hands at work. The Book of Deuteronomy contains several clear references to a Temple at Jerusalem that can only be the one re-built by Zerubbabel. And the literary style of Deuteronomy clearly shows that it was once a part of a three-volumed work, the Books of Deuteronomy, Joshua and Kings. The author-editors of this self-contained work within the Bible are known by a simple tag; 'the Deuteronomist'. Similarly, the ghostly author-editors who compiled the first four books of the Pentateuch, equally unified in their style but showing very different preoccupations from the Deuteronomist, are called 'the Priestly Writer'.

The Old Testament itself emphasizes not the authors of its books but the accuracy and authority of the writing and the *authenticity* of its divine inspiration. Clearly the Deuteronomist relied on much older works for his compilation. Yet out of this material he put together a clear message for the people of his own age in the time of the Persian Period. His three-part history shows that the divine retribution detailed in his Book of Kings followed the breaking of the Law set out in the first of his books, the Book of Deuteronomy. Biblical Ezra the Scribe reads the Law to the people of Jerusalem because he believes that only its observance will bring prosperity and that the weakest link in the chain of the national covenant with Jehovah will bring disaster to the new-born nation. Yet sources both inside and outside the Bible show very clearly that not all Jews shared Ezra's opinion. And the debates between these different factions also had great effect upon the Bible and its books.

Many Jehovahs

Not all exiled Jews of Babylon returned to Jerusalem. Many had stayed in Babylonia. Others, taking advantage of the new freedom of movement within the Persian Empire, had settled in other eastern lands. In the fifth century BC, when Ezra and Nehemiah were at Jerusalem, a settled community of Jews at Aswan in Egypt served as part of the Persian garrison.

The town of Aswan was a border town, built beside the granite cataract over which the Nile followed northwards into Egypt. For thousands of years, priests of the Temple of Khnum on the little island of Elephantine, had measured the annual rise of the river waters, to gauge the flood on which Pharaoh's yearly harvest was dependent. Beyond Aswan was Nubia with its wild tribes and desert nomads while to the north the land of Egypt lay under Persian domination. Documents found in the present century have given vivid glimpses into the life of the Jewish colony at Aswan, and these fragments provide a counterbalance to Ezra and Nehemiah's one-sided descriptions of their people and the religion of Jehovah.

To begin with, unlike the returning exiles at Jerusalem, the Jews of Aswan mixed freely with their neighbours. They happily married outside their faith, though they kept distinctively Jewish names and recognized David's City as the spiritual centre of their faith. But they were not intimidated by Jerusalem and dared to petition the High Priest, asking for permission to rebuild their local temple of Jehovah at Aswan which had been burned down in a riot, when the priests of Khnum discovered the Jews sacrificing a ram which was Khnum's sacred animal. It is clear, too, that this was a full-blown temple and not just a simple meeting-house. The letter-writer understood very well the scandal that his request would cause to the orthodox in Jerusalem, for whom there could be but one Temple. So, in his letter, he concedes that worshippers at Aswan will no longer sacrifice animals upon its temple altar. A convenient compromise with local sensibilities as well as with Jerusalem.

The destroyed Aswan temple had been a substantial building of stone, with bronze doors and fittings of silver and gold. Today, when our understanding of ancient Judaism comes almost exclusively from the pages of the Old Testament, it seems extraordinary that the Jews of Aswan could so calmly ask the Jerusalem High Priesthood, those pillars of orthodoxy, for permission to rebuild their grand and obviously heretical temple! But, clearly, the Jews of Aswan did not think that their request was strange and neither was their attitude unusual. For the biblical histories of Israel relate that there had been several temples of Jehovah outside Jerusalem in more ancient times, just as both archaeology and the Old Testament testify that there were also many pagan shrines in Israel and even in Jerusalem. Two hundred years after the request from Elephantine, a son of a Jerusalem High Priest opened another temple of Jehovah in the land of Egypt!

So if the Books of Ezra and Nehemiah reflect something of the condition of the Jewish people and their religion at Jerusalem, and there is no reason to think that they do not, then you can see several strands of Judaism at this time. One orthodox, believing that Jehovah's temple was the Jerusalem Temple, that marriage with non-Jews was strictly forbidden, and that the strict letter of the Law must be observed; this was the Judaism of Ezra. While another kind of Judaism was rather more in the usual manner of the ancient world. The Jews of Elephantine, for example, gathered for regular worship in their temple, sang biblical Psalms, observed the traditional festivals and considered themselves no less pious than their cousins in Jerusalem. But in their temple they had also, in the ancient way, a place for other gods besides Jehovah. In this and in their practice of inter-marriage they showed that same ancient liberality of faith that had so distressed the earlier biblical prophets.

In these two strands of Judaism, then, were two different perceptions of Jehovah. For Ezra Jehovah was the infinite, universal Deity, as potent in Egypt as in Israel; but his sole earthly temple was in Jerusalem. For the Aswan Jews, the Jehovah in Jerusalem was the god of that city, just as their Jehovah of the temple on the granite island of Elephantine was the God of Aswan. Khnum, the neighbouring Egyptian god, had other temples in Egypt – there was a 'Khnum of Memphis' and a 'Khnum of Thebes' – so the Aswan Jehovah was similarly earth-bound and similarly divisible. This is why the Jews of Aswan did not realize that their request for permission to rebuild their temple was anathema to the priests they so respected. Like all ancient gods, Khnum and Jehovah in Elephantine were part of the society that sustained them. There was an intimacy between the gods and their followers. But Jerusalem's Jehovah, however, was a universal god surrounded by a mass of law and theology which required a detailed specialized knowledge to understand and obey. A hierarchy of priests and teachers grew up who taught that they alone could interpret holy Law, and thus insure the harmony of the community and the salvation of the people. This then is the birthplace of modern Western religion. But even in the city of Ezra and Nehemiah this attitude was far from universal. And these differing perceptions of god, and what he demands from man, had their effect upon many of the Books of the Bible. For example, it has been suggested that the Book of Jonah is a satire aimed at the religious priggishness of some of the returning exiles. This story of a stubborn old man swallowed by a whale, who would sacrifice anything for his personal standards to the point of appearing ridiculous, is an odd one. Though an apparent mention of Jonah in the Book of Kings attempts to set the story in the age of ancient Israel, the strong Aramaic flavour of the prose – Aramaic was the language of the Persian Empire – suggests that the story was written in the Persian Period.

There were other, practical divisions inside Judaism. The Jewish exiles released from Babylon were not just a group of pious nationalists but a well-structured section of urban society sent off to govern the new Persian province that had once been their ancestral homeland. The returning nobles came back to an impoverished provincial city. But to aid them in the work of restoration, the Old Testament tells us, they brought back not only Persian subsidies but also a new sense of national purpose and a determination to live by the ancient Law whose breach had caused their exile and the destruction of the ancient kingdom.

It is hardly surprising, then, that these 'children of the captivity' (Ezra 10:7) found themselves at odds with the indigenous inhabitants of the city. The Book of Ezra tells how the pious scribe separated many of these poor people from their 'strange' (i.e. foreign) wives: on that sad day 'all the people sat in the street of the house of God, trembling because of this matter, and for the great rain' (Ezra 10:9). These were the same people who, for reasons of their ritual impurity, had already been excluded from the rebuilding of the Temple. Tradition has it that this quarrel between the 'children of the captivity' and the indigenous Jerusalemites was exacerbated by the Persian governor of the province to the north of Jerusalem who allowed these Jerusalemites to build their own temple on a hilltop close to the old Israelite citadel of Samaria. There, as the 'Samaritans', they followed a schismatic faith which recognized only the books of the Pentateuch as the authoritative Bible.

[117]

The Old Testament calls these people 'the people of the land' – they were the sons and grandsons of the 'weakest class of the people . . . vine dressers and labourers' (Jeremiah 39:10 NEB). Many of these people had intermarried with the foreign settlers that the Babylonians had brought to the city after the blinded King of Judah and his court had been led away into captivity. It should never be forgotten that most of our ancient history is but the history of kings, courts and armies. Historic changes occurred at the top of society, for very few conquerors were foolish enough to deprive the land of its working peasantry. The biblical 'people of the land' were a part of the vast mass of humankind that stood in their fields and observed the passing antics of rulers and armies. They lived out their lives in anonymity, and the practices of their faith are as obscure to us as their names.

This evidence of different religious factions within the city of Jerusalem has led scholars to trace the influence of these attitudes in the biblical text. It has been claimed that some biblical passages reflect a sympathy with the plight of the 'people of the land', while the Books of Chronicles, Ezra and Nehemiah (another integrated block of text with a unity of style and content) give the priestly point of view. The 'author' of these orthodox books is known as the 'Chronicler'. Like the Deuteronomist, the Chronicler has also compiled a religious history of Israel, tracing a genealogy from David back to Adam and relating the problem of the 'children of the captivity' to roots deep in Israelite history. The difference in attitude between the Deuteronomist and the Chronicler is often seen as representing two differing factions among the returning Jews.

One thing, however, is certain. During the Persian Period, there was never a single shelf of books that, with some additions, would become the Old Testament. What must have been in existence was a hefty mass of ancient material. Brand new texts had been recently composed, and more would follow: the perfection of the Hebrew Bible was still a long way off. And in the beautifully direct manner of ancient scribes the Books of Esdras tell us this same thing. Though these Books were later rejected from the sacred canon and relegated to the Apocrypha, they are, nonetheless, old writings and provide us with interesting testimony. In the second Book of Esdras, chapter 14:23ff., the writer reveals how Ezra the Scribe received divine inspiration directly from Jehovah after drinking 'a cup of what seemed like water, except that its colour was the colour of fire', and then he dictated the Holy Books afresh. 'a flood of understanding, and wisdom . . .' grew up inside Ezra, he opened his mouth to speak and 'continued to speak unceasingly . . .' dictating the Holy Books to five scribes 'trained to write quickly'. The writer seems to be describing a process whereby an ancient, possibly even a partly oral tradition was reformed and rewritten. One old commentary remarks that 'If Moses had not anticipated him, Ezra himself would have received the lamp of understanding'. Such was the regard for Ezra among ancient Jewish scholars. He was seen as holding all the old wisdom of the faith within his head, and uttering it anew. Such were these elusive years of exile and return; a time as crucial to the Old Testament as anything that had gone before.

Glittering Cities

At about the same time that Jehovah was lighting 'the lamp of understanding' in the mind of Ezra, the Greek historian Herodotus was in Tyre, a port to the north of Jerusalem, to visit the Temple of Hercules and 'to get the best information about the origins of this god'. Herodotus (c. 490–425 BC) spent much of his life travelling through the ancient world to collect the diverse legends and histories from which he put together the long narratives now often called the world's first history books. Indeed, even after a century of scientific archaeology, the great bulk of our knowledge of the ancient world still comes from the writings of such men. The myths of ancient Egypt, the sagas of Osiris, Isis and all the other gods, were written down not by Egyptians but by literary Greeks who gathered up the age-old fragments of ritual and belief and cast them into long adventure stories.

This Greek sense of historical narrative was also shared by the writers of the Old Testament. Both Greek and Jewish writers saw history and their religions not as the rest of the ancient world had usually seen them – in terms of endless cycles of planting and harvesting according to a cosmic harmony, in victories granted by the gods to good men – but as a succession of single, unrepeated events. These unique happenings, previously thought to be chance interruptions in the timeless relationship of gods and men, now held the centre of the stage in Greek and Jewish histories. History now became a record of unique events moving in a continuum and related by cause and effect. Now only the peasants still laboured in rhythm with the gods of nature. Kings and their courts, educated men, could now move in their own time. So during the Persian Period, the biblical editors shifted the stories of the Patriarchs out of the ancient cyclical time of myth and saga into this vigorous new linear time based on happenings in men's own lives. Israel's past was transformed from theology into history.

This new vision also affected daily life: for now men felt they could control their own future. By living strictly in accordance with the Laws of Jehovah, the Jews would achieve victory in battle and prosperity at home. The future of Israel rested in its people's hands. This idea of history is not a notion from the most ancient east from the ages of the Book of Genesis. It is a notion from the new age of Herodotus, an age that also included the Deuteronomist, the Chronicler and the other biblical editors of the Persian Period. They were men of their own time and place, and this is why, after their editing of the ancient texts one sometimes feel that the ancient forefathers of whom they write are people living in advance of their times.

Jews and Greeks shared in an intellectual climate that was quite widespread at the eastern end of the Mediterranean, but nothing prepared the East for the effect that these ideas had upon the Greeks. Unlike the Jews, the Greeks did not believe that control of the future was dependent on careful observance of ritual laws. They saw man's destiny depending upon political, financial and military choices as much as fate. The future would be shaped by the arts of war and trade. Kings and princes could make decisions with conscious political ends in view, and the unfolding of events according to their choices would become the stuff of history. Judaea and all the ancient cultures between the Mediterranean and India would be broken by the whirlwind of this potent Western ideology.

The missionary of the new ideology was the Macedonian king, Alexander the Great. Before he died in Babylon of a fever at the age of thirty-three, Alexander and his armies had conquered Egypt and the Persian Empire (gobbling up Judaea on the way) and had fought across Afghanistan and into the Indus Valley. Much of the ancient world was ruined and plundered by his advance; startling new cities were founded in his wake. After his sudden death, his generals scrambled for the pieces of this huge *Imperium*. Ptolemy in Egypt and Selucius in Syria made themselves the masters of new kingdoms which they ruled from these new cities set like Greek gems in an alien landscape. For some 800 years these kingdoms lasted with varying success, haunted by the tremendous image of Alexander, looking back to the golden age of his life-time. And in this reformed eastern landscape, Judaea occupied but a small impoverished niche; impoverished by its harsh climate and poor land, and increasingly by foreign armies that marched and counter-marched along its age-old routes. In the three centuries after the death of Alexander in 323 BC, more than 200 campaigns were fought across Judaea, chiefly by Egyptian or Syrian armies. In the midst of this turmoil, the people of Judaea, pressed by these contending forces and the new Greek way of life, held on to their ancient Law.

When Alexander and his army had begun their campaign through the ancient east, all sorts of people had been attracted to his nomad court, many of them brilliant, some of them mad. One of them, a young Rhodian architect called Deinocrates wanted to build a statue of Alexander so big, he said, that the open

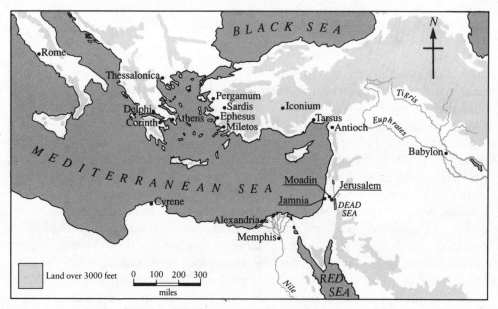

The Hellenistic Mediterranean with sites referred to in the text

palm of its right hand would hold a city; a city watered by streams that ran from the statue's leaden veins and filled with water collected from the condensation of clouds vaporizing around the statue's head. Alexander took Deinocrates into his court not, he said, because of the statue-city which he thought impractical but because of the size of the young man's imagination. After he had conquered Egypt, Alexander ordered Deinocrates to design the City of Alexandria, that most renowned of all Alexander's cities, built on a sandbank at the edge of the delta of the Nile.

Alexander's cities gave birth to a new and international way of life. Suddenly Chinese silks became high fashion by the Aegean Sea, and Greek sculptors opened studios on the edge of the Gobi desert. Buddhist missionaries preached in Egyptian Alexandria. Colossal quantities of wheat and wine filled the cities' warehouses. International merchants dealt in luxuries produced by large slave-based manufacturers: papyrus, parchment, pearls, incense, jewellery and ornaments of gold and precious stones; in the huge warehouses of cities like Alexandria all the wares of the ancient world were laid out like the goods on the shelves of a supermarket. Everything was up for sale. Ancient Alexandria, however, has long been devoured by its success – modern Alexandria is Egypt's second city. But beautiful Ephesus in modern Turkey, half-abandoned and sacked when its docks silted up and the sea-coast retreated, still shows you something of how such cities must have appeared.

To ancient sailors, rounding the headland of the bay and beating towards Ephesus at the mouth of the river Cayster, the city must have appeared to be an epitome of civilization itself; temple roofs and gilded statues flashing in the sun and the open arms of the semi-circular theatre standing on the hillside above. The marble docksides led to a wide marble road, the first night-illuminated road, that ran straight into town. 'The Greeks', an ancient rabbi observed, 'boast of their lust for learning but are shamed by their equal lust for gold.' Nonetheless, the evidence of wealth was overwhelmingly present in the warehouses, the palaces and the public buildings.

The sea view at Ephesus was dominated by the great Greek theatre, the huge structure that announced that the city, like all Hellenistic cities, was dedicated not to the gods, as was the case in Babylon or Jerusalem, but to man's pleasure. In the first century AD, according to the Book of Acts, the silversmiths of Ephesus demonstrated in this theatre, angrily claiming that St Paul's missionary zeal would harm their trade in little silver shrines and statues of Diana, Ephesus' goddess. The shops of the silversmiths were close by the theatre, standing on one side of the large market square, the *agora*, the communal centre of the city. These huge paved rectangles were a hallmark of all Alexander's cities, areas for trade and public recreation that would later be taken up by the Romans with great enthusiasm and yet remain in Italy in the beautiful piazzas that are to be found in most cities. The *agora* was the supreme architectural expression of these new cities. The ancient cities of the east – Babylon, Jerusalem, even Elephantine – all had temples at their centres, lavish statue-houses of the gods served by a traditional, hierarchical priesthood. Here, people lived in houses built like beehives, stacked up tightly and joined by dark alleyways with no open public spaces. They were cities built round the ancient gods. But the new cities of Alexander's empire were built around the recreation and labours of mankind. Just as man and not the gods now determined the course of history, so he had also moved into the light at the centre of these cities.

Today, walking in their remains we feel more at home in the open spaces of Ephesus than in the more ancient cities of Babylonia or Egypt. For our modern cities are derived from these classical forms. In these man-centred cities we instinctively understand the powerful order and the designs of the streets and the spaces. In the cities of Alexander's empire, though the gods still have a place, life has become essentially urban. To the Jews and other peoples of an older tradition, these cities filled with great white streets and squares, with Greek pillars and marble statues, had elevated man at the expense of God and were a blasphemy. Even the Christians of a later age found these cities cold hard places and often they cut small crosses into their pavements and stonework. To the people of the ancient East, these cities must have seemed places where ancient civilization, that compact between gods and men, had completely broken down.

The arrival of Alexander's armies and Hellenism at Jerusalem had hardly been a surprise to the Judaeans. Jewish mercenaries serving in foreign armies had already encountered the self-confidence and new competence of the Hellenes. Constant wars and the impoverishment of their own land following Alexander's death led large numbers of Judaeans to move into the new glittering cities of the East. They wanted to join this new international culture, Alexander's eastern legacy, a nervous super-Greek style based on classical Greek art of earlier centuries became the essential decoration of all ambitious men. Now commerce and diplomacy were carried on in the Greek language. You were either a Hellene or a barbarian, there was little alternative. The idealized portrait of Alexander came to embody the image of a master race. Dynasties of kings from Libya to Afghanistan, black, brown and blonde monarchs, all affected Greek manners, all dressed up like the legendary Alexander and in the portraits on the coins that they issued, gazed into distant Hellenic eternities. And they all built marble markets and theatres and had Greek inscriptions incised on walls and architraves. They employed Greek artists and orators to celebrate their courts and in a suitably Hellenic spirit of accommodation allowed ancient local manners to be absorbed into the new style. At Ephesus, the famous city-goddess Diana no longer appeared as an Anatolian mummy but as a plump matronly virgin in the best Greek manner. In Alexandria, composite gods were invented that fused venerable Egyptian deities with lively Greek gods and everyone was pleased with the results. With such cleverness, with such flashing style, with such promises of richness and great tolerance the confrontation between pliant, pushy Hellenism and the adherents of Jehovah's intransigent Law was postponed for centuries. But still the seeds of that conflict were always present in the marble cities: that coming calamity that would push the Hebrew Bible, the Old Testament, into its final form.

Yet for more than 300 years Alexander's cities had large, prosperous Jewish communities eagerly participating in this new city life. The practice in these cities was for each large ethnic group to have its own quarter with its own administration. Within this civic structure, Jews filled every role from merchant prince to small craftsman, from soldier and courtier to slave. And in the countryside that surrounded and supported these huge urban populations Jews were farmers and farmhands. At Miletos, close to Ephesus, leaders of the Jewish community had some of the best seats in the public theatre. Still today, their inscriptions are cut into the white marble in Greek letters: 'The place of the Jews, also called the god-fearing'.

The population of these cities, then, was as mixed as the people in an international airport, and they shared, too, many common attitudes. The pyramids of Egypt and the hanging gardens of Babylon had now become tourist attractions. Most celebrated, however, was the huge lighthouse of Alexandria – the technical wonder of the age with a vast lens that magnified an oily fire to make a beam that drew the ships of all nations towards Alexander's city. This was the beacon of a brash and confident culture whose marbled halls and columned marketplaces promised all manner of seductions – slaves, gold and silver, silks, statues and civic pride, fast horses, whores, exotic foods. It held a fascination for the ancient cultures of the East every bit as strong as Western culture, with its jeans, whisky and *laissez-faire* capitalism, does in the Middle East today.

When Alexander the Great began his ten-year war across the world he not only took his army and its generals the friends of his youth, with him, but most of the Macedonian court as well, the musicians, priests and scholars, some of them elderly men quite unfit for fighting and trekking, but who bravely followed their young king to the end. Alexander's love of Greek learning was famous – it is said he kept his copy of Homer in a jewelled box taken from the Persian emperor and used that Greek warrior epic as a Baedeker of behaviour and courtly custom. And all his Empire followed him. All the Hellenistic kings prided themselves upon their learning and their libraries. Many rulers assembled teams of scholars to copy ancient texts so that their marble cities might hold the wisdom of the world. Huge libraries with staffs of scribes and librarians handled hundreds of thousands of scrolls. In open competition with the Attalid dynasty at Pergamum, in present-day Turkey, the Ptolemaic kings of Alexandria built the greatest library of the ancient world. Just as the offerings to the gods had once promised the ancient world security and prosperity, so now the rulers of the Hellenistic cities saw public benefaction, libraries, baths, fountains and marble streets as working for the common good. Eastern Hellenism had found its own dynamic: the marble cities became as living organisms.

The Jewish communities of these Hellenistic cities had taken to this new culture with alacrity. Even in Alexander's lifetime, a traveller spoke of Jews who were 'Greek not only in speech but in spirit'. These Jews used the city vernacular call *Koine*, the lively demotic Greek that developed out of the classical tongue. Generations of Jews now lived Greek lives. They spoke *Koine*, wrote their names in the Greek way, bought and sold in Greek drachmae – though the pious used this coinage with its forbidden images for secular transactions only. As in the days of the Babylonian Exile, when the archaic Hebrew of the sacred books was translated into the Aramaic of the Persian Empire, so now the sacred texts were translated into Greek *Koine*. Moses' Books of the Law – the Pentateuch – were first translated in Alexandria in the period around 250 BC, and the rest soon followed. These translations were the professional work of scribes well used to making transcriptions from one language to another, for that was part of the ordinary business of the great libraries of the day.

Not all Jews approved of these translations. Many considered that the work held them and their faith up to ridicule. In the light of the new civic virtues the Patriarchs, the fathers of the nation, seemed to be a dynasty filled with cheats, liars, thieves and profligates, while stories such as that of Tamar (Genesis 38:6ff.) seemed filled with ancient barbarisms. Tamar, who after her two husbands had been killed by Jehovah, prostituted herself in the traditional way and conceived two sons by her father-in-law Judah, the Jewish Patriarch. Today, of course, we may read this as a lesson in the imperatives of survival or even as an example of antique marriage customs, but not as a demonstration of modern morality. Similarly in the tale of Jacob and Esau, Jacob's sheep-stealing brings prosperity, not divine wrath. And likeable lazy Esau, who guards neither the prosperity nor the purity of Abraham's tribe, has to be overcome by his voracious brother Jacob whose energies are entirely concentrated on the well-being of his family. Many of the sacred stories revolved around questions of the ritual purity of the Israelites, and the permitted relationships between the people of Jehovah and the gentiles: issues that the Jews who lived in the marble cities still faced every day of their lives. Here, then, lay a profound contradiction.

There is a splendid legend about the translation of the sacred texts into Greek. It is said that seventy-two scholars, six from each of the Twelve Tribes, were set to work on the orders of King Ptolemy Philadelphus in Alexandria. They retired to huts on a sandbank in the harbour, each man inspired by God, just as Ezra had been, each with the lamp of learning burning in his brain. In seventy-two days they completed seventy-two identical translations! This was the Septuagint – the 'Book of the Seventy-two' – and it came to exercise a special influence upon early Christianity and the New Testament, for until the fourth century AD this was the only version of the Old Testament used by the Christian church.

The act of translation, however, had inevitably affected the flavour and direction of the ancient texts. Unlike written Hebrew and Aramaic, literary Greek was the product of the public orator and philosophic discourse. Greeks reading the Septuagint in search of novel definitions of divinity and holiness would have quickly bumped their heads against the odd angles of a manner of writing from a very different tradition. But there were also points of similarity. The mystic visions of the prophets were couched in the kind of language quite familiar to Hellenistic religious sects. And the adherents of these same sects were also intrigued by the Hebrew name of God. By tradition this was represented in the sacred texts by the letter JHVH, called the *Tetragrammaton* in Greek, and pronounced *Jahweh* in Hebrew and later rendered erroneously as *Jehovah* in Elizabethan English. In the Septuagint, this term had been represented by the Greek letters IO, a strange conjunction that swiftly entered the vocabulary of the mystic sects as 'an unutterable name of the divine essence'. By such misunderstandings this most practical and rugged of ancient texts came to be regarded as an obscurely symbolic source of esoteric wisdom, where each word could be studied as if it were a portmanteau of hidden meanings. Gentile cults grew up alongside the Jewish communities in the marble cities, and in the first two centuries after Christ these affiliated communities became especially receptive to the preaching of Christian missionaries.

Another product of the meeting of Judaism and Hellenism was the Synagogue. Though none have physically survived from before the time of Christ, they were common enough in the Hellenistic cities. Alexandria alone is said to have had more than 300 of them: the very word synagogue is Greek. There was never an Israelite predecessor of these buildings that were born in Hellenism; civic buildings shaped like a classical council chamber or a *basilica* where the community elders held conference and alms were distributed to the poor. Here circumcisions and weddings were enacted with the appropriate ritual; the Sabbath prayers were recited and the Books of the Law, kept in a secure central place, were paraded and read in public assembly. The Pentateuch was read out and discussed in public over a three-year cycle, and teachers, called rabbis, began to lead these Hellenistic congregations.

The synagogue became the centre of Hellenistic Jewish communities. Jewish travellers, like Paul, gravitated naturally to the assembly place where the sacred books and the traditions of the faith were stored and celebrated. And here in their faith, Jews stood quite apart from the life of the marble cities. Hellenistic society, like most of the ancient world, was tolerant in religion, happy to accommodate all gods. But the Jews, of course, could never compromise: Jehovah was a jealous god and the Jews were his chosen people. In general, the cosmopolitan communities of the big cities respected Judaism. Like all non-Hellenes they were thought of as barbarians, but barbarians with a difference. For they had certain affinities with the Greeks, both people indulging in abstract thought and both recognizing the supremacy of abstract ideas. The Jews, then, were seen as philosophers, barbarian philosophers, and to that extent worthy of respect. And that was the extent of the accommodation.

In the marble cities, Jews were perceived as being different, but their peculiarities were not threatening. It was recognized that no Jew, whether merchant prince or slave, would work on his Sabbath day, nor would they treat humans as gods – not even Alexander, and certainly not the Roman emperors who later ruled the Hellenistic world. Among themselves the Jews achieved a balance inside these great godless cities, happily living inside their walls, but always prohibited by Jehovah's Law from full membership of the glittering society that moved around them. A central element of city life that Jews could never properly join were the *gymnasia*, huge houses dedicated to the cult of the body.

All Hellenistic towns had their *gymnasia*. In the major cities like Alexandria and Ephesus, the baths and exercise areas were truly vast. And in all these cities, marble statuary in the manner of the old Greek masters, celebrated the public image of the ideal man: a fine-tuned body housing a wise and manly mentality. These statues were key ingredients of Hellenism, essential in any new city. Just as the libraries and teachers trained and tuned the mind, so the gymnasium and its professional athletes trained the urban body. The gymnasium was a major element of Hellenistic life. There all free men exercised together in the nude, then bathed in the large marble public baths so beloved of Hellenistic and Roman society. If you wished to get on in Hellenistic society, membership and use of the gymnasium was essential. The Macedonian gymnasium had been the training ground for Alexander's army. He and his generals had trained together as children learning the skill of war and an understanding of each other that would give them the assurance to take their army from Macedonia to India and back again to Babylon. But in the fat cities of Hellenism the gymnasia became like luxurious city clubs. At their centre were statues of divine emperors and princes, the pinnacles of the Hellenistic establishment, in shrines attended by a staff of priests. Outside on the palestra, the exercise court, the free men of the city were seen, tested and summed up by the great men of the city; their public presence, their characters evaluated. As the young men competed with the athletes and with each other, the old men watched and talked together.

Jehovah's Law hardly permitted entry to such pagan institutions. And should ambition dissolve a young man's fear of sin, then the ritual scarification of his faith, the mark of circumcision, would set him apart. In sad response to this dilemma, a painful operation called the epispasm was devised by which circumcision was disguised. Some Jews had the operation done and undone several times with the waxing and waning of their faith.

Slowly and inadvertently, Hellenism and its prizes were attacking the most basic Jewish values. Within a century of Alexander's death, great numbers of Jews had gone to the new cities and out of the orbit of the traditional ways described by the sacred Law. They became Hellenistic Jews, working as hard as their pagan neighbours for the prizes offered by the glittering cities. Caught between the old, uncompromising faith and the brave new world, tremendous tensions developed inside Judaism. First there was a warm embrace between the two. Then, after centuries of fretful accommodation and self-doubt, there was a deep revulsion and a violent and devastating reaction. It was in this last period that Jesus lived out his life, and in this period also the Old Testament that we have today was finally born.

Herod and Hellenism

Even by the third century BC Hellenism stood like a demon at the very gates of Jerusalem, re-built now around Jehovah's Temple. Palestine had fallen to the armies of Alexander the Great in 332 BC, a year before he brought the Persian Empire to its end. By the second century BC the High Priest of the Temple, the virtual ruler of Israel since the return from exile, was said to be curtailing the evening ritual at the Temple so that the priests could watch the athletic events taking place at dusk in the city *gymnasium*. And at this time, too, under the rule of Syrian kings, a dynasty founded by one of Alexander's generals, the position of High Priest was on sale to the highest bidder. The history of the doleful period is laid out in the two Books of the Maccabees in the biblical Apocrypha; Jewish texts written in Greek with all the clarity and intelligence of a good Hellenistic historian. They tell of the plundering of Zerubbabel's Temple and its treasures, of plots and wars and of the terrible sufferings that in 168 BC had accompanied the enforced proscription of the Jews' religion by the Syrian king Antiochus Epiphanes. His generals burned the sacred scrolls, banned circumcision and the celebration of the Sabbath, and set up a pagan altar and established ritual prostitution inside the Temple. The indignation of the common people was immediate and ferocious and caught the Syrians by surprise – many were already angry at the leaning of the Jerusalem priesthood toward Hellenism – and a full blown rebellion began when Judas ben Mattathias, a countryman from a town outside Jerusalem struck down a Jew and a Syrian army officer who were both making an offering to the Syrian king upon a pagan altar. The wars that followed ran through several generations and cost the lives of Mattathias's five sons.

In a century of pride and power these priestly warriors – the Maccabees – established their own dynasty of priest-kings that ruled Judaea from Jerusalem. The Syrians were driven out and the ancient Law restored. Once again it seemed, just as in the days of David, that obedience to the Law was the bastion of the nation against defeat and oppression. The rule of Jehovah was hard, but without it the people of Israel could not succeed; an alternative, political explanation of events, however, is that the Syrians lost Judaea because the ruling dynasty was weakened and diverted by petty internal wars. One thing is certain; all such upheavals in the Near East worked against the interests of the rising power in the area: that of Rome. All contending factions in Judaea – the Syrians, the Egyptians, even the pious Maccabees – courted Rome, but none understood the ruthless self-interest of the Romans. Even their manners were blunter than those of any Hellenistic monarch. When a Syrian king on military manoeuvres demanded more time to consider the orders of the Roman Senate, the Roman general Pompilius Laenus drew a circle around him in the dust and told the Syrian to make up his mind before he left it. A new order had arrived in the East.

'The plan of a theatre,' wrote a Roman architect Marcus Vitruvius, 'is to be constructed as follows. Having fixed upon the centre, draw a line of circumference of what is to be the perimeter of the bottom of the theatre and inscribe four equilateral triangles, at equal distances apart and touching the boundary line of the circle as do the astrologers in a figure of the twelve signs of the zodiac ... The Roman platform has to be deeper than that of the Greeks because our artists perform on the stage whilst the orchestra contains the place reserved for the seats of the senators.' The Roman theatre was as essential to Roman cities as it was to Hellenistic ones. Vitruvius advises that it should be put in as healthy a position as possible, 'For when plays are given, the spectators sit spellbound and their bodies, motionless with enjoyment have their pores open, into which blowing winds find their way.'

The theatre of Caesarea, on the coast of Palestine, is built upon the beach. From its seats, if they were bored with the spectacles the audience could see the huge new port, built by Roman engineers, and watch the ships of the Roman empire, from Africa, Asia and Europe, sailing in and out carrying cargoes, soldiers and administrators. Caesarea was the capital city of Herod, King of the Jews, a prince of Idumaea to the south of Judah. First, Rome had granted King Herod his royal title, then allowed him to fight his way to power, finally murdering the last generation of the Maccabee family to take hold of their kingdom of Judaea and then expanding it to include Samaria, Galilee and most of Syria. First backing Mark Antony (and putting up with Cleopatra) Herod then sided with Augustus, the future emperor, a shrewd move for which he was rewarded with new cities to administer and new provinces to rule. Herod supplied soldiers for the eastern Roman armies and cash and flattery to a succession of Roman emperors, two of whom were personal friends. At the centre of Caesarea stood a great white temple, visible from far out to sea. Herod had dedicated it to Caesar and Rome, the butter on his daily bread. Like most of his subjects, Herod was a Jew, his ancestors having been forcibly converted to Judaism during the time of the Maccabee wars. Unlike most of his subjects, however, he was convinced that prosperity was to be found by adopting the manners of Hellenism and the cause of Rome. In his palace at Caesarea he was a splendid Hellenistic king, a man decorated with silks and jewellery, a man with stables filled with fine desert horses, a man who built a dozen Corinthian palaces, the rococo desert dreams of a fierce and wily warrior. At holy Jerusalem, however, Herod was a pious Jew, relatively sober, god-fearing and mindful of Jehovah's Laws.

In 15 BC, Herod made a proclamation which was recorded by the historian Josephus: 'With God's assistance, I have advanced the nation of the Jews to a degree of happiness which they never had before . . . Our fathers, indeed, when they returned from Babylon, built this temple of God Almighty, yet still it wants sixty cubits in size, but let no one condemn our fathers for their negligence or want of piety, for it was not their fault that the temple was no higher . . . But since I am now, by God's will, your governor, and have had peace a long time and gained great riches and since, most importantly, I am a friend to everyone, well-regarded by the Romans who, if I might say so are the rulers of the whole world, I will do all I can . . . to make a thankful and pious return to God for the blessing of this kingdom by rendering His Temple as complete as I am able.'

At the Temples of Baalbek and Palmyra, Judaea's neighbours had already dressed their old religions in the costumes of Hellenism, and now Herod wished to do the same for the religion of the Jews. But his proclamation had frightened the priesthood at Jerusalem. For, if the old Temple of Zerubbabel were torn down and the new one built in a manner that deviated from the prescriptions of Holy Law, then the new building would be unusable. With tact and energy and a considerable outpouring of money, Herod managed to assuage the fears of the priests. By degrees, all the requirements of the Law were complied with, and to the astonishment of Jerusalem the enormous project was completed inside ten years. On the summit of Mount Moriah, where Abraham had offered to sacrifice Isaac and where David had planned the first Temple, Herod's architects and engineers raised a gleaming Hellenistic citadel. The entire hilltop was now framed by a huge rectangle of stone which more than doubled the size of the old Persian platform, and all was made 'with stones that were white and strong and measured 25 cubits,' – about 40 feet (see Plate 15). The centre was occupied by Jehovah's new Temple, built according to the dreams of the prophets and the Laws of Moses, a cube-like building, similar in proportion to the *Ka'aba* at Mecca and sheathed with gold that could be seen flashing in the sun for miles around. Inside was the dark sanctuary of Jehovah, built by priests and so sacred that even Herod never saw inside it.

All around the sanctuary was a succession of wide courtyards, decorated in the grandiose Corinthian order, with the colossal columns so beloved of Rome and Eastern Hellenism. Beneath the Temple platform, huge stairs and walkways carried the faithful up to their devotions. Vast vaults and arches carried a stone bridge that spanned the valley isolating the profane city from its sacred hill. International Hellenism and Roman engineering had been set to work to make a brand-new house for an ancient god, and all done strictly according to the letter of the Law. The Temple was a triumphant meeting of two cultures, and it epitomized the tightrope that Herod had walked throughout his long life.

Judah under Rome
What then did the people of Judaea think of this Hellenistic invasion? There is little evidence that as an architectural style it was in any way disliked, and so deep had the manners of this international culture become ingrained in the life of cities like Jerusalem that the plainer, ancient styles had all but disappeared. Now upon the holy Sabbath, the Judaeans might sit in synagogues designed in the manner of Hellenistic council chambers, all decorated with classical colonnades. In the centuries after Herod, drawings of the great seven-branched candlestick of the Jerusalem Temple, the *menorah*, might appear among the flowing acanthus leaves on the capital of a Corinthian column (see Plate 12). The four festive plants of Judaism – myrtle, tamarisk, willow and citron – would find their way into the elaborate decorations of a Hellenistic marble frieze. And on one occasion, a synagogue frieze even included a small picture of the synagogue's Ark, the box that held the sacred scrolls, drawn as a little wheeled cart. Even the six-pointed 'Star of David' and the five-pointed 'Star of Solomon', ancient magical patterns, were woven into the Hellenistic designs. But though forms of the classical world were happily accepted by the people of Judaea, the way of life that gave birth to them was sharply rejected by the synagogues' teachers, the rabbis. 'One may not descend in matters of holiness,' one of them observed, and the language of this holiness was still the ancient

Hebrew of the holy texts. But in Roman Judaea the everyday language of the people was Aramaic and that in heavy local dialects. There was a need for the sacred texts to be rendered in the popular tongue and this was done by specially trained rabbis whose translations, *targammim*, were widely used. Abroad, among the Jewish communities in the cities of the Roman Empire, the Greek text of the Septuagint was popular alongside Latin versions. But despite all these translations, Hebrew remained the essential language of the faith. Pious scholars who devoted themselves to the Law, who guided the people on all matters of observance, used only the Hebrew texts. To such people schooled in the sacred text of ancient Israel's history, the benefits of strict observance seemed obvious. The short reign of Herod's grandson Agrippa (AD 41-44), for example, was looked on as an exemplary time. The king had given much of his energy and fortune to the Temple and the faith. In his reign, it was said that grains of corn grew as large as shekel pieces and beans as large as kidneys. At Jerusalem the priests kept specimens of these miraculous crops to demonstrate the practical results of such obedience to the Law. (But even pious Agrippa died 'struck down by God' after he had awarded himself the trappings of divinity before an admiring audience in the Roman amphitheatre at Caesarea.)

Spurred on now by new Roman masters, Hellenism was relentlessly infiltrating every aspect of life in Judaea. The ancient holy texts needed the most careful scholarship and interpretation to fit their injunctions to the realities of this new world; the New Testament's Gospels show Jesus constantly arguing about the interpretation of holy Law in Hellenistic society. In Jerusalem rabbis founded schools of scholarship that dealt solely with these same problems. A fresh discipline based upon those interpretations was established that covered every aspect of daily life. To many people, the Hellenized priests of the Temple now appeared remote and corrupt, leading Greek lives with Greek names. Holy men denounced them as idle and wicked, a stumbling block to the progress of the faithful. Terrific tensions were slowly building up inside Judaea. Several contemporary commentaries upon the ancient books are filled with ominous undertones and lightly veiled references to contemporary events, and told of the coming battles between the faithful and the heathens. Some texts tell of a Messiah who will free God's chosen people. Others prophesy the last trumpet that will announce the end of the world.

And through them all runs the theme that the Law held no compromise in it. That there was but one Temple and one God, and that he was not the Emperor of Rome and that even to pretend for a moment that he was was a deep sin. Yet the idea of empire to the Romans was to some extent a religious idea and to deny its sacredness seemed to deny its authenticity. Most eastern nations cheerfully accepted the Roman emperors and gods. The Jews would not. A large part of Herod's success had depended on his subtle accommodation inside Judaea of the few outward marks of power on which the Romans insisted, a balancing act of the greatest delicacy. In the Temple, offerings on the emperor's behalf were made daily to Jehovah and when in AD 66 the priests rejected them, the Romans quite correctly interpreted this as an official act of rebellion, an act that neither city riots nor peasant rebellions could have proclaimed.

When the great new Temple had been under construction Herod had a huge relief of the imperial Roman eagle placed over the main door and this greatly offended many pious Jews. Years later, as he lay dying in his desert palace at Jericho, a group of pious men took this eagle down. But even on his deathbed. Herod had not lost the tough instincts that had kept him on his throne for so long: he ordered the burning of the culprits, including two rabbis, and had one of his own sons executed, who had seemed, somehow, to be implicated in this insult to Rome. Five days later the old man died leaving orders for a number of leading citizens of Jerusalem to be killed so that there would be a show of real grief inside Jerusalem on the day of his funeral. But his sister Salome set them free and Herod went unmourned to a secret tomb. Seven years later Jesus of Nazareth was born. In the aftermath of Herod's death the remaining members of his family murdered and plotted their way into oblivion and exile; Roman governors were appointed to rule the land. Judaea became a third-rate province governed by unexceptional imperial bureaucrats who had neither sympathy for, nor understanding of the people they controlled. Yet like more modern imperial powers the overall policy of Rome was not ungenerous; implacable in face of opposition, sometimes foolish in matters of policy, Rome was self-effacing in the cause of self-interest, preferring prosperous cities to smoking ruins. As long as Rome's own interests were safe, people could get on with their lives as they pleased.

In general, then, Roman policy towards Judaea was designed to mollify religious sentiment. The Roman practice was to respect Jewish faith. There are records of soldiers being transferred, or even executed, for offending Judaism. The marching legions often had the tact to by-pass Judaea so that the sacred standards that bore the imperial portraits would not be carried onto Jewish soil. Apart from mad Caligula who had insisted that a statue of himself should be set up in the Jerusalem Temple and had nearly caused a rebellion, the emperors raised neither statues nor temples on Jewish soil. Judaea was the only Roman province where coins did not bear the emperor's face.

Yet the inevitable pressures to conform to the manners of the Empire led Jewish scholars to ever stricter and more precise interpretations of holy Law. Some now said that all the earth beyond the holy land of Israel was impure and that the people of God could not suffer contact with such ritual impurity. Others declared that all gentiles and all their works, even their crops and animals, were equally impure. Arguments raged over the minutest details. Was bread lawful when baked in an oven inadvertently heated with wood cut by a gentile? Did a weaver's shuttle cut from foreign wood make lawful cloth? The ancient texts were silent on these matters and scholars combed the written works for precedents and guidance. The appalling consequences of lax practice had been emphasized again and again in the histories of Israel, in the Books of Kings and Chronicles.

Under the negligent rule of a succession of poor provincial governors, there grew up in the Roman provinces of Judaea and Galilee a conviction that all misfortune would be reversed by a purer, stricter and more rigorous observance of the Law. The complete observance of the Law would bring victory to a Jewish army fighting the Roman legions. But if success did not attend the Jewish army, this would be because of breaches, deliberate or inadvertent, of the Law. Such attitudes did not appeal to the rich priests, merchants and princes of Judaea, who knew very well the reality of Roman power and were unwilling to accept such literal interpretations of the holy texts. Though these men might be fastidious in their personal devotions, they had long developed a more accommodating public faith. By Herod's day a split had developed between religious conservatives and Hellenized city dwellers, many of whom had grown rich through their contacts with the Hellenistic world. One popular northern preacher, John the Baptist, was beheaded for denouncing the unlawful marriage of the local Hellenized prince of Galilee; doubtless, for many people, the words of Jesus of Nazareth, seemed to hold similar nationalistic aspirations of purity and piety. A great many Gospel stories concern the contradicting cultures of Hellenism and Jewish piety. Jesus, a country preacher, must also have passed under Herod's blasphemous Roman eagle as he went into the temple of Jerusalem to cast out the money changers, those associates of the Hellenized priesthood. To many Judaeans, both the Romans and the Jewish nobility were godless sinners whose presence was keeping the people of Israel from ritual purity and unity with their Lord Jehovah.

The Veil Rent

Herod's Temple is gone today, but still, on the stairways that lead up into the colonnaded squares in which the temple stood, you can sense something of its history. These steps worn shiny-smooth by ancient sandals are Herod's steps, the top of a long staircase where the ancient rabbis met their followers before walking with them to the squares above where they conducted their classes, in

Hellenic style, under the grandiose arcades. These steps, too, were the ones up which Jesus would have walked on his way to overturn the money changers. This switching of money from pagan Roman coin to that of the local currency, so that the purchase of animals for offering would be ritually pure, had strains of nationalism about it which are echoed on a present-day trip to the Temple platform; you pay for entrance in Israeli shekels but receive a ticket that is priced in Jordanian pounds.

The main doorways to the ancient Temple are still half-visible in the western wall at the top of the stairway. But stones block off the ascending staircases that run now under the al-Aqsa Mosque, but once rose to a huge open court. From here you would have seen the outer wall of the Temple's enclosure beyond which non-Jews, warned by multilingual notices, passed at their peril. Today all this has gone, and all that remains of Herod's buildings are the underground entrance tunnels, the walls of the Temple platform and the blocked doorways on the ancient steps. The splendid cornice above the northern doorway is probably early Byzantine, perhaps even Islamic. Three courses above it, now set upside down in the wall, is the base of a Roman statue inscribed to the Emperor Hadrian. In the second century AD all Jews had been banished from Jerusalem and forbidden, on pain of death, even to look upon the city. Jehovah's Temple had been swept off the face of the earth. Jerusalem, the Holy City, was reduced to ash and rubble and ceremonially ploughed by the Roman priests. Hadrian gave the city a new name Aelia Capitolina and stationed a legion there; his statue base is from that legion's imperial temple – the whole doleful story is held in the beautifully bronzed stones.

For a brief period Herod's Temple had stood flashing brightly in the sun, and the priests cared for Jehovah in his temple and made daily offerings. But the Romans were engaged in wars to the east of Judaea and the eastern provinces were taxed hard to pay for the armies. At the same time the fighting also stopped the trade that was the life-blood of Hellenism. Poor government and severe taxes both exasperated and impoverished much of the eastern Empire. In Judaea, the Hellenized merchants and priests lost sympathy with Rome and ordinary citizens, long horrified by the blasphemies of their overlords, found common cause with their native masters. Economics joined religious sentiment, and to no one's surprise but the Romans, thirty years after the crucifixion of Jesus, rebellion broke out, the Temple priests throwing down the gauntlet by refusing the daily imperial offering. Judaea and Galilee were lightly garrisoned, and that gave the Jewish leaders valuable time to prepare for the inevitable Roman onslaught. The defence of Galilee in the north was entrusted to Flavius Josephus, a nobleman of Jerusalem, who years later wrote the long and detailed history which holds virtually all we now know about the terrible events that were to follow.

Perhaps it was their faith in the power of piety and learning which had prompted the Jews to give the scholarly Josephus, who had already advised against rebellion, such a powerful military role. Soon he was in the midst of the war as the Roman army came down from Syria into Galilee. Some of the northern cities were heavily fortified and offered brave and bloody resistance. But Josephus seems to have fought with his fellow countrymen as much as he did with the Romans. At the end he was wounded, then trapped by the enemy in a cave where he and his men made a suicide pact on which, by his own account, he reneged at the last moment. Brought in chains before the victorious general Vespasian, he so charmed the Romans that they not only took him into Judaea for the rest of the campaign but also, when the war was over, gave Josephus an estate and a pension in Rome – a fact that many later historians have been unable to excuse. When Titus, Vespasian's son, and the legions arrived beneath the walls of Jerusalem it was heavily defended by several different factions including many of Josephus' own commanders, refugees from Galilee. So fierce was the rivalry among these diverse groups that the Romans simply encamped and waited while street battles, a real reign of terror, ravaged the besieged city. After six months of murder, starvation and populist rule, the Romans built siege towers against the walls and stoned the Temple Mount, which was burned out in the attack. Then, as Jewish leaders hid in caves under the city, the Romans slowly occupied and sacked it.

Following another war across the same small hills in 1967, Israeli excavations cut through much later ruins to uncover some of the ash and debris from the Roman sack of the city in AD 70. In the ruins of the well-to-do house of Kathros, a Temple priest, the violence of those days was still to be seen: an iron-tipped spear still leaned against the kitchen wall; a severed arm lay in the ash behind an upturned table; the kitchen equipment, the pots, pans and pestles were all broken.

PLATE 12 (Opposite): Detail of a column capital from the Great Synagogue at Capernaum, showing a menorah *– a seven-branched candlestick of the type used in the Jerusalem Temple – nestling among the acanthus leaves of the Corinthian Order. Late second century* AD.
PLATE 13 (Overleaf): A Dead Sea Scroll still showing the marks of the ancient priestly hands that used it. One of the first scrolls to be found, it is a copy of the Book of Isaiah and was made in the first century BC.

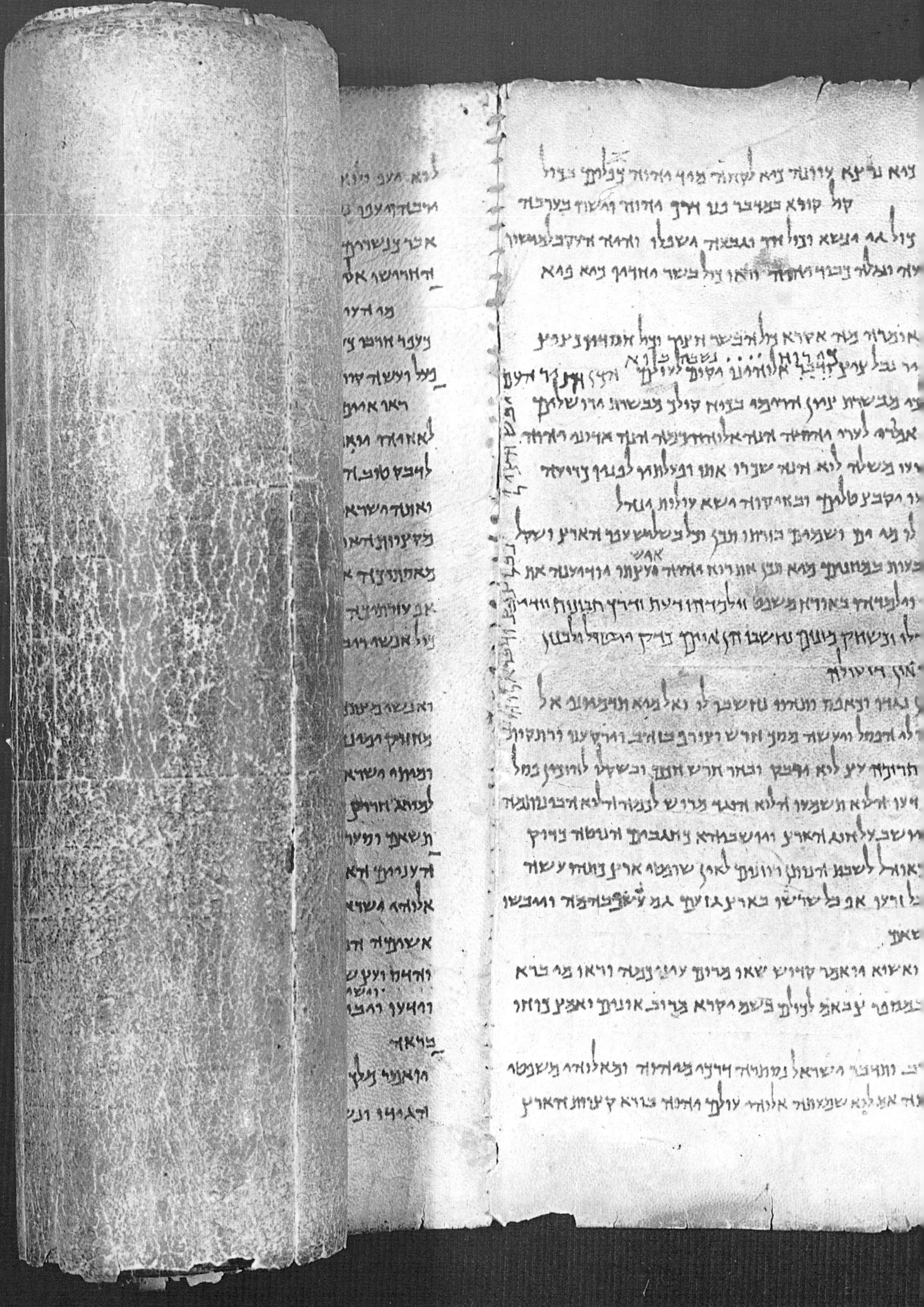

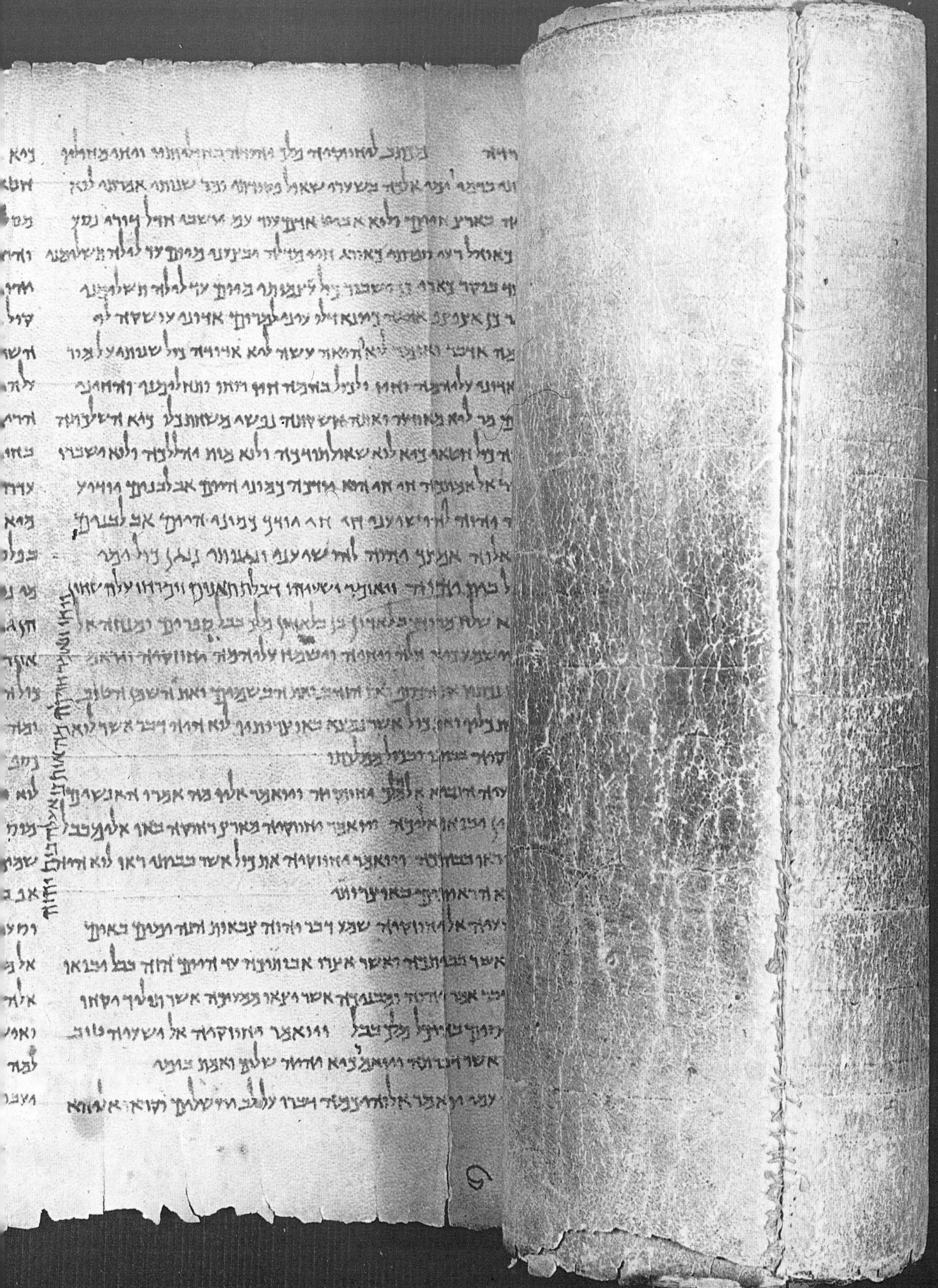

Josephus records that after the Roman troops had taken the Temple Mount, Titus had called on the rebels in the upper city to surrender. But as he allowed them no passage to freedom they had little choice but to stand and fight. Then Titus had the valley between the city and the Temple where the priests lived set on fire. It is tempting to think that the ruin of Kathros's house was the result of this action. But it is just as likely to have resulted from the fierce internecine fighting that had taken place during the time of the siege. The priestly families were notorious; one text specifically mentions Kathros's venality, so it is not unlikely that they had already received short shrift at the hands of the rebel leaders.

After the fall, Josephus walked in the streets of the ruined city. On the Temple Mount, he saw women and children gathered for sale into slavery and obtained the release of a hundred or so people he knew. On an outing with the Roman cavalry, he came across a place of mass crucifixion and was alarmed to see old acquaintances hanging on the crosses. He 'begged of Titus with tears in my eyes' for these to be taken down and some were successfully revived by the Roman doctor. Titus, we are told, asked Josephus what he wanted from the ruined city: he begged for the release of his friends and of his brother and for the rest he merely asked to be allowed to take the 'Holy Books'. It was a prophetic request. One that must have been in the very front of the minds of all surviving Jewish intellectuals. With the heart of the nation burned right out and the people crucified or enslaved all that remained of ancient Israel now was the Law and the Holy Books. Many of the surviving Jewish scholars would, like Josephus, set about building the literary memorials of their ancient culture.

Dead Sea Scrolls

Josephus' histories provide us with a marvellously detailed story of his times; his autobiography tells us of the dilemmas that faced all educated Jews living in Judaea in the century after Christ, the last years before the final reshaping and selection of the texts of the Hebrew Bible, the Old Testament. Josephus tells us that by the time he was thirty he had already visited Rome to plead the cause of

PLATE 14 (Opposite): The caves close to the ancient fortress of Qumran where, in 1947 a family of bedouin shepherds discovered the first cache of Dead Sea Scrolls.

some friends in prison, and with the help and friendship of the notorious Poppaea, whom he describes as 'Nero's wife, a religious lady', he obtained their release. Later, when he faced the Romans in Galilee, Josephus had no illusions as to the fearsome power of the legions. He had a respect for Rome and a reverence for classical culture but also a filial devotion to his own culture and its Holy Law. Before his journey to Rome, Josephus had spent three years living in the Judaean desert with a hermit called Bannus, a man 'who used no other clothing than what grew on trees . . . no other food than what grew of its own accord, and bathed himself in cold water frequently, both night and day, in order to preserve his chastity'. From the temptation of prosperous Roman hedonism to the rigours of the cenobitic life, young Josephus had explored most of the possibilities of his contemporary world.

Josephus was born in Palestine in about AD 37. His parents were nobles and as a youth he was considered to be wise enough for scholars to consult him on 'points of the Law'. Before his stay with Bannus he had already 'made trial of several sects', first studying with some Sadducees to whom he was related. These were the half-Hellenized priestly nobility that controlled the Temple and its vast revenues. Then he studied with the Pharisees, the group of teachers and rabbis dedicated to the elucidation of the Law who, in Josephus' day, increasingly demanded that Jews live a life of strict observance. He also visited a monkish sect called the Essenes who lived in male communities strictly bounded by the Law. Though the members of this sect were reticent in their dealings with the world, their piety and austerity attracted the attention of many writers. Pliny the Elder, the Roman historian, wrote of them with enthusiam: 'they inspire our admiration more than any other community in the whole world. They live without women . . . without money, and without any company save that of the palm trees.'

Excited by such antique enthusiasm, eighteenth-century church historians suggested that the Essenes had been practising a sort of proto-Christianity. Even the acerbic Gibbon observed that 'the community of goods which had so agreeably amused the imagination of Plato . . . subsisted to some degree among the austere sect of the Essinians [sic].' And he went on to observe that in the remote Egyptian oasis that became the cradle of Christian monasticism, an Essene community called the *Theraputae* had offered 'a very lively image of primitive discipline'. With the nineteenth-century passion for finding the sources of everything from rivers to the human race, the Essenes were often put forward as the precursors of Christianity. Perhaps John the Baptist, and even Jesus himself, had studied with these mysterious people? Yet the only evidence regarding the Essenes came from the same sparse classical texts that Gibbon had known a century earlier.

Then in the 1940s and 1950s the mysterious Essenes were dragged into the bright light of day; when the treasure-troves of ancient texts known as the

Dead Sea Scrolls were first discovered, they were said to be the product of an Essene community. Suddenly the Essenes assumed a tremendous importance in the history of the Bible. For the Dead Sea Scrolls had all been made before the Roman sack of Jerusalem in AD 70; most of them were biblical texts, and these were at least one thousand years older than any others that were known. Here was an extraordinary opportunity to read the sacred texts in their pristine condition before they had been garbled by centuries of copying.

The Dead Sea Scrolls promised nothing less than a revelation; some of the first scholars who worked on them claimed that they would change our understanding of Judaism and the Bible for ever. First, of course, the authenticity of the scrolls had to be established. That they were genuine ancient texts was never doubted. But who exactly had written them, and where had they been used? Were they from the library of the Jerusalem Temple? Had they been made by the Pharisees or the Sadducees – did they reflect in some way the attitudes of these parties? Or even, perhaps, the attitudes of mysterious sects such as the Essenes? Could they, in short, be taken as orthodox versions of Holy Scriptures?

The scrolls had been found mostly by bedouin shepherds and sold, piecemeal, to Israeli and Jordanian archaeologists. Much of the material was in thousands of fragments. Only four scrolls were virtually complete, splendid fat rolls of sheepskin still bearing the marks of ancient hands that had opened and closed them 2000 years earlier (see Plate 13). A visitor to the laboratories in Jerusalem, where many of the scrolls were stored, said that they resembled 'autumn leaves that had lain in the forest all winter'. The process of sorting and joining these fragments could, quite literally, take centuries of careful scholarship. And in the meantime who could guess what surprises they had in store? For both Jews and Christians, the situation was one of extraordinary interest.

Apart from biblical texts, there was a variety of other writing found in the Dead Sea caves. Among the very first to be found were some lists of rules, apparently made to govern the life of a Jewish sect, and beside these rules were descriptions of ceremonies of initiation and ordination. From the first, it was suggested that these were the rule books of the Essene order. Yet the three separate texts of rules frequently contradict each other. Nor did the word Essene appear in any of them. More recently it has been proposed that these rules were sets of ideal principles, rather like the credo of King Arthur's Round Table. Certainly, other copies of the same rule books were cherished well into the Middle Ages and little or no attempt was made to put them into daily practice. But when these texts had first been deciphered, it had seemed to the scholars that these had been the rules of a real ancient holy order and this they identified with the Essenes. Then, close by the first of the scroll caves to be found, a modest group of ancient remains called the Khirbat Qumran – the ruins of Qumran – was excavated. The archaeologists' report described the buildings as an 'Essene monastery' and identified – though this was disputed – one room as the scriptorium where the scrolls had been written and stored.

Since those early days a veritable industry has sprung up around the decipherment and interpretation of the Dead Sea Scrolls. The attractive scenario of this golden monastery by a bright blue sea, filled with pious, scribbling monks at work on mountains of religious texts, appealed to many historians and the public alike and was quickly enshrined in several bestselling books. This had the great advantage of distancing the Dead Sea Scrolls' texts from the contemporary schools of Jerusalem. Any deviation from orthodoxy in the scrolls could be put down to the oddity of the Essene order. According to this view, the scrolls were the work of a long dead schismatic sect of interest largely to students of religious history. Doubts about the theory were seldom aired.

Yet the archaeological evidence from Khirbat Qumran was insufficient to prove that the scrolls had ever been there, or indeed that it had been the house of a religious community, Essene or otherwise. Not one religious object was found there, nor could any of the buildings be proved to have a specific religious use. Like so many sites in the Holy Land, Khirbat Qumran had suffered from over-hasty acceptance of a pious literary theory without any hard evidence. As the excavators themselves reminded us, 'archaeology is not an exact science' – they knew that they had never proved their assertions.

All, however, are agreed that the finds at Khirbat Qumran show that it was originally built as a Judaean fortress at some time between the ninth and seventh centuries BC; that it had been refortified for the last time a century or so before Christ and finally destroyed, perhaps by an earthquake, after a siege in which some of the building walls had been sapped. Roman arrowheads found in the ashes suggest that this sack of Qumran took place during the Jewish rebellion of AD 66-70 as the legions had travelled down the western shore of the Dead Sea. The little acropolis with a wide sweeping view was in an excellent strategic position. Its watchtower commanded the important routes to Jericho and Jerusalem. A Roman road on the desert behind Qumran shows that the Romans too realized the value of this high point guarding the crossroads at the north end of the Dead Sea. Yet the communal arrangements of a Jewish garrison suggested to the excavators the form of an Essene monastery. Pliny had described the Essenes as living under palm trees, without money or women, and at Khirbat Qumran the archaeologists had found exactly the reverse. Women were buried in the settlement cemetery, money was stashed under the floors, and there had never been any palm trees growing on the dry desert bluff. Khirbat Qumran was not an oasis; its survival depended on an elaborate water catchment system that fed large, plastered cisterns. But for the nearby caves with their sensational treasures, the tumbled buildings of Khirbat Qumran would have been left to lie in sandy ruin, identified merely as one of the ring of strategic outposts that surrounded ancient Jerusalem.

Similarly, without their cache of scrolls, the caves by Qumran would have been identified as convenient storerooms for the fortress; for identical pottery was discovered in both caves and fortress, and these caves were designed as cool larders, with carefully made vents to trap and circulate the desert winds (see Plate 14). That the garrison of the Qumran fortress had helped the keepers of the scrolls to hide them in the caves would seem to be a reasonable assumption. Archaeologically, the connection between the Fort of Khirbat Qumran and its caves seems clear enough. But, just as David and Solomon still await archaeological evidence of their earthly existence, so Khirbat Qumran still awaits proof that it ever served as an Essene monastery. Nor is there any evidence at all that the Dead Sea Scrolls were produced or even owned by that mysterious sect.

Whoever it was that made and hid the scrolls, however, one thing is clear: they are a vital link in the history of the Bible. Before their discovery, texts of such antiquity were few and far between, existing only in isolated fragments. There were some Samaritan versions of the Pentateuch of indeterminate age – this schismatic sect recognized only the Five Books of Moses. There were also some later copies of the Greek translation of the Septuagint, made by early Christian scholars. But before the discovery of the scrolls, apart from these few fragments, the oldest surviving Hebrew texts were copies of the 'correct and clear manuscripts prepared by the master Aaron ben Moses ben Asher' in Tiberias, by Lake Galilee, in AD 1008. Though none of these ancient versions differed profoundly from each other, scholars could only guess at their relative ages and correctness. Even in the 1940s, after a century of intense study, leading biblical scholars were still wondering if our Old Testament was a completely accurate copy of an ancient Hebrew original. And there seemed little hope of ever finding an answer. Then, in the 1950s at a single stroke, the Dead Sea Scrolls gave the world another thousand years of the Bible's history. Of the 80 texts presently identified from among the material in the caves, 175 are copies of Bible books, and 70 of these are of the Pentateuch. There are 48 scrolls of the prophets, the majority being of the Book of Isaiah, and 57 copies of the Books of Psalms and the historical writings. The oldest of all the texts yet found in this colossal jigsaw puzzle is one of the four copies of the Books of Samuel, and this has been dated by the style of its writing to the third century BC. Curiously enough, this is a version of the same text that had been used to make the Greek translation – the Septuagint – and contains many variants from the orthodox Massoretic text of ben Asher of Tiberias.

The different versions of Bible texts found in the Dead Sea Scrolls have been separated into a number of different families – the material is from very diverse sources. Some texts are apparently revisions of the Samaritan Pentateuch, others show marked similarities to the later Massoretic text (as Ben Asher's text is called), many are mixtures of several different types, and that some of the ancient scribes had recognized these differences is emphasized by the many alterations they contain. Yet all these different versions were hidden in the caves, side by side, with equal care. And this is remarkable when you consider that in later centuries, the addition or omission of a single dot or hyphen in a manuscript would lead to the rejection of an entire scroll! To preserve the absolute integrity of the holy writings not one misplaced jot or title was allowed to pass the rabbi's eagle eye. Clearly, this was not the case in the eras of the Dead Sea Scrolls before the destruction of Jerusalem in AD 70. So the question whether our Old Testament is an accurate copy of an ancient Hebrew original is no longer relevant; it seems that there never was a single original of the Holy Writings. The best that we can say, from evidence of the Dead Sea Scrolls, is that by the time the last of them were made in the first century AD, the different versions held but small variations in them; but nonetheless each version still had its own integrity and its own ancient pedigrees.

So far all these different versions have given us no blinding revelations. Fresh facts gleaned from their variant readings may well undermine theological arguments that depend on the precise meaning of, say, the word *Lord* as opposed to the word *God*. But the practical effects of the Dead Sea Scrolls upon our understanding of the modern biblical text have not been large. A few passages, previously obscure because they had become garbled in their copying, can now be understood. It seems that the watchman in the Book of Isaiah (21:8) did not mysteriously shout, 'A lion: My lord, I stand continually upon the watch tower'; much more reasonably, he cried out *like* a lion, 'My lord, I stand continually upon the watch tower' – a difference that resulted from the reversal of just two letters in the Hebrew text. Yet there is still a great number of questions raised by these scrolls which their keepers, Bible scholars, have yet to answer.

The first question is why on earth this mass of diverse material was hidden in the desert at all. The traditional answer is that the texts were the contents of the Essene scriptorium and the monks placed them in the nearby caves at Qumran for safekeeping. If that was so, the little room at Khirbat Qumran must have been a sort of Judaean United Nations, full to overflowing with texts from different backgrounds and different traditions. Research, unfortunately, is still hampered by the scandalous fact that today, forty years after the initial discoveries, more than half the 800 texts remain unpublished. But we may be sure that had any documents been found to support the conventional picture of the 'Essene scriptorium' they would have been published long ago! Slowly, as more of the Dead Sea Scrolls are studied, younger scholars are questioning the connection of the scrolls with the Essenes. There is a growing belief that the scrolls were not written in the Qumran scriptorium, nor were they placed in the caves by the members of a schismatic sect; in the words of one doubting scholar, 'that was nothing but science fiction.' The ancient Essenes, it has been pointed out, were quite a large, probably international, organization. They were sufficiently well-known for Pliny to have heard of them, and Josephus describes them as people of 'the third way' after the Sadducees and the Pharisees. Even if Khirbat Qumran could be proved to have belonged to the Essenes, it must have been an extremely insignificant part of their organization. The Essene headquarters were certainly at Jerusalem. Quite possibly the Dead Sea Scrolls had connections with an Essene library, and several other religious libraries, but this is pure speculation.

Despite the bustle of activity surrounding the scrolls, one piece of evidence concerning their origins has, until quite recently, been ignored. This is the text of one of the scrolls themselves, a strange list engraved on a roll of copper, which in itself is a unique document, for all the other scrolls are written with ink upon parchment, leather or papyrus. At first, the content of the Copper Scroll was considered so incredible that it was taken for the product of a deranged mind; perhaps a folk story or an enigmatic game. Anything, in fact, but the simple truth. But it is difficult to see why such an elaborate object, the only one of its kind and so carefully hidden in the desert hills, should contain only twaddle. At the same time, it is easy to see why this strange text was so ruthlessly dismissed, for it suggested that the Dead Sea Scrolls had originated in Jerusalem and not Qumran at all.

When it was found, the Copper Scroll was heavily oxidized and so fragile that it had to be sliced into spill-like sections rather than risk the disintegration that threatened any attempt to unroll it. After its ingenious dissection in a Manchester laboratory in England the Copper Scroll revealed that it had been but one of a pair of identical documents. 'Near the caves, is a hole opening to the north,' a typical line reads, 'there is a copy of this book with explanations, measurements and details'. The two texts had recorded the hiding places of a large list of treasures that had been cached in an area that ran from the caves and valleys of the Judaean desert to the walls of Jerusalem herself. The topography described in the scroll has never been exactly identified. The treasure, if it exists, may still lie undisturbed.

Unlike all the other texts of the Dead Sea Scrolls, this odd document is written in first-century colloquial Hebrew and in the down-to-earth manner of ancient book-keepers. The Copper Scroll is unique among the Dead Sea Scrolls in that it was engraved on metal, presumably for its greater security. Moreover, it is the only purely secular document found in the caves and it was made in the period during which the Dead Sea Scrolls were hidden. This, then, is an authentic document from the time of the destruction of Jerusalem in AD 70.

For thousands of years before the Romans arrived in Judaea, the local people had hidden their precious possessions in the preserving desert. Many hoards have been found in this century: mysterious masks from a Stone Age settlement from 7000–8000 BC; the equipment of the Bronze Age temple from 4000–5000 BC; the domestic treasure, house-keys and even the corpses of refugees fleeing from Roman troops in the second century AD. But the vast quantities of treasure listed on the Copper Scroll were well beyond the resources of a religious sect, or the private wealth of Judaea. Moreover, the religious rule books of the Dead Sea Scrolls specifically forbade such accumulations of wealth. And this is partly why the text of the Copper Scroll was at first considered a fantasy! Yet the accumulated wealth of the Temple in Jerusalem, the economic heart of Judaism that administered a national system of tithes and offerings might conceivably have amounted to such quantities. When Titus returned to Rome after the conquest of Jerusalem, his triumphal procession boasted only Jewish slaves and Temple fitments, none of the wealth of the ancient city and its priesthood. Presumably it had not been found. Among the hiding places listed in the Copper Scroll for its lost treasures are also eight locations specifically designated for scrolls. From the centuries after the sack of Jerusalem, Christian records describe two separate discoveries of jars holding Bible texts; the discovery of the Dead Sea Scrolls was the third occasion when ancient scrolls were recovered from the Judaean desert. A pattern begins to emerge; and a more plausible theory of the origin of the scrolls presents itself.

At face value, the Copper Scroll seems to be a genuine inventory of the treasures and documents hidden before the destruction of Jerusalem in AD 70 when the priests and elders, as Josephus tells us, realized that destruction was pressing close upon the city. The earthly and spiritual treasures of Jerusalem were buried all together. This explains the extraordinary diversity of the scrolls – why, for example, three contradictory rule books were found quite close together and why several different versions of sacred texts appeared in the same place. The texts had been gathered up from a larger mass and taken to the desert caves for no other purpose than their storage. Probably taken from the libraries and synagogues of Jerusalem, the scrolls represent many ages and traditions of Hebrew writing, with their contradictions, variants and repetitions. The theory of the Essene scriptorium makes a romantic tale; but, unfortunately, little sense. As texts from Jerusalem, the Dead Sea Scrolls take on a much wider significance. For these are documents from the age when the rabbis and scholars who would later shape the Hebrew Bible, Christianity's Old Testament, received their education. The evidence of the Dead Sea Scrolls shows that the ancient books of Judaism were at hand in AD 70, but before the destruction of Jerusalem, the work of making a Hebrew Bible had not yet begun.

As well as Bible books and books of rules, the Dead Sea Scrolls had preserved an extraordinary Jewish literature that was purely a product of the Hellenistic age; esoteric records, ruminations, even rages and meditations reflecting upon the gross impieties of the age that had pressed so hard on Judaism. Some texts speak of the misfortunes of a Teacher of Righteousness, other of a Wicked Priest and the enigmatic if rather splendidly dubbed 'Seekers-after-Smooth-Things'. Veiled references hark back to historical events, and it is generally agreed that these texts describe the times when Jewish patriots like the Maccabees fought the Hellenized High Priests of the Temple and the vicious kings of Syria. One of these texts, known as the War Scroll, tells of the battle that will take place at the end of time. It describes precisely the ritual battle order, drawn up strictly in accordance with the ancient Law, by which the Sons of Light will triumph over the Sons of Darkness. The battle order lists everything from the specifications of the field latrines to the ages of baggage porters and the ritual order of advance that will secure the final victory. Such dreams sustained many Jewish fighters as the Roman legions advanced through Judaea, and nowhere was the dream more persuasive than at another fortress by the Dead Sea, the famous rock of Massada, where a garrison held out for three long years after the fall of Jerusalem.

Massada began its ancient life as a Hellenistic fortress, but was later elaborated at the whim of King Herod to become a villa-palace on the high rock that overlooked the gaudy beauty of the Dead Sea. In Herod's day the rock's plateau held swimming pools and storerooms; the palace, its public rooms, with pretty sandstone columns and painted plaster, ran straight up into the cliffs. Josephus tells a grim story about this fairy castle. Of how a community of nationalists withstood a long siege there, then killed themselves as the Roman army broke onto the plateau. The remains of the defenders have never been found; but blown into nooks and crannies of the palace storerooms and carefully buried under the floors of a little synagogue, fragments of some fourteen of their scrolls have been found, fragments of both biblical and apocryphal texts, including a Book of Psalms of a variant type known previously only from the Dead Sea Scrolls. Now, if these scrolls were also the product of the Qumran 'monastery', then the only explanations for the presence of the fourteen scrolls at Massada are that the 'Essene Monks' of Qumran gave the texts to Massada's defenders, or that some 'Essenes' broke the strict rule of their pacifist order and came to Massada with their scrolls to fight alongside the nationalists! If however, as is more likely, these fourteen scrolls are simply further examples of the living religion of AD 70, then the texts discovered at Massada merely provide further evidence of the nature of Judaism and its sacred texts at the time of the destruction of Jerusalem.

Of all the themes in the non-biblical texts of the scrolls, none is more interesting than the pre-occupation with the future. The sacred texts were ransacked for prophecies and intimations of the apocalyptic battles long felt to be imminent by many pious Jews. The sacred histories gave a form, a roundness, a feeling of destiny to the story of Israel. People saw that the Exile and the

Return had provided an end and a new beginning, just as the Prophets had promised. And now another catastrophe, another ending, was at hand. As the Romans destroyed Jerusalem and the Temple fell for a second time it must have seemed that this second apocalypse was imminent. For the defenders of Massada the formula for surviving this end-time lay in the strict observance of the Law. As the Roman legions cut down through Galilee, the story of the final battle between the Sons of Light and Darkness must have taken on direct and poignant significance.

'The priests shall blow the trumpets of massacre, and the Levites and all the blowers of the ram's horn shall sound a battle alarm, and the foot soldiers shall stretch out their hands against the host . . . and at the sound of the alarm they shall begin to bring down the slain. All the people shall cease their clamour, but the priests shall continue to blow the trumpets of massacre'. High in the fortress of Massada, the defenders stood alone. Jerusalem had fallen, the rest of Judaea was lost. On the hills below, a Roman army was encamped in good order. From their high rock, listening to the calls of the sentries and the conversations in the camps, the defenders watched the hardened professionals of the legions move steadily about their work. In their simple houses built amid the ruins of Herod's palace, they followed the patterns prescribed by the Law, and their lives took on the timelessness of ritual. The defenders of Massada were living in an end-time: the Books of the Prophets told that the destruction of the Temple marked the ending of the world. Now they lived in the sterile desert on their giddy rock with the deep blue sea beneath them, the hard blue sky above, and all encircled by the Sons of Darkness. Whoever it was who composed these texts has allowed us a unique glimpse of his times and of its writings too from which the Hebrew Bible, the Old Testament, would be made.

Making the Book

An ancient Jewish text tells that during the seige of Jerusalem in AD 70 when Jewish factions were fighting among themselves, the Rabbi Johannon ben Zakkai ordered a coffin and had himself carried in it to the Roman army beyond the walls; a symbol of the division and subjugation of his people. The rabbi then begged the general Titus to be allowed to establish an academy away from the condemned city, and his request was granted. So Rabbi

Johannon and his pupils travelled along the road that led westwards to the coast, and in the town of Jamnia, close to Jaffa, he opened the academy called *Beth Hamidrash*. For the next fifty years, the survivors among the Jewish scholars came to Jamnia and fixed for all time the canon of the Hebrew Bible.

It is no exaggeration to say that the destruction of Jerusalem in AD 70 is the single most important event in the history of Judaism: 'Rabbi Johannon sat and watched in the direction of the walls of Jerusalem to learn what was happening, and when he saw that the Temple was destroyed and the Holy of Holies burnt, he stood and rent his garments, took off his *tefellim* (the small leather cases containing passages from the scriptures worn during prayers) and sat weeping, as did his pupils with him'. The rabbi wept not for the loss of King Herod's golden Temple but for Jehovah's own house: the centre of the world and the only place on earth where Jews could atone for sin. With its destruction and the cessation of daily offerings, the single continuous link between Jehovah and his people had been broken. In the manner of the ancient world, where there was no firm distinction between civil and religious authority, Rome had destroyed the centre of a faith and an earthly kingdom. As he watched Jerusalem burn, Rabbi Johannon had foreseen a profound vacuum opening in the lives of the survivors. The large Jewish communities outside Judaea, in Egypt, Babylonia and throughout the Roman Empire, were without leadership. The centre had been burned away. Rabbi Johannon's frame of mind can be seen in his ruling that stated that as murder and promiscuity had become commonplace, the traditional rites of purification that surrounded death and trials for adultery could be discontinued.

At Jamnia, however, Rabbi Johannon soon gathered a number of distinguished scholars around him and the academy was quickly recognized as the educated voice of Judaism. Johannon, already old when he fled from Jerusalem, was succeeded by Rabbi Gamaliel, called the Younger, a descendant of an august line of Sadducees who had controlled the supreme Jewish council and high court in the days of Herod's Temple. In those days Rabbi Johannon, a Pharisee, had been a severe critic of the priesthood. Now, however, the remnants of the old Jewish hierarchy had come together and slowly a new religious government was established under the direction of a *nasi*, a prince, and there are many bitter stories about the arguments and debates that accompanied the birth of this new administration.

Outside the circles of scholarly politics, where he fought hard for the power of the *nasi*, Gamaliel was much admired. A contemporary called him 'the heavenly voice that was heard in Jamnia'. Above all, the rabbis and scholars now wanted to reform Judaism and to help the people survive the loss of the Holy City. Gamaliel, for example, is credited for fixing many of the rules that govern Judaism to this day – many of the rituals of Passover Eve, and the obligation to pray three times a day. At the same time, under the direction of the academy, new translations of the Sacred Writings into Greek and Aramaic were prepared. These were done by two converts to Judaism, a rich Roman courtier named Aquila and a Greek named Onkelos. Aquila's translation has survived only in fragments but the *Targum Onkelos* has remained the standard Aramaic translation, much used by scholars to this day. Both these translations point to a new breadth inside Judaism and show the Jamnia scholars attempting to come to terms with the new age. But many Jews resisted all aspects of life that had originated in foreign cultures. Oiling the body, for example, which had long been the practice in Greek and Roman baths, was deemed impure and even bathing came in for close scrutiny. Following Rabbi Johannon who had described bathing as an act of charity for an old friend, Gamaliel caused a scandal by bathing in a Hellenistic bath-house that had paintings of the Greek goddess Aphrodite on the walls. Gamaliel defended himself by arguing that the goddess was there to decorate the baths, and not the baths the goddess; many of his pronouncements are still debated among the orthodox. It was said of Gamaliel that he dabbled in science and astrology, and used seals with figures engraved upon them. He was friendly with many gentiles, though he also made the first Jewish ordinances against the rising faith of Christianity.

There are many stories about Jamnia and its fifty-year academy, these recorded in the vast mass of Jewish religious literature written in the centuries after the fall of Jerusalem. Some stories tell how the most celebrated leaders of the faith in those days came to the prosperous farming town to discuss, in its quiet gardens and cool Hellenistic arcades, the precise order and contents of the Hebrew Bible. Throughout this time Rome pressed hard upon the Jews. Wherever there were Jewish communities, ill-recorded but often enormous wars and insurrections took place; from Alexandria to Cyprus and Babylon thousands of people tortured and killed each other. But throughout the turmoil scholars from all over the Jewish diaspora came to Jamnia. The Jewish records are usually discursive, anecdotal, and they allow fascinating glimpses of the last stages of the making of the Hebrew Bible. Not the least of its makers, certainly one of Jamnia and Judaism's most extraordinary personalities, was a rabbi named Akiva. He would come from his own academy in a nearby town, accompanied by a large group of his students; all fire and brimstone nationalists to a man, they had clear visions of a Messiah who would rise like a star in the evening of the world. Rabbi Akiva preached that laughter led straight to immorality; that 'if you would hang yourself use a large tree'; that every dot and comma of a sacred text held meanings of their own. Akiva, tradition tells, saved the Song of Songs for the Bible but forbade its singing in beerhalls; his pungent personality shines right through the diffuse records, an embodiment of the stubborn spirit of a hard-pressed people.

Akiva was about twenty when Jerusalem fell, and tradition has it that he studied at Jamnia under Gamaliel, apparently a difficult apprenticeship. 'More than fifty-five times,' a colleague recalled, 'was Akiva punished before Rabbi Gamaliel.' Akiva's firm judgments and forceful character dominated many of his fellows, and his followers were equally aggressive. 'When will Rabbi Johannon's eyes be freed of earth so that he might see . . .' says one of them at the start of a debate. And very often, what was under debate was which of all the mass of ancient texts truly held God's authority and which being merely the works of pious people did not: and which of the many differing versions of these sacred books were the most accurate. There is a pretty picture in the record of one rabbi 'burning a thousand measures of oil', working through the warm night with the crickets and the fireflies, so that he could prepare the Book of Ezekiel in time for work of the daily council. The problem was that certain passages of the text seemed to be at variance with the Law; such anomalies had to be resolved so the rabbi burned the midnight oil.

Other texts, not so fortunate, were rejected completely; this not because they were not old or much beloved or venerated, but because the burden of what they said did not support the Law. So the Books of Maccabees, of Tobit and Ecclesiasticus were all excluded and only after considerable argument were the Books of Proverbs and Ecclesiastes admitted. The Book of Esther, the only biblical book said to have been written by a woman, was halved. Eighteen psalms, known as the 'Psalms of Solomon', were detached and excluded from the main body of the book. The opulent poetry of the Song of Songs caused much debate. For a prolonged contact with the seductive attractions of many gentile religions (a major theme in many Old Testament stories) had long prompted pious Jews toward reticence and modesty. It must have seemed that the Song of Songs would go the way of Tobit and Ecclesiasticus. But Rabbi Akiva, though a fierce conservative, was no prude and he had the final word. 'God forbid,' he said, 'that any man of Israel deny that the Song of Songs is a holy text; for all the ages are not worth the single day on which the Song of Songs was given to Israel. All scripture is holy, but the Song of Songs is the holiest of all.' And this carried the day. It was as if the rabbis had seen that the Hebrew Bible was not only a record of Jehovah's Law and Israel's culture but a living being that not only praised God and held memories of the past but also held the human emotions of love and lust. Rabbi Akiva was not merely defending the emotions of the Song of Songs, but the extraordinary symbolic image of Israel as the bride of God, a common theme of Jewish mysticism.

It has been suggested that the Song of Songs was originally the *libretto* of a small opera, a little Hellenistic drama cast in the manner of the day. Jewish synagogue paintings of the second century appear to be representations of plays that were sometimes performed in front of synagogues, and the Song of Songs has a stage-like air about it. But despite the great weight of Rabbi Akiva's endorsement, it took many years for such books as the Song of Songs to be accepted as sacred by the congregations, just as it also took many years for books like Maccabees and Ecclesiasticus to be thought of as profane, merely books of wisdom and history.

At the end of this long process, however, the Hebrew Bible emerged, divided into three parts: the Law, comprising the Five Books of Moses; the Prophets, comprising the Books of Joshua, Judges, Samuel, Kings and all the books of the Prophets except Job; and the Writings, comprising all the remaining books. In the Christian Old Testament these divisions are muddled, but the Hebrew Bible keeps them to this day.

Beside his work on the canon of the Hebrew Bible, Rabbi Akiva is also credited with bringing order to the great mass of traditional teachings upon the Law and the Sacred Books. Commentaries were prepared which linked scripture stories to recent historical events. A commentary upon the Book of Genesis, written in Akiva's day, suggests that the reason why Abraham's strength had been sapped during his war with the raiding kings was because a temple to a Roman emperor was later erected on that same battlefield, an interesting inversion of the usual principle of Israelite histories which generally demonstrates that the causes of such disasters were sins committed *before* the defeat. The story is also a very early example of the use of biblical stories as moral parables. The continuing problem concerning the morality of some of the actions of the Patriarchs also occupies the compilers of the *Midrash*, as these commentaries are called. The terrible tale of Abraham's preparations to sacrifice his son showed such austere devotion that it clearly worried the ancient rabbis who expressed their alarm in a speech that they wrote for Abraham as an address to Jehovah. 'Only yesterday you promised me a large prosperity; now I must burn his bloodless body upon your altar?' The rabbis' clear delight at Jehovah's last minute substitution of an animal for Isaac shows in their joyous elaboration of the fate of the ram: it had been made on the first day of Creation: its ashes would become the foundations for the Temple of Jerusalem; King David used its sinews for his harp strings; Jehovah used its horns as a trumpet on Mount Sinai, and the same trumpet would sound once more on the Day of Judgment.

All this wisdom, all the traditions that had grown up around the sacred books in the schools of Jerusalem and the decisions of the learned courts were gathered up, written down and carefully categorized. Though the Temple no longer existed, all its rituals and even the measurements of its architecture were minutely recorded. All of Judaism, the faith, the Law, its customs and rituals, were committed to writing, a labour later described as one 'in which a whole people has deposited its feelings, its beliefs, its soul'. Thus Rabbi Akiva, credited with being a driving force in the early stages of this work, was called by his contemporaries 'one of the fathers of the world'.

Now, too, the texts of the Hebrew Bible became endowed with a new sanctity. The rule of the Law became its own justification; unclean things, it was said, might not of themselves be defiling; they were unclean because the Law had pronounced them so. The sacred texts, especially the Pentateuch which was their heart, came to be seen as a divine exhalation. Rabbi Akiva held that alternative spellings and punctuation, even the decoration of certain letters in the texts, contained special meanings. There is a story that Moses himself could not understand the teaching of the learned Rabbi Akiva in this respect, but he was re-assured when he was told that it was indeed correct for it had been 'given to you, Moses, on Mount Sinai'.

Such was the sensitivity of the editors to the tiniest details of the sacred texts that they allowed many of their more obvious contradictions to remain. How easy it would have been, for example, to have settled on one consistent age for Abraham and Sarah, or on a consistent number of Esau's wives. Though the texts were minutely checked for deviations in matters of the Law, such internal inconsistencies were carefully preserved.

The cataclysmic destruction of Jerusalem and the Temple had created an explosion of scholarship. There was a determination that whatever might happen in the future, the Law and sacred writings of Israel would be preserved. The holy texts, the Hebrew Bible, had been fixed forever. There would be no more writings recording the relationship of Jehovah and his chosen people. The faith that had lived with its god in time now moved into a timeless limbo.

Rabbi Akiva would attend the ending of this religious tradition. In his old age he saw the last phases of this holy history rising around him. About AD 130 he went on the warpath, travelling through the Jewish communities of the Eastern Empire preaching an imminent apocalypse and the establishment of the direct rule of Jehovah on earth. He named and anointed a resistance leader as the Messiah come to free the Jews. The cold light of revolt flared like a comet over Israel. While scholars sat in Jamnia copying Books of the Law, charting Jehovah's path through the nation's history wild-eyed fighting men saw the same deity as a modern ally who could destroy the mighty resources of Rome. Like an ancient prophet, Akiva set his hand upon a guerrilla leader named Ben Kosebah. A son of the house of David, just as the ancient prophets said the Messiah would be, Ben Kosebah was renamed Bar Kokhba, Son of the Star. The revolt, as had happened sixty years earlier, had an initial success. Coins were issued decorated with a picture of the destroyed Temple with a star over its door, dated from the first, second or third years 'of the freedom of Zion'.

Yet not all the rabbis were convinced of Bar Kokhba's divine role.\'Grass will grow through your skull, Akiva,' a fearful colleague declared, 'and still the son of David will not have come.' Once again the Roman legions were marshalled in force and war ravaged Judaea. But this time there was no Josephus to record the sad details. We can only judge the terror from the records which report a succession of small pungent incidents. It is said that at the end the Roman cavalry charged crowds so dense that the blood of the slain washed the withers of the horses. It is said also that to prevent the enslavement of their children some Jews wrapped them up in sacred scrolls and set fire to the parchments. Judaea was virtually destroyed. The Romans pursued the last survivors into the desert to frightful, lonely endings. Sometimes their sad remains still come to light – a little basket of letters and deeds, a child's toy, a mirror, a fine bowl made of bright blue glass, some balls of wool with which a woman was knitting a winter cloak, and the desiccated bodies of the dead.

Although he escaped the massacres, old Rabbi Akiva was arrested for continuing to preach adherence to the Law which the Romans, exasperated by the terrible battles, now forbade. After AD 135 all Jews were banished from their Holy City, forbidden even to set eyes on it. A new city called Aelia Capitolina was raised on the ruins. New temples housed the gods of Rome, and a boar, the emblem of the garrison legion, decorated the city's gateways. But even in his prison cell Akiva was yet asked for rulings upon matters of the Law. One of his pupils, an Alexandrian rabbi called Johannon, would pose as a cobbler and ask questions through the window of the cell. Would civil rituals, once performed before the rabbi, be considered valid if now they were performed in private? It was a desperate sign of the times – Judaea was by now virtually depopulated – that Akiva said that they would be.

Though the Romans forbade it on pain of death, Rabbi Akiva would not stop teaching the Law. To those begging him to stop and save his life he answered with a parable about the fox who urged a fish to escape the net by coming onto the river bank. 'If we are afraid in the element in which we live,' said Akiva, 'how much more should we be afraid when we are out of that element. For then we should surely die.' So finally he was executed by the Romans who combed the skin from his body with 'combs of iron'. And while they flayed him he began to recite the *Shema*, the great prayer of Moses from the Book of Deuteronomy (Deuteronomy 6:4). 'Hear, O Israel: The Lord our God is one Lord: And thou shall love the Lord thy God with all thine heart, and with all thy soul, and with all thy might.' So he began, the story tells, 'and it filled him with joy.' 'Old man, old man,' cried a Roman officer, 'are you a sorcerer, or do you defy me by showing joy in the midst of your pain?' 'Calm yourself,' replied Akiva. 'I am neither a sorceror nor a mocker; all my life long, I have read this verse of the Pentateuch, and sorrowfully said to myself, when shall I fulfil the three ways of worshipping God: I have proved that I love him with all my heart and all my means, but I have not yet undergone the test of love with all my soul. I undergo it now, and thus this is the moment in which I shall recite the *Shema*.' Beginning again those ancient words, he gave up his soul to God.

Scribes and Printers

Thousands of fragments of paper, tea chests full, all gathered from the tiny bricked-up storeroom of a Cairo synagogue are virtually all that remains of the Hebrew Bible from the centuries that followed Rabbi Akiva's execution. Mixed with these fragments were pages from old book catalogues which show that, during the ninth and tenth centuries, a trade in Jewish texts extended through the Mediterranean and reached as far as the Jewish communities in Babylonia and the Yemen. The scraps of sacred texts show that a considerable change had taken place since the days of the Dead Sea Scrolls; the process of hand-copying lends itself to slow and subtle change. A scribe might unconsciously scramble a familiar phrase, reverse or repeat the order of the words or even miss out entire passages. He might also discover impieties in the ancient words which he would then 'correct'. Fragmentary texts show, for example, that in Akiva's day Jehovah was sometimes described as standing in front of Abraham; in these ninth-century texts it is always Abraham who is attendant upon the Lord. But in general the differences were very minor. The insistence of Akiva and his fellow rabbis that every letter, every jot and tittle had its place helped to ensure an extraordinarily accurate transmission of the text.

There was, however, a problem in reading and understanding ancient writings. Traditionally, words were written with no gap between them and most vowels were omitted. This system worked well so long as reader and writer shared the same pronunciation of Hebrew and a single tradition of interpretation. But over the centuries, the Jews had spread throughout the ancient world and in the course of time, they evolved into communities whose traditions and very language and accents were affected by contact with other peoples.

While the letter of the sacred texts had been preserved, there was a growing danger of a real loss of understanding. Traditionally, interpretation had depended on the common training of scholars and rabbis and the use of a large body of written commentary, some of which went back to the days of Akiva. But as the community of Judaism had spread wide, so the traditions had long been stretched and the ancient words began to take on different meanings. By the eighth century, several religious centres – Babylon, Spain, Alexandria – had seen the problem and were devising ways of overcoming it.

A system of writing was devised that was eventually adopted by almost all of Judaism; one was developed over several generations by a family of rabbis of Tiberias in Galilee which since the loss of Jerusalem had become a centre of Palestinian Jewry. The ben Asher family devised a written method of recording precisely the traditional vocalization of the Hebrew language, and they also introduced the precise separation of words, sentences and paragraphs and of every column of the Hebrew Bible. What had formerly belonged only to verbal tradition was now set down clearly on the sacred scrolls. Now, too, the middle letter of the middle words of every book was noted and numbered so that merely by the mechanical process of counting a quick and accurate check could be made of every manuscript. Jewish law had long decreed that all imperfectly made copies of the sacred books should be burned, and that only undamaged texts could be used in the synagogue. Damaged documents were placed in a special storeroom called the *geniza*, and it was from just such a storeroom that the fragments in Cairo were collected.

Similarly stringent laws also specified every step in the production of the sacred texts. The exact specification of the ink was given; the parchment had to be made from ritually pure animals; the spacing of lines, words and letters was precisely detailed. And it was written: even if a king addressed a scribe as he was writing the Holy Name, the scribe must complete the holy word before he looked up to answer the king; and before beginning the Holy Name, the scribe must recharge his pen with ink, lest the pen run dry. Nothing, not a word or a dot should be set down without reference to a perfect manuscript, and all must be prefaced by a solemn prayer. Such perfection of reproduction seemed to cry out for the new technology of printing, and when printing from movable type was invented in Europe in the 1440s, Jewish scholars immediately took an interest. Within the first decade, Jewish apprentices were working in an Avignon printing shop. The first dated Hebrew book appeared in 1477 and in 1488 the first and perhaps the most beautiful of all printed Hebrew Bibles was produced in Italy by a family of German Jews who had settled, with the permission of the Duke of Milan, in the little town of Soncino near Cremona. By this time the libraries of Italy were being filled slowly with the magnificent productions of the Renaissance printing presses; to their fresh and elegant style, on which all modern books are based, the Soncino printers now added Hebrew typefaces of their own design to make a beautiful and exotic hybrid. In 1495 one of the Soncino presses produced a Hebrew Bible small enough to be carried in a bag or pocket, an ideal size for many Jews who were continually on the move. It was also, it transpired, a convenient size for the fugitive monk Martin Luther, who used this little Hebrew text when he made his German translation of the Old Testament, the book that became the basis of German Protestantism. In the sixteenth century the Soncino printers took their printing presses right through Europe to Naples, to France and Spain, to the Jewish communities along the Rhine, and even to Constantinople where they introduced the first printing press. All the while they produced edition after edition of the Hebrew Bible, many with the Soncino press-mark, a little Italian *castello* with high battlements.

It was, however, the printing shop of a Christian publisher that produced the Hebrew Bible that would become the standard version of the text. After his expulsion from Tunis, the venerable scholar Jacob ben Khayim had found work in Venice where as he says 'God sent me a highly distinguished and pious Christian.' This Christian, a printer named Daniel Bomberg, asked ben Khayim to revise his earlier edition of a Hebrew Bible, 'to correct the mistakes and purify the style and examine the works till they are as refined silver and purified gold'. Bomberg's second edition of the Hebrew Bible published in 1524 under the direction of Jacob ben Khayim became the standard printed text of the Hebrew Bible. At last, in a corrected text deriving from the manuscripts of the ben Asher family in Tiberias, the heritage of Rabbi Akiva and the most distant past had been delivered to the Western world.

Daniel Bomberg was a remarkable man. Born in Amsterdam of a wealthy merchant family, he was fascinated by the technology of printing. Most unusually for a gentile of his time, he was specially interested in Hebrew and taught himself to speak and read it. 'On this book,' he wrote of the Hebrew Bible, 'the entire structure of Christianity rests.' One of the first and finest of the Venetian printers, Bomberg employed the most skilled craftsmen of the day, cast his own type and even, on occasion, manufactured his own paper. At that time, Jews in Venice were constrained to live in an area near the foundries for casting cannon called the *Ghetto*. Bomberg obtained special dispensation for his Jewish workers to travel freely in the city and to leave off the yellow hat that they were forced to wear. Not only did his workshops print Hebrew Bibles, but a large range of other Jewish literature too, and all in the careful order and style that, in many cases, has remained the standard until today. Little is known about Bomberg's motives in all this; his care was beyond any demand of Christian duty or scholarship. Certainly he lost a fortune, his son followed him in his profession and they both remain the most enigmatic if talented members of their new profession.

There were many other printing houses publishing Hebrew books, for as the correct observance of the Law depended upon knowledge of a large literary tradition, there was a high rate of literacy in Judaism and a great demand too for such books. Christian scholars, too, were printing Hebrew versions of the Bible texts alongside Greek and Latin versions. In the sixteenth century there was a growing urge to reform the sacred texts of Christendom; a new style of literary piety. At first this was frowned on by the clerics who traditionally regarded alternative versions of the Bible text as irrelevant and probably heretical. Those who read Hebrew, it was asserted, would become Jews: as for the Greek of the Septuagint, that was merely the book of a schismatic church. But the scholars' awakening interest would not be stopped, though the popes banned the printing of most Jewish books and printers were often hounded from pillar to post. No one yet understood the power of this technology; but certainly it could not be denied, it was a vital part of the spirit of the Renaissance.

The first of a series of multilingual Bibles was produced in Spain. Known as the Computensian Polyglot, it was printed in Alcala (the Latin name of Alcala is *Computensis*) and issued around 1522. The Old Testament of this splendid book reproduced the Greek text of the Septuagint – printed here for the first time, and a text in Hebrew taken from a Soncino Bible. These were printed on either side of the Roman Latin text, in the manner, the commentary explained, of the two thieves that hung on either side of our Lord at the Crucifixion. This great work was entirely successful and many other European countries printed similar Bibles. The holy texts of ancient Israel, the preserved scholarship of an ancient, hard-pressed people, had been delivered to the Christian world.

Chapter Four
JESUS AND
THE NEW TESTAMENT

Introduction: The Marketplace

Broadly speaking, it is true to say that the Bible was made in the wake of two invasions of the Holy Land. The first, from the east in the sixth century BC, had resulted in the capture, exile and then the liberation of Judah and the priests of Jehovah – events that had prompted the Jewish scribes to re-make the ancient records of the national faith into the book that would eventually become the foundations of the Old Testament. The second invasion, from the west in the fourth century BC, had brought Hellenism. Alternatively tempted and repelled by its unholy delights the Jews were finally goaded into a tragic series of conflicts which terminated in the deadly wars with the Romans. In turn, this prompted the rabbis to fix for all time the order and contents of the Hebrew Bible. The cultural and political insecurities of this last age, the moral problems that this foreign order raised in Judaea and Galilee, would also prompt the rise of Christianity and the writing of its sacred books; those of the New Testament.

The first Christian converts outside Palestine were citizens of the eastern Roman Empire in the societies of the Hellenistic cities. The Apostles took their message and their faith straight to the great cities at the heart of the Empire – Antioch, Ephesus, Alexandria, Corinth and Rome. The New Testament, written during the two centuries after Christ, was aimed at this world and its people. And so it was that the preaching of an obscure Palestinian Jew was received in the centres of world culture. Christianity's initial success lay in the fact that it provided potent remedies for Hellenism's discontents. The marble cities also had their vulnerabilities; behind their confident façades and private fortunes was a darker side and often you may see this in the statues of their gods.

Having lost a mythical music competition the marble satyr, Marsyas, hangs waiting for Apollo, god of light, to flay him alive. A famous image, an epitome of Hellenistic taste, first made in a kingdom of Asia Minor founded by one of Alexander's generals, marble Marsyas hangs tremulously waiting for the flaying knife. His hands and feet are bound as tight as corn sheaths, his skin is ultra-sensitive in expectation. The satyr awaits the fate of martyrs. He is a forerunner of all the images of crucifixions; torsos that hold in them the tension and death of the cross. If Hellenism brought the Bible one thing, it brought this brand new sense of time. The Old Testament patriarchs live in timelessness, Marsyas hangs between myth and reality. Jesus hangs on his cross in modern time; our calendar starts with Jesus. He is the beginning of the West; though he is the son of God, his earthly body is tuned to the savage moment.

With its terrible new awareness of time as an aggressive pushing force Hellenism brought discontents that are still with us. Again, the sculpture of Marsyas can serve as an example. It was made in Pergamum, a splendid Hellenistic city built with the fortune of one of Alexander's baggage trains, a fortune that had dropped randomly into the hands of a chamberlain when a general had died unexpectedly. The mythic life of Marsyas, too, has a similar train of randomness running through it. For Marsyas, a celebrated flautist, had found his flute by chance after it had been thrown away by a goddess when the gods had laughed at her distorted face as she had played upon it. Marsyas had also entered into the musical contest with Apollo after a random suggestion and had almost won it. The sculpture shows him, then, as a man suffering a random, accidental but inevitable fate, a major theme of Hellenistic sculpture; giants, gods and mortals all participate in terrible but mindless combat, like the flickering films of the Battle of the Somme. There is no hope in these heavy, earth-bound battles, only the acute awareness of solitary vulnerability.

This is another side of Hellenism. The brash confidence that had built the marble cities had also brought a loneliness, a separation from the gods which rarely occurred in more ancient societies. A new, impersonal cruelty now haunted daily life. The slave industries that sustained the ancient city state of Athens in the days of Socrates (the slaves manning mines so rich in silver that all free men of Athens had received regular issues of coin) greatly expanded in Alexander's empire and also sustained the Roman world. A Roman philosopher described slaves as a 'sort of tool'; neither ancient Assyria or Babylonia had so robbed people of their dignity. By its silence, Rome had dismissed its multitudes of slaves to oblivion, yet in the severity of the slaves' punishments, such as crucifixion, there is a strong scent of fear.

But the problems of this empire were not merely those directly connected with slavery. The Gospels show Jesus of Nazareth dealing with a range of problems such as the Old Testament Patriarchs never knew and could not have understood. There was, for example, the possibility of immense private wealth, of fortune and influence based neither upon blood nor rank but upon the produce of money-based economies. There were problems born of social change and disruption, problems of standards of commercial honesty and its relationship to individual morality. There were problems also of allegiance in the new cities, of civic duty, of taxes and tax evasion, of the relationship of the new world to the old gods; these, of course, were problems of prosperity.

All too often, this 'age of early Christianity', the age in which the New Testament was written, is distorted by those who would use it merely as a backdrop on which to set the beginnings of their faith. But the pagan empire of this age was hardly an 'old, tired and brutal world thirsty for a new faith' as a well-worn cliché would have it, just as Alexander the Great was never a pure young Greek, fresh from Aristotle's academy, bent on bringing wisdom to sadistic orientals. One could argue equally well that the embattled eastern kingdoms which Alexander's generals had inherited were vigorous spiritual environments, and that Christianity, one of their products, was later marketed in the tough commercial world of Rome as cannily as Coca-Cola.

With all its cruelties and alienation, this international society for which the New Testament was written was no harder pressed than it had been in previous centuries. Certainly, it was more prosperous in the two centuries after Christ than it would be under the later Christian emperors, when slavery along with poverty would become more common, and the churches and the imperial courts and armies were given to ever greater and more lavish display. It was certainly not true, therefore, that the adoption of Christianity, this minority religion, brought any material ease to the empire at all.

Here then, as the New Testament was being written, was a lively world, a world with gods and spirits all around, a world relatively prosperous and well-regulated. This was the world in which the words of Jesus and the Apostles were preached, and if the East had provided this new vision of spirituality, the West would give it a firm shape and organization and allow it the means of its dispersal. The vast empire of Rome was better organized and infinitely more powerful than any of its predecessors. That the written word of a country craftsman from an eastern Roman province held meaning for some of the inhabitants of Egypt and Northumbria alike speaks of an incredible regularity: the common denominator of Hellenism that Rome had turned so cleverly to its advantage. Greek and Latin were international languages and literacy was high. The international trade that so enriched the empire carried Christianity and its books, along with several other faiths, to its furthest outposts. Jesus would become the first religious leader not to have been a prince or a courtier; in Rome's great empire, such noble sponsorship was no longer required to establish a new faith; such was the power of the written word. Yet this Jesus in the Gospels had not been born of this urban internationalism and had lived, so the Gospels tell us, largely inside the highly conservative society of Judaism. In the four Gospels, Jesus acts like a Pharisee from Galilee; a statement that can only be made after studying local Jewish writings. Yet the most powerful, the most central images of Jesus are those of the four Gospels, and these were written for the people of the empire of Rome. These literary portraits, then, span two separate worlds: and what then of this man who is the centre?

Gospel Truth? Jesus and Archaeology

Time and time again, the Gospels tell us, Jesus aroused the curiosity of the people of Galilee and Judaea and gained popularity, too, as a miracle worker and healer of the sick. By the convention of the day, these powers would have led to him being regarded as a holy man, one skilled in religion and religious law. 'Rabbi,' says Nicodemus to Jesus, 'We know that thou art a teacher come from God: for no one can do these miracles that thou doest, except God be with him' (John 3:2). The Gospels tell us that this practical ability to heal the sick in mind and body was used as an advertisement for the teachings that followed, a pattern that contributed, we are told, to Jesus' prosecution and death. The chief priests and Pharisees are reported as saying, 'What do we? for this man doeth many miracles. If we let him thus alone, all men will believe on him: and the Romans shall come and take away both our place and nation.' (John 11:47–48).

As a healer and preacher in Jerusalem Jesus visited the sanctuaries of the sick, which, like those of most Hellenistic cities, were usually situated close by water. John's Gospel (9:7ff.) describes Jesus using the clear warm waters of the Siloam spring, the ancient water supply of David's city, to heal a blind man. 'What sayest thou of him, that he hath opened thine eyes?' asked the rabbis of the healed man. 'He is a Prophet,' was the reply. And again at the Pool of Bethesda, 'the sheep pool with five colonnades': 'In these colonnades there lay a crowd of sick people, blind, lame, and paralysed. Among them was a man who had been crippled for thirty-eight years.' Jesus said, 'Rise to your feet, take up your bed and walk' (John 5:3–9 NEB), and the man took up his bed and walked.

This was a common treatment in the Hellenistic world. At a grander sanctuary at Corinth in Greece a certain Hermodikos has left a dedication in the Temple of Aesclepius, the god of medicine, describing a similar cure. 'As an example of your goodness, Aesclepius, I have dedicated this rock which I lifted up, clear evidence of your art, for all to see. For before I came into your hands and those of your sons, the sanctuary physicians, I was laid low by a hateful disease with an abscess in the chest and paralysis of the arms. But you, persuading me to raise this rock, made me sound.' Five centuries after Jesus' time, a Christian pilgrim who visited the Sheep Pools reported that this was the place where 'Lord Christ cured the paralysed man, whose bed is still there'. As at healing shrines today, such places in the ancient world were decorated by testimonies of efficacy.

In Jesus' day, Jerusalem was still a Jewish city, the great revolts which would destroy it were still some forty years off. But Herod's Hellenistic architecture, the great Temple, the royal palace and the fortresses, the Hellenistic villas of the priests, had cut through the close weave of ancient streets and alleys. There was, too, an Aesclepium, a sanctuary for the sick, and one prestigious enough to appear upon some of Jerusalem's coins, where it is pictured as a classical temple. It was situated at the Sheep Pools where the Temple priests, who required ritually pure water for washing the animals to be offered on the Temple altar, used the rainwater gathered from the surrounding slopes and stored in two large pools. The fine porticos under which, John's Gospel tells us, the sick lay were probably those recently built by Herod as part of the work upon the Temple. The five colonnades of John's account used to be something of a puzzle, for it was difficult to imagine the arrangement of five-sided cisterns. Then excavations in the 1960s solved the problem, uncovering a part of the architecture to show that there had been two rectangular colonnaded pools separated by a narrow central causeway, a 'fifth' arcade. Close to these excavations is the beautiful Gothic church of St Anne, built by Crusaders in the twelfth century on the ruins of a Byzantine basilica. Both these churches had been built on the traditional location of the Sheep Pools in John's Gospel. It was gratifying to know, from archaeological evidence, that even when the New Testament's descriptions were not readily understandable they could still accurately reflect conditions in the Holy Land at the time of Jesus. The great Byzantine basilica had straddled the causeway between the two pools, its courtyard set high on arches that once overhung the ancient pools.

When the archaeologists had cleared the rubble of the Byzantine church out of the Sheep Pools, they also found remnants of the foundations of the Aesclepium, over which a part of the Byzantine church had been built. As in so many other places, Christianity's triumph over the pagan gods had been celebrated by the building of a church on the ruins of a temple; but here, the church had also celebrated Christ's healing at this pagan shrine. Though the Aesclepium had been largely destroyed by the Byzantines, some small underground chambers remained; perhaps the little rooms where, traditionally, invalids would sleep and hope for consultations with the healing god. John's Gospel (5:4) says that healing here only happened after 'an angel went down at a certain season into the pool, and troubled the water'; this seems to be part of the common Hellenistic belief that moving water was necessary for a cure. The archaeologists also found some broken classical reliefs strewn by the pools: an elegant ex-voto of the woman Poppaeia Lucilia whose foot had been healed here by a god; some fragments showed scenes of people bathing in the miraculous water; another was a fragment of a carving of a snake, Aesclepius' frequent companion and still to be found writhing around the staff of Caduceus, the emblem of doctors to this day.

It may seem surprising today that this pagan cult was permitted so close to Jehovah's Temple – indeed, should share with it the use of the ritually pure waters – but it should be remembered that the ancient city had always supported such pagan cults within it, much to the anger of the biblical Prophets. A Christian father of the fourth century describes this 'pool with five porches' and adds that still in his day 'a great many sick people lay there, and the incredulity of the Jews was great'. By that time, of course, Christ and not Aesclepius was the supreme healer and shortly after, the huge Byzantine church that dominated the two pools showed tangible evidence of his triumph. Nevertheless, just like healers at Aesclepia all over the empire, Jesus had effected cures at this sanatorium by word and touch, and the people around him had accepted this treatment because it had been a part of Hellenistic medical practice for centuries. A modern view might have a psychological explanation for these cures or put them down to hypnosis, but it makes not a jot of difference to the reality of the ancient world where such cures were expected of wise men and the healing gods. Such an explanation of ancient realities may comfort those who wish to believe Jesus' teachings but not his miracles, but it takes a large bite out of the reality of the world through which he and his Gospel writers are moving. The trick is not to 'explain' these ancient happenings but to use them to try to understand a world where everybody believed that such things happened every day. It was a world with its own wisdom and subtlety and very different from our own. We must treat it with sympathy. No two people, of course, not even two Gospel writers, report precisely the same facts about the same event; for everybody has their own vision of things. But the four Gospel writers instinctively share the common vision of their day. Still, in the fourth century, the Lady Egeria who visited the Holy Land as a pilgrim, tells us that the stones which Jesus had used as a table when he had fed the multitude by Lake Galilee had been made into an altar and that 'people take away small pieces of the stones to bring them prosperity and they are very effective'. And this too is part of the same ancient reality.

Another part of the problem of treating the Four Gospels as a straightforward documentary account of Jesus' life is that they were written at a time when the church was in the process of rapid expansion and the memories of its founder, of Jesus' acts and sayings, had already taken on fixed regular forms. Indeed it is generally agreed that the New Testament Gospels are four attempts to capture, in part, this living oral tradition inside the early church. This would mean, as well, that the four Gospels, being compilations of earlier records, already reflect, to some extent, the needs of this early church. Was Jesus the *real* founder of this church, or only its inspiration? The Gospels seem to show that he had intended its foundation – but also show Jesus as a typical Jewish prophet of his day. Already Jesus has become a character in a book.

Today, the archaeological site of Capernaum underlines the difficulties in getting closer to this man, and shows, too, something of the passions and opinions involved in modern debates about him. For if this ruin really is the site of the ancient town by Lake Galilee where Jesus lived and preached, then it is likely that the synagogue where, the Gospels tell us, he taught and healed was the predecessor of the splendid monument that stands there still today, now carefully restored. Indeed, the strange angle of its white stone walls set slightly askew upon a black basalt foundation may well reflect a deviation from the line of the earlier building now demolished.

After the destruction of Jerusalem, the daily prayers in this splendid synagogue, as in all synagogues, included a curse upon those who had left the Jewish faith, the *minim* as they were called. This is often interpreted as a reference to early Christianity. Of four great sages who had entered into the forbidden garden of Christianity and sampled its exotic fruit, it was said that only one, Rabbi Akiva, had not been poisoned. The tale implies that Akiva, like Saul of Tarsus who had also been a student of the most illustrious rabbis, had been attracted by this new faith along with many other Jews. Several Jewish sources mention communities of Jewish converts living by Lake Galilee.

A short distance from the Capernaum synagogue, amid the ancient houses of the lake-side town, it seems that some of these Jewish-Christians made themselves a house-church. Later, by the fourth century, this little church and the rooms beside it were celebrated as the house of St Peter the Fisherman – the same house where Jesus had lived when he started his preaching. That indefatigable pilgrim, the Lady Egeria, visited Capernaum in the 380s during her pilgrimage to the Holy Land and had this to say about it: 'In Capernium, the house of the prince of the Apostles has been made into a church with its original walls still standing. It is where the Lord cured the paralytic. There is also the synagogue where the Lord cured a man possessed by the devil. The way is up many stairs, and is made of dressed stone.' A hundred years after Egeria's visit, the old buildings and the church-house had all been incorporated into a large octagonal church with fine mosaic floors and walls of limestone blocks. In the process much of the old building had been lost, taken down and used as fillings in the new foundations. But the new building was a fine Byzantine church with rooms for the clergy, greater space for the worshippers and a baptistry where more souls could be brought into Jesus' congregation.

Like the four Gospels, these ancient churches, one above the other, have never lacked interpreters. When Franciscan archaeologists began excavations at the side they must have trembled at the extraordinary prospects that awaited them beneath the sandy soil – perhaps the recovery of the very house, the actual rooms where the Apostle Peter, even Jesus himself, had lived and worked! And that, they claimed, is what they found: first the octagonal church built over the little church-house, the latter probably the building that the Lady Egeria had seen; and under this, a group of village houses that went back to the first century BC. And these houses were made of the same black volcanic stone that had been used in the foundations of the synagogue in the village. The houses had been used and re-used for some two hundred years, floor upon floor laid down one atop the other, as the embedded pottery sherds and the numerous fragments of small oil lamps proved. The archaeologists were particularly impressed by the absence of any of the usual domestic objects in the small square room at the centre of the church-house. They also saw that the walls and floors of this room had been painted and re-painted many times, a unique feature in the village. Fourth-century graffiti scratched into the plaster of the church-house mentioned both Peter and Jesus and included typically Christian signs and symbols and even hinted at the church rituals of the day.

But unfortunately there was no evidence that any of the rooms of the earlier village houses beneath the house-church had ever been inhabited by Peter, and the fourth century was precisely that era when scores of such holy sites in Palestine were being identified in dreams and visions, then memorialized by fine Byzantine churches. Nonetheless, the archaeologists were convinced of the tremendous value of their discovery, and finds like the fishing equipment from the ancient houses were sufficiently suggestive to inspire the title of their archaeological report: 'The House of St Peter at Capharnaum' (an alternative spelling of Capernaum).

Now, it is usual in such scientific reports to present the evidence recovered from the archaeology separately from the excavators' interpretations of what that evidence might signify. Nothing the Franciscans excavated had proved beyond reasonable doubt that they had uncovered St Peter's house; the title, therefore, is contentious and hardly commended itself to archaeological opinion and consequently the work has been largely ignored by other scholars working in the same field. One eminent authority simply remarked that 'claims that the house of Peter has been found at Capernaum based upon the find in it of a fish hook, must be regarded with some scepticism'. Already embroiled in a bitter controversy with Jewish scholars about the dating of the synagogue, the Franciscan archaeologists replied to their fellow scholars' criticism in high polemic style, noting 'discussions that were not always serene', pointing to their opponents' 'futile and childish theories', their 'ridiculous expedients' in debate, and their 'utterly gratuitous hypothesis'! All of which would be but a storm in a scholarly tea cup until it is remembered that Capernaum is a very important archaeological site for both Christian and Jewish archaeology, but one so bedevilled now by this debate that the excavated church, once regarded by centuries of ancient pilgrims as containing the very walls of St Peter's house, is seldom mentioned in religious circles today. 'Here', one tour guide tells his audience on his weekly trip around the excavations, 'you either take it or leave it'. At the end of the day, then, Capernaum contains the remains of the finest ancient synagogue in the Holy Land and, close by it, an ancient pilgrimage church built over the traditional site of St Peter's house. And underneath all that are the grey-black ruins of a first-century village standing under billowing eucalyptus trees on the beach of the flashing lake. No evidence of the presence, of the earthly existence of Peter or Jesus has ever been found there.

But many Christians do believe that these ruins hold the remains of St

Peter's house, and, similarly, that the four Gospels too may only be understood by believers and not by those who stand in the darkness of scepticism. Yet for more than a century now, many convinced Christian scholars have held that nothing at all remains of this man Jesus or of his humble life, that he has become a mythic, literary figure. Yet this does not mean that, according to the normal criteria of historians, Jesus may be said not to have existed. Most history, after all, requires some degree of faith for its comprehension. Both Alexander the Great and Queen Victoria, for example, lived lives that are now deeply buried in legend and sentiment and yet, although there are few people alive today who actually met the latter, no one would deny the presence of genuine historical beings at the centre of the considerable auras of myth and tradition. Often it is this aura, not the simple reality of the past, that so affects us and seems so real. But the concrete reality of the past is so very important, for it is out of the reflections caught in this quicksilver that all the myriad interpretations of such ancient lives are made. And there is something of this ancient reality to be seen in the old village at Capernaum. Yet, as at dozens of sites throughout the Holy Land, as the Gospels and history move closer together, at the last moment they always jump apart. So many times is this repeated with the Bible's stories, indeed, that it almost seems as if their ancient authors were deliberately refusing to connect the two, as if they did not care to degrade the truth with mere historical fact: they invite you to make a leap of faith.

Yet this man Jesus lived, of that there can be little doubt. Consider the life of Alexander the Great. As with Jesus there are a number of legendary biographies about his career written after he died, eulogistic accounts of a departed demigod. But we are convinced that he lived. His effect upon the world was so tremendous; Hellenistic towns and temples that he founded are scattered from Egypt to India; the kingdoms of his generals changed the ancient world for ever. It is by the effect of the man, ultimately, that you may say that Alexander lived: according to such widely accepted standards of historical probability, Jesus too must once have lived. Unlike Alexander, of course, Jesus was a humble man; there are no coins with his face upon them, no contemporary inscriptions telling of his passing. And neither should we expect there to be any; no names of any of the villagers of Capernaum were found in the excavations there. Such humble people rarely leave records of their passing. It is unreasonable to expect to find contemporary records of Jesus or Peter in such a place. Yet from a village by this lake and from the words of the Gospels came such an energy, such an effect, that unless the whole movement was a confidence trick of unparalleled dimensions, it is more reasonable to assume that a man called Jesus really lived in Palestine during the Roman Governorate.

There still remain, of course, the widely varying interpretations of Jesus' identity, his aims and his ambitions. True or false, the Gospels are gloriously ambiguous. Is their Jesus simply a holy teacher with no great plan for the world or a church? Is he consciously engaged in acting out throughout his life the prophecies that cement the four Gospels so securely to the Old Testament, and so promising mankind a very specific destiny? Is he a divine vagabond, an ineffable being with no plan or direction that mortals can understand? Are all such interpretations gleaned from the words of Jesus or merely from the expectations that he aroused among the Gospel writers and their followers? The first Christian writings that have survived were the letters written some twenty years after Jesus' death by the Apostle Paul, and they show that, already at that time, the church on earth was well-established and beginning to grow into a highly complex organization with rules and rituals more intricate and elaborate than anything that Jesus teaches in the Gospels. This period, then, between the death of Jesus and the first of Paul's letters to the Western churches, is the single most significant time in the history of the New Testament, for this was when its readership was being created, the readership for whom the Gospels were later written. Yet we have very little information about these vital decades; Luke's Book of Acts that describes the period in some detail was written, it is reliably estimated, at least thirty years later, at the same time as the Gospels themselves. What continuity is there, then, between these letters of Paul and the Four Gospels?

Paul's Church: The New Testament Audience

There is an early Christian text that tells of a man called Onepheros, the leader of a congregation of a city in Asia Minor, waiting by the roadside for a sight of Paul, who was travelling from town to town across the Anatolian plateau. 'And he saw Paul coming, a man little of stature, thin-haired upon the head, with eyebrows joining, and nose somewhat hooked, full of grace: for sometimes he appeared like a man, and sometimes he had the face of an angel. And when Paul saw Onephoros, he smiled.'

This is the Paul who stands out so clearly in the uncertain mists of early Christianity – an itinerant preacher. An extraordinary, vigorous man, blunt, committed; a man who had seen a vision and was for ever after driven by it. 'I must make it clear to you, my friends, that the gospel you heard me preach is no human invention. I did not take it over from any man: no man taught it

[167]

me; I received it through a revelation of Jesus Christ.' (Galatians 1:11—12 NEB).

Such a close familiarity with divinity was not uncommon in the Hellenistic cities. In the previous century, a certain Aelius Aristides had been on such good terms with a god that by secretly making offerings and prayers he had managed to save the splendid city of Smyrna from a devastating earthquake. Aristides had desperately wanted to tell his fellow citizens of his success, he admits, 'though I had intended to say there is no need to be afraid . . . I stopped so that I might not seem to be some demagogue.' Such reticence, such a constriction of passion, had sent Aristides into a lifetime of illness but no such brake operated upon the Christian Paul. Nowhere else in the Bible does language take on such urgency and passion.

Paul's biblical letters are the oldest surviving Christian texts, written, in all probability, before AD 60. Certainly, there is little reason to doubt that they are genuinely ancient documents. Since the last century, excavations have re-covered evidence of many precise circumstantial details mentioned in Paul's letters but unknown for centuries. With such information the very order of his journeys has been accurately re-constructed. The style of the letters, too, is of Paul's day, with the usual elaborate forms of address and manners of composition. Such letters were usually the work of professional scribes who composed them around the words of their masters, but Paul's overwhelming desire to communicate his new-found faith has stretched these traditional forms into long and vigorous tirades. Historically they show us a busy man dealing briskly with the day-to-day affairs of the new church. Rapidly growing congregations were slowly coming to grips with the effects of Christianity on their daily lives and establishing their joint identity in the pagan world of the Hellenistic cities. Much of Paul's advice to them has a practicality and a sensitivity that many later missionaries would have done well to emulate. When, for example, a congregation at Corinth in Greece inquires of him whether or not they should eat meat that had been offered on the altars of the pagan temples before appearing in the butchers' shops – a common enough custom in those days – Paul replies: 'You may eat anything sold in the meat market without raising questions of conscience; for the earth is the Lord's and everything in it. If an unbeliever invites you to a meal and you care to go, eat whatever is put before you, without raising questions of conscience. But if someone says to you, "This food has been offered in sacrifice", then, out of consideration for him, and for conscience' sake, do not eat it – not your conscience, I mean, but the other man's. . . give no offence to Jews, or Greeks, or to the church of God. For my part I always try to meet everyone halfway' (1 Corinthians 10:25—33 NEB). Sometimes, however, Paul's 'halfway' was a long way from local inclinations. 'You stupid Galatians! You must have been bewitched – you before whose eyes Jesus Christ was openly displayed upon his cross! Answer me one question: did you receive the Spirit by keeping the law or believing the gospel message? Can it be that you are so stupid? You started with the spiritual; do you now look to the material to make you perfect? (Galatians 3:1—4 NEB).

Paul's argument here is directed against a congregation that was being encouraged to follow Judaic Law inside their Christian church. Paul's 'gospels' were, of course, the Old Testament in its Greek translation – the Septuagint. In the earliest days of the Church, when Paul and his fellows were preaching in synagogues, there was much uncertainty and argument around whether Jesus' church should observe Judaic Law and whether it could embrace gentiles as brother Christians without them living according to the Law. Paul, who believed that he had in a dazzling vision been charged to preach to the Gentiles, was in absolutely no doubt about the matter. Physical observance of traditional Law was unimportant, and so incensed was he by the enquiry of the Galatian congregation about the need for circumcision that at the end of the letter he took up his secretary's pen himself, 'You see these big letters? I am now writing to you in my own hand. It is all those who want to make a fair outward and bodily show who are trying to force circumcision upon you; their sole object is to escape persecution for the cross of Christ . . . Circumcision is nothing; uncircumcision is nothing; the only thing that counts is the new creation! . . . The grace of our Lord Jesus Christ be with your spirit, my brothers. Amen.' (Galatians 6:from 11—18 NEB).

As you would expect of one who had rejected the faith of his family and his people, Paul's attitude to Judaism was sensitive and often emotional. But though as a Christian, he rejected the need for the observance of the Law, he never rejected the social attitudes of contemporary Judaism, and so the Christian church has inherited, for example, Paul's repugnance for orgiastic ritual, a common feature of the Hellenistic world, and his social code regarding the proper behaviour of men and women: 'Does not Nature herself teach you that while flowing locks disgrace a man, they are a woman's glory? For her locks were given for covering.' (1 Corinthians 11:14—16 NEB). When Paul argues for the veiling of women in church he appeals not to God, but to Nature; this 'natural' law is from the familiar world of his childhood. As he himself says, Paul was often willing to meet people halfway, but he always attacked vigorously when he detected the infiltration of pagan ritual or custom into the church. Unlike Paul, gentile converts to the church came from the richly varied background of Hellenistic paganism. It was as natural for them to fill their new found faith with the rites and attitudes of their childhoods as it was for Paul to fill it with the responses from his. Born in the Jewish community of a large Hellenistic city, he would have had experience, and an automatic suspicion, of pagan attitudes and practices.

Paul's letters allow us vivid glimpses of the young church slowly defining itself inside Hellenism; they show us, too, how the church was indelibly printed with some of Paul's own piety and prejudices. Lacking any reports of what Paul actually said as he converted the pagan and preached to the faithful, we find in these letters the closest thing we possess to a description of the church in the days before the four Gospels were written. And there is no doubt that these congregations were those for whom the Gospels would later be written. But there is nothing in Paul's letters that either hints at the existence of the Gospels or that even talks of a need for such biographical memoirs of Jesus Christ. Paul, the New Testament says, never saw the earthly Jesus but was totally convinced of his divinity. He was, he says, 'an apostle, not by human appointment or human commission, but by commission from Jesus Christ and from God the Father.' (Galatians 1:1 NEB).

The Gospels: The Art of Sacred Biography

Tradition has long held, and there is no great reason to doubt it, that Paul was executed at Rome late in the reign of the Emperor Nero. A few years later, the Roman legions devastated Judaea and destroyed Jerusalem; Paul had been in a hurry to complete his mission because he believed that the end of the world was nigh; 'the time we live in will not last long' he asserted in his first letter to the Corinthians (7:29), restating a constantly repeated theme; he had the whole of Rome's empire to visit before, as he says, his 'life is poured out upon the altar'. Between Paul's letters and the writing of the Gospels, a gap in time no longer than half a century, there was a whole world of difference. Jerusalem had gone; a tangible earthly cataclysm had occurred.

There is not a single mention or even a hint of Paul's letters in the Gospels. Their vision seems far removed from the practicalities that are spelled out in Paul's letters. His main theme is Jesus' message of God's love for the world and also Christ's assertion that the ending of the world is imminent; his historical view is sharp and certain. In comparison, the Gospels often seem uncertain of their central message and of their central character; Jesus' purposes on earth seem curiously elusive. As writings dealing with the sacred personage at the centre of the faith and not, like Paul's letters, with the day-to-day affairs of the church, it is, of course, appropriate that the Gospels are written in a very different way. But there is more to it than that. The Gospels' portrait of Jesus seems to be separated from real time. The central character is set in a rambling series of incidents and sermons, engaged in a mysterious progress revolving around an unstated drama that finally ensures his capture and death. Perhaps in response, modern histories, too, often lose all sense of reality as they approach the Holy Land. Neighbouring countries have economic histories and bloody political wars. All too often, however, the Holy Land is portrayed as a fairyland of country folk, wicked kings, corrupt priests, tax collectors and stock revolutionaries. But did these ancient Galileans really live with eyes fixed only upon the infinite? How, for example, did Jesus see his career on earth? Just as a healer and preacher? Did he consider the political or social consequences of his teachings? Just as the Gospels themselves are elusive on these subjects, so the relationship between church and state in Christendom has remained ill-defined, even into modern times.

But slowly through the haze, as the reality of the Holy Land in those times is better understood something of the real life of this lonely man at the centre of the Gospels is beginning to emerge. Jesus' mission on earth begins, so the Gospels all agree, with his baptism in the Jordan by John the Baptist. The story is of a young Galilean countryman come down from his home province to see a famous preacher, a young man who through all his life's work will use the agricultural metaphors of his childhood; a countryman to whom the most beautiful things that came to mind were the 'lilies of the field'. Throughout the Gospels, Jesus seldom refers to cities and their ways. Indeed, the greater part of his teaching was conducted in three towns so small that they are barely mentioned in texts and inscriptions outside the Gospels themselves. Yet so precise are the Gospel's descriptions of this Galilean landscape that their writers surely knew it well.

With the Gospels, in common with many studies of ancient history, we are left, not with firm facts, but with a scale of probabilities ranging from very high to very low. Working inside this scale, modern New Testament historians would generally agree on a short list of statements about Jesus, a sort of historian's creed, you might say: at the beginning of his mission Jesus was baptized by John the Baptist, a man known from other ancient records: Jesus came from Galilee and preached and healed inside the borders of Palestine with a group of followers; he became embroiled in a controversy about the Jerusalem temple; he was subsequently crucified by the Roman authorities. Naturally, as a modern historical list, this contains neither miracles, nor a resurrection! And, because there is still strong disagreement about certain key issues – which party, for example, was responsible for his execution – the list, at first glance, seems to be very short. Nonetheless, it is born of historical probability rather than pure faith and it contains sufficient information to attempt a reconstruction of Jesus' earthly career.

In any attempt to find this man in the Four Gospels the central problem always revolves around the question of *how* the Gospels describe Jesus' life, of *how* they report his words and deeds. For although they describe Jesus' birth, life, death and resurrection, they are not written in the usual manner of ancient biographies and it is difficult to see the man developing – how his ideas, actions and teachings follow one upon the other.

Part of the problem seems to stem from the Gospel writers' own uncertainties about Jesus' identity. Even Jesus seems to have had his doubts as to how he had appeared to his fellow men. 'Who do men say that I am?' (Mark 8:27) he asks a disciple; there remains, and must always remain, many different interpretations of him. The account of Jesus' baptism by John the Baptist is certainly the key to the story of his earthly career. This baptism contains the political seed of his ending on the cross. For, like John the Baptist, Jesus promised redemption from earthly sin, not by the orthodox Jewish method of making offerings at the Jerusalem Temple but by the simple gesture of genuine personal repentance. The acceptance of God was signified not by an expensive journey to Jerusalem and an offering at the Temple but, in John the Baptist's case, by immersion, by baptism in the free-flowing waters of the River Jordan, and in Jesus' case by an internal act of will and faith.

When the Romans destroyed the Temple forty years after Jesus' time they destroyed the political as well as the spiritual heart of Judaism. Most ancient kings raised revenues through taxation which was often called an offering to the state gods. In Jerusalem also the elaborate system of Temple offerings was central to the fiscal power of the state. By proposing the redemption of sin outside the Temple and its system of offerings, both Jesus and John not only denied the spiritual efficiency of the priests but also hit at the source of their wealth. John the Baptist and Jesus were both executed; and both of them had struck at the heart of this priestly state. The Gospels describe the baptism of Jesus as a personal visionary experience; the account of the event is said to come from Jesus himself: 'and, lo, the heavens were opened unto him,' Matthew tell us 'and *he* saw the spirit of God descending like a dove' (Matthew 3:16). Naturally, his vision took the common Jewish form for such things, 'a voice from heaven'. From that moment on, Jesus, like John the Baptist, preached the possibility of personal redemption outside the structures of organized Judaism. Unlike John, however, he did not preach with the rough fervour of a desert hermit, but with a great calmness and a love of life. Both John and Jesus, though, viewed their mission as preparing people for the establishment of the Kingdom of God on earth – Paul's end-time. And all of them believed, so the New Testament says, that this end-time was very near.

In AD 70, after the Temple had fallen to the legions, the remnants of Jerusalem's defenders retreated to the western end of the city, to Herod's great fortress palace with its three stout towers named after members of his ill-fated family: Phasaelus, Hippicus and Mariamne. In August AD 71 the last Roman assault took place, storming up earthen ramps piled against the western walls of the palace. Weak with hunger, the Jews abandoned the fortress and surrendered. The Roman troops ran through the narrow streets killing the remaining civilians. Orders were given that the Temple and the city should be destroyed, only the three towers and their walls were to remain to house a Roman garrison. Part of the tower of Phasaelus stands today, embedded in the walls of a Turkish citadel, whose shape reflects the order and design of Herod's fort. This was the building that, after Herod's death, the Roman governors of Judaea had used as their residence in Jerusalem. In this building would have been the room where Jesus was interviewed by Pontius Pilate. Though the Gospel descriptions of the events that led up to the trial of Jesus never tell us why he was put on trial for his life, today it seems most likely that his fatal contact with Rome was the result of his being considered a threat to the peace and well-being of the province. Although, the Gospels tell us, Jesus insisted that his kingdom was not of this world, and he had no aspiration to earthly power, in ancient times there was little distinction between religion and politics; indeed, in the next century, Jesus' own church would become embroiled in a protracted political struggle. In Jesus' time there was much talk of a Messiah who would liberate the Jews by force; the Romans executed several of these would-be Messiahs as well as Jesus of Nazareth. This label of Messiah automatically challenged both Roman and Jewish authority in Judaea and Galilee; for the belief that a Messiah would arise and, with the help of God, expel the godless was often expressed in Hebrew Scripture. It had become a deep popular dream which the holy texts had promised would become a reality at the end-time. There remain, however, several alternative explanations for Jesus' own attitude to this popular image of the Messiah. Did he deliberately embark upon his fatal path, representing himself as the Messiah to his people, intending by his execution to still the suicidal dream of a victorious war against the Romans? If so, the great gesture failed. Indeed, there are many devout historians who have suggested that Jesus' execution was just such a failure; the fulfilment of the Prophet's prediction that the Messiah would be 'despised and rejected of men; a man of sorrows and acquainted with grief' (Isaiah 53:3).

The period of Jesus' ministry was a time of rising passions and repression in Judaea, a doom-laden age when people braced themselves for the coming apocalypse. This, it was widely thought, would come after the final war against the 'Sons of Darkness' – the Romans. The Gospels describe it as an age of seers, of visions and shooting stars, of miracles and prophecies. Although in the Gospels Jesus declines all claim to earthly power, it must have been very difficult for his contemporaries to divorce daily reality from Jesus' preaching. This was a man, the Gospels tell us, who foresaw the ending of the Temple and wept openly for the Holy City. There would have been a great gulf between Jesus' understanding of his role on earth and the roles that he played in the eyes of his contemporaries. As Jesus stands in Pilate's court about to undergo the processes of Roman civil law, the Son of God and earthly history jump apart again, as they do at Capernaum. The Gospel account of his trial is enigmatic. Jesus has become a mirror of earthly passions and political tensions apparent in his contemporary Jerusalem; there were underground movements like that of the Zealots who may well have seen him as a military Messiah; Caiaphas and the other priests of the Temple surely would have wanted him out of their way. Part of Jesus' preaching seems to attack both the authority and livelihood of the priests – as his physical attack on their Temple's money-changers, that bazaar brawl, makes clear. And in his turn, Pontius Pilate would have seen Jesus of Nazareth as just another focus of civil unrest; in an empire ruled by divine emperors, Jesus' claim to be the Son of God would have been sufficient cause to have him condemned to death.

Such was the ring of opinion that would have surrounded Jesus on that day in Herod's fortress. And beyond that generation, in the following decades, stand the Gospel writers who have left us the only record of the event. They, of course, wrote their texts after the destruction of Jerusalem with the benefit of a hindsight which also saw Jesus' trial as the prelude to his resurrection. They wrote about their Lord, Jesus Christ, and they addressed a gentile church. They were eager, too, to excuse the Roman authorities for Jesus' death, for the inheritors of that government were now targets for conversion. So Pontius Pilate, who is known to have been a ruthless and insensitive adminis-trator, is portrayed in the Gospels as a bemused bureaucrat and the 'Jews' – the population of the city – are seen as a single vociferous voice in the hubbub of Jerusalem. But the order of the Jewish council that the Gospels describe is the order of the council *after* Jerusalem's fall as we know from Jewish records, not that of the time of Jesus at all, and that helps to set the Gospel writers in their own time.

Nowadays, of course, accumulated ages of opinion stand between us and the Gospel writers' accounts of the trial. Each of the churches, too, have created their own visions of Jesus; often he is not seen as a man at all, but as a being whose life was a series of moral parables and holy lessons. Little wonder then that many modern churchmen regard the trial, like the rest of Jesus' life on earth, as a mythic history whose truth lies in the ethics of his teaching. And this elusive man at the centre of it all? The man who in the Gospels barely bothers to defend himself against his accusers and prompts from Pontius Pilate the question 'what is truth?' stands somewhere between all these hopes and dreams and apprehensions.

Matthew	Mark	Luke	John
and they bound him and led him away and delivered him to Pilate the governor.	and they bound Jesus and led him away and delivered him to Pilate.	Then the whole company of them arose, and brought him before Pilate.	Then they led Jesus from the house of Caiaphas to the praetorium. It was early. They themselves did not enter the praetorium, so that they might not be defiled, but might eat the passover.
			So Pilate went out to them and said, 'What accusation do you bring against this man?' They answered him, 'If this man were not an evil-doer, we would not have handed him over.' Pilate said to them, 'Take him yourselves and judge him by your own law.' The Jews said to him, 'It is not lawful for us to put any man to death.' This was to fulfil the word which Jesus had spoken to show by what death he was to die.
		And they began to accuse him, saying, 'We found this man perverting our nation, and forbidding us to give tribute to Caesar, and saying that he himself is Christ a king.'	
Now Jesus stood before the governor; and the governor asked him, 'Are you the King of the Jews?' Jesus said,	And Pilate asked him, 'Are you the King of the Jews?' And he answered him,	And Pilate asked him, 'Are you the King of the Jews?' And he answered him,	Pilate entered the praetorium again and called Jesus, and said to him, 'Are you the King of the Jews?' Jesus answered,

Matthew	Mark	Luke	John
			'Do you say this of your own accord, or did others say it to you about me?' Pilate answered, 'Am I a Jew? Your own nation and the chief priests have handed you over to me; what have you done?' Jesus answered, 'My kingship is not of this world;
'Do you think that I cannot appeal to my Father, and he will at once send me more than twelve legions of angels?'			if my kingship were of this world, my servants would fight, that I might not be handed over to the Jews; but my kingship is not from the world.' Pilate said to him, 'So you are a king?' Jesus answered,
'You have said so.'	'You have said so.'	'You have said so.'	'You say that I am a king. For this I was born, and for this I have come into the world to bear witness to the truth. Every one who is of the truth hears my voice.' Pilate said to him, 'What is truth?'
But when he was accused by the chief priests and elders, he made no answer.	And the chief priests accused him of many things.	So he questioned him at some length; but he made no answer.	
Then Pilate said to him,	And Pilate again asked him,	The chief priests and the scribes stood by, vehemently accusing him.	
'Do you not hear how many things they testify against you?' But he gave him no answer, not even to a single charge; so that the governor wondered greatly.	'Have you no answer to make? See how many charges they bring against you?' But Jesus made no further answer, so that Pilate wondered.		

A count of the stories of the four Gospels reveals a shared corpus of about three hundred and sixty separate events and these may be grouped under two general headings: those that deal with Jesus' teaching and those that tell of incidents from Jesus' life. These biographical stories are broadly set into a consecutive sequence, but there is no reason to assume that they are all in chronological order – indeed the different Gospels often show variations in the order of the same stories. Further, there is no way of knowing how much time passed between the narrative of Jesus' entry into Jerusalem, 'Palm Sunday', and the arrest and crucifixion. It is also impossible to discover any concrete relationship between Jesus' teachings and the events of his life. There is no development of his thought; his words are described as a largely unrelated succession of teachings – a traditional body of stories that grew up around the person of Jesus.

Many of the Gospel stories are designed to show how Jesus' life fulfilled the Messianic predictions of the Hebrew Prophets. The use of ancient archetypes to explain contemporary events was common in ancient Israel. Just as the Patriarch Jacob had wrestled with an angel, had been wounded, then changed his name and founded a nation; so also Saul had a vision upon the road to Damascus, changed his name to Paul and preached a new faith. These were familiar ways of behaviour in biblical Palestine and the Gospel writers who took many of their stories about Jesus' life from ancient prophecies were further fortified in their method by their belief that Jesus had been the Messiah and *must* therefore have fulfilled the ancient predictions about this appearance on earth. To them, to have recorded the Messiah's life in any other way would have been historically incorrect and sacrilegious to boot. Jesus, therefore, must be born of a virgin in the town of Bethlehem with a star hanging in the night sky over his stable precisely because the Prophets have told that this is how the Messiah will be born.

Similarly, Luke's account of the circumstances of Jesus' birth, 'In those days a decree was issued by the Emperor Augustus for a registration to be made throughout the Roman world' (Luke 2:1 NEB), is an inaccurate historical fiction, introduced in all probability to enable the Messiah to be born in Bethlehem and so fulfill the Prophet's words. Similarly, the Gospels give Jesus a Messianic pedigree. Matthew's lengthy genealogy of Jesus includes a suitably fantastic measure of ancestors; Tamar, for example, whose children were born of incest, Bathsheba whose offspring were born of adultery: all this to demonstrate an illustrious precedent for Jesus' illegitimacy and also to provide extraordinary and miraculous antecedents for this divine man. Though such passages tell a great deal about the Gospel writers, they do little to advance our understanding of the earthly Jesus.

But there are also very many details in the Gospels, both historical and topographical, that are circumstantially correct and have a ring of truth about them. Sometimes, it is the story's very oddness that convinces; and this is the case with Jesus' inconvenient assertion in Matthew's Gospel (15:24) that he was sent only to the 'lost sheep of the house of Israel', and his following description of some gentile neighbours as 'dogs', an insult that in the East is still considered to be highly offensive. This tale seems to show Jesus abusing part of the very audience for whom the Gospels were written, and it remains in the Gospels, perhaps only because it was part of the authentic tradition of Jesus' life; surely no churchman would sensibly have ever invented such a tale.

Similarly, the act of Jesus' crucifixion convinces because of its extremely degrading nature. In the Roman Empire crucifixion was a most shameful death, even in the minds of the early Christian congregations, as Paul's letters make clear. It was not until the third century that Jesus' cross of execution became a common symbol of the Christian faith; the taint of its shame was so strong. No one but the most bizarre of contemporary theologians would have invented such a miserable ending for the Lord of Heaven. There is, as well, the conviction of truth about the Gospel account of Jesus' way to the cross; it has the authenticity of experience. If the traditional site of the crucifixion in Jerusalem is the correct one, and this is entirely plausible, then the road that Jesus would have taken from Herod's fortress to Golgotha follows the main street of the modern bazaar. This runs down the site of an ancient city wall, then turns sharp left to a rocky knoll that would have been the Roman execution ground. Ancient descriptions of such executions talk of criminals, weak through loss of blood after their flogging, carrying the instruments of their death upon their backs to the place of execution, through streets that were no wider than their modern successors. Jesus' progress through these alleys, bleeding from his wounds, would have had a brutal immediacy for the people of Jerusalem. Onlookers and passers-by would have been but a few feet away from the condemned man on his way to death. And this is a fragment of the reality that the Gospels so poignantly convey, an immediate truth beyond the facts of history and the conviction of faith.

Before his last, fatal battle with the Roman legions, Spartacus, a leader of the slave rebellion of 70 BC, had a prisoner crucified in the centre of his camp to show his followers what awaited them if they should lose. Crucifixion was considered to be one of the most severe Roman punishments, worse than decapitation, burning, or exposure to wild beasts. Only very rarely was it used on anyone but the poor or enslaved, which gave it its special stigma, and then only for such crimes as spying, desertion, rebellion and forgery. Crucifixion was also the traditional fate of all the slaves in the household of a man murdered by a servant; it was also the fate of slaves who betrayed their masters. The victims were usually lashed to a horizontal beam, then nailed to its vertical support in whatever position caught the executioner's fancy. At mass crucifixions the executioners sometimes made tableaux to amuse themselves and passers-by. Death usually came as a result of exposure, as Juvenal, the great Roman poet describes.

> [The vulture] from the cross the felon's carcass tears,
> and with her brood the gory relic shares

Like all societies who hold large numbers of their people in subjection, the Romans were frightened of the latent power of their slaves. The common but terrifying fate of crucifixion is not often mentioned in Roman texts; even usually humane writers simply accepted this traditional torture as an inevitable measure of slave control. Crucified corpses were a normal decoration to a city's gateways, where the dead upon the cross shared the desolate landscape with graveyards and rubbish tips.

Jerusalem's place of crucifixion, Calvary, an important symbol of Roman imperialism derived its biblical name from the word skull, which in Aramaic is Golgotha. Recent excavations underneath the Church of the Holy Sepulchre – the traditional site of Jesus' crucifixion and burial, of Calvary and the Tomb – have traced the ancient levels of the bedrock up from the subterranean limestone quarries, as old as the kingdom of Israel, up through the underground chapels built amid ancient quarryshafts and water cisterns, up fine Crusader staircases covered with the pious crosses of medieval pilgrims, onto the modern ground level of the church. For many centuries these pits under Calvary were bricked off from the church above because, it was believed, they led straight to Purgatory and the cries of suffering would disturb the congregation in the church above.

The rock of Calvary emerging from the floor of the church is cleft, and this crack, according to Christian legend, appeared when Christ was crucified. And down the same crack, the legend says, Jesus' blood flowed to splash on Adam's skull, who was thus given life. In an upheaval of time itself, Christ crucified appears at man's beginning: our history is here transformed into a cosmic drama. On the top of Calvary two chapels mark the place where Jesus was nailed to the cross, and then raised up on it into the air. The socket that once held the wooden cross is still to be seen; today, however, the rock has largely been chipped away through the generations by the chisels of the faithful.

Down the stairs from Calvary is a slab of stone that marks the spot where, by tradition, Jesus' body was laid for anointing. The stone lies on what would have been the centre of the ancient road which once led up to a city gate. Jesus' tomb, nearby, was on the other side of the road from Calvary; nowadays it is marked by a curiously ugly kiosk, thick with alabaster curlicues, candle smoke and supporting girders erected by the Royal Engineers during the British Mandate in Palestine (see Plate 20). Excavations have shown that an ancient Jewish cemetery once stood here, a small one probably, set amid a suburb of Hellenistic villas of the Roman period.

In the darkness at the back of the church lies the decrepit chapel of the Syrian Christians, deserted now, save for one poor oil lamp, and here, in a dank corner, are ancient Jewish tombs cut into the rock and dating to the time of Jesus. These, traditionally, are ascribed to the family of Joseph of Arimathea, the man who gave up his own new tomb to Christ. Burials of that period would have left the body exposed upon a rock ledge in the open tomb until the flesh decayed, then the bones would have been collected and placed in a small ossuary, often mingled with the remains of other members of the same family. The three women of the Gospels who brought unguents to anoint Jesus' corpse in the tomb were performing a tender act for, as the story of Jesus at Lazarus' tomb makes plain, quickly decaying corpses usually required that the tomb chamber be sealed until such time that natural desiccation had cleared the air in the tomb.

Once again piety has transformed this ancient landscape and used the Bible as its guidebook. Christian emperors ordered the rock around the hillside tomb ascribed to Christ to be cut down so that the simple chamber was left free-standing, a small kiosk of living rock. Thus exposed, the tomb was later attacked by the quarrymen of a deranged caliph and almost completely destroyed. Since those days, following fires and earthquakes, the kiosk has been rebuilt and restored many times over. Today the entire complex is ardently contested by half a dozen different churches, each with its regiment of burly monks, and the effect has been to ensure that the strange old edifice seems to have no proprietor other than the patient Muslim family which, since the earliest days of Islam, has been assigned ownership and control of the keys of this contentious place. Uniquely the church belongs to its visitors.

At the front door of Christ's tomb, where there is always a queue of visitors, there stands a piece of the rock said to be part of the rolling stone with which the tomb was closed. Here, it is believed, the white angel sat and talked to the three women as they came to anoint the body of their Lord. Here, too, Jesus is said to have appeared to Mary Magdalene as she sat weeping by the empty tomb. The precise spot is now marked upon the floor: in such places science bows to faith.

And when the sabbath was past, Mary Magdalene, and Mary the mother of James, and Salome, had brought sweet spices, that they might come and anoint him. And very early in the morning the first day of the week, they came unto the sepulchre at the rising of the sun. And they said among themselves, 'Who shall roll us away the stone from the door of the sepulchre?

And when they looked, they saw that the stone was rolled away: for it was very great. And entering into the sepulchre, they saw a young man sitting on the right side, clothed in a long white garment; and they were affrighted. And he saith unto them, 'Be not affrighted: Ye seek Jesus of Nazareth, which was crucified: he is risen; he is not here: behold the place where they laid him.

(Mark 16:1—6)

Gospel Beginnings: The Archaeological Evidence

The writing of the Gospels, a leading churchman once suggested, was an early manifestation of the operation of original sin: a loss of nerve within the church as the founding fathers, preachers all, slowly died, and following generations attempted to preserve their stories about Jesus by writing them down. The oldest examples of the Gospels yet discovered came from the ancient sand-bound towns at the edge of the Sahara desert in Egypt – from the Hellenistic cities in the huge oasis called the Fayuum and from some of the ancient monasteries that stood at the desert's edge alongside the river Nile (see Plate 17). Two centuries ago the Hellenistic towns and cities of Egypt were buried deep in heaps of ancient dirt. Most of them were ruins, showing as dark stains on desert sand dunes. For many centuries, canny local farmers had taken their donkeys to these city mounds and loaded up their small panniers with the rich, ancient dirt. Then scientists discovered that this dirt which embalmed the old cities was a magical nitrate-rich compound of ancient dusts, soot and dung, a splendid agricultural fertilizer for the farmers of Egypt pressed by foreign debt, their fields washed clean of nutrients by imperial irrigation schemes. So with the efficiency of government, huge camel trains and special rail-head terminals were established to mine the ancient houses. By the 1890s one archaeologist estimated that something between 100 and 150 tons of *Sebakh coufri*, as the black dirt was called, was being removed from a single city on every working day. So, most of these ancient cities were demolished and quarried, their mudbrick walls broken up and the old dust spread over Egyptian fields. Until the First World War, agricultural manuals compiled by British scientists cheerfully discussed the merits and drawbacks of the use of Hellenistic cities as fertilizer; and they noted with alarm that this valuable black earth, this excellent source of revenue, was beginning to run out!

As the quarrymen – the *sebakhim* – cut into the cities they knew that there was always the possibility of finding buried treasure. Only a few collectors realized that the strange little objects coming out of Egypt, glass and bronzes, pottery, even papyrus, represented the detritus of an entire civilization. Nevertheless, the plunder was enormous; antiquities flooded into Europe and the United States. In England a small body of antiquaries gathered together to excavate and record some of the fast-disappearing cities, raising their funding largely on the possibility of making biblical discoveries. So these fertilizer quarries became the 'Cities of the Exodus', the 'granaries of Joseph' and so on, and many of the claims made by the first rescue archaeologists in the 1880s and 1890s have stuck in the popular mind as 'proof' of the Old Testament. Working in lonely and remote locations, threatened by disease and bandits, a handful of archaeologists rapidly traversed the Nile Delta, making rough excavations and crude plans of the ancient cities as many of them were literally quarried away before their eyes. In this hurried and inexpert work, the science of Egyptian archaeology was born; at the same time, the cities that had stood in northern Egypt for thousands of years largely disappeared. As well as Greek and Roman antiquities, there were also large amounts of ancient papyri coming onto the antiquities' market of the West. These fragments contained every conceivable kind of text, from vast masses of ancient bureaucratic writings to previously lost masterpieces of Greek and Roman playwrights and philosophers. Young men more at home in university libraries than desert excavations now came to dig for papyri, and they found them, in their thousands. Texts that had once been torn up or thrown away, then trapped in the wind-blown sand, tiny precious flakes of papyrus, blown into the corners of the ancient houses, or buried in the vast rubbish tips that surrounded the ancient cities. The oldest known fragment of the New Testament was probably found in just such a place, though its precise spot is not known. Other pieces of papyri having served their ancient purpose had been re-used as papyrus papier-mâché, moulded into brightly painted mummy cases and buried in the city cemeteries. Sometimes the ancient dead also had their favourite texts buried with them – any number of religious tracts, one of Homer's poems, even an

Old Testament Psalm. Altogether, an incredible variety of ancient texts was found by the scholars in the cities or were bought from local antiquity dealers; there were letters from emperors to their officials, receipts, bills, all the little legal agreements of daily life, and in such quantities that still today, almost a century later, an international group of scholars is still at work preserving, examining and publishing them.

The most successful of all these papyri hunters were two young Oxford men, Bernard Pyne Grenfell and Arthur Surridge Hunt. Usually they began their search by digging a deep trench through an ancient mound, cutting through the sand upon the surface, perhaps through the remains of Arab cities and Byzantine houses, until they arrived at the Hellenistic levels of the town. Then they looked for a distinctive loose-packed band of earth which the workmen called the *akfsh*. This, Hunt says, was not as fine as the usual powdery *sebakh* which was used as fertilizer, nor as hard as the tamped earth of the ancient house floors. Usually, under the weight of the covering debris and attacked by the acids in the *sebakh*, the fragile papyri were destroyed. The *akfsh*, on the other hand, was a gossamer-soft stratum that lightly held the dust and debris of the ancient world above the floor levels. In the ancient environment, where the floors and walls of most houses were made of sun-dried mud that continually shed layers of its own fine dust, the *akfsh* could sometimes be quite deep. 'The gold digger does not look for gold where there is no quartz,' Grenfell observed, 'similarly, the papyrus seeker may practically disregard any kind of earth other than *akfsh*.' Though today it is easy to bemoan the random destruction of these ancient cities, one cannot but admire the energy of these men who recovered such vast quantities of ancient writing.

Though they often ignored the smaller fragments of papyrus, it was the *sebakhim* that made the most notable discoveries in these ancient cities, and before beginning their winter excavations, Grenfell and Hunt, along with many holidaying vicars and travelling scholars, made the rounds of the antique dealers to see what the efforts of last season's *sebakhim* had brought to light. It was in this way that Grenfell bought the oldest fragment of the New Testament yet known, a tiny snippet of a Gospel of John; he found it in 1920 in a shop in Cairo. But it was not for some fifteen years after this chance discovery that the little flake of papyrus, by that time reposing in the collections of the John Rylands Library at Manchester in England, was recognized for what it was and dated, by the style of its handwriting, to about AD 130 – around a century after the crucifixion of Jesus.

This fragment of papyrus has proved to be remarkably informative. Careful examination of the text, the margins and the cut edge led to the deduction that it had probably been part of a small booklet bound with string, which, if it had contained 132 pages, each one with about 18 lines upon it, would have been large enough to contain the whole Gospel of John.

If the little fragment had been discovered at the turn of the century, it would have caused a sensation. For at that time, leading New Testament scholars were broadly agreed that John's Gospel had been written at a very much later date, the last of the four, it was supposed, to have been written down. The fragment contains snatches of the report of the trial of Jesus before the Jewish Council on one side; and Jesus' interview with Pilate on the other: 'and Pilate said "what is truth?"' (John 18:38). The brief text confirms the reliability of the later versions of the same story and is virtually the same as modern Bibles. Indeed, there is very little in all the known variations in the ancient versions of New Testament texts that gives any grounds to suppose that there have been major changes in them; the original Gospel message has remained intact.

The Rylands Fragment proved to be the forerunner of a dozen or so slightly later Gospels, all from Egypt, all written on pages of papyrus rather than on the

PLATE 15 (Opposite): Jerusalem. The walls of the stone platform on which Herod's temple once stood. The North Wall in the sunlight, retains its ancient gateways, now blocked, which once stood at the top of a broad flight of steps that led up into the Temple courtyards.
PLATE 16 (Overleaf): Two papyrus pages of the oldest known Book of the Gospel of Luke, dating from about AD 220. The two passages – Luke 12:18–37 (left) and 12:42 to 13:1 (right) – contain some of the Parables, the left-hand page holding Jesus' famous words 'Consider the lilies how they grow. . . .' This is also one of the oldest surviving books – known as biblia in the ancient world. Note the central gutter with the holes that once held the stitching. Chester Beatty Library, Dublin.

ΚΑΝΑΠΑΥΟΥ ...
ΤΗΙ ΤΗΙ ΝΥΚΤΙ ΤΗΙ ...
... ΙΛ ΚΑΙ ΤΙΝΙ ΕΣΤΙΝ Ο ...
... ΛΥΤΟΝ· ΕΙΠΕΝ ΔΕ ΠΡΟΣ ΤΟΥΣ
... Η ΜΕΡΙ ΛΝΑΤΕ ΤΗ ΨΥΧΗ ...
... ΤΙΕΝ ΔΥΣΗΣ ΔΕ ... Η ΨΥΧΗ ΠΛΕΙΟΝ
... ΤΟΥ ΕΝΔΥΜΑΤΟΣ· ΚΑΙ ΚΑΤΑΝΟΗΣΑΤΕ
ΤΟΥΣ ΚΟΡΑΚΑΣ ΟΤΙ ΟΥ ΣΠΕΙΡΟΥΣΙΝ ΟΥΔΕ
ΘΕΡΙΖΟΥΣΙΝ Ο ΙΟΥ ΚΕ ΕΤΙΝ ΤΙ ... ΕΙΟΝ ΟΥΔΕ ΑΠΟΘΗΚΗ ΚΑΙ ΚΑΙ Ο ΘΣ ΤΡΕΦΕΙ
ΑΥΤΑ ΠΟΣΩ ΜΑΛΛΟΝ ΥΜΕΡΙΣ ... ΦΕΡΕΤΕ ΤΩΝ ΠΕΤΕΙΝΩΝ· ΤΙΣ ΔΕ
... Υ ΛΙΩΝ Λ ΜΕΡΙ ΛΝΟΝ ΔΥ ... ΤΗΝ ΡΙΜΝΑ ΔΕ ΕΙΝΑΙ ΕΠΙ ΤΗΝ ΗΛΙΚΙΑΝ
ΤΟ ΥΠ ΛΙΧΥΝ ΕΙΣ ... ΙΟΥ ΔΕ Ε ... ΧΙΣΤΟΝ ΔΥ ... ΛΣΘΕ ΤΙ ΠΕΡΙ ΤΩΝ ΛΟΙΠΩ(Ν)
ΕΡΙ· ΛΕΓΩ ΡΙΝ ΟΥ ΔΕ ΣΟ ... ΤΑ ΚΡΙΝΑ ΠΩΣ ΑΥΞΑΝΕΙ ΟΥ ΚΟΠΙΑ ΟΥΔΕ
... ΕΝ ΤΟΥΤΩΝ ΡΙ ΔΕ ΕΝΑΙΣΡΟΙ ΣΗΛΙΕ ... ΜΙΟΝ ΕΝ ΤΗ Ι ΚΟ ΣΗΙ Λ ... ΛΑΜ ... ΟΥ ΠΕΡΙΕΒΑΛΕΤΟ
ΕΙΣ ΚΛΕΙΒΑΝΟΝ ΒΑΛΛΟΜΕΝΙΝ Ο ... ΡΟΝ ΤΟΝ ΧΟΡΤΟΝ ΟΝΤΑ ΚΑΙ ΑΥΡΙΟΝ
... ΛΙΑΣ ΟΡΙΚΟ ΠΙΣΤΟΙ ΚΑΙ ... ΔΙΕ Λ ΗΖΗΤΕΙΤΕ ΤΙ ΦΑΓΗΤΕ ΚΑΙ ΤΙ ΠΙΗ
ΤΕ ... ΗΜΕΤΕΩ ... ΖΕΣΣΕ ... ΠΑΝΤΑ ΤΑ ΑΙΘΝΗ ΤΟΥ ΚΟΣΜΟΥ ΕΠΙ
ΖΗΤ ... ΥΜΩΝ ΔΕ Ο ΠΡΟΙΣΕΝ Ο ... ΧΡΗΖΕΤΕ ΤΟΥΤΩΝ ΠΛΗΝ ΖΗΤΕΙΤΕ
ΒΟΥ ΤΟ ΜΙΚΡΟΝ ΠΟΙΜΝΙΟΝ ΟΤΙ ... ΑΥΤΑ ΠΡΟΣΤΕΘΗΣΕΤΑΙ ΥΚΑΙ ... ΜΗ ΦΟ
ΤΗΝ ΒΑΣΙΛΕΙΑΝ· ΠΩ ΛΗΣΑΤ ... ΗΥΔΟΚΗΣΕΝ Ο ΠΡ ΥΜΩΝ ΔΟΥΝΑΙ ...
... ΣΣΥΝΗΝ· ΠΟΙ ΣΑΤΕ ΕΑΥ ... ΤΑ ΥΠΑΡΧΟΝΤΑ ΥΜΩΝ ΚΑΙ ΔΟΤΕ ΕΛΕΗ
ΡΟ ... ΑΝΕΚΛΙΠΤΟΝ ΕΝ ΤΟΙ ... ΒΑΛΛΑΝΤΙΑ ΜΗ ΠΑΛΑΙΟΥΜΕΝΑ ΑΝΕΚ
ΔΕΟ ΣΔΙ ΑΦΘΕΙΡΕΙ ΟΣ ... ΙΣ ΟΠΟΥ ΚΛΕΠΤΗΣ ΟΥΚ ΕΝΓΙΖΕΙ ΟΥ
ΔΙΑ ΛΙΩΝ ΕΣΤΗ ... ΕΟ ... ΗΘΗΣΑΥΡΟΣ ΥΜΩΝ ΕΚΕΙ ΚΑΙ ΗΚΑΡ
... ΥΧΝΕΙ ΚΝ ΟΣΦ ... ΣΦΥΕΣ ΠΕΡΙ ΕΖΩΣΜΕΝΑΙ ΕΝ ΚΑΙ
ΤΙΝ ΚΝ ΕΑΥΤ ... ΠΟΙ ΣΙ ΠΡΟΣ ΔΕΧΟΜΕΝ ...
... ΤΑ ... ... ΟΝ Τ ... ΙΩΝ· ΤΙ ΔΕ ΑΛ
... ΚΑ ΜΑΚΑΡΙΟΣ ΔΟΥΛΟΣ ...

ΙΝΑΤΟΙCΑ..ΩΤΗΝΗ̣CΙΟΛ
ΚΑΡΔΙΑΝΤΟ̣ΥΧΡΟΝΙΖΕΙΟ
ΠΑΙΔΑCΚΑΙΤΑCΠΑΙΔΙCΚΑCΕ
CΘΙΕΙΝΗΠΙ̣ΝΚΟΤΟΥCΙΑΓΟ̣ΥCCEΙ
ΗΟΥΡΕΙΝΟCΕΚΕΙΚΑΙΔΙΧΟΤΟΜΗCΕΙ
ΤΩΝΑΠΙ̣CΤΩΝΘΗCΕΙ ΕΚΕΙΝΟCΟ
ΤΟΥΚΑΙ ΠΟ̣ΙΗCΑCΠΡΟCΤΟΘΕΛΗ̣ΜΑ
ΛΗΓΝΟΥCΠΟΙΗCΑCΔΕΑΞΙΑΠΛ
ΩΕΔΟΘΗ ΠΟ̣ΛΥ ΖΗΤΗ̣ΘΗCΕΤΑΙΠ̣ΟΝ
ΠΕΡΙCCΟΤΕΡΟΝΑΙΤΗCΟ̣ΥCΙΝΑΥΤΟ̣Ν
ΚΑΙΤΙΔΕ̣ΛΘΕΙΗ̣ΜΑΝΗΦΑΗΒΑΠ̣
ΠΩCCΥΝΕΧΟ̣ΜΕΘCΟ̣ΥΤΕΛΕ̣CΘ̣Η̣
ΝΟΜ̣ΗΝΔΟΥΝΑΙΕΠΙΤΗCΓΗCΟΥΧΙΕΤΩ̣Υ
ΕCΤΑΙΑΠΟΤΟ̣ΥΝ̣ΥΝΕΝΟΙΚΩΙΕΝΙΠΕΕΤΕ
ΕΠΙΑΥCΙΝ...CΑ̣ΙΕΠΙΤΡΙCΙΝΔΙΑ̣ΜΕΡΙC
ΠΡΕΠΙΠΟCΙΝΜΗΤΗ̣Ρ̣ΕΠΙΤΗΝΘΥΓΑΤΕΡΑ
ΠΙΕΝΘΕΡΑΕΠΙΤΗΝΝΥ̣CΦΗΝΑΥΤΗCΚΑΙΝΥ
ΕΛΕΓΕ̣Ν ΔΕ̣ΚΑΙΤΟΙCΟΧΛΟΙCΟΤΑΝΙ̣ΔΗΤΕ
ΥΑΝΑΠΟΔΥCΜ̣ΩΝ ΕΡΧΟ̣ΜΕΝΗΝΕΥ̣ΘΕΩCΛΕΓΕΤΕ
ΥΔ̣ΩΡΟΚΑΙΤ̣ΑΝΟΤ̣ΑΝΝΠΝΕΟΝΤΑ̣ΛΕΓΕΤΕΚΑΥΔ̣
ΡΙΝΕΤΑΙΥΠΟΚΡΙΤΑΙΤΟΠΡΟCΩΠΟΝΤ̣ΥΓΑΝΟΥΚΑΙΤΗ̣C̣
ΚΙΜΑΖΕΙΝΠΛΗΝΤΟΝΚΑΙ̣ΡΟΝΤΟ̣ΥΤ̣
ΑΦΕΑΥΤΩΝΟΥΚΡΕΙΝΕΤΕΤΟΔΙΚΑ̣
ΔΙΚΟΥCΟΥ ΕΠΙΤΟΝΑΡΧΟΝΤΕΝ
ΔΙΑΥΤΟΥΜΗΠΟΤΕΚΑΤΑCΥ̣Ρ̣
ΔΩCΕΙCΕΤΩΙΠΡΑΚΤΟΡΙΚΑ
ΛΕΓΩCΟΙΟΥΜΗΕΞΕΛΗ
CΩΤΟΔΑΠΑ̣ΡΗCΑΝΔΕ̣
ΡΙΤΩΝΓΑΛΙΛΑ̣

long scrolls favoured by both Jewish and classical scribes (see Plate 16). All these early examples of New Testament texts have been bought on the European antiquities' market since the 1930s. Most of them seem to have come from a single ancient library in Egypt, perhaps that of a Christian meeting-house or an early church; their precise origins will never be known; nowadays they bear the names of the industrialists or bankers who bought them. Remarkably, all these documents were written in exactly the same style of handwriting as the secular documents from Hellenistic Egypt. The bulk of them were written 70 or 100 years after the Rylands Fragment. Some of them are virtually complete books and remarkably well preserved; indeed, some of them still have fragments of their original bindings. But, of course, they are but a tiny fraction of what was once buried in the cities and sands of Egypt, and are but a hint of what once must have been. For these are but the fragments from provincial libraries; the diversity of the contents of the great libraries, such as those of Alexandria and Pergamum subsidized by kings, must have been astonishing. One of the reasons why it is so difficult today to isolate the influences, the styles and manners of the Gospel writers is that we lack detailed knowledge of the literary world of this vital period. What remains, however, is the environment in which they were found, the ruins of these early provincial cities.

These Hellenistic desert cities had been established in Egypt as commercial enterprises, part of huge irrigation and farming schemes that thrived for centuries in the Egyptian oases until their fields salted up and became useless. From the governors and state officials to the workmen and slaves, the people of these cities were bound together in a tight bureaucratic organization that carefully extracted the maximum it could from the land and the peasants. The cities were Hellenistic microcosms, mixtures of Egyptian, Greek and Jewish cultures set side by side, sometimes with an Egyptian-style temple at the centre that housed hybrid Greek gods. Invariably there would be a sandy Greek *agora* and modern bathhouses made for aspiring Hellenes. From the cemeteries of such towns has come a brilliant series of life-like portraits. These pictures were first hung in the houses when their owner was alive, then after death buried with the owner as part of the coffin. These are startling portraits. Real people look at you, their ancient eyes seem to catch yours: young men, women, girls and boys, brothers, bureaucrats, hard-faced matrons all dressed up in the Roman manner, sparkling sometimes with gold-leaf ornaments – Hellenistic Egyptians getting on with life in their brand-new cities, the people who wrote and read the oldest Gospels that we have today.

PLATE 17 (Opposite): Karanis, one of the numerous Graeco-Roman cities of the Egyptian Fayuum where most of the oldest Bible fragments were found. The desert will preserve organic material such as papyrus almost indefinitely.

Just as Christianity must have come to these desert cities from the Egyptian capital, Alexandria, so Christianity and its texts must also have spread right through the eastern Empire at this time. Most of the literary texts in the Roman world were written by professional scribes, usually slaves working in commercial studios, where publishers controlled production lines of scribes producing hand-written editions of thousands of copies. These Egyptian Gospel texts, however, were not written in these conditions but were the work of clerks and businessmen, men who usually wrote only of their work and family affairs, but who now copied out these Christian texts in their spare time so that they might have a copy for themselves. Though sometimes their handwriting imitates the formal elegance of the professionals, the natural speed and economy of their style gives them away – perhaps explains, as well, why these oldest Gospels are not written upon the traditional scroll but in the convenient notebooks, the *codices*, usually used by merchants. Paul also used notebooks; in a letter to his friend Timothy he asks that 'when you come, bring the cloak I left with Carpus at Troas, and the books above all my notebooks' (2 Timothy 4:13 NEB).

The rapid workmanlike style of these ancient Gospels also shows that in those days there was little sense of reverence surrounding these notebooks – unlike the books of the Hebrew Bible, for example, which were made with ritual care and precise control. These Gospels were made by Christians for their own use, not for ritual, but for reading. Nonetheless, the dozen surviving texts show a remarkable consistency and care in their copying; there is not one line of the New Testament whose meaning has been deeply compromised by the discovery of alternative versions among these texts. These night-time scribes did not, however, limit their activity to the Four Gospels. Certainly, the collection of books that is now the New Testament had not then been gathered together as a single volume and there were also many other Christian texts of similar age, many of which have also been found in Egypt. Grenfell and Hunt's first publication of their discoveries, in 1897, was of two ancient and fragmentary documents that recorded some previously unknown 'Sayings of Jesus'. It caused an appropriate sensation for here was an ancient collection of Jesus' own words in a form that possibly pre-dated the more elaborate Gospels. It reminded many scholars of the ghostly source 'Q' – Quelle (see page 190) that had been detected in the Gospels of Luke and Matthew. Many Christians, too, were delighted to read sayings that some sections of the early church had attributed to Jesus himself. A complete version of these 'Sayings of Jesus' was found in Egypt just after the Second World War; its ancient title proved to be 'The Gospel of Thomas'. But by that time, Grenfell and Hunt's publication had introduced several of these new sayings of Jesus into church literature by way of the hymn book – 'Raise the stone and you will find me, cleave the wood and I am there' being perhaps the most celebrated example. It seems clear that there were also more of these 'Sayings of Jesus' circulating in the early church, 'sayings' that were not included in the Gospels, and have now been lost to us. This hints at a vital oral tradition inside the early church that went right back to the first days of Christianity when the faith was preached just as Jesus had; when the faith was spread by word of mouth with passion and conviction and not be the written word. In such a world the written Gospels introduced a barrier between men and the passionate words of the Apostles, a barrier encrusted too with all the artificialities of literary Hellenistic Greek.

These earliest writings, then, represent the beginnings of the formalization, the ordering of Christianity. Perhaps this is why the Bible scholar, R.H. Lightfoot, declared that the writing of the New Testament represented the Church's first collective loss of nerve. But then, Jesus' church and its Bible both have a most human history.

Gospel Beginnings: Antioch and the Evangelists

In Jesus' day, the city of Antioch on the river Orontes was one of the largest cities in the world. It was also close to Jerusalem. Today the ancient city and its port have long been silted up by the river and both are buried in thirty feet and more of mud. Great Antioch had been one of sixteen similarly named cities built by the Syrian dynasty founded by one of Alexander's generals. To the Romans it held the essence of the East, filled with the fierce pleasures and exotic aesthetics of oriental Hellenism. After Olympia in Greece, Antioch had the most famous Games in the world. Its chariot races were legendary, as were the riots of the fans. Antioch had a two-mile long main street, the first in the world to be paved with marble and donated, it was said, by the admiring King Herod of Judaea. The only thing the people of Antioch took seriously, boasted Libanius, a local philosopher, was love – to this he might have added, good food, good houses and a healthy scepticism. Excavations in the city suburbs have uncovered the finest mosaics of the ancient world, an amazing series of brilliant floors covered in gambolling *putti* and *erotes*; here also are portraits of the city's actors, charioteers, and gladiators. And mosaics that show, too, the great market that ran along the two-mile street covered with pillared arcades and backed by great merchant houses and the city temples. There are lucky mosaics as well, pictures of phallic hunchbacked dwarves, the evil eye pierced with a dozen sharp, superstitious amulets. And from the houses of international

[187]

merchants there are exquisite pictures of old Neptune and fishermen: great seascapes filled with fish and birds, winds and gods, all fashioned in the luxurious style for which Antioch was famous. Downriver near the springs of the rich suburb of Daphne, it was said that Apollo had chased the eponymous nymph who had turned into a laurel bush in his arms. There it was that Antony had taken Cleopatra in the first year of their affair; and shortly afterwards canny Herod, their reluctant supporter, paved the city's straight street to honour Octavian, Antony's executioner. Here, too, after the destruction of Judaea and the burning of Jerusalem, Titus came in triumph and erected an altar inscribed 'from the spoils of Judaea'. He also built at Daphne a huge temple on the ruin of the city's largest synagogue.

Jews had lived in Antioch since its beginnings and they had prospered with the city. Rabbis from Jerusalem visited Antioch regularly to collect tithes and attend the court of the Roman governors of Syria, and in turn many of Antioch's devout Jews returned to Jerusalem in their old age. These close connections with Jerusalem made it inevitable that Antioch would be among the first cities to receive the Christian missionaries when they started to move through the Roman East after the death of Jesus. The Book of Acts tells us that Paul, Peter and many others of those early preachers went to Antioch. It tells us, too, it was in Antioch that the followers of Jesus were first called Christians, that the phrase 'the catholic church' – i.e. the 'universal' church – was also first used at Antioch and this was the first indication of the church's ambitions to penetrate the gentile, imperial world. It was from Antioch, then, that the Christian church entered the big cities of the Roman Empire. But our knowledge of these vital years is founded solely upon the Book of Acts and later church tradition. There is no mention at all of this period of Christian history in any other literature. We know only what later churches wanted to tell us. And this is also true of the beginnings of the Gospels. We are left with the evidence that can be gleaned from the Four Gospels themselves and a large number of conflicting statements made in the writings of the early church fathers.

So the beginnings of the Gospels are almost impossible to find. Certainly they were written several generations after Christ. Like Jesus who, John's Gospel tells us, wrote but once – a mysterious line upon the sand (John 8:6) – the earliest church was much more interested in word-of-mouth preaching than in the composition of written texts. The first faith was verbal and passionate. Paul's letters, he says, were written because he could not visit the recipients himself; for him, writing was second best. In this sense, it is true to say that the Gospels were the churches' first loss of nerve, the first dilution of the word that previously had been spread directly from one person to another. For the Gospels were compiled so that the stories about Jesus told by the first preachers would be preserved for the following generations. But of course they reflect something else too: the needs of the audience for whom they were written; the needs that is of the church at the time of the death of the Apostles. The New Testament's Four Gospels are not simply the authentic unadulterated work of four biographers who followed Jesus around on earth recording his words and deeds, but authentic witnesses of the extraordinary explosion of Christianity that burst out around the Mediterranean in the first and second centuries.

The Four Gospels began as a series of anecdotes, proverbs, reminiscences and stories; they were 'sayings of Jesus' which circulated among the earliest preachers of the faith as they founded churches in Syria, Asia Minor, Egypt, Greece and Italy. Only Matthew's Gospel had no traditional connection with Antioch; it was written, according to tradition, in various places between Ethiopia and Sicily. Of the other three, John's Gospel has an authentic trace of the Christian teaching that is known to have developed in Antioch and the Gospels of Mark and Luke are directly linked to the city by early church historians. It is said that Peter went to Antioch and preached there in a cave high above the city – a cave that Crusaders later decorated with a fine starred facade. Excavations at this church, claimed to be the oldest in the world, have uncovered mosaic floors that date, perhaps, to the fourth century but certainly no earlier. At the back of the church, however, by the altar is a spring of fine cold water that, legend tells, Mark the Evangelist used to make his ink when he took dictation from St Peter, who was relating his experiences in the inner circle of disciples that had surrounded Jesus Christ. This text, it is said, became Mark's Gospel. But an equally strong tradition tells us that Peter *really* dictated the Gospel to Mark in Rome, and that after Peter's martyrdom Mark travelled to Alexandria where he finished writing a public Gospel and then wrote two 'secret' ones which, though they are mentioned in second-century writings, have since disappeared. Unfortunately the earliest surviving writings of the church at Rome, the Epistles of Clement, do not mention Mark's Gospel; a lack of knowledge of this allegedly 'Roman' book which strongly suggests a more eastern origin for it; possibly Antioch as the tradition says. Similarly Luke's Gospel, too, is traditionally associated with Antioch; Luke was the secretary of Paul and he also wrote the Book of Acts which, though separated in the traditional order of the New Testament Books, is a direct continuation of his Gospel. But it is also said that, after escaping martyrdom with Paul in Rome, Luke went to Greece to write both his Gospel and the Book of Acts, and he died there, a bachelor, at an advanced age.

Each of these ancient stories has an equally convincing alternative, and for every alternative there is a fresh objection. But the very diversity in the accounts allows all these stories and traditions their own element of truth. Just as Hellenism itself was international, so was Christianity. From the earliest days, the faith and its books were both portable, as Paul's note to Timothy about his notebooks clearly shows (see page 186). Today, international newspapers and magazines are written in several different countries, then edited and published in many more and sold and exchanged in yet others; so the geographical spread of these stories of the Gospel's origins - Rome, Alexandria, Antioch and all the rest – reflects Christianity's precocious internationalism. The Four Gospels are not the writings of four men, but the products of different traditions, different churches, that had accumulated many of the same stories of Jesus and his life. These Gospels were collected and most carefully collated by these early churches to make the Four Books that we have today.

Of these four Gospels, John's is clearly the odd one out. It has different stories and themes in it and it is more abstract in its expression. None of the other three, for example, can begin to approach the intellectual beauty of John's first lines, 'In the beginning was the Word, and the Word was with God, and the Word was God'; these sentiments had been part of Middle Eastern theologies for thousands of years, but are here set to work for a new faith. In this, John's Gospel seems to inhabit something of the same world as Paul's Epistles; both are addressed to an erudite, middle-class Hellenistic audience. John's abstract definitions of God and Jesus later raised many an eyebrow among the fathers of the early church. On the other hand, the other three Gospels are not only different in their tone to that of John, but are also extremely closely related to each other in the stories that they tell and the words and sentences that they use to tell them. So close are these Gospels to each other that comparable passages in them can be analysed, set side by side, in the manner of the extracts that describe Jesus' trial (see pages 175–176). Clearly these three Gospels are intimately related, their texts interdependent and interwoven. For this reason they are called the Synoptic Gospels. In the nineteenth century, when analysis of the Gospels began in earnest, it was quickly seen that some of the long-accepted traditions concerning these three Gospels were mistaken. St Augustine's statement, for example, that Matthew's Gospel, the longest and most eloquent of the three, had been the first to be written and that Mark's shorter, less-polished Gospel stood in relationship to it 'as a footman', was wrong. In fact, analysis showed that the shorter, less polished text of Mark was embedded in the texts of both Matthew's *and* Luke's Gospel. This meant that far from being a 'footman', Mark's Gospel had provided much source material for the other two. Such analysis also showed a second source of the stories which was shared by both Matthew and Luke and this second group was called 'Q', abbreviated, it is said, from the German *Quelle* or source. It was reasonably suggested that as both the Gospels of Matthew and Luke were primarily based upon Mark plus Q, the differences between the two of them represented the separate traditions of two different churches. More importantly, the analysis of Mark and Q also led to the startling realization that it was unlikely that these same two Gospels, Matthew and Luke, had been written by people who had actually known Jesus on earth. No first-hand witness of the events that these Gospels describe would have needed to draw upon earlier written sources for his text, as both Matthew and Luke had done. Of the other two Gospels, Mark's, though heavily edited, was conceivably the work of a man who had known Jesus; while John's Gospel, scholars generally agreed, was the last to have been written, perhaps at the ending of the first century, but this was based more on opinion than on hard fact.

But even if it could be *proved* that John's Gospel had been the first of the four to be written down, there would still be considerable confusion as to who 'John' was. For the various styles of the New Testament texts ascribed to John – the Gospel, the letters, and the Book of Revelations – are each so different in their style that it is extremely unlikely that they had been written by one person. Modern theory inclines to the opinion that these writings of 'John' are the work of a group of scholars in Asia Minor who followed an Apostle John, perhaps John the son of Zebedee, Jesus' cousin. One tradition tells that John wrote his Gospel in Ephesus in Asia Minor; at Ephesus there is a 'Tomb of John' that has been revered since the second century as the tomb of John the Apostle, and this is a very early date for such a shrine, reaching back almost into the generations of the successors of the Apostles. After the calamities of Jerusalem in AD 70 and the growing hostility of the Jews to the Christians, early church tradition tells that many of its founders moved to Asia Minor – one of Antioch's first bishops is said to have heard 'John' preach when he had been a boy. But then, John's Gospel also bears strong traces of Egyptian Alexandria; it holds many of the abstractions and expressions invented and used by the religious philosophers of that most learned city. Once more the circle of probabilities and contradictions starts to spin. Recent linguistic analysis of all four Gospels, however, has tied them not to these grand cities of the Empire but to the verbal culture of Palestine itself. The construction of their Greek texts, the shading and colouring of the writing strongly suggest that much of them has been translated from Palestinian Aramaic, Jesus' own language. In this ancient international world where the sayings of a Palestinian holy man could convert congregations in Asia Minor, in Italy, Greece and Egypt, the Gospels had picked up something of the flavour of the international cities while, at the same time, they had held true to their own beginnings and the sayings of the man, Jesus, at the centre of the faith.

'Crooked harps and customs'

> I hate, in Rome, a Grecian town to find:
> To see the scum of Greece transplanted here;
> received like Gods, is what I cannot bear.
> Obscene Orontes diving underground,
> Conveys his wealth to Tiber's hungry shores,
> and fattens Italy with Foreign whores:
> hither their crooked harps and customs come;
> all find receipt in hospitable Rome.

So, in Dryden's spry translation, Juvenal's lament runs its curiously modern course. As Juvenal wrote, the 'obscene Orontes', Antioch's river, was not only bringing 'hungry Greeks' to Rome, all 'quick witted, brazen faced and fluent tongued', but also the first Christian missionaries too; another group of quick-witted, streetwise foreigners. Ancient graffiti scratched upon the plastered walls of Pompeii and Ostia hint that Christianity was already installed in those ports by AD 79. The Book of Acts tells us that Paul's arrival in Rome – innocently welcomed by a group of Jewish elders who had no idea of the problems Paul would cause them when Nero began to persecute the first Roman Christians, after blaming them for the disastrous fire of AD 64 – was accompanied by an attack upon the city's Jewish community. Unlike the later persecutions which revolved around issues of loyalty and imperial politics, Nero's little pogrom was based on malice and expediency. Tradition tells that St Peter was crucified during these Neronic persecutions and buried, eventually, under the site of the present altar of St Peter's church; nowadays in weekly services the Pope sits sixty feet above the founder of his church.

Despite persecution, by the second century Christianity had spread, as Paul had directed it, outside the Jewish communities and into pagan Rome's middle and upper classes. The remains of the early churches, simple meeting-houses, have sometimes been discovered deep under the foundations of Rome's great churches. The basilicas of Santa Cecilia, San Clemente and Santa Pudenziana were all founded in the ordinary Roman town houses of Cecilia, Clement and Pudenziana, these citizens attaining their sanctity in later times when it was imagined that the churches built above them must have held the tombs of martyrs. So the beautifully painted semi-circular apse of San Clemente stands directly over Clement's buried house of the second century; the nave being built over the atrium of the house – an open courtyard that Clement and his successors seem to have adapted as a shelter for the sick and poor. Out of such beginnings arose the beautiful church, just as the vast baroque shell of St Peter's now shelters the simple shrine of the Apostle.

At some point before the church of San Clemente was built, the atrium of Clement's house had also served as a pagan temple, a shrine of Mithras, a god who, like Jesus, had been born in an eastern cave but who had come to Rome not from Judaean Bethlehem but from distant Persia. The cult of Mithras had been taken up with great enthusiasm by the Roman legions and had travelled with them from Iran to Rome, to Tunis, to the Rhine and even on to London and Hadrian's Wall. Mithras' cult satisfied many of the same urges that would also attract people to Christianity. It was a brotherhood where rank and mutual obligation were based not upon accepted social codes but on the secret bonds of a closed circle, an underground network of close allegiances operating right across the strong social fabric of the Empire. Juvenal's complaints were not only directed at the odd Greek juggler or Syrian sex maniac, but also against these underground sects which were flowing down the Orontes into the Tiber and slowly eroding the public structures of Roman society. For Juvenal and for many other noble Romans, their city was mankind's greatest creation. But by Juvenal's day the public ambition and high sense of honour that had once fuelled the system and built an empire was threatened by the foreign ideas and cults that Rome's internationalism had brought home.

Eastern religions, Christianity among them, were attracting support at all levels of society. Ancient foreign faiths quickly became urban hybrid sects. Outside the great cities of the Roman east, the vast mass of the population in the Empire were poor villagers who kept their native faiths with them as they passed through the Roman worlds as soldiers, servants and slaves. In Rome these foreign faiths were often reduced to dull supersitions or secret cabals of initiates; they also quickly became an unwitting expression of resistance to the imperial machine. Similarly, the great eastern cities, those marvellously mixed communities bound together in a economic unity, had engendered their own peculier sects; faiths that were often born of rich, disaffected groups of people who viewed the imperial order as a hindrance to their own personal salvation. Often influenced by Hellenized versions of local religions, these sects usually created their own rites and lurid, savage and frequently orgiastic rituals through which, it was claimed, one could gain through physical ecstasy and extremity, self-awareness and ultimate truth. Passing through the Empire many of these faiths were also finding their way to Rome.

In the Roman basilica of the Porta Maggiore is rare and tangible evidence of these faiths which competed with Christianity and which would influence inadvertently the words of its Bible. So perfect is this little underground building that something of the ancient ambiance is still held under its stuccoed vaults and arches. Here is much that Christianity would adapt for its own purposes; the use of a basilica for a place of worship; the gesture of out-stretched hands as an attitude of prayer, which appears in the poses of some of the figures on the elegant stuccoed reliefs on the walls and ceilings.

Many of the strange sects held Persian, even Indian, conceptions of the world in them: universes that were held in two oppositions, dualisms of goodness and sin, of light and darkness, of god and the devil, opposing forces that were drawn up to face each other in a creative tension. The powers of darkness controlled man's world. Light and intellect were their opponents; earthly organization and authority were its allies; and the organized Christian church was seen to have been made by the Devil to pervert true faith. Among these underground sects, people aimed for perfection. They might eat, for example, what they thought of as magical foods, like moist cucumbers, glistening and filled with light. Later, the residue would pass through the body and emerge as dark excrement, while the light element emerged in orgasm as semen. Many of the rituals involved the anointing and swallowing of this sacred substance, an orgiastic ritual that had been the bane of the Old Testament prophets a thousand years before and now afflicted the early church. Paul in his Epistles clearly defines the differences between sacred and profane love – to many Hellenistic Christians these differences were not quite as clear.

A splendid Christian legend tells of St Peter's combat with another of these eastern prophets who was preaching salvation at a price to the people of Rome. Magnificent Simon Magus, 'the Power of God', was a Samaritan magician among other things and was said to fly about through the air with the greatest of ease. Simon had been baptized as a Christian in Palestine, then adapted many Christian rituals to his own purposes, despite the fact that when he had offered to buy Peter's holy powers from him to add to his magical repertoire, he had received a blast worthy of John Knox. 'I perceive', says Peter in the Book of Acts (8:9ff.), 'that thou art in the gall of bitterness, and in the bond of iniquity'. Undeterred, Simon, like Peter, went on to Rome accompanied by the beautiful Helen, whom he had reputedly rescued from the fleshpots of Levantine Tyre where he had recognized her as the First Principle of All Things. Helen the Harlot, as the Christians called her, was Simon Magus' Mary Magdalene (it has even been suggested that Simon himself is but a malicious literary caricature of St Paul). In Rome, according to the legend, Simon the flying prophet got his come-uppance. One day when he was flitting around the Roman forum in a display of religious aerobatics he was gunned down by St Peter's prayers and suffered a broken ankle. This legend, however, is but a pretty allegory of the very serious threat that he and many others like him posed to the Christian church. For not all of St Peter's competitors were on this Barnum and Bailey level. Many of them were pious and learned men with different views of Jesus and of God.

They preached as confidently as did Paul, who also had never seen Jesus, and they felt secure enough in their understanding of the true religion to claim their faith as divine, even to the extent of disagreeing with some of Jesus' disciples. And like Paul, who wrote the oldest known Christian texts of the New Testament, many other Christians were also writing mystical narrations, poems, stories, abstract speculations; these were people who saw their faith as Paul did, in terms of the culture from which they had come. By the second century, there were more than a dozen gospels circulating, along with a whole library of other texts. These included letters of Jesus to foreign kings, letters of Paul to Aristotle, histories of the disciples and of many other characters in Jesus' life and times. And despite the fact that they were all outlawed by the later church, many of these writings quietly survived in Christendom to become a source, a secret source, of mystic Christian knowledge. Indeed, their influence upon Christian art and literature is much greater than is generally realized. In a religion where faith is usually held in the written word, much of the gesture and symbolism of Christian ritual can be traced to these forgotten and once-forbidden sects.

Many of these writings were made in eastern cities like Antioch, Ephesus and Alexandria and, alongside their Christianity, they also reflected local beliefs and ways of thinking. Since the beginning of civilization many eastern religions had held that gods who died and then were resurrected, gods like Jesus, were the underlying powers that provided nature's annual fertility. Christians born in such cultures easily joined Jesus to gods like Osiris, god of the rising of rivers and the sprouting of seed. In Egypt the ancient *ankh* sign, a hiero-glyphic sign for life, became Christ's cross, the sign of lives reborn. And like

Christ, Persia's Mithras had been born in a cave and from there he sent his light to the world. Some saw in Christ's promise of salvation and redemption an immediate release from the sins of the world, a freedom that could be acted out in the age-old rites of orgiastic ritual and bacchanalia. God's universal forgiveness, as preached by Jesus, was the key to *individual* salvation; so the Gnostics believed that the church itself was a device of the devil made to keep man from God and from realizing his true nature. So powerful was the knowledge held in these sects that often it was never allowed into the light of day.

Groups of initiates practised secret faiths; they called themselves 'knowers' or Gnostics. They alone, they felt, held the keys of the universe. In all this ferment of esoterica, Jesus Christ was usually seen as an enlightened teacher, perhaps one of many – a wise man, a magi. Stories of his secret life were woven into the Gospel narratives. Second-century bishops writing of these secret Gospels say that they were only to be shown to initiates. One passage describes Jesus taking naked young men off to secret initiation rites in the Garden of Gethsemene, rites that could be duplicated in the underground lodges of the Gnostics. And like Mithraism, these sects not only operated across the social fabric of society, but penetrated different faiths as well. In the first and second centuries, they were a powerful part of the identity of the Christian church. And this, of course, is why, even today, their 'wickedness' is so reviled by the faithful. Yet in those first centuries of Christianity there was no such thing as orthodoxy; and when orthodoxy finally came, it was defined, almost inadvertently, in argument against many of these gnostic sects.

There is a strange problem of language nowadays when describing all these different sects that existed inside early Christianity. We see them from the wrong end of the telescope. We understand Christianity to be the church of Peter, Paul and Jesus of Nazareth, of the Four Gospels and a volume of accompanying holy texts. For 1800 years Christian churches have drawn common lines between true faith and heresy. Westerners, whether professing Christians or not, can usually detect the difference. But the ancient world of Peter, Paul, Simon Magus, Mark and 'John' was very different. There was a multiplicity of churches, of teachings, of holy books; it was a world with no clear Christian creed, no single body of accepted truth and no New Testament. This book, like the faith itself, was still a soup with many exotic ingredients – a mixture that went right back to the church's early years. The Book of Acts tells us there was considerable debate among the Apostles about whether or not Jesus' message should be preached to the gentiles at all. Many of Paul's letters, on the other hand, deal with the problem of whether or not this budding gentile church should be obliged to keep Jewish Law as part of the Christian faith. Clearly these churches still lacked 'orthodox' identity. And though Paul's tough arguments carried the majority of the churches with him, there remained, for example, the remnant of the first Jerusalem church that had once been led by Jesus' brother James. After persecution, we are told, the followers of James fled to Syria, where they used their own separate Gospel book, known later to the gentile church as the 'Gospel of the Hebrews'. Such divisions had been with Christianity since its beginnings. And for Romans, even this catholic soup was but one of many bowlsful steaming on the imperial table.

In the mid-second century a bishop's son, a wealthy ship-owner from Asia Minor named Marcion, made the oldest-known list of Christian books – a list of contents for a New Testament. Marcion preached a Christianity that denied all Jewish connections with Jesus and with the Old Testament. Jesus, Marcion believed, had not been born but had sprung, like Zeus, fully grown from God. This Jesus was set down on earth to preach a ministry of redemption; he offered a God who, unlike capricious and cruel Jehovah, was primarily a God of Love. Marcion thought that all Jewish connections with God had been inspired by the devil and elaborated by sinful men. None of Marcion's works have survived the wrath of the orthodox, but the church's careful and numerous attacks upon his heresies have happily, for the Bible's history, preserved many of his ideas for us, including Marcion's own list of what constituted the authentic writings of the faith. Marcion's non-Jewish Bible is necessarily rather short, consisting of some of Paul's letters and just one Gospel, basically Luke's but carefully abbreviated to exclude all mention of the Jews! A little later, however, the church itself adopted Marcion's notion of defining orthodoxy by listing a sacred canon of texts – the Christian Bible – and then attacking those who would disagree with or alter it. So the *idea* of the Bible as a single, sacred unalterable corpus of texts began in heresy but was then extended and used by churchmen in *their* efforts to define orthodoxy.

A Roman document written just a few years after Marcion's preserves part of another list of sacred Christian texts. Written about AD 170, this is called the Muratorian Canon after the eighteenth-century historian Lodovico Muratori who first recognized its significance. In very rough Latin, the ancient author seems to list four Gospels including Luke and John and, in all probability, that of Mark, though the text is very damaged. It also lists the majority of the other New Testament texts, except some of Paul's letters. But, although it rejects Marcion's writings together with many other early Christian texts, it also includes in its New Testament two now long-forgotten texts. Interestingly, this fragment also rejects, as modern Bibles do, a text known as the 'Shepherd of Hermas', a Roman collection of sayings that reflect some of the oldest rituals and traditions of the Roman church, and which, it has even been proposed, is so early that parts of it might even underlie some passages in the Four Gospels themselves! The little Muratorian fragment of seventy lines, ill-written and badly spelt, is our first indication that the New Testament we know today was being compiled during this period in the late second century.

[197]

Making the Choice: Irenaeus of Lyon

The eastern gods were not only flowing down Antioch's Orontes into the Roman Tiber, but also into every province in the Empire. In the mid-second century the river Rhône in Gaul carried Christian missionaries from the churches of Asia Minor to the town of Lyon; Greek-speaking bishops and pastors who had been trained by men like Bishop Ignatius who, early church histories tell, was a successor of St Peter as Bishop of Antioch. These were men grounded in the earliest traditions of the church. Lyon had been founded in AD 43 on the orders of the Senate as a new city for retired legionaries. Roman engineers built an enormous system of aqueducts to bring water to the top of a rocky spur standing over the misty confluence of the rivers Rhône and Saône, and there they placed a splendid hillside city with theatres, public squares and courtyards and a huge temple for the eastern goddess Cybele, all set upon terraces overlooking the plain below. And so successful was this elegant new town that it became the region's capital. Here, Herod's fractious relatives had passed their last years in exile and, it is even said, the notorious Salome found her burial place. And here, too, from the east had come not only Christians, but followers of Persian Mithras and Cybele.

'If you wish to know the mortal reposing here,' says a Greek gravestone excavated at Lyon, 'there is nothing to hide; of his works the inscription here says all. Euternios is his surname, Julianos his name; Laodicea his country, an admirable ornament of Syria: His lineage was of note on his father's side, and his mother was of similar fine rank. He was of service to his fellows and just to everyone, earning in return the affection of all. When he spoke with the Celts, [i.e. the native population of Gaul] persuasion ran from his mouth. He travelled in many countries; he knew numerous people and was courageous in foreign lands. He travelled in ships on the sea without respite, bringing to the Celts and the Western lands all that God required to be brought from the East. Because he was the man he was, he was fertile in all things; because he loved, he pushed the three tribes of Celts towards dignity'. Julianos from Syria was a good Hellene.

Lyon's first Christian Bishop, Pothinus, had come from Smyrna with Irenaeus, an assistant, who like Julianos would learn the barbaric local language so that he could preach the word of God to the Gauls. By Pothinus' day, official Roman attitudes toward the Christian church had changed from general disinterest to erratic persecution and many Christians now faced such capricious torments with a passive courage. Their new faith, their new-found community in Christ, gave them a strength that often preferred death to apostasy. This exclusive Christian God could not recognize the Emperor's divinity; in the eyes of the imperial administration this was clearly a political issue. Juvenal's complaint against all the foreignness that was washing through old Rome, diluting the original force of the empire, was a symptom of a common urban anxiety, and many provincial administrators were also finding difficulty in coming to terms with the ever-more exotic world of the enlarging empire. Early in the second century Pliny the Younger who was then serving as governor in the Asia Minor province of Bithynia, had uncovered some of these new Christian groups and wrote directly to the emperor. 'It is my custom, Lord Emperor, to refer to you all questions of which I am in doubt.' He had found that these Christians, who were widespread throughout his province, met 'to recite by turns, a form of words to Christ as God', that they bound themselves by oaths not to steal, not to commit adultery or lie, and then to eat together. Here was something strange thought Pliny, and because they would not worship the divine emperor, he tortured two maidservants called 'deacon-esses', but discovered from them, he reported, 'nothing but perverse and extravagent superstitions'.

In reply, the Emperor Trajan told Governor Pliny that Christians were 'not to be sought out' and that, if they were accused, they were to be released 'if they worshipped the gods'. But, slowly, opposition stiffened. After a testy interview with the Emperor Trajan, during which Bishop Ignatius of Antioch had told this earthly divinity that he was mistaken, Ignatius was taken to Rome in chains and thrown to the wild beasts in a public stadium. And this, he wrote, was exactly what he desired, 'the wheat of God . . . ground by the teeth of wild beasts'. Ignatius' friend Bishop Polycarp of Smyrna, too, was later martyred, burned in the city's amphitheatre. According to one of Irenaeus of Lyon's pupils, Polycarp had also 'sat at the feet of John, with the rest of those that had seen the Lord'. To Irenaeus and his bishop at Lyon, it must have seemed that they had sailed away from trouble, but it was not to be. Twenty years later, Pothinus was arrested with a group of Christians and the old man was so badly beaten during an audience with the city governor that he died a few days later in a prison cell. Many other Christians were publicly tortured to death in the Lyon amphitheatre, and these were among the first martyrdoms of Western Europe. Facing such direct pressures, many Christians gave up the faith in this trial of nerve, which seems to have been the object of public butchery. Some, however, did not submit. A recent convert, the slave girl Blandina, and her friends were burned and whipped, then exposed to wild beasts and tied in nets and thrown to wild bulls. This, indeed, was a clash of wills between authority and the masses on the one hand, and a few disparate, ill-assorted citizens on the other; but those people had found fortitude and comfort in a faith that overcame all threats. Spectators in the front seats, only yards from the arena floor, must have been splashed with blood. But Blandina 'the small, the weak, the despised, had put on Christ, the great champion' and even the citizens of the world's most powerful empire could not make her do what she did not want to do. The final act of her martyrdom, which was preceded by the young girl being bound to a stake in the amphitheatre where she offered words of comfort to a boy who had chosen to die with her, is one of the most moving records of early martyrdom. Slowly, the spectacle of these quietly committed people singing their songs and praising their God in the face of such public horror began to impress the spectators. Goaded by this strange new religious resolve, the authorities increased the persecution.

Irenaeus was in Rome when Bishop Pothinus and his fellows were martyred; he had been appealing through the offices of the Roman church for the persecution of the Lyon church to be stopped. At Lyon Christians who witnessed the terrible events had seen that gnostic Christians showed themselves every bit as steadfast as Pothinus' own congregation. And in Rome, too, Irenaeus found the church filled with all manner of different cells and sects. On his return to Lyon, in the manner of revolutionaries, as ardent against schismatics in their movement as against the common foe, Irenaeus turned his attention to these internal divisions. Perhaps he wanted to make a clear statement of the faith which the audiences in the amphitheatres had seen people die for. Irenaeus felt that the faith he had known in Asia Minor was being muddied and obscured by the elaborations and secrecy of many Christian sects. Like St Paul before him, Irenaeus possessed an instinctive knowledge of the true faith, of the traditional teachings of the Asia Minor church, of the unity of God the Father and God the Son, of the redemption and salvation of all mankind. Irenaeus attacked the gnostic sects in a lengthy series of writings that first described the principles and rituals of each heresy in turn, then attacked them, root and branch, with 'common-sense' theology, insinuations and straightforward ridicule. And in the course of this vast polemic, almost inadvertently, Irenaeus also laid out the orthodoxies of the Christian church, its faith, its preaching and the books that it held as sacred authority. So popular did Irenaeus' work, *Against the Heresies*, become that fragments dating to the century of its composition have been found right through the Eastern world.

In his book, Irenaeus was not only concerned with the fragmentation of the church but also with the social effects of the Gnostics upon some of his parishioners at Lyon. He writes, for example, that 'one of our deacons received Marcus [a Gnostic] into his house. His wife, a woman of remarkable beauty, fell a victim both in mind and body to this magician, and, for a long time, travelled about with him'. 'This Marcus' Irenaeus observes, 'devotes himself especially to women, well bred, elegantly attired, whom he frequently seeks to draw after him, by addressing them in such seductive words as "I am eager to make thee a partaker of my *charis* . . . receive me as a spouse".' Many of the more innocent faithful had a somewhat mistaken notion of the proper Christian concept of love. But eventually, 'the brethren' wrote Irenaeus, 'managed to reconvert Marcus' acolyte, and the poor woman spent her whole time, afterwards, in the exercise of public confession'. Such experiences must have been extremely disruptive, and this at a time when maximum cohesion was required. Although

[200]

Irenaeus battled mightily with the theological obscurities of these disparate sects, one cannot escape the feeling that the real and the immediate problem in the church was understanding and organizing this huge wave of new-found emotion and fellowship that Christianity had brought to the world; and this was an emotional and physical problem rather than a conviction based on philosophical or theological argument.

Irenaeus fought his literary battle on a variety of fronts. He shows that Christian authority was twofold, derived both from Scripture and from the preaching of men who had known Jesus' disciples at first hand. Before Irenaeus' time, there are but sporadic allusions to Gospel texts, often occurring in the official records of the proceedings of magistrates intent upon suppressing the Christians and their books. 'What have you in your defence?' the proconsul Saturninus had asked some Christian prisoners during his investigations at the city of Scilla in Lybia in AD 180. 'The books, and the letters of a just man, one Paul,' was the reply of one of them, Speratus, before he and a little band of like-minded people were led off to their deaths thanking God and trusting in the preachings and the books of the church. A decade earlier the gnostic Marcion had produced his own strange list of Bible books to support his claim to doctrinal authenticity, and now Irenaeus did likewise but in a manner that completely éclipsed his gnostic predecessor. For Irenaeus not only gave a pedigree of authenticity to his beliefs and to the scriptures, but to the very church itself, showing the origins and the succession of the Bishops of Rome and of those of other churches too. As for the New Testament, he says, its contents had long been authenticated by the use of them by the church fathers who had gone before – men like Ignatius and Polycarp and the earlier generations, 'those that had seen the Lord'. As for the Gospels, Irenaeus said that they were four in number; like the four zones of the world, the four winds, the four divisions of man's estate, and the four forms of the first living creatures – the lion of Mark, the calf of Luke, the man of Matthew, the eagle of John. Irenaeus' defence and definition of the canon of Gospels soared like a hymn. And at a stroke, he had delineated the sacred book of the Christian church. His writings also went out and did battle with the gnostic confusers of his faith; proving that the visible world had not been produced by a demon known as Achamoth, that the very idea of the Demiurge was a 'stupid ignorance', that neither Jesus nor Almighty God was made of the Twenty-four Elements, nor the world by fifty angels. So Irenaeus' great book not only became the yardstick of major heresies and their refutations, the starting-point of later inquisitions, but simply by saying what Christianity was *not* it also, in a curious inverted way, became a definition of the orthodox faith.

Irenaeus' writings moved the church and its holy texts into a new era: Paul's end-time had been indefinitely postponed. Perhaps this is Irenaeus' greatest contribution, not his arguments against heresies, nor even his inadvertent definitions of the faith or the New Testament, but his vision of the *future* of the church. Irenaeus had seen that gnosticism was a holy anarchy, a closed sectarian faith built for a few initiates, not for the mass of the Empire's people. Irenaeus saw *his* church as the true church, as a universal church, the church of the great masses and therefore inevitably the faith of the Empire itself. That is why he gives us the history of the Roman clergy. Irenaeus laid out the precise descent of the Roman Bishops for us because he knew where the real seat of power lay; in the capital city of the Empire. And he saw the church as the future of that Empire.

This does not imply for one minute that Irenaeus ever conducted a political debate in the pages of *Against the Heresies*. He saw all its detailed arguments about the nature of God and the Universe and Jesus and the angels as being as important as the heretics did. But his arguments also held in them a particular attitude to power – both in this world and in the next, for both were linked – and this may be called a political attitude. Irenaeus held that the Gnostic's division of universal power between good and evil was an attempt to divide God himself. Just as he looked to Rome as the single seat of earthly power, so he also saw one God as the single supreme universal power. The order of heaven was to be mirrored by the earthly order. Down the ages, theologians and politicians would stake their lives for such ideas about deity and earthly rule.

Chapter Five

DEO GRATIA: BY THE GRACE OF GOD

Introduction: Pagan to Christian

'Dear me!' the Emperor Vespasian, the destroyer of Judaea, is supposed to have said when, late in the first century, he lay on his death bed, 'I must be turning into a god.' Two hundred years later, legislation and force of arms had streamlined the process. The Emperor Diocletian attained deification while he yet lived, and this was a bonus for his architects who were then able to use a temple design, a god's house, for Diocletian's tomb. Another two hundred years on, this splendid mausoleum came to house a further god; Christianity had taken over the Roman Empire and the Bible had become its imperial guidebook. Neither the Emperor Diocletian nor his subjects had been particularly convinced with this new-found role of god-on-earth, it was simply part of the new order which this clever man had imposed upon the ramshackle empire. By that time too, the empire needed a stronger cement than the notion of imperial divinity and within two generations it found it in the Christian church. The story of how Diocletian's successors achieved this brand-new balance between heavenly power and earthly rule is a story of how the Bible was interpreted to justify the Christian empire and its rulers, men who found a new balance of earthly and divine power that would last a thousand years and more. But the forms and the order of this Christian society had begun in the days of the divine emperors.

Diocletian's sober mausoleum tells a great deal about his age. Such buildings, with their high simple vaults, were intended to set the divine emperors in the darkness of infinity, a somewhat lonely ending for the career of a god on earth. In earlier centuries, the classical decorations of lintels and columns had all been filled with life. By Diocletian's day, however, these same forms, capitals, borders and friezes were used like encrusted wallpaper. Stone drills were used to make the outlines of the decorations instead of the traditional but far slower chisel work and odd bits of stone taken from older ruined buildings were often used as lintels and columns. The beautiful ancient language of classical architecture was broken down into simple functional forms that were efficient, plain and built to last.

In just this way Diocletian streamlined his empire. In the muddled era that preceded his reign the emperors had mostly ruled from Rome; many of them had been both mad and bad, the majority were murdered. Massive invasions along the imperial borders from Germany to Syria had thrown the weak government into high relief. Diocletian, an old soldier, had restructured this empire. Recognizing that it was too big to be ruled by one man, he divided it into two halves, east and west, with two rulers called *Augustii*, each one with a deputy Caesar, so that if the senior partner should suddenly die, succession would be automatic and continuity would be assured. These four posts were filled by the ablest men available, with the legions sanctioning their rule. The two *Augustii*, Diocletian and Maximian, another soldier, celebrated their official birthdays upon the same day; when they met they sat side-by-side, the elaborate imperial ritual was now doubled to accommodate the situation. And as the *Augustii* talked together they clasped hands; when they travelled together they sat in the same golden carriage. Poets said they were like the heavenly twins, but the joint deification was not like that of the lesser gods, Castor and Pollux but of Diocletian-Jupiter and Maximian-Hercules. The reality, however, was that Diocletian had chosen his old comrade as a co-ruler in their joint reign which Diocletian had determined was to be of an ungodlike, fixed term, both *Augustii* retiring simultaneously on 1 May AD 205. On that day at Nicodemia, Diocletian's capital in Asia Minor, his armies were drawn up around a steep hill crowned for the occasion with a column topped by a figure of Jupiter. The emperor, pale from a winter-long illness, wept as he addressed his troops with whom he had campaigned for so many years. He told them that his job was done and, placing his imperial cloak of purple silk around the shoulders of his successor, publicly proclaimed the two new *Augustii* and their new Caesars. Both Diocletian and Maximian left their armies and their capital cities on this same day in May, Maximian to retire, in all probability, to a fine villa in Sicily. Diocletian travelled back in a plain country carriage to Dalmatia, the land of his birth, now part of modern Yugoslavia. Diocletian's parents had been born slaves but their son now chose to live in a huge palace which would stand as an ideal of ancient imperial style for centuries. And just as the form of Diocletian's mausoleum inside his palace at Split became a favourite form for early Christian churches, so, in these last monuments of the classical pagan world you may find the foundations of Christendom.

Diocletian, the one-time countryman, remembered his childhood with nostalgia; the little stream that flowed into the sea beside his palace had once supplied him as a boy with good fat trout. Diocletian, the old soldier, planned his palace on the lines of a military fort; just like one he had already built at the oasis of Palmyra in the Syrian desert. The building was a fortified square of walls and towers with central gateways giving access to two central avenues that intersected and divided the fortress into four parts. The half-square closest to the sea housed the private apartments of Diocletian and his Empress, Pisca, the other half held the guards and palace servants. For a palace the plan was a great innovation; but then, no emperor had ever retired before.

Diocletian had long set a new style for the embattled Empire and, to support his new military order, he had already transformed the entire Empire. The old easy-going imperial ways which had allowed a general if erratic tolerance had gone. Diocletian and his co-emperors had made a state where animals, land and people were all tightly organized and controlled; one writer complained that there were more tax collectors than tax payers, but at last the unruly legions were well supplied and properly controlled and once again protected the imperial borders. Under the new organization, the old system of independent cities whose citizens owed loyalty as much to their town or municipality as to the Empire had gone. Diocletian's Empire was split into *diocese* and these were governed by officials called *vicarii* who were controlled directly from the two seats of imperial administration. The bureaucracy was supervised by the *vicarii*, civil judges and local militia. So successful, so carefully controlled was this new streamlined empire that Diocletian even tried to impose a common price on all commercial goods, in an attempt to end the ruinous inflation of previous reigns. This extraordinary decree demonstrates much of the spirit of the age. Christianity would soon inherit the same civic ethic, and the Bible would be used to illuminate and validate it: 'Since fear has always been ingrained as the most influential teacher of proper duty, it is our will that anyone who shall resist the regulation set forth in this statute, shall for his daring be subject to the death penalty . . . We therefore appeal to the loyalty of all our people that a law created for the public good may be observed with willing obedience and due fear of God.'

The beginnings of this abstract notion of the 'public good', may be traced back to the previous century when, in the reign of Antoninus Pius, a number of state employees who did not work hard had their salaries stopped; the emperor himself had commented that such people who lived off the state and gave nothing in return were 'mean and heartless'. In Diocletian's time a sort of elemental socialism had evolved, a system under a living god, a sanctified governmental structure that, under the dual pressures of invasion and inflation, was hard and cruel and emphasized conformity and regularity.

Quite obviously, the multitude of foreign faiths and sects that had long penetrated the empire – Mithraism, Christianity and all the rest of them – hardly conformed to this new imperial ideal and could easily be seen as a disruptive threat to the new order. About AD 295 the divine Diocletian issued on behalf of the four rulers of the Empire a decree that outlawed the Manichee Gnostic faith along with its 'abominable scriptures', on the grounds that this Persian hybrid had 'tampered with what has been laid down absolutely and definitely by the ancients'. 'Peace,' Diocletian observed, 'sometimes allows the spread of the most foolish and base doctrines by wicked men.' The writings of the prophet Mani proposed a different sacred order to the one formulated by Diocletian and his fellow emperors. Seven years after the start of the Manichee persecutions another imperial edict, the first of several, outlawed Christianity, ordering the submission of its clergy to the imperial cult, the shutting of churches and the destruction of the sacred books. By Diocletian's day, Christianity was especially widespread throughout the Eastern Empire, more popular even than the other eastern sects which were traditionally influential in the legions. But still, the converts to this Palestinian faith counted for less than ten per cent of the population of the Empire.

The ancient visitor to Split, arriving either as a prisoner or as a supplicant – for although Diocletian had resigned as Augustus, he still held court as a living god – would have passed through the great *Porta Auria*, the huge northern gateway, walked straight on down the main street of the palace, passing the great mausoleum to the east and the little Temple of Jupiter to the west, and into the heart of the palace, the colonnaded vestibule where visitors waited for an audience with the Emperor. Here Syrian architects had placed Roman arches high on Corinthian columns running rhythmically down towards a façade based upon the forms of a triumphal arch, a design that would later be repeated in thousands upon thousands of Christian churches. Here, however, it was the living Emperor and not the cross of Jesus that appeared at the architectural centre of the show. The decoration on a fine silver plate from Spain shows just such an imperial audience of a slightly later date, when similar palace courts had also been built in Germany, Italy and Asia Minor. On the plate, the largest central arch of three holds the seated figure of the Emperor with two little Caesars sitting on either side of him and all of them flanked by their soldiers. Around them are the fields of paradise – the heaven of good rule – filled with little *putti* that, under Christian emperors, became the angels themselves. Edward Gibbon wisely observed that the two planks of Diocletian's rule were division and ostentation.

A visitor to Diocletian's audience chamber would have felt as if he were about to meet a god. As petitioners waited for his appearance, his procession would have been making its way from the private rooms of the palace, gathering up courtiers and priests, taking the salutes of officers; a private imperial progress that a courtier compared with the coming of spring and the warming sun rising over a cold land. As the Emperor's party appeared, sacrifices were conducted in the Temple of Jupiter and simultaneously in the Emperor's own mausoleum where Diocletian himself was worshipped as Jupiter, the father of the gods. Such ritual would form part of the pagan imperial legacy to Christendom and its churches. Then, the sacrifices concluded, courtiers might address Diocletian with poems, 'Even though you have retired into one and the same place, your divinity is present everywhere, the whole earth and the seas are filled with you ... your immortal soul is greater than any power and fortune, yes, even greater than the Empire.' So this divine being entered his court and all present fell to the ground, those who were especially favoured being allowed to kiss the hem of his silken gown, a rite copied, like the palace architecture, from the east. Senior ministers were sometimes allowed to pass this atrium to meet the Emperor in the huge throne room behind the open court, where, framed by three arches looking onto the sea, Diocletian sat in state. Grouped together in a little domed room behind the atrium, in mysterious perfumed gloom, these ministers would have waited for the court chamberlains to guide them into the throne room, where, at a gesture from a court official 'the clouds [i.e. the curtains] which conceal the light of heaven' were pulled back to reveal the Emperor clothed in silks, pearls and golden fabrics, with a halo of lighted torches about his head. Shouts of praise and hymns issued from the assembly, incense, that most ancient of mediums to join heaven and earth, men and gods together, was censed all around the throne. The Emperor sat stiffly with orb and sceptre, heavy with jewellery and cosmetics, a living icon of imperial power. Here, then, the divine Diocletian conducted state business, advising the new *Augustii* and their two Caesars. And here, perhaps, he also listened to the reports of the investigations and persecutions of the Christians, for this faith had become so widespread through officialdom that even court officials were rumoured to cross themselves at the ceremonial offerings to Diocletian's cult. (It was rumoured, indeed, that Diocletian's own family had been questioned about their sympathy with the growing faith; but such rumours were Christian rumours, just as it was Christian historians who wrote the vituperative histories of these events.) So severe were the persecutions of Diocletian that the Egyptian church still reckons its calendar from their beginnings in AD 302.

Aided by pagan priests, the investigating officers quickly recognized the importance of the New Testament books to the growing faith, and they were banned and burned. A government report tells that when investigators arrived at the church of Cirta, existence of Christian writings was betrayed by empty bookshelves; the books were out on loan, the imperial officials were told, and when demands were made for the names and addresses of the readers the sub-deacons refused to tell. This lonely act of bravery in a small town must have been repeated unknown times in a hundred other places. At Cirta, on the North African littoral, it must have been an especially hard decision, for the deacons knew that the speedy acquiescence of two of their colleagues had already resulted in their immediate freedom. Such contests of will, under the threat of torture, set fear of the God-Emperor against faith in the power of Christ. At Cirta the investigating magistrates also took the church treasure, silver candlesticks and the like; 'you would have been a dead man if you had not produced them for us' warned one of them. It is hardly surprising that many Christians gave up this struggle. But many did not; 'We are not traitors: here we are, order us to be killed' said the deacons of Cirta. That so many copies of the New Testament existed in such small towns shows the extent of the Gospel's diffusion. Martyrdom became a public spectacle and was often of a brutal ingenuity intended to test the martyr's faith and to amaze and terrify the audience. These martyrs were not large in number, but their deaths served to give the faith a wide celebrity. Indeed, it came to fill the Roman world. And it is strange indeed that the carefully devised cult of the emperor, who was the mortal enemy of the church, would become within a short time the ritual that Christian emperors would adopt for both their courts and their churches. The rich bindings of the imperial Bibles, all gold and precious stones, were clothed with the same impulse that had once decked the emperors themselves in eastern silks and pearls and sat them upon golden thrones. And like the hem of the emperor's cloak, the covers of these jewelled Bibles would be kissed by the faithful, carried in procession and perfumed with precious incense.

So the imperial court of Diocletian's palace where the Emperor had sat in state became the model for the churches of the Christian empire. And the place where once the imperial throne stood, where the Emperor had sat as a living icon of imperial power, was now taken by a Christian altar, and this was attended by priests dressed in the rich robes of late Roman courtiers.

Yet all this pagan paraphernalia could not provide a firm glue for Diocletian's empire. By his resignation he almost seemed to acknowledge the impossibility of holding it together. Diocletian had proposed a commonwealth of purpose, with honest officials and integrity amongst the rulers. Yet within two years of his resignation they were all fighting with each other. The new ethics were not sufficient for the empire; as Diocletian says in a report of an imperial conversation, 'statecraft and government are the most difficult things on earth.' In his palace at Split, the retired Emperor was even unable to help his family caught inadvertently in the new wars; his wife and daughter were publicly beheaded in Thessalonica and thrown into the sea. In the following years, whole families of little emperors, their wives, concubines and children, legitimate and illegitimate were executed. Poor Diocletian must have had few illusions about his own divinity. Yet, when, from his villa in Sicily, Maximian suggested that the two of them should return to rule the Empire that their successors were fighting over, Diocletian sent his old friend a letter telling him that if he could only see the splendid cabbages that he, Diocletian, had planted in the palace gardens with his own hands, he would no longer urge him to give up his enjoyment of happiness for the pursuit of power. Maximian went back to public life alone and within a few years committed suicide after losing a battle. The solid old soldier chosen by the crafty Diocletian for his integrity had been no match for these young imperial wolves who were hunting in bigger and yet bigger packs.

Diocletian had no daughter to put coins upon his old eyes as his corpse was carried to the porphyry sarcophagus which had long stood waiting at the centre of his octagonal mausoleum. In his last years he had seen the disintegration of his great creation; that hard world, centred on an imperial *mysterium* of shadowed gold and shot silk. The Empire had slipped away into its separate provinces. The centre had been hollow; no common bond had held the people of this commonwealth, only abstract civic duty inside a faceless state. Even the Emperor had preferred growing fine green cabbages. It was becoming a misty disembodied age where not even the vast imperial wealth held men's imagination. Porphyry, a contemporary of Diocletian, says that his teacher, the philosopher Plotinus, 'gave the impression of being ashamed that he dwelt in a body and as a result of this attitude he could not endure to discuss his lineage, nor his parents, nor his fatherland'. Plotinus had deemed it degrading to submit to being the subject of a portrait; he had said to Amelius the sculptor that it was 'sufficient just to carry that image which nature has imposed upon us, without making concessions to it by deciding to leave behind a more lasting image of the image, as if it were one of those things which is particularly worth seeing'. Plotinus is a true voice of an age when cabbages were more enjoyed by emperors than the golden glow of deification. Although a clever critic of the early Christians, he shared with them strong sentiments of earthly disgust and the desire to retreat from civic obligation and the pursuit of fame. Similar sentiments were also prompting many Egyptian Christians to leave their urban middle-class society in the Hellenistic cities and live as hermits in desert caves, clad in rags, dying alone.

The ancient world had grown cold. In Diocletian's time, pagans might literally manufacture gods of their own choice from elements of various exotic pantheons; gods that were used just as the Christians would use their saints, to mediate between the human and the divine. At the same time, there was also a tendency towards monotheism; Diocletian's edicts refer to 'God' as a single entity. But this was not new: the tendency to think of deity as a single force alongside a growing disillusionment with political, earthly power, had long found expression inside the imperial court. Septimus Severus, an emperor of Diocletian's youth, had maintained an imperium as splendid as that of Diocletian, yet he would only marry a woman who shared the same sign of the Babylonian Zodiac. He, too had been searching for a faith that would unit the Empire under the emperor. The ancient Middle Eastern religions, born in the world's first nation-states, which had mixed kings and gods together in fruitful coalition, and formed populations into a single coherent mass, were obvious models. The city gods of ancient Rome had never been large enough to encompass the huge Empire.

One by one, the ancient eastern faiths had come to Rome and seemed to be absorbed into Roman life, their ancient purposes diminished. Yet in the second century, when the emperors had elected to become living gods, a truly regal religion, a sun-cult of the Syrian Kingdom of Emessa had come into its own. Its beginnings at Rome were hardly auspicious; the establishment had watched in horror as a young Syrian Emperor Heliogabalus of most unusual sexual proclivities had acted out a living syncretization of faith by marrying a Roman Vestal Virgin! Suitably sanitized for Roman tastes, a new solar faith, the third-century Emperor Aurelian's Sol Invictus, had begun to achieve some level of acceptance. It was a sensible choice, for this particular *Sol*, the Sun of Victory, was already a popular army god. Aurelian had introduced his deity with remarkable coolness, as one might market a soap powder. He had surrendered up the coinage, traditionally a most public medium for the celebration of the emperor, to the new god. Coins were stamped *Deus Sol Invictus* and not with the head of Aurelian, the Emperor having assumed the title of *Pontifex Maximus*, the Chief Priest. A great octagonal temple had been built for Sol Invictus at Rome, bread and circuses had kept the population happy and the volatile Romans had enjoyed their new religion. But Aurelian's god had died with him. Indeed it was the chaos of Roman politics that followed Aurelian's murder that had led Diocletian, the new emperor, to neglect Rome, to run the Empire from eastern cities and to establish himself as an earthly deity on par with the traditional Roman gods. But though the Empire found Diocletian's religious abstractions unconvincing, the population remained fascinated with the universal faiths from the east and their single universal deities. At last, rising from the battles of the *Augustii* and the *Caesarii* that followed Diocletian's resignation, the Empire finally found its spiritual salvation. A new emperor, Constantine, one of the greatest of all emperors, achieved a balance of earthly and divine power that even the genius of Diocletian had not found. Constantine used Christianity: the New Testament books, burned in Diocletian's day, supplied the models and the justifications for this splendid new creation – the Christian Roman Empire.

Idolized by Christian biographers, hated by pagan contemporaries, Constantine the Great remains a strangely elusive man. Nowhere is he seen better than in his colossal marble portrait at Rome (see Plate 18). Like Constantine, it is considerably larger than life and very much a product of his age. 'Dextrous, intrepid and affable' was Edward Gibbon's splendid assessment of him; 'a sovereign with the conviction of a personal mission entrusted to him by the Christian God' is the opinion of Professor Baynes, a more recent authority. Whether or not the man *was* a devout Christian, what, indeed, was his understanding, his conception of Christianity, we may never know. The man has gone, but his church yet remains as do some of his letters and decrees, and it is this public face that is his legacy. The famous head of the Emperor at Rome once formed part of a colossal statue which must have stood at least fifty feet high. Its body was probably made of bronze. You may imagine that its ancient sculptor took the customary delight in modelling the fine thin silks that Constantine would have worn under the traditional leather kilt and cuirass of a Roman army commander. And how the imperial face has changed from the lifelike portraits of the earlier emperors! Though the head is still turned slightly in the classical manner, Constantine's huge eyes now stare straight out of his face, focused on eternity. The head is built like a piece of architecture; the hair locks together like the stones of a huge arch, the dome-shaped cranium above reflects the great round chin; the fleshy mouth is over-large, weighty; the lids fit over the orbs of the eyes like brick vaults: the whole, a vast immoveable icon. A contemporary writer described Constantine's son marching into Rome at the head of his armies, 'He looked stiffly ahead as if he had an iron band around his neck and he turned his face neither to the right nor to the left, he was not as a living person, but as an image'. This, too, was Constantine's presence, built into his great marble portrait. The sheer size is daunting; another image of the imperial presence, that mysterious god-like power, which Diocletian had attempted to conjure with lighted torches, silk, incense and burnished gold.

Constantine's great statue, famous even in antiquity, was set up inside an enormous basilica built in the centre of Rome. He had taken the city in a battle with a rival Caesar and had impressed his own identity on it. His architects changed the design of the basilica so that the imperial statue stood right upon the central axis in a huge apse opposite the entrance portal dominating the public life of the huge hall: the nave of St Peter's Rome shares its design and measurements with much of Constantine's great basilica. And just as these basilicas are the direct ancestors of many Christian churches, so Constantine's huge dominating head is an ancestor of the image of the powerful bearded God that appears in so many eastern churches, those powerful haggard portraits that glitter in the golden gloom high above the altars and incense.

When Constantine's portrait was made at Rome, he had ruled for about ten years and was halfway towards his goal of re-uniting the Eastern and Western Empires. He had grown up in Diocletian's court. Called to York by his dying father, a Caesar of the Western Empire, he was proclaimed an *Augustus* by the troops of the northern legions on 25 June AD 306 at the age of twenty-one. Seven years later, after a convoluted and brilliant career, he had entered Rome in triumph after defeating and killing another emperor outside the city. Before that battle Constantine told his army that he had had a dream in which he was promised victory if they fought on that day under the sign of the cross and, as superstitious as everyone of the time, Constantine had ordered his troops to paint Christian monograms on their shields. But the coins struck in celebration of his great victory at the Milvian Bridge were not dedicated to the God of Jesus Christ but to his legion's perennial favourite, Sol Invictus.

After this daring victory which Constantine had won despite his being greatly outnumbered, there were just two emperors: Constantine in the west, Licinius in the east. In council at Milan, these two *Augustii* agreed, among other things, to ban the persecution of the Christians which, in any case, had all but ceased. Indeed, Constantine himself had been involved in the politics of the church for some time, ajudicating disputes and receiving church petitions. Twelve years after this Milan conference, after declaring that Licinius had revived Christian persecution in the east, Constantine defeated and killed him. Then he convened the first general council of the Christian church at Nicaea in Western Asia Minor. At this council, the precise nature of the Christian faith and its relationship to Constantine and his imperial successors would be negotiated.

The Council at Nicaea: Striking a Balance
It is a measure of Constantine's genius, as Dean Stanley once observed, that 'Every church feels that it has some standing place in the Council of Nicaea'. Authentic records of the Council are very scanty; most of our history is church legend, yet the effects of the Council are still felt in the Christian church and in Western government, so successful was Constantine's solution to the problems of his Empire.

In AD 325, the year of the Council, Constantine was unpopular in Rome. His huge new Empire was also extremely stressed, divided by different faiths and by various political allegiances. Even the Christians were themselves divided on matters of doctrine. Despite Constantine's personal intervention, the churches of North Africa had already partially split from Rome, and nothing could heal the rift. The Eastern church, too, was threatening to split between north and south. Yet it was the whole church, vigorous, growing and deeply fascinating to Constantine himself – and still only comprising about ten per cent of the population – that the Emperor now convened almost as a parliament for his new Empire. Constantine would use the Christian bishops to broadcast his new rule and order, both temporal and spiritual, throughout the Empire. The Council of Nicaea was a convocation of church leaders brought from the four corners of the ancient world, from Spain to Persia, from North Africa to northern France, from Egypt, Syria, Armenia and Palestine. Constantine established and controlled this gathering, the first ecumenical conference, carefully creating the first image of Christendom. 'It might have seemed the likeness of the Kingdom of Christ,' declared an eyewitness as he described the appearance of the Emperor surrounded by his bishops and guards. Following generations widely believed that Constantine's Council had been guided directly by the Holy Spirit. And here the enthroned Emperor and his bishops appear as the prototype of Western government, for it was at Nicaea that this dual order of temporal and spiritual power first received sanction. At the centre of this new Christian empire stood the Holy Books of the Bible.

The Council began with Constantine seizing the initiative from the eastern bishops who had already called a smaller council to settle a question of heresy. In his letter announcing his imperial convocation, Constantine says, 'It was formerly agreed that the Synod of Bishops should meet at Ancyra of Galatia, but, it has seemed to us on many accounts, that it would be as well for a Synod to assemble at Nicaea, a city of Bithynia, both because the Bishops from Italy and the rest of the countries of Europe are coming, and because of the excellent temperature of the air, and in order that I may be present as a spectator and participator in those things that will be done . . .'.

Constantine's letter contains no mention of the intended excommunications that were to have been the main event of the Ancyra conference. His desire was for unity not further confrontation. Moving the intended conference to Nicaea was also a clever stroke. Now the bishops were summoned not by contentious and contending churchmen but by the Emperor himself; they would travel under *his* orders to *his* conference to be held at *his* chosen location, and Nicaea was just twenty miles from the palace of the executed Licinius in whose apartments Constantine was living. At a stroke, the Emperor filled the church council meeting with his imperial presence and purpose.

Today, the ancient council halls of Nicaea lie deep under the rubble of the Turkish town of Isnik. Traditionally, the main council chamber is said to be sited close by the city's walls, by the ancient harbour of the beautiful Lake Ascania. It is easy to see why Constantine, who chose to live in waterside palaces for much of his life, picked such a verdant place with its 'excellent temperature of air'. Nicaea was the centre of the most beautiful province of Bithynia, a rich volcanic plain filled with vineyards and orchards abundant with dusty sugary grapes, bright yellow quinces, cherries and pears. Constantine's lakeside palace is represented today by a few blocks of fine white stone, some columns and high walls that overlook the town's neat allotments. A hundred years ago, the Christian Bishop of Nicaea used to tell visitors that Constantine's throne was set up where an ancient plane tree now grows. Eyewitnesses described the opening session of Constantine's Council taking place in a large rectangular hall at the centre of the palace. Tradition tells that a copy of the Gospels holding, it is said, the presence of Christ himself, lay in the middle of the chamber; according to legend some heretics, finding nowhere to sit, threw the Gospels onto the floor and sat down in their place!

The authentic proceedings of the Council make a very slim volume, but a vital one for all that. The chief results were a creed of faith called the Nicene Creed and a list of twenty statements that lay down rules of behaviour for the clergy, rules that are still generally observed by many churches to this day. In these articles we can discover, for example, that usury – the perennial problem for Christian bankers – was defined as *excessive* interest. As normal rates in the Roman Empire ran at about twelve per cent, presumably usury was defined as a higher percentage. There were also rules that govern the order of standing and sitting during church services. There was also a re-statement of the rules governing the re-admittance into the Church of those who had broken from the faith during the persecutions and this, more than anything, showed the continuing desire of the Church – the dream of Irenaeus of Lyon – for true universality. Another rule, excluding clergy who had emasculated themselves, was clearly aimed at those who had been pagan priests of Sol and the like, for many of these had regarded castration as a supreme offering for god. Other provisions laid down the proper conduct of the clergy, though the vivid description of an aged and celibate Egyptian hermit pleading passionately for the right of the clergy to marry – 'lay not this extra burden upon the clergy; marriage itself is a continence' he cries – is a later invention. The monk in question is now a saint of the Eastern church where a clergyman must be a married man.

As for the great Creed, contemporary records indicate that it represented a compromise, guided by Constantine himself, intended to reconcile the adherents of the two factions that were threatening to divide the Eastern church. The argument concerned the precise nature of divinity. Theologians were interested in the nature of God: Constantine was concerned with the extent of divinity. If Jesus had first been conceived in Mary, as some heretics were arguing, then there must have been a time when God was not born, so there was a family hierarchy of deity; God the Father being the senior of Jesus, God the Son. (Continuing such speculation, it would also be noticed that there had been a time before God created the world, and the question was asked, what then had he been doing? In the following century St Augustine would succinctly answer this by declaring that 'He had spent His time building a special hell for those that asked such questions'!)

Such disagreements about the nature of deity, about Jesus' relationship with

God the Father, may be traced right back to the first days of the church. But then many Christians had believed, like Paul, that the physical end of the world was close and the church had not worried itself with such carefully made definitions. But now, the sons of that church were sitting in the marbled halls of the Emperor taking on the appearance of a spiritual government, and they required an earthly hierarchy for themselves, and one that Christian doctrine could affirm. What Constantine sought in all this was a pre-eminent position for his imperial self. The heretical splitting of God into a hierarchy of sacredness served to muddy the issue. For if God was divided into Father, Son and Spirit, then small fractions of this sacredness might still run throughout man's world just as Jesus, the Son had once done. And if sacredness could run unchecked through the order of the world, the role of emperors in such a universe of democratic holiness would come but a poor second! Constantine wanted *his* Imperium to resemble the order of heaven, with the role of emperor echoing the role of God in heaven. Arguments about the nature of God were far from being theological abstractions: they were about power in this world and the next.

The Nicene Creed, that basic statement of Christian faith still used by most churches in one form or another, was the result of careful compromise at the Council. Two creeds were proposed, one heretical; the second amended to include a term which defined the nature of God precisely as being 'of one substance'. This Creed was proposed by Eusebius of Caesarea in Palestine, whose diocese included the city of Jerusalem. Its wording was that of a Jerusalem baptismal creed that had its origins in the very earliest days of the church. As Irenaeus had done at Lyon with his defence and selection of the four Gospels, the church once again returned to its very roots at the critical time when it was pressed to define its nature and substance.

The Holy Trinity, that supreme mystery of Christian theology which holds that God exists in Three Persons and One Substance, came to serve the cause of the Christian empire. God had become a remote and ineffable unity of Father, Son and Holy Ghost. His time on earth as Jesus Christ was fixed precisely to one event in the historical past from which the new imperial calendars would be dated. Christ's birthday, fixed on 25 December, took over the feast day of an earlier favoured deity of Constantine, *Sol Invictus*. In all this, the church and its officers became a vital part of the earthly hierarchy, the organization through which people might reach to God. And at the very top of this worldly pyramid of power stood Constantine, the holy emperor, whose earthly order reflected that of Heaven itself.

This is why the Council of Nicaea and its Creed, which so carefully defined and separated the heavens from the earth, was of fundamental importance to Constantine the Christian and to Constantine the empire-builder. And for that reason the Council of Nicaea may be said to have been about the redefinition of imperial power. In later letters and decrees, Constantine continually reminded his subjects that these sacred definitions were drawn up by 'three hundred bishops remarkable for their shrewdness'. In return for the imperial acceptance of the bishops and their faith, the Council tacitly validated the emperor's earthly rule, the sanctity of which Constantine, raised at Diocletian's court, had not doubted for one moment.

In his desire for church unity, Constantine went out of his way to assimilate the heretics who insisted upon the splitting of the Godhead into earthly and heavenly parts. Even when he later exiled some of the more vocal heretics he did so only after personal interviews with them and a barrage of letters. Constantine knew that, like many of the bishops at Nicaea, these men would undergo torture and death rather than submit to alien beliefs, as many of them had already proved during Diocletian's ruthless persecutions. Requiring their acceptance rather than their denunciations, Constantine needed tact and subtlety, qualities that the Emperor possessed in abundance.

It is hardly surprising that the surviving descriptions of Constantine's first entrance into the Council chamber, to take his place at its centre at the behest of the bishops, has something of the air of Diocletian's entrances at Split. Every speech of the Emperor, his every gesture, even the precise position of each of the bishops in the hall, has become the subject of later legends, the justification of much church custom and ritual. Legends tell of a shepherd bishop, Spyridon of Cyprus, who brought a sick ewe along with him; other bishops, who had been mutilated in the earlier persecutions, had their wounds and scars kissed by Constantine himself. The Eastern churches call the Council the '318' after the number of bishops traditionally said to have attended. In Greek, this number reduced to equivalent alphabetic notation makes the letters, TIH: 'T' has become the cross, 'IH' the name of Christ. This number 318 was also the number of Abraham's slaves in the Book of Genesis and was therefore especially auspicious. As each bishop was allowed to bring two presbyters and three slaves with him, this would have made about 2000 people present at the gathering, a burden that the fruitful plain of Nicaea could well have supported for a season or so.

PLATE 18 (Opposite): Constantine the Great. From the colossal contemporary portrait in marble and bronze (circa AD 315) whose fragments are preserved in the courtyard of the Palazzo dei Conservatori, Rome.
PLATE 19 (Overleaf above): The Holy Sepulchre at Jerusalem. A new dome crowns the drum of Constantine's rotunda built to cover the Tomb of Christ. Most of the architecture visible in the photograph is medieval, dating from the times of the Crusaders.
PLATE 20 (Overleaf below): The Holy Sepulchre, interior. The entrance to the Tomb of Christ, which was last rebuilt in the nineteenth century.

Another legend about the conference tells that its first sessions were dominated by a gaggle of bishops skilled in the Greek arts of rhetoric and debate, and that the unlettered bishops of Egypt and Africa sat confounded and bemused as these eloquent men debated the nature of God. Finally, one of the Egyptian clerics, a man blinded and hamstrung by Diocletian's torturers, rose and limped exasperatedly towards them. 'Know you not,' he said, 'that Christ and his Apostles left us not a system of logic, nor a vain deceit, but a naked truth, to be guarded by faith and good works.' With these legendary sentences we may see how the formal perfections of the classical world would be transmuted into the strange intensities of early Christian art; how the precise architecture of the pagan temples was transformed into the haphazard, intensely beautiful architecture of the early church, made as much by faith and prayer as by civil engineering. Here is the profound rejection of the slave-wrought 'arts of Rome', the cold polish of the classical tradition. And the learned bishops were forced to acknowledge the justice of the old hermit's words. 'My learned friends,' one of them says, 'so long as it was a matter of words, I could oppose words to words, and whatever was spoken I could overthrow by my skill in speaking; but when, in the place of words, power comes out of the speaker's lips, words can no longer resist power, man could no longer resist. If any of you have felt as I have felt, let him believe in Christ and let him follow this old man in whom God has spoken'.

Thus did Constantine's Empire seek not only to reform its politics and faith but also to build an art that expressed not the visual appearances of things, their external elegance, but the fire of faith in a flashing eye and the spiritual power of a praying hand. So, too, the Bible's texts came to be used, not as Paul had written his letters, as straightforward exhortations to a Christian life, or even as a record of Jesus' sayings and life, but as sacred words, the breath of God, a fount of imagery, of spirituality.

PLATE 21 (Previous page above): The apse mosaic of Santa Pudenziana in Rome. Though bearing the scars of many restorations, the outlines of this mosaic, which dates from Constantine's own century, show the Emperor's new buildings in Jerusalem, including the rotunda built over Christ's Tomb and the huge gold cross that he set on the top of the Rock of Calvary.
PLATE 22 (Previous page below): The court of Constantine's successors at Constantinople. A relief on the base of an ancient Egyptian obelisk showing the Emperor Theodosius I (ruled 379–395) in his box at the hippodrome receiving the homage of a group of kneeling captives.
PLATE 23 (Opposite): The Mausoleum of the Empress Galla Placidia at Ravenna, made and decorated about AD 450. The dome of heaven holds a mosaic cross at its centre; its vaults are supported by the Evangelists. Closer to earth, a portrait of St Lawrence (right) is balanced by a bookcase holding the four bound volumes of the Gospels (left). In this period, illustrations of biblical stories are rare, but literary allusions to the Bible and its authors permeated every aspect of Christian art.

Constantinople: A Christian Rome

While the Emperor fought his last campaigns in the Eastern Empire, one of his armies had besieged the small town of Byzantium on the Bosphorus and it was probably during this minor siege that Constantine saw the city's strategic potential: a site at the eastern-most tip of Europe facing outward towards Asia and set between the two rivers that formed the Empire's most vital borders – the Danube to the north and the Euphrates to the east. As several of his predecessors had done, Constantine now resolved to build himself a new capital to take the place of Rome. Unlike his predecessors, however, Constantine built himself a Christian city, and the nature of Constantine's Christianity may be seen most clearly in his plans for this bright new metropolis by the Bosphorus; a new Rome that rose in the space of a very few years. This gimcrack city, Constantinople (now Istanbul), survived to become the most fabled city of the world, celebrated everywhere from Ireland to China and everywhere renowned for its riches, its learning and its sophistication. On 11 May 330, all that was still in the future and Constantine was busy performing the city's foundation ceremonies on the spot where his tent had been pitched during the siege of Byzantium. His camping ground, enclosed inside a huge oval piazza, remained the heart of the city until its fall. Constantine's elaborate ceremonies mixed traditional pagan rites with Christian ritual. Priests of both persuasions accompanied the Emperor as he sacrificed and prayed, and buried a rich collection of ancient objects in the foundations of his new city. Among the objects was an antique wooden image of Pallas Athena called the Palladium, which had been sent down to earth by Zeus and had been taken from the burning city of Troy by Aeneas. Thence it came to Rome where its presence, it was well known, had on many occasions saved the old city from invasion. Along with this most holy object Constantine had also buried fragments of Jesus' cross, brought especially from Golgotha.

The place of Constantine's dedication ceremonies is marked nowadays by a blackened column of seven huge drums of imperial porphyry, wreathed in iron hoops, now partly hidden by old Turkish repair work. In Constantine's day the column supported a colossal bronze statue of Apollo, made, it was said, by Phidias but changed into a portrait of Constantine; the rays of Apollo's golden headress turned into a gilded halo which was made from the metal of one of the massive nails from Jesus' cross. (Legend has it that another of these holy nails served as the bit of the bridle of Constantine's favourite horse.) The great gilded statue stood with an orb in one hand and a sword in the other, and the people of Constantinople came to believe that if invaders should enter their city the golden emperor would jump down from his plinth and drive the enemy away. The statue has gone now, but the ancient column still stands on one side of the main street running between the bazaar and the great mosques that crown the hills of Istanbul.

Constantine decreed that on every anniversary of the city's foundation a special statue of himself ensconced on a wooden carriage should be paraded down this main thoroughfare and around the hippodrome, the racing stadium which, in imitation of Rome, had been built alongside the imperial palace. For centuries Constantine's successors honoured the old statue as it was carried past the *Kathisma*, the imperial box, in front of the assembled population, treating the ancient effigy as if it were a pagan god. Not only was the hippodrome the centre of Constantinople, in many ways it became the centre of the Eastern Roman Empire – the Byzantine world. Here it was that most civic events of the capital city were played out.

Constantine had plundered the Empire to decorate this extraordinary city. Nothing was wanting there, said a cynic, except the souls and the intelligence of the illustrious men whose memorials now stood in its streets and squares. Thousands of sculptures had been gathered up; the city was a museum of classicism. Constantine placed an especially splendid collection of antiquities along the central spine, the *spina* of his hippodrome. Here were the famous four bronze horses of Lysippus, in Constantine's day already some six hundred years old, which, looted once more, would later stand along the façade of St Mark's in Venice. Still standing today in its original place, however, is a huge bronze column of three twisted snakes, an offering made to Apollo at Delphi in 479 BC, in thanksgiving for a great Greek victory. Two obelisks still stand on either side of this Greek tripod – one of them a great granite shaft already some two thousand years old when Constantine removed it from Egyptian Thebes. And on its base there are scenes of the Emperor Theodosius and his court having a day at the races half a century after Constantine's death (see Plate 22).

Just as Constantine took an empire and changed it to his design, so the artists of these splendid scenes have subjugated individual figures, placing them in rectangular units. All the free air of their ancient world has gone. The blocks of figures are pressed into a thin envelope of space, as if they were up against a shop window. The classical human figure in all its individual dignity has disappeared. In the new Empire of Diocletian and Constantine, slavery and poverty had greatly increased; life inside this Empire was harder than it had ever been before. The most important figure in the scenes, the Emperor, is also the largest, his flanking courtiers reducing in size according to their political importance. High in a stand, the court watches the racing chariots, spearmen hover behind them, dancing girls and musicians perform on the sand of the arena: an eerie preview of the scenes of the Last Judgment which will decorate so many of the churches of Christendom in later centuries.

Though these emperors and their court seem far from Western Christendom, in this polity lay the roots of the hierarchy of Christendom and the order of its art. There yet remained one essential step. With God in his Heaven now, and Constantine ruling by God's Grace: *Deo Gratia* upon the earth, the imperial power had to be seen as the essential link in the scheme. So Constantine built vast imperial churches not only across the seven hills of Constantinople and through the ancient city of Rome, but right throughout his empire. But the most remarkable feat, the most extraordinary creation of this elaborate architectural ceremonial was in the eastern province of Palestine, the land of Jesus Christ. For there, Constantine used the Bible's stories and local memories to mark out Jesus' life on earth in monuments. This small stony province with its passionate and tragic history was transformed into a biblical landscape, a distant theatre for a Western deity marked out by a Roman emperor. Constantine, that great collector of antiquities and relics, made this land itself into a relic, a literary landscape, a Holy Land.

Making the Holy Land

In Constantine's day, Jerusalem was a typical small Hellenistic town, little changed since the days when the Emperor Hadrian had established the Roman city of *Aelia Capitolina* in the ruins of the Israelite capital two centuries before. At the centre of the platform where Herod's great temple had once stood were two statues of Hadrian; on one day each year a delegation of Jews was allowed to return and anoint the venerable rock that marked the site of the Temple, and to mourn its loss. Right over the place where local Christians believed the tomb of Jesus had once stood was a large temple dedicated by the Emperor Hadrian to Jupiter and Aphrodite. Though somewhat decayed, it was still active in Constantine's day. The first Christian church in Jerusalem seems to have been a small building on Mount Sion where, tradition held, the disciples had gathered after Pentecost – this would also become known as the Room of the Last Supper.

After the Council of Nicaea, Constantine decided to change the landscape of this pagan city: 'Constantine, Maximus, Augustus, to Marcarius, [the unsuspecting Bishop of Jerusalem] you are an able man, and it is your task to make the arrangements and plans for the construction of a basilica finer than any other. . .' The letter then discusses, at some length, the plans and the materials to be used and concludes with typical enthusiasm: 'I desire to know from you how the roof of the basilica is to be made. Is it to be coffered? If so, it may be gilded as well. God preserve you, dear brother.'

[220]

So Jupiter's temple, 'the gloomy shrine of lifeless idols dedicated to the impure demon Aphrodite, where they poured foul libations on profane and accursed altars' was taken down. Even the earth and foundations which had supported this 'devil worship' were 'dug away to a considerable depth and removed to some distance'. And as they stripped the ground down to bedrock again, the Christian overseers discovered to their great delight, a small cave cut into a hillock which had been buried in the rubble under the base of the temple. Inside the cave there was a ledge for a body, and outside its door a rock stood close to the entrance: they had found the tomb of Christ. 'The holy of holies, the cave, was, like our saviour, restored to life.' It was an identification based, like Christianity itself, on faith.

Just a stone's throw away from this tomb stood the traditional site of Calvary, another rocky outcrop bearing on its top the sockets that had once held the three fateful crosses of the Gospels. This too was now cleared of debris. Stonemasons were then set to work to cut down the rock which held the tomb and to square up the Rock of Calvary until these two outcrops faced each other as two rectangular blocks of living rock. It was these two biblical sites that became the starting points of an ambitious architectural plan.

At this time, Constantine's aged mother, the Empress Helena, came to Jerusalem on a pilgrimage, just as ever-increasing numbers of Christians from all over the Empire were now doing. In those days, this sacred area must have lain under the white haze and loose chippings of a stone quarry. Aided by the equally aged Bishop Marcarius, using prayers, dreams and diligent questioning, Helena discovered the True Cross of Jesus, with Pilate's wooden label still beside it. These, together with two nails and the crosses of the thieves, were lying in an ancient water cistern dug close by the Rock of Calvary. With the nails which Constantine would employ to great effect in his new city, most of the sacred wood was shipped back to Constantinople; since those days it has been distributed in thousands of splinters throughout Christendom. After carefully measuring all of these fragments that he could find, a French divine of the nineteenth century concluded that their combined volume would not amount to sufficient wood on which to crucify a man! But such rationalism, however well intentioned, belies the relics' true power. Like the sacred spots that Constantine's architects were busy memorializing, such relics stand as testaments to the direct link between heaven and earth, tangible symbols of the grace of God on earth. Constantine saw his role as emperor in a precisely similar light; as a link between these two worlds, human and heavenly. And this role would be inherited, along with appropriate collections of holy relics, by all the kings of Christendom.

It is difficult today to discover the authentic buildings of Constantine's Holy Land. Down the centuries his monuments have been endlessly embellished, attacked and rebuilt so that all that is left of them is the memory of the sacred spot they once enclosed, and a few stone walls and columns (see Plate 19). If, however, you walk down into the *souk* of Old Jerusalem, along through the food markets of the *Khan el Zeit* you will still see, behind the little oven of Zalotimo's Greek Bakery, parts of the door jambs of the church that Constantine built over Calvary and the tomb of Christ. Bishop Eusebius of Caesarea, Marcarius' superior and Constantine's biographer, has described the view from this spot, looking into what was the finest of all Constantine's churches. In his day, as now, the doorway was in the middle of a street of shops. The door was a 'marvellous ornate entrance, which, when open allowed a breath-taking view of the interior to those passing by'. The church was a masterpiece, 'enormously lofty and of generous proportions'; its walls were decorated in coloured polished marbles, its ceiling carved and coffered and all 'brightly gilded', making 'the whole church shine and sparkle'.

Deep under the present church of the Holy Sepulchre, which is built inside Constantine's great monument, are the ancient water cisterns where, it is said, the Empress Helena found the True Cross. From here you may walk up the rock of which Calvary forms the summit. You enter the chapels of Calvary today up steep stone stairs that run up the side of Constantine's rock cube. At the top you will find two chapels, one 'Greek', one 'Latin'; Constantine's imperial church now divided into its Eastern and Western halves. Both these chapels are relatively new; the Greek one holds the ancient socket, which you may see in the candlelight beneath the altar.

As you cross the church between Calvary and the Holy Sepulchre, you walk over the floor that Constantine's quarrymen levelled some seventeen centuries ago. Then you walk into echoing darkness under a high dome, Constantine's cover for the tomb of Christ. Various churches have altars in the ambulatory around the dome. A bright Roman Catholic chapel marks with a marble star upon its floor the spot where, the Gospels tell us, Mary Magdalene stood when she heard the news of the resurrection. A little distance away there is another chapel, now soot-black and desolate, decorated only by a burned painting; lit by a single tiny lamp fuelled by green olive oil, this is the Chapel of the Syrian Church where Jesus' followers were first called Christians.

In a corner of the Syrian chapel, in a dangerous dark hole, is a group of Jewish tombs which may be dated by their shape to the first century. This is the proof that in Jesus' time this area of Jerusalem was indeed a graveyard and lay, therefore, outside the city walls – a necessary requirement for the location of Calvary as well as for the Tomb. But this archaeological affirmation introduces a further question; for even if this is indeed the location of Jesus' execution and burial, how did Jesus' tomb come to be identified from among the unmarked chambers of the ancient graveyard? Here we are thrown back onto the stories of Helena and her contemporaries. Like their Emperor, these people lived in a world filled with miracles and faith.

During her pilgrimage Empress Helena dedicated two other churches in Palestine, one on the Mount of Olives at the site of Christ's Ascension into Heaven, and one where he was born at Bethlehem; three churches, then, stand at spots where divinity directly touched the earth. These three spots memorialize some of the most fundamental passages of the Nicene Creed. For this asserts that Jesus was born of the Holy Spirit and the Virgin Mary (the Nativity Church in Bethlehem), was crucified and died and rose again on the third day (the Church of the Holy Sepulchre), and ascended into Heaven to sit at the right hand of the Father (the Church of the Ascension).

A mosaic in the basilica of Santa Pudenziana at Rome, made in Constantine's own century, celebrated this brand new Bible land and its buildings, showing them as a backdrop to the figure of Christ who sits like a Greek philosopher amid his pupils (see Plate 21). The jewelled cross over Christ's head is a drawing of the huge triumphant cross Constantine had set into the Rock of Calvary. The fine new building with its domed roof to the left of Christ is the canopy that Constantine's architects built over Christ's tomb; the building to the right, the octagon that they built around the Rock of the Ascension. In the sky above are the signs of the Four Evangelists looking down upon this city that they celebrate in their Gospels. The mosaic has made this scene into a heavenly city; Jerusalem is now a city halfway between man and God, its strange sky shot-red seems to vibrate supernaturally. And underneath all this, Christ opens a jewelled Bible.

The Imperial Bible

Constantine died in 337, in the thirty-second year of his reign; the Council of Nicaea had marked his twentieth jubilee, his thirtieth had seen the dedication of the Basilica of the Holy Sepulchre. So tremendous was his earthly presence that when he died at a spa close to Constantinople, his corpse was brought back to the capital where it lay propped up to rule the Empire through the medium of his ministers' words for several months. Whatever the personal beliefs of this most extraordinary of rulers, Constantine had ensured the success of this faith, Christianity, and that to his contemporaries seemed a miraculous proof of its truth. By the end of the fourth century a great part of the Empire had accepted the faith. But what was the precise nature of Constantine's personal religion? The man was a man of his own times, a man of transition. From his letters and edicts it is clear that he saw himself in the manner of an Old Testament monarch; as a chosen vessel, a tool of God. And naturally enough, Constantine saw all his enemies as evil opponents of divine will, anti-Christians, persecutors of the faithful simply because they opposed him.

Constantine had already planned his own tomb, for which the holy Emperor gathered, as it were, the New Testament all around him. Bishop Eusebius of Caesarea describes the monument as having twelve cenotaphs, one for each of the Apostles with Constantine the thirteenth apostle lying at the centre of the cross that formed the church's ground plan. Legend says that he was buried in the white robes of baptism, a ceremony not unusually performed late in life in those days. By his own lights, then, Constantine was indeed a Christian.

This church was dedicated to Christ's triumph; the cross, the Christian sign of victory, seals the place. This is how Constantine wished to be viewed by posterity and with his keen awareness of architectural symbolism, the Emperor would certainly have sympathized with Sultan Mehmet, the Islamic conqueror of Constantinople, who had the Emperor's old mausoleum torn down and his own funerary mosque built upon the same spot! There are several literary descriptions of this famous church, but its most beautiful memorial is surely a drawing of a small part of its architecture made three centuries after the Emperor's death. The church's bright-painted columns support a line of arches springing, in the old manner of Diocletian's palace, from fine capitals still in the full classical tradition. Here, too, are twelve Roman-style portraits of the Apostles – copies, perhaps, of the originals that once decorated Constantine's church.

This golden page was discovered, cut-down and bound as a decoration, in a medieval Greek Gospel. Originally, it had decorated a long table of contents that listed corresponding passages of the Four Gospels, so that a single Gospel story could be quickly consulted in each of its different versions – a so-called 'Canon Table'. Attached to this same sheet was a copy of a letter written by

Bishop Eusebius of Caesarea, the man who first compiled these lists and who is a considerable figure in the early history of Christianity. Without Bishop Eusebius' copious collections of letters, church records and written history, without the Ten Books of his *Storia Ecclesiastica*, there would be precious little history of the early church surviving, and even Constantine the Great would be considerably diminished. Bishop Eusebius also provides the next chapter in the history of the Bible. For although Irenaeus wrote in defence of the Gospels, it is the writings of Bishop Eusebius that provide the first complete surviving list of what, precisely, the Christian Bible should contain. Irenaeus had coined the name of 'New' Testament to stand alongside the 'Old'; now in his *Storia Ecclesiastica*, Bishop Eusebius counted out, one by one, the list of New Testament books that we have today. He also discussed other texts which he calls 'doubtful ones' and which, for the most part, were only finally excluded from the sacred canon in the half century that followed his death. Eusebius fitted his list of New Testament books into his great Church history, placing them into the period in which he thought they had been written, which was shortly before the turn of the first century. Even in Eusebius' day, however, some two centuries later, information about such distant times was already sparse. Just as we would today, he quotes from Josephus, the Jewish-Greek historian, and from fragments of Irenaeus' writings. Then after telling us a lively tale about St John, he introduces his list of New Testament books into the ancient scene that he has conjured up. Modern historians might use a different method to suggest the texts' true age, for in this we are better informed than the old bishop. Nonetheless, his list of sacred books is the same as that of the modern Bible:

> It will be well, at this point, to classify the New Testament writings. We must, of course, put first the holy quartet of the Gospels, followed by the Acts of the Apostles. The next place in the list goes to Paul's Epistles, and after them we must recognize the Epistle called 1 John; likewise 1 Peter. To these may be added, if it is thought proper, the Revelation of John, the arguments about which I shall set out when the time comes. These are classed as Recognized Books. Those that are disputed, yet familiar to most, include the Epistles known as James, Jude, and 2 Peter, and those called 2 and 3 John, the work either of the evangelist or of someone else with the same name.

Among Eusebius' spurious books are the 'Acts of Paul', the 'Shepherd of Hermas', the 'Revelation of Peter' and the 'Epistle of Barnabas'. He went on to consider Revelations:

> as for this Revelation of John, if this seems the right place for it: as I said before, some reject it, others include it among the Recognized Books and so it has remained; but not without argument! Moreover some have found a place in the list for the "Gospel of the Hebrews", a book which has a special appeal for those Hebrews who

have accepted Christ. These would all be classed with the Disputed Books, but I have been obliged to list the latter separately, distinguishing those writings which according to the tradition of the Church are true, genuine, and recognized, from those in a different category, not canonical but disputed, yet familiar to most churchmen; for we must not confuse these with the writings published by heretics under the name of the apostles, as containing either Gospels of Peter, Thomas, Matthias, and several others besides these, or Acts of Andrew, John and other apostles, all these being second and third-century works. To none of these has any churchman of any generation ever seen fit to refer to his writings. Again, nothing could be further from apostolic usage than the type of phraseology employed, while the ideas and implications of their contents are so irreconcilable with true orthodoxy that they stand revealed as the forgeries of heretics. It follows that so far from being classed even among Spurious Books, they must be thrown out as impious and beyond the pale.

Like Irenaeus before him, the Bishop of Caesarea relied heavily on the traditions of the Church for his definition of the New Testament.

In his biography of Constantine, Eusebius recorded one of the Emperor's more remarkable commands: nothing less than an imperial order for the manufacture of bibles for the churches of Constantinople:

I have thought it expedient to instruct your Intelligence [Constantine here directs Eusebius] that you should command to be written fifty volumes on prepared vellum, easy to read and conveniently portable, by professional scribes with an exact understanding of their craft – volumes, that is to say, of the Holy Scriptures, the provision and use of which is, as you are aware, most necessary for the instruction of the Church. Letters have been dispatched from our Clemency [i.e. Constantine] to the accountant of the province, advising him to supply everything requisite for the production of the books, and it will be your care to ensure that they are prepared as quickly as possible. Using the authority of this letter you should commandeer two public carriages for their transport, for by such means will these fine volumes be most readily brought before our eyes, this duty being performed by one of the deacons of your church, who on reaching our presence will experience our liberality.

Constantine's order is a truly imperial one – the vellum required for fifty bibles would have taken the skins of some four and a half thousand animals. Though it is not proven, it seems highly likely that the famous *Codex Sinaiticus* was one of these fifty bibles. Split now between Leipzig, St Catherine's Monastery in Sinai and London, where the British Museum holds the lion's share of the manuscript, the beautiful *codex* is one of the world's oldest surviving bibles. Certainly it is of a standard that Constantine would have expected from Eusebius' workshops, plain, elegant and of great quality. Eusebius was the right man to ask for such books for the Bishopric of Caesarea had long held a famous library and had been at the very centre of Bible studies for more than a century. Origen, the great theologian, had settled there after fleeing from a jealous Bishop of Alexandria in the year 231. Though Origen's theology was later condemned by the Church Councils and his literary works largely destroyed, at Caesarea he had made a vast compilation of the different versions of the Old Testament and this work had enduring fame and prestige. The great volume remained a treasure of the Church's library, until its destruction by invading Arabs in the seventh century. In this huge book, known as the *Hexapla* or 'six', six differing versions of the Old Testament were written out side by side. The first of the *Hexapla*'s columns held a Hebrew text and was followed by five Greek versions, four of them made anciently by Hellenized Jews and one, the final version by Origen himself, a version compiled by careful comparison of all the others. Origen had taken the Hebrew text as his prime source, carefully indicating with signs and symbols where his version differed from it. By listing all these different versions side by side, Origen saw, as many modern Bible scholars have also affirmed, that there never was a single Bible text, simply different schools of tradition each one with its own, usually quite small, variations. Origen also saw that the most accurate text was to be made by a comparison of the available versions. Origen's huge book was never copied in its entirety but it was the most influential Greek text of the Christian Old Testament and fragments from ancient copies of it have been found in libraries from Milan to Cairo.

In his youth, Origen's mother had saved him from an ardent martyrdom; as an old man in 254 he finally suffered this fate, dying after lengthy torture during persecutions in Caesarea. Sixty years later one of his pupils, Pamphilius, suffered the same fate in the same city. The *Codex Sinaiticus* itself provides a remarkable postscript to these events in a rare note copied onto the manuscript that tells us of its ancestry. This *Codex*, the note says, has been checked against another 'exceedingly ancient Bible' which had borne the following inscription:

> Copied and corrected from the Hexapla of Origen, corrected by himself. Antonius, the confessor, collated, and I, Pamphilius, corrected the volume in prison by the great favour and enlargement of God. If one may say so without offence, it would not be easy to find a copy comparable with this copy.

In a chapter of his history of the Church, Bishop Eusebius records that as a young man he himself had been imprisoned alongside Pamphilius and that the older scholar so impressed him that he had changed his name to 'Eusebius [son] of Pamphilius'. There is, therefore, a direct line from Origen to the *Codex Sinaiticus* and this is a pedigree that very few old texts can match. Together with a few hundred fragments of similarly ancient texts, and the celebrated *Codex Vaticanus* at Rome which is of the same age, though of completely unknown origin, these few Greek Bible texts represent a tradition of determination and good hard scholarship that was at the heart of the early church right from the grim days of its persecution up to the imperial extravagances of Constantine himself. *Codex Sinaiticus* was written out by three scribes who, as their spelling mistakes and copying errors clearly show, worked from dictation. Though the copies of the scribes betray different educations, they write in very similar hands; no doubt they had learned their trade in the same scriptorium. Either Egypt or Palestine must have been their home. Mistakes in their understanding of the dictation – on one occasion, for example, a scribe writes 'Caesarea' in mistake for a word he has misheard – provide clear evidence that either the three scribes, or the text that was read to them, had been near to Palestine. Similarly, the division of the *Codex* into the so-called 'Eusebian Sections' reflects the numbers used by Eusebius in his canon tables and betrays a direct connection with the Bishop of Caesarea, though the *Codex* also contains three whole books of the second century which had been dropped by the church of Eusebius' day. *Codex Sinaiticus* is perhaps most remarkable for the meticulous processes of correction through which it has passed. Hardly apparent to the naked eye, though clearly revealed by infra-red photography, are some 14,500 alterations to the text, some of them made by the three scribes as they checked through their dictation, others by much later hands carefully perfecting the ancient text. The preparation of *Sinaiticus* is an example of the care that was continuously expended upon the Bible until the invention of printing made standardization of the text convenient and quick. The greatest works of ancient Greek philosophers never merited the care that has been lavished on Bible texts from the earliest days. Like old stones dug from the ground, these texts might well lack the precise hard edge of new compositions but the ancient message of the volume that was now the most holy book of the Christian Empire remained intact.

Pagans and Heretics

For a brief moment one of Constantine's imperial successors tried to turn the new world from its path and back into pagan ways. It was said that this Emperor Julian, a cousin of Constantine, sent his friend Orobasius to ask the advice of the Oracle of Delphi, the heart of the ancient classical world. When he arrived, around AD 360, Orobasius would have found the ancient sanctuary looking like a plundered cemetery. Forty years previously Constantine himself had visited the sacred hillside, and after attending ceremonies in his honour had left with a collection of its finest bronze sculptures – the huge bronze tripod now standing in Istanbul and the four fine horses of St Mark's at Venice. And Constantine had been but the last of a long line of imperial plunderers.

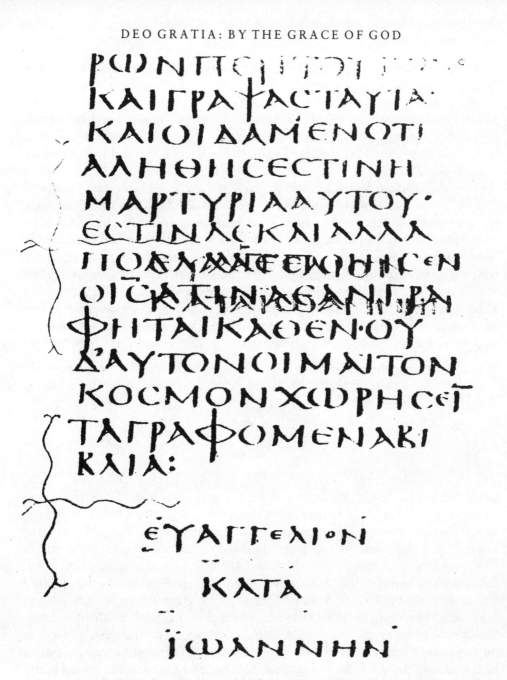

But in Orobasius' day the Temple of Apollo would still have held a *Pythia*, an old woman through whom the millennia-old oracle of the god gave voice. Orobasius would have washed in the sacred spring, the *Kastalia*, which, pagans believed, endowed its imbibers with the art of poetry; then he would have offered a small animal, a sheep or a goat, upon Apollo's altar, skinning the animal then pouring the ice-cold spring water over its corpse to see if it

[229]

trembled auspiciously. Only then would he have walked into the temple and presented the Emperor's question. There, in an underground vault sat the *Pythia*. She also had purified herself in the spring, then offered burned laurels and barley-seed upon the temple altar. She sat upon a tripod set up over a crack in the rock beneath the temple, slowly chewing upon the sacred laurel leaves, sometimes gently stroking the *Omphalos*, the oval stone that marked the centre of the world.

From the crack volcanic gas issued, and this along with the small doses of cyanide in the laurel leaves induced a heady trance. Into this darkness, then, the Emperor's question was cast: what hope was there for the Emperor's intended revival of the pagan gods? The *Pythia* would have replied incoherently from her deep trance. Later, her priests would have presented the interrogator with her answer set into beautiful and often deliberately ambiguous verse, just as 700 years earlier they had advised King Croesus and later, the Etruscans. For a thousand years the Greeks had honoured this oracle and its sanctuary. Now an emperor had spoken to the ancient god once more, and for the last time the answer was set in the beautiful archaic cadences of classical verse:

> Tell the king that the glorious dwelling has fallen to earth; that Apollo no longer has a Temple nor a prophetic laurel; the sacred spring is dry; its waters no longer speak.

Julian the pagan should not have worried about the old gods. Christianity was a religion of a book and a religion of dogma; a literary and verbal faith. Subtly, so subtly that the bishops themselves had not seen them, the old gods had entered their churches like the air of the Mediterranean. And they live still in Christian ritual, in the iconography and the festivals of Christianity. When Julian arrived in Antioch in 362 on his way to fight the Persians, he was amazed and rather annoyed to find himself alone. The great Christian city was in mourning, bewailing in the Levantine manner the annual death of Adonis, Venus's beautiful lover. At Ephesus, though the sanctuary of Diana, goddess of the city, was taken down and the temple stones were used to make a public bath house on the site of an old brothel, her statues were carefully buried in dry sand. And when the Third Council of the church assembly at Ephesus solemnly voted that henceforth the Virgin Mary should be honoured with the title of *Theotokos*; the God-bearer, Ephesus, itself for centuries the city of the virgin huntress Diana, became the city of the Virgin Mary, the Mother of God. In Egypt, too, the ancient sign of life, the *ankh*, which the gods had carried in their sculptures for thousands of years, was easily transformed into the Christian cross; the figure of Isis nursing her child Horus, *Isis Lactans*, became the figure of the Virgin with Jesus at her breast. And even 300 years after Julian's death, the gods lived on in southern Egypt until, to the desolation of their priests, the Byzantines took the little wooden figures away to Constantinople and burned them in the hippodrome.

At Rome, Romulus and Remus were swapped for the biblical saints Peter and Paul. And still in the fifth century, the Pope had to stop the early morning congregation of St Peter's from walking up the church steps backwards so as not to offend Sol, the rising sun god. Similarly, 25 December, now Christ's birthday, was also the day of Sol Invictus' festival and Constantine's birthday. This festival was celebrated by cutting green branches and hanging little lights on them, and presents were given out in the god's name. Sol's weekly festival Sol-day – Sunday – became the Christian Sabbath. Just as Apollo of Delphi had made a beautiful transformation to become the Roman Sol Invictus, so later he became a Christ of the sun. All three of them are sometimes pictured in their fiery chariots, tall straight-nosed classical youths with blonde curly hair and radiant haloes, in the manner of Constantine's lost statue at Constantinople with its sun-ray halo beaten from the nails of the True Cross. In this sense Christianity was a reflection of the changes in the Empire, rather than the cause of them.

The young Emperor Julian had come to believe that the goddess of Victory had abandoned the Empire because the Empire had abandoned the old gods. He saw his conversion to the ancient gods and their rituals – Julian had been brought up as a Christian – as a means of galvanizing the Empire with a new faith, just as Constantine had done. But after a fourteen-month reign, the young man was stabbed in a skirmish deep inside the Persian Empire and he died shortly afterwards.

Even in his understanding of the terrible threat that now faced the Empire, young Julian had been mistaken, a man in the wrong place at the wrong time. His Empire was indeed threatened, but not by Persian armies. Even during his lifetime Asian tribesmen were on the march again; twenty years after his death they had dislodged the Gothic tribes of eastern Europe – a million of whom had settled in Dacia (modern Romania) with the consent of the reigning emperor at Constantinople. Twenty years later these Goths were moving south into Greece, destroying Delphi and Athens and heading ominously towards Italy herself. These barbarians who would so wantonly destroy the Western Empire were of that faith which Julian so despised; they were Christians. The Gothic tribesmen marched with Bibles at their head and when they came to deal with the senators of Rome, they dealt, for the most part, with pagans. When some of these tribal armies ejected the priests from Hippo, the city of St Augustine in North Africa, it was because they considered them to be heretics. But the Christian Empire had condemned the beliefs of the Goths themselves ever since the Council of Nicaea; everyone knew that it was the tribesmen who were heretical.

That they should have professed any sort of Christianity at all was remarkable and due largely to a quirk of imperial history. Bishop Ulphilas – *Wulfila* in Gothic or 'Little Wolf' – had been appointed the Goth's first bishop when the tribesmen were settled in Dacia. As his name suggests Ulphilas was raised among the Gothic tribes, though he had received his education at the court of a bishop in Constantinople, a schismatic bishop who through Ulphilas would pass on his heresies to the barbarian tribes. And it was Ulphilas who translated the Bible that the tribesmen carried into Greece and Italy. The Bible that was at the side of Alaric, their greatest warlord, when he died in Italy; the Bible that was carried with the Vandals, as they roamed through France and Spain leaving Gaul 'burning like one great funerary pyre', and it was with them still when they destroyed imperial North Africa. When he started upon his translation Ulphilas decided to ignore the Books of Kings because as he says: 'They are a mere narrative of military exploits, and the Gothic tribesmen are especially fond of war, and are more in need of restraints to check their military passions than of spurs to urge them on.' With or without the Books of Kings, restraint was a vain hope; the Goths and their fellow tribesmen carried the Gothic Bible with their spears. Rare fragments of a fifth-century text known as *Codex Gissensis*, a bilingual Latin/Gothic Bible, have been found in Egypt, and others in Italy and Germany. But nowhere does a complete copy of Ulphilas' Bible survive; the most complete, the *Codex Argenteus*, holds little more than half of it.

The story of Ulphilas' translation of the Bible was one destined to be repeated many times. So important is the Bible to missionaries that its translation is one of their first tasks. Like Ulphilas, they are often obliged to devise a new script to suit a non-literary tongue, to invent words to hold the Bible's arguments and ideas and fit them into a foreign culture, often one that has no books at all. Ulphilas' translation is a scrupulous one, word for word, accurate and reverent. He rendered it from the original Greek into a script that he invented himself so that the barbarian language might find a proper written reflection.

By the time the beautiful *Codex Argenteus* (see Plate 30) was written out, in gold and silver inks on purple-stained vellums, all with fine conceits and decorations, the text had changed from Ulphilas' original version and shows not only the influence of Ulphilas' Eastern original but traces of the Bible's Western texts too. The book was perhaps made in a scriptorium in the Gothic city of Narbonne in south-west France. The Bible reflects the long migrations of this wandering people.

It is difficult today to imagine the attitudes of these tribesmen to the theological wranglings about the nature of the Holy Trinity. Certainly the tribesmen were seen as perfidious schismatics by the orthodox in Rome and in the East. As with so many religious conflicts, there is a strong impression, despite the impassioned rhetoric of the priests, that it was not *what* your precise beliefs were, but *who* held your allegiance. Orthodoxy was as much to do with power and procedure upon earth as it was with the court of heaven. Thus the day of Easter, which varied according to different churches, did not so much spring from spiritual convictions as from the church to which you belonged. And so it was with the Goths. Though, in his youth, Alaric, that famous Gothic chieftain had wanted to be a commander of the Roman armies and to live like a Roman, when his tribesmen conquered Italy and Gaul they had kept to the heretical beliefs that Ulphilas had taught them – 'that the Father was greater than the Son'. They shouted it as one of their battle cries as they rode out to meet the Roman legions. In such cultural and social differences did these arguments about Christianity find their real force. Faith and reasoned argument made precious little difference to the terror of the times.

Jerome and the Roman Bible

Striking south into Greece, the Gothic tribes had inadvertently exploited a bureaucratic weakness of the Empire. For at that time the province was under dispute between the Western Emperor at Rome and the Eastern Emperor at Constantinople and was not adequately defended. After the reign of Julian, Constantine's Empire had been split in two once again with the senior emperor in Constantinople. But real power rested not in these petty rulers – it was said of one of the Eastern Emperors that to him Rome was but the name of a pet hen – but in a succession of military men. This re-division of the Empire had a special effect upon the Western church for it was isolated from Constantinople and the East, the heart of Christianity, and forced back upon its own resources. Slowly, an individual Western church – a Latin church – was developing. Set firmly in the ancient traditions of patrician bureaucracy, the Roman bishops were beginning to exercise a magisterial control over their congregations and even Eastern churches began to look westwards for guidance in ecclesiastical disputes. But Rome was still far from the centre of the faith. The Bishop of Rome had not even attended the Council of Nicaea; Rome itself was no longer the centre of the Western Empire, which had moved north to face the barbarian threat directly, and the city had few churchmen of the first rank in it; indeed, even the language of Rome, Latin, set it apart from the literary heart of the faith for the Christian Bible was written in Greek, and Greek was the language in which the majority of the writings of the church had been set down. Yet Latin, that age-old and richly traditional language, was the natural language of the Western Empire and the language of its church, too.

'Theodorus, Felix, Divvante deo Omnipotente poemnio caelitus ... [sic]: Theodorus, the happy one, with the help of Almighty God and of the flock entrusted to him from on high had made this well and dedicated it gloriously'. So the Bishop of Aquileia wrote in mosaic on the floor of his church, secure in the belief that the majority of his congregation could understand his text and enjoy the extraordinary pictures that surround it. And here, too, doubtless across this same splendid floor once walked a young man who would translate the Greek Bible into a Latin text that the Western church would use on each and every day for more than a thousand years; the translation that still remains the Latin Bible of the Roman Catholic church; the Vulgate or the 'common' Bible as it is known, which has been approved and protected by Popes and church councils down to this day. Eusebius Hieronymous called Jerome, the man who would make this Latin Bible, was born near Aquileia in 342, fifty years before the barbarian invasions, in a town, he tells us, called Stridon that Attila and the Huns destroyed so definitively that today even its location has been lost to us.

Jerome, however, is well known to us through his translations, his Bible commentaries and his richly varied, often autobiographical, letters. At once a saint and among the greatest doctors of the church, Jerome was yet a man of whom it has been said that he was canonized not for his qualities of saintliness, but for the services he rendered the Roman church. Hot-tempered, outspoken, passionately devoted to his work and his friends, Jerome is certainly one of the most extraordinary figures in church history. And doubtless, it is due to this special temperament that his Latin Bible has come to be regarded by many people almost as if it were the unmediated word of God himself.

The fine floors of Aquileia cathedral, virtually unaltered since Jerome's day, tell us a great deal about the Western church of Jerome's youth, this relatively unsophisticated partner of the Eastern church. The Aquileian mosaics show the mix of paganism and Christianity that runs through so much Christian art of that time. Beside representations of the bread of the Eucharist is a winged figure of Victory, the goddess that only fifty years before Constantine had stamped upon his coinage. There are isolated scenes of which one may only guess the meaning; pictures of a cockerel fighting a tortoise, for example, may refer to the battle between Christ, the cockerel, and the heresies which were condemned at the Council of Nicaea. And here, too, amid the pictures of lobsters, fish, *funghi* and fine good foods, is an almost gluttonous celebration of Aquileian life. Jerome once said that the people of his town loved their bellies more than God, and that their clergy were a suitable lid for such a pot: but he remembered the delights of their table throughout his life. Here, too, on these mosaic floors are personifications of the seasons, each one a pagan motif, and nearest to the high altar are marvellously pagan scenes of *putti* and cupids all fishing, swimming and playing in the blue Mediterranean. The Christian artists have taken these images of Paradise directly from the pagan world. Nonetheless, biblical subjects are carefully introduced as well. So one of the pagan fish is a sea monster, the whale that swallows Jonah the biblical prophet, while in another part of the scene, in suspended time, another fish spews him out. Even the *putti* fishing traditionally in these Egyptian-style scenes seem to have been turned into Christians – into fishers of men. Appearing once again, Jonah sits serenely in his Paradise under a bower of gourds.

Later in life, when Jerome was hard at work on his Bible translations, this same scene – a popular motif of early Christian art where the swallowing and release of the Old Testament prophet was seen as a pre-figuration of the death and resurrection of Jesus Christ – must have sprung straight back into Jerome's mind, especially when he received a letter from North Africa from his friend Augustine, the Bishop of Hippo. For Augustine had written to tell him that the Christian congregation of a nearby town, Tripoli, rioted when Jerome's new translation of the Book of Jonah had been read at the Sunday service! So indignant had they become that some of the members had gone into the Jewish quarter of the town to ask Hebrew readers their opinion of the true meaning of the words of the text. At that time Jerome had been meeting Jewish scholars for some twenty years and surely knew exactly where the truth of the matter lay. What Jerome had done was to replace the traditional reading of the Hebrew word *qiqqayon*, changing it from the Latin *cucurbita* meaning a gourd, to *hedera* meaning ivy, and this had brought into question a favourite image of the artists of his day, the gourd bower of Paradise. Nor were the literary-minded congregations of North Africa, where Bible study was very popular, the only ones to be annoyed; artists too were very loath to give up their splendid gourds for mere clinging ivy, though some of them did meet Jerome's translation half-way by twining strands of ivy around the gourds!

The incident is typical of Jerome; he would have known the trouble that such a change would cause yet he still questioned the conventional images of Jonah that he had known from his youth. And as he candidly admitted in his reply to Augustine his 'ivy' was not a perfect rendering of the Hebrew either! Here is that grand mix of contradictions, complications and candour that makes Jerome such a strange yet suitable candidate for such a work. And Jerome's youth and middle age were, indeed, the perfect training ground for the task. After his Aquileian childhood he was sent by his parents, wealthy landowners, to the finest school in Rome, and there he first imbibed the classical authors who sustained his prose and haunted his Christian soul. Later in his life when Jerome was almost at the point of death, he dreamed he was hauled up before a Heavenly Tribunal where the Almighty himself told him that he was a follower of the pagan Cicero, the Roman rhetorician, not a Christian at all! Even *in extremis* Jerome's mind seeks to resolve the inner contradictions of faith and temperament: contradictions that he had once tried to resolve in the austerity and loneliness of a hermit's cell in Syria. He himself later recalled: 'Many years ago for the sake of the Kingdom of Heaven, I cut myself off from home, parents, sister, relations, and, what was harder, from the dainty food to which I had been used. But even when I was on my way to Jerusalem to fight the good fight there, I could not bring myself to forgo the library which with great care and labour I had got together at Rome. And so, miserable man that I was, I would fast, only to read Cicero afterwards. I would shed bitter tears called from my inmost heart by the remembrance of my past sins; and then I would take up Plautus again. Whenever I returned to my right senses and began to read the Prophets, their language seemed harsh and barbarous.'

While the other monks living all around Jerome's little cell practised extreme mortifications of the flesh, Jerome's mortifications were mainly of a literary nature. The scholar had taken donkey-loads of books into the desert with him yet other, less defined temptations also haunted him.

When I was a young man, though I was protected by the rampart of the lonely desert, I could not endure against the promptings of sin and the ardent heat of my nature. I tried to crush them by frequent fasting, but my mind was always in a turmoil of imagination. To subdue it I put myself in the hands of one of the brethren who had been a Hebrew before his conversion, and asked him to teach me his language. Thus, after having studied the pointed style of Quintilian, the fluency of Cicero, the weightiness of Fronto, and the gentleness of Pliny, I now began to learn the [Hebrew] alphabet again and practise harsh and gutteral words. What efforts I spent on that task, what difficulties I had to face, how often I despaired, how often I gave up and then in my eagerness to learn began again!

My unkempt limbs were covered in shapeless sackcloth; my skin through long neglect had become as rough and black as an Ethiopian's. Tears and groans were everyday my portion; and if sleep ever overcame my resistance and fell upon my eyes, I bruised my restless bones against the naked earth. Of food and drink I will not speak. Hermits have nothing but cold water even when they are sick, and for them it is sinful luxury to partake of cooked dishes. But though in my fear of hell I had condemned myself to this prison-house, where my only companions were scorpions and wild beasts, I often found myself surrounded by bands of dancing girls.

Jerome's love of women and his fascinated observations of the ladies of Rome – to whom he later recommended the harsh regimes of the Eastern hermits – were, to his contemporaries and even to some more modern churchmen, a strange fixation for such a holy man. 'Widows [are] wont to paint their faces with rouge and white lead, to flaunt in silk dresses, to deck themselves in gleaming jewels, to wear gold necklaces, to hang from their pierced ears the costliest Red Sea pearls, and to reek of musk.' Jerome was in love with everything from Latin prose to the curve of a knee; and he was certainly never daunted by lesser mortals, even when they forced him, a senior churchman, to leave Rome after one of his circle of admiring Roman matrons, virginal ladies sworn to serve God at his encouragement, had died from the severity of her mortifications. And this had been the last of a series of public scandals which dogged Jerome throughout the first half of his life. Even as a young man when he had finished his Roman education and returned to Aquileia filled with the idea of establishing a small group of Christians that would aim to lead an austere and holy life, his plans had been violently disturbed, as Jerome himself tells us, by a personal scandal. This he never names; but it had been his remorse for this lapse that had impelled him eastwards into a Syrian hermit's cell where he had stayed for many years. It is all too easy today to assess Jerome as one would a modern man – to show, by the hints that he himself continually gives us in his letters, that he was driven into the burning desert of devotion by remorse and guilt. But the man's candour is of a very different age to ours, and we should not easily allow the indignity of such brisk interpretations. But somewhere between the explosive invective of his literary arguments and his frank use of sexual imagery in some of his letters lies the essence, the fire of this Bible maker.

By the time he was forty, Jerome had survived two public scandals, spent years in a Syrian desert and travelled right around the Christian East. He had attended a general council of the church in Constantinople and talked with the finest scholars of his day from Didymus the Blind, the celebrated biblical scholar of Alexandria who had dedicated four studies to him, to the greatest Greek theologians of Antioch and Constantinople. He had also been the secretary to a pope in Rome, Pope Damasus, who had commissioned him to begin the task of translating the Bible into Latin. Jerome spoke Latin, Greek and Hebrew, a unique accomplishment for his day; he also understood Syraic, a language akin to Aramaic, the biblical language of Jesus Christ. Bundled on a boat in Ostia in 384 after the death of Pope Damasus and in the aftermath of his Roman scandal, Jerome had set sail for the East once more, this time for ever. Six years earlier Aquileia had been sacked by Attila and the Huns: Jerome's hometown and his family estates had been completely destroyed.

Translations and Transitions
'Bethlehem now ours, and the earth's most sacred spot . . . was overshadowed by a grove of Tammuz who was Adonis: and in the cave where the infant Christ once cried, the paramour of Venus was bewailed.' So Jerome introduces us to the small town that would be his home for almost forty years. When he arrived there in 384, the pagan grove was long gone, consumed both by workmen's fires and Christian indignation. In the town's centre stood Constantine's bright new Church of the Nativity, dedicated by his mother, the Empress Helena some fifty years beforehand. A steady stream of pilgrims visited the church as part of a round of sacred sites marked out by fine churches and local traditions. Today,

it must be said that of virtually all the holy sites, Bethlehem, the birthplace of Jesus, is the one that makes the most call upon faith. But to Jerome and the monks of the monastery he founded, the little town was the spot where God had come down to earth, and it was here that he chose to finish his translations.

Even as he had started the work in Rome, Jerome had had few illusions about the rumpus he would cause and he had begun by providently arming himself against prospective critics. 'You urge me' he had once written to Pope Damasus, 'to make a new work out of an old one, and, as it were, to sit in judgment on the copies of the Scriptures now scattered throughout the whole world; and, since they differ from one another, to decide which of them agree with the true reading of the Greek original. The labour is one of love, but at the same time both perilous and presumptuous; for, in judging others, I must myself be judged by all; and how can I dare to change a language that is old and carries the world back in its hoary old age to the early days of its infancy? Is there a man, learned or unlearned, who will not, when he takes the volume into his hands, and perceives that what he reads does not suit his settled tastes, break out immediately into violent language, and call me a forger and a profane person for having the audacity to add anything to the ancient books, or to make any changes or corrections therein?' This last statement is particularly pungent. It would be difficult to see Jerome reacting to the biblical translations of someone else in any other way than the one he describes.

Within a year of his arrival at Bethlehem, Jerome and his monks were joined by the saintly Paula, one of his Roman followers, and her daughter Eustochium. They would help Jerome in his work until they died, not only with his biblical translations for which purpose Paula had learned Hebrew, but also with the copious correspondence which Jerome conducted with a variety of people in North Africa, Gaul, Rome and Asia Minor. Paula founded three monasteries in Palestine; along with Jerome's community they were among the first religious groups from the West to establish themselves in the Holy Land, the forerunners of the communities whose high-walled silent buildings give towns like Bethlehem and Jerusalem a special quality.

Jerome's first task in his Bethlehem study was to finish the translation of the New Testament from the Greek which he had begun in Rome. That done, though he had discharged Pope Damasus' original request, he began work on the Old Testament, translating first the Book of Job from the Greek of the Septuagint, then making another translation of the Book of Psalms – the first, which he had made for Damasus at Rome, is, so tradition tells, the version called the Roman Missal which is still used in St Peter's to this day. This time, however, Jerome did not work exclusively from the Greek but also checked his readings against the original Hebrew. This experience seems to have encouraged Jerome to make translations directly from the Hebrew; and it is this final splendid translation, begun in 391, which, along with his earlier New Testament, serves as the bones of the Vulgate Bible. As he finished each Bible book, copyists from churches all around the Western Empire prepared manuscripts which were sent to Jerome's friends, and back to their own churches – distant places from which Jerome received lively criticism of his scholarship.

It was the new translation of Job which in 403 had brought on the riot in Tripoli. In his letter Augustine wondered whether or not Jerome should have translated those texts. Though they were probably quite incorrect in their older versions – Augustine says that he himself could not judge as he had little Greek and no Hebrew – they had served the faithful well enough. Less sensitive critics simply questioned Jerome's right to tamper with the sacred words at all, especially with the traditional translations of the words of Jesus, some of which he had changed considerably. To all this, the great scholar had a rich reply:

> I am not so dull-witted nor so coarsely ignorant as to suppose that any of the Lord's words is either in need of correction or is not divinely inspired; but the [old] Latin manuscripts of the Scriptures are proved to be faulty by the variations which all of them exhibit, and my object has been to restore them to the form of the Greek original, from which my detractors do not deny that they have been translated. If they dislike water drawn from the clear spring, let them drink of the muddy streamlet, and when they come to read the Scriptures let them lay aside the keen eye which they turn on woods frequented by game-birds and waters abounding in shellfish.

Jerome was not insensitive to the power of tradition, nor to the fondness that people have for the familiar texts; despite his famous dream, he never tired of the classical authors whose phrases continued to haunt his own prose until the day he died. So he says, 'to avoid any great divergencies from the Latin which we are accustomed to read, I have used my pen with some restraint; and while I have corrected only such passages as seemed to convey a different meaning, I have allowed the rest to remain as they are'.

Nonetheless, as Jerome believed that all the New Testament had been written in Greek, it appeared to him to be fruitless to spend time correcting earlier Latin versions when older Greek texts were available. 'Why not', he asks, 'go back to the original Greek and correct the mistakes introduced by inaccurate translators and the blundering alterations of confident but ignorant critics and, further, all that has been inserted or changed by copyists more asleep than awake?' In such work Origen's great Hexapla in nearby Caesarea must have been of especial use.

It was all a delicate question of balance, a balance that required just the mixture of hard scholarship and transparent honesty that Jerome possessed in such large measures. Even as he had begun his translating work in Rome, he had acknowledged the impossibility of making a mechanical translation that precisely copied the original; all one can do, he says, is to perceive the real meaning of the text and render it as well as possible.

Where the sweet reason of his letters and his biblical commentaries failed to impress his critics, Jerome enthusiastically resorted to a biting invective. His opponents, he says, are 'little asses with little pointed hooves'; he suggests that a Scots critic had porridge for brains – a dish whose full horrors Jerome must have experienced in northern Europe, a memory which had lingered in his mind for decades. As he grew older, Jerome continued working on new translations and each day also wrote commentaries upon points of scripture, and in these commentaries he included thoughts upon the experiences of his life. Jerome even describes the feelings of guilt and laziness that commonly afflict writers when they are not at their work, the little mechanisms of self-delusion, too, that often serve to put off the moment when pen touches paper.

> If we spend more than an hour in reading, you will find us yawning and trying to restrain our boredom by rubbing our eyes; then, as though we had been hard at work, we plunge once more into worldly affairs. I say nothing of the heavy meals which crush such mental faculties as we possess. I am ashamed to speak of our numerous calls, going ourselves every day to other people's houses, or waiting for others to come to us.

Though wrapped in the style of the late classical world, and not always to our contemporary taste, Jerome's commentaries and letters sometimes have the force of an early Christian stream of consciousness: a beautiful self-portrait.

In 410, six years after Jerome's last translation of the Old Testament, Alaric's Goths finally sacked Rome, the city having twice withstood a siege in the previous decade. During the first siege the Pope had even consented to secret pagan sacrifices, that, it was said, had saved other cities. Alaric, embittered and obdurate after a decade of fighting and negotiating with a dozen generals and imperial legates, had demanded all of Rome's gold, silver and moveable treasure. 'What will be left to us?' the city's senators asked him. 'Your lives', Alaric replied. But he had taken less and so returned with his tribesmen for the second siege a few years later. Then the Romans had staved him off with more loot, including 3000 pounds of pepper, 5000 pounds of gold and 400 silk tunics; old Rome was stripped bare. Finally, in 410 after another quarrel the infuriated Goths had marched to Rome yet again, starved her in a long siege, then sacked and burned the city in three days of pillage. Even the emperor's own sister, Galla Placidia, was taken away as a hostage.

Although Jerome had left Rome abused and in disgrace, the old imperial city was still the centre of his world, as it was to all the citizens of the Western Empire. 'I was so stupefied and dismayed that day and night,' he later wrote, 'that I could think of nothing but the welfare of the Roman community'. Far away in North Africa, Augustine, too, saw the sack of Rome, the first in a thousand years, as an ominous and fateful happening, and was prompted to begin his immense work, *The City of God*. The destruction of Rome, he said, showed how transient were even the mightiest of man's creations which should be made, therefore, to mirror the image of eternal God. Jerome lamented the tragedy which had shaken the whole classical world, in the introduction of his commentary upon the Book of Ezekiel. 'When I heard that the bright light of all the world was quenched, or rather that the Roman Empire had lost its head, and that the whole universe had perished in one city: then indeed, I became dumb and humbled myself and kept silence from good words'.

Jerome, Augustine and many of their contemporaries had clearly seen the ending of their world: a world where an Italian translator living in Bethlehem could dispute in lengthy letters with bishops in North Africa and Spain; a world which shared an international Latin culture where joint responses to events, to catastrophes and blessings alike, could be formulated by those with a common language, education and ideas. They saw that their age was ending and they put their faith in the Christian God. Jerome's Latin Bible and Augustine's flood of writings would become the most influential texts of the Western church, the bridge between the ancient classical world and the Christian faith of later ages.

Jerome lived on some ten years after the sack of Rome, Augustine ten more still, dying as the Vandals were besieging Hippo itself. Augustine's last written work was a carefully reasoned response to the problem of whether or not his priests and sacristans whom the Vandals were torturing and killing as heretics, should remain to minister to their hapless flock or flee to safety.

In Bethlehem Jerome's friend and helper, Paula died before him, and he saw that she was buried in a cave cut in the rock close by the Holy Grotto, where, it was said, the Christ-child had been born. Jerome became blind and could work only by dictation; Paula's daughter Eustochium helped him until she, too, died and was buried beside her mother. And all the while Jerome's correspondents told him of the terrible progress of the barbarian tribes as they moved through Italy, Gaul and Spain and right across North Africa. In the old man's mind these modern wars mixed freely with the Bible's texts. In his letters, as he bemoans the destruction of the Western Empire, his voice becomes like those of the Old Testament prophets with whom he had spent so many hours. In a letter he wrote to a baby at the request of her parents, he advises them to keep their little girl away from the sinful joys of this world whose end, he says, is fast approaching. This little girl, Patacula 'who babbles softly in her mother's arms, and finds honey sweeter than words', must learn to read and study says Jerome, 'because she thinks that the world was ever thus, she knows not of the past, she shrinks from the present, she fixes her desires on what is to come . . . my affection for you, brother Gaudentius [Patacula's father], has induced me to write this rough discourse and in my old age write a letter to an infant. I preferred to answer your request inadequately rather than not to answer it at all. As it is, my own inclinations have been paralysed by grief; in the other case you might have doubted the sincerity of my friendship'.

Jerome, it is said, worked in the cool darkness of a cave cut next to the site of the Holy Manger in Constantine's church; and there, in 420 at the age of seventy-three the old man was buried beside his two faithful Roman ladies.

Nine hundred years later, as the Crusader armies fled from Palestine after the fall of the Christian Kingdom of Jerusalem, the bones of St Jerome, St Paula and St Eustochium were taken off to Rome along with the five boards of the Holy Manger, all bound in silver, just as Jerome had described them. The remains of a man who left the imperial city disgraced and insulted had returned revered and sanctified – a Christian saint who would hear prayers and could make miracles. Nowadays both Jerome and the five wooden boards lie amid the splendours of the ancient Basilica of Santa Maria Maggiore. And Jerome would surely have been delighted; for he had known this church in his own time at Rome as Papal Secretary, when it had stood high among vineyards in a fashionable residential suburb. In those days the Roman church had serious problems. When Jerome's Pope Damasus had been elected, a rival had contested the papal throne and fierce battles had taken place in the city's streets. Barred from entering the Basilica of Santa Maria Maggiore, Damasus' supporters had climbed onto the church roof, stripped it of its heavy tiles and thrown them down onto the rival congregation below. More than a hundred people had died and the pretender had fled.

In later years, when Jerome was his secretary, Damasus did much to reconcile the pagan noble families of Rome to Christianity. This was no mean task. Jerome himself became a victim of the noble pagans' continuing suspicions about Christianity, when he was forced to leave the city in AD 384. As Jerome and Augustine had done in their youth, the pagan Romans thought the prose of the Christian Bible barbaric, and were scornful of the strange, rough, Eastern book, which, before Jerome's translations, existed in many varied and piecemeal versions. Jerome's Vulgate provided a text appropriate for sophisticated and intelligent Roman taste, and lent weight to the primacy that the Roman church now claimed. For a struggling and embattled church, it was a pearl almost beyond price.

Chapter Six
DARKNESS AND
ILLUMINATIONS

Introduction: Into the Dark

As the Western Empire died, it left behind it empty cities with marble ruins lying like great skeletons at their centres. Slowly the population was transformed into separate and modest nations of small farms and savage armies. There was little international trade and almost total illiteracy. Ironically just as Christianity had arrived in the west, the Empire started to dissolve. Even in Jerome's day, Rome had long since been deserted by the Western emperors, their courts having moved first to Milan where Augustine had come from North Africa to study and preach, and then to Ravenna, a marshy city in the flat delta of the river Po, a difficult and unhealthy city that discouraged all but the most organized invaders.

So Ravenna took on all the trappings of an imperial city and as it was less central to the affairs of Europe than either Rome or Milan many of its ancient buildings have survived. The imperial palaces, from which several mercenary armies marched in brave attempts to turn back the barbarian tribes, now lie under half the modern city, unexcavated in the marshy soil. But the splendid court churches remain, some of the greatest treasures of Europe and the last monuments of the Western Empire, hinting at what the artists of imperial Christianity might have achieved had their courtly patrons and the Empire survived. They also show how Christianity and its book had already transformed the hard art of pagan Rome. And this is a transformation at once moving and strange, something alien yet so beautiful as the patterns and colours of the mosaic-covered vaults unfold all around you.

Legend says, and there is little reason to doubt it, that the famous little cross-shaped tomb chamber known as the Mausoleum of Galla Placidia was used as the burial place not only of that famous empress but also of two of the last Emperors of the West, her brother and her son (see Plate 23). Archaeologists tell us that the little cruciform building once stood at one end of a courtyard in front of a large basilica; the modest monument was once an adjunct to a great court church. Empress Galla Placidia was no mere adjunct of the court but a tough old lady who ruled the dying Empire for twenty-five years. Her life was an amazing microcosm of the era. The daughter of the Eastern Emperor Theodosius I, Galla Placidia had been brought up at Split in Diocletian's huge palace, where the divine emperor still lay inside his mausoleum, and she was educated in the palace at Constantinople. A beautiful young woman, she was carried off by Alaric at the sack of Rome and was married, decked in furs and silks, at the Gothic capital of Narbonne in France to one of Alaric's sons. Her dowry at this strangely barbarous Christian wedding was a palace full of Roman booty, including some of the antique treasures of the Jersualem Temple, which the Goths had removed from the temples of the Roman Forum. The young Queen then went on campaign with her new husband. They buried a young son in a silver coffin at Barcelona before her husband was assassinated and she was led in chains over the Pyrenees by her husband's killers. Ransomed by the Eastern Emperors for 600,000 measures of wheat – the improvident Goths were starving – Galla Placidia then lived again in Constantinople, having been exiled from Ravenna by her brother. There she married again and raised a Greek family, before invading Ravenna at the head of an Eastern army virtually to rule the West as Empress and regent for a quarter of a century up to her death. On one occasion she locked up a daughter who, already pregnant by a court chamberlain, was attempting to elope with Attila the Hun!

Until the twentieth century it was said that you could see the old lady sitting bolt upright on a chair inside one of the three marble sarcophagi in her Ravenna mausoleum. Then one day a guide dropped his candle into the box and the mummy burned. Though it is unlikely that the Empress could ever have survived so long, burials in this position were not uncommon in her time. But there is nothing at all in the little chapel that gives even a clue to the imperial owners of the three huge marble sarcophagi that fill the space.

That this beautiful building is of Galla Placidia's time and of imperial origin there is no doubt; it is the work of court artists, built by architects, perhaps brought from Milan, and decorated in exotic mosaics by international crafts-men. But how Christianity has transformed these artists' touch! How the inhumanity of much earlier Roman architecture, with its mechanical smooth columns and dead flat marble walls, has been transformed into live surfaces that gently ripple as they roll across the walls and vaults. All these hard surfaces bear the handmarks of the men who made them. The walls, the vaults and the dome are all made without strict control, without the foreman's whip and plumb-bobs, the tools that controlled the slaves who made Diocletian's great cold tomb at Split. And, unlike the deep darkness of that pagan monument, here the dome above is filled with heaven's stars.

But these Christian artists still dwelled inside the old classical world. A mosaic Christ sits in an imperial arch, a fresh-faced young Christ, a shepherd with blonde hair and a Greek nose. But on the opposite wall, there is a surprising and very different scene. In a tomb where two emperors and an empress were probably once laid, there is not one word of memorial, no celebrations of their names and achievements, but simply a mosaic picture of a dead church deacon, St Lawrence, who, legend tells, was martyred at Rome in the persecutions. St

Lawrence had been ordered to take the treasures of the church to the magistrates; he then gave away the church plate and money, and took some of Rome's poorest people with him to the court: 'These are the treasures of the church,' he told them, and was roasted alive on a grid-iron for his trouble. That emperors were now entombed with images of men like St Lawrence on their walls shows something of the new world that was beginning to be made as the Empire fell to the barbarian armies. Yet above Jesus and St Lawrence in their vaults are all the age-old classical decorations, but here triumphantly transformed into something beyond decoration, something with its own interior life. Pattern intensified has become art. And above these low vaults your eyes move upwards into heaven, to a little dome supported by the signs of the four Evangelists. And above these images, shimmering in the night-sky of heaven and burning like church lamps, is the cross, the keystone of heaven. The *mysterium tremendum* of the pagan emperors has become Christ's.

By the side of St Lawrence, and forming part of the same scene, is a bookcase holding four leather-bound books – each one of them a Gospel. Deacon Lawrence would have been responsible for just such volumes as part of his church duties; bookcases like this one were to be found standing inside the doors of many churches, the books intended for the use of their congregations. Here in Galla Placidia's mausoleum this bookcase with its books, drawn as large as St Lawrence himself, is laid out as a witness to the incredible impact of this eastern faith built around the Gospels. Christianity, it was said, had been a success so absolute that it could only have been ordered in Heaven itself. Though it is very rare in these early Christian monuments to find illustrations of the biblical stories, the Word, the books themselves appear. The symbols of the Four Evangelists hold up the mausoleum's central dome, the very vault of heaven.

There is also at Ravenna another, darker imperial tomb, an ominous tough little stone octagon that stands like a full stop at the ending of classical history: this is the tomb of Theodoric the Ostrogoth. Built seventy years after Galla Placidia's mausoleum, the making of Theodoric's stone-domed tomb required the resources of the Empire, just as Diocletian's buildings had done – masons from Syria and eastern architects, even Egyptian porphyry for its sarcophagus. Yet the building is still part nomad, its low dome reminiscent of the round tents, the yurts, of Theodoric's Gothic ancestors. The strange decorative band cut into the tomb's eaves, sheltered under the deep ring of the dome, is covered with the age-old Asian spiral decorations adapted by the Syrian stonemasons from the patterns on horse harnesses and cloakclasps of northern tribesmen. Archaeologists have found these artefacts in burials in Italy, Greece, Spain and even North Africa, in tombs in St Augustine's own church at Hippo. Theodoric the Ostrogoth was a Christian monarch albeit, like most of the northern tribesmen, an ardent follower of Bishop Ulphilas, whose heretical views upon the Holy Trinity had been condemned by every church council since Nicaea.

The shafts of light that filter through the gloom of Theodoric's tomb chamber down onto the purple sarcophagus pass through small windows shaped like eastern crosses. The sarcophagus itself is protected by a huge four-square cross painted onto the underside of the dome, a cross drawn like the jewelled and golden cross that Constantine had placed upon the Rock of Calvary. Shells that had once borne Venus on the Mediterranean waves and which stand in early Christian art as a sign of Paradise, decorate the smaller niches of the burial chamber. The mausoleum's architecture is sophisticated and beautifully made, an extravagant mixture of barbarian and classical style. It is also ruthless and rather frightening.

This is the essential memorial of Theodoric, a pious, clumsy, suspicious, well-intentioned man, who brought some of Rome's finest scholars and diplomats to his court, a barbarian who, the scholars felt, might be made into a Roman emperor. So the prodigious scholar Boethius came with several other senators to try to 'tame the wild beasts' – the northern tribesmen who now ruled Italy. And Boethius advised the Gothic court about lutes and water clocks and upon framing proper Christian laws for the Ostrogothic kingdom. In his writing, Boethius comments ominously upon Aristotle's optimistic assertion that knowledge inevitably increases; he says that in his own time the problem was not the increase of knowledge but the preservation of it. At the end of his long reign, growing ever more suspicious and frightened of such cultivated Romans, Theodoric had Boethius imprisoned, then killed with a bowstring, which, it was observed, was tightened around his temples until his eyeballs stood right out of his head.

Neither the fine words of Roman senators nor the prayers of Italian Christians had kept the barbarians out of the Empire and neither would they save the imperial government from complete destruction. By Theodoric's time – he died in 526, some seventy-five years after Galla Placidia – Africa and the northern provinces were abandoned, and both the Eastern and Western Empires were forced to rely on some of the tribes themselves to fight off the later waves of barbarians, all of them hungry for the rich crops and treasure of the Mediterranean lands. In just such a way, Theodoric and his eastern Goths had been invited into Italy in 476 by an Eastern emperor after the last Western one, Romulus Augustulus, had sent the imperial insignia back to Constantinople and resigned. After a lengthy siege Theodoric had reduced Ravenna, that impregnable marsh-bound city, to starvation, then slaughtered the defenders after concluding a peace treaty with them. Upon such inauspicious beginnings, Theodoric had built his thirty-year rule. Aided by Roman statesmen like Boethius, Theodoric drew up a long series of edicts encouraging peaceful co-existence between the Romans and the tribesmen that wandered through Italy. 'They visit you', wrote a Roman poet, 'at dawn, breathing leeks and ardour; great friendly souls, with appetites much bigger than your larder'.

Yet Theodoric's court was hardly as impoverished as his tribesmen. Another of his ministers, Cassiodorus describes the imperial dining-table of Ravenna holding fish from all the rivers of the Empire, from the Rhône, the Danube, the Rhine and the Po. But these Romans must have been lonely men at this foreign table. In jail and under sentence of death, Boethius wrote *The Consolation of Philosophy*, perhaps the finest of all such prison books, in which he meditates on fame, fate and destiny. It is the swansong of the classical tradition. Though a Christian who wrote commentaries upon religious themes, Boethius the old aristocrat resolutely refused in his last days to mix his faith with his classical education.

PLATE 24 (Opposite): The church of Haghia Sophia, consecrated in 538. The extraordinary visual riches of Justinian's original building survive almost intact.
PLATE 25 (Overleaf above): Abel and Melchizedek offer up a sheep and bread and wine on a Byzantine altar. Mosaics from the time of Justinian in the church of San Vitale at Ravenna, consecrated in 547.
PLATE 26 (Overleaf below): Justinian, his bishops and his army go to celebrate the Eucharist. San Vitale, Ravenna.

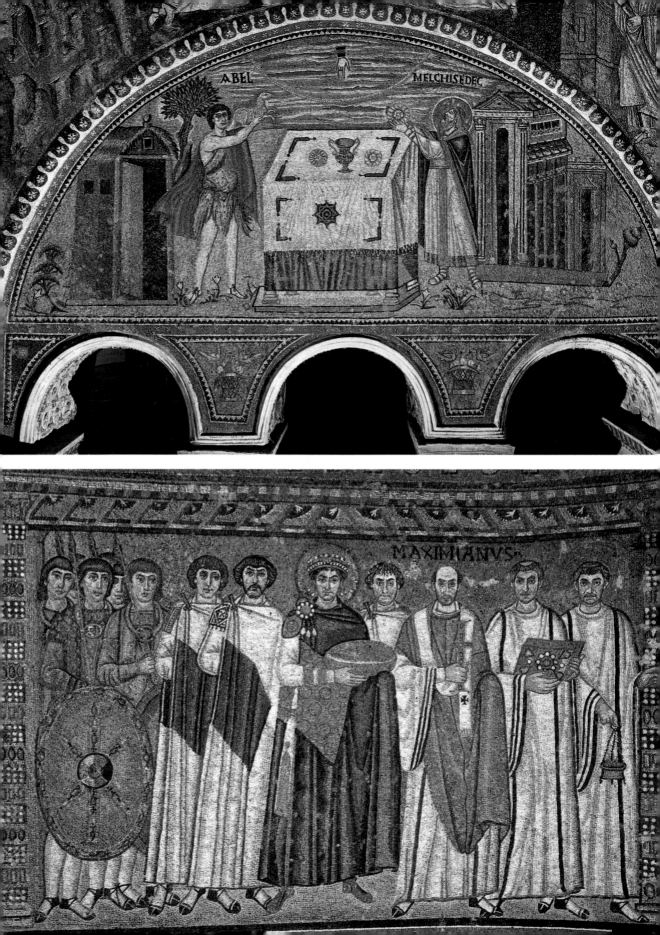

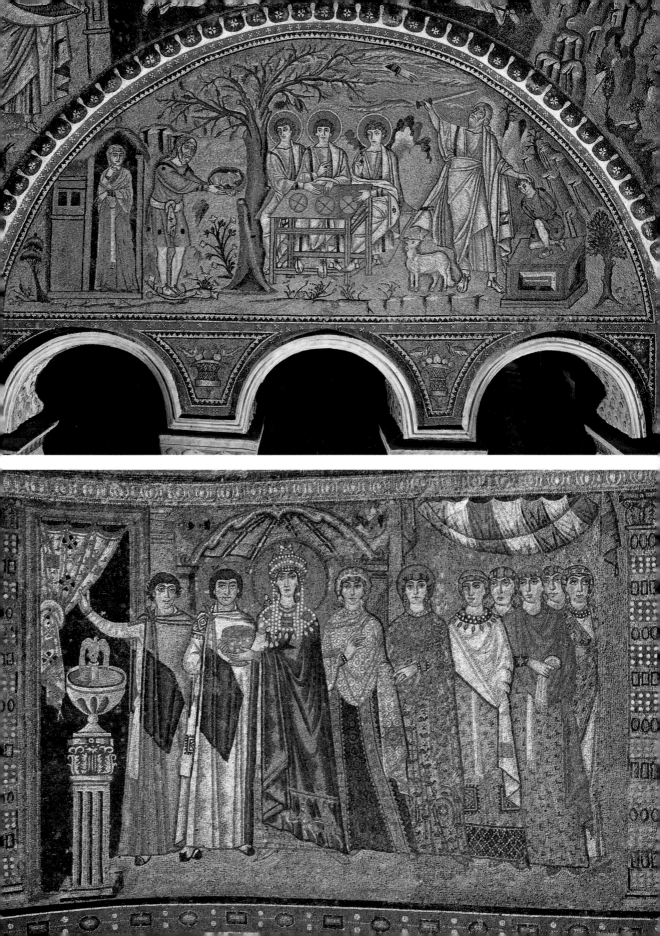

This man, this man sought out the source
Of storms that roar and rouse the seas;
The spirit that rotates the world,
The cause that translocates the sun
From shining East to watery West;
He sought the reason why spring hours
Are mild with flowers manifest,
And who enriched with swelling grapes
Ripe autumn at the full of year.
Now see that mind that searched and made
All Nature's hidden secrets clear
Lie prostrate prisoner of night.
His neck bends low in shackles thrust,
And he is forced beneath the weight
To contemplate – the lowly dust.

Boethius' humility is perhaps a Christian virtue. Certainly *The Consolation of Philosophy* became one of the most influential books of the Christian Middle Ages, its reflections and sentiments affecting Dante and Petrarch. (In England, King Alfred the Great, Chaucer and Queen Elizabeth I all translated it.) According to a medieval legend, shortly after Boethius' execution, Theodoric himself died of regret and a broken heart; another tale relates that to avoid divine retribution he took refuge in his great stone tomb but was killed by a thunderbolt which split the massive stone dome and struck him where he stood.

In his lifetime Theodoric had promoted a certain peace and prosperity in his kingdom; after his death the Western Empire descended into greater poverty, local wars and illiteracy. In 540 the armies of the Eastern Emperor entered Ravenna after a long and bloody campaign up through Italy. This conquest, however, promised not civilization, but more chaos. The Gothic Empire was finished and Cassiodorus, the chief minister, left the north for his home town in the south of Calabria where he founded a religious community, an academy of learning where monks studied, copied and translated classical texts, both pagan and Christian. In this beautiful retreat called Vivarium – the 'fish pond' – all the letters and decrees which he and his fellow senators had composed for the Gothic kings with such clarity and humanity were collected and edited; later they became the models for the chancellories of medieval Europe.

PLATE 27 (*Previous page above*): *Abraham offers bread and wine to the three angels, and (right) prepares to sacrifice his son Isaac. San Vitale, Ravenna.*
PLATE 28 (*Previous page below*): *Theodora and her ladies go up to the women's galleries of the church. San Vitale, Ravenna.*
PLATE 29 (*Opposite*): *The church of Haghia Sophia, a view from the gallery down to the apse, where the High Altar once stood.*

But the most important undertaking of Cassiodorus at Vivarium was the collection and revision of the Latin Bible, the book that would eventually supply re-born Europe with its models of earth and heaven, government, dignity and morality. In the ages before printing when all texts were individually hand-written, it was extremely easy for the copyists working in the scriptoria to misread or misquote as they wrote. Through generations of such errors, mistakes, even of spelling or of punctuation, could slowly deform the words of the text. Since ancient times it had been recognized that perfect copies of sacred texts were essential. Scribes copying the Jewish Bible were obligated under Holy Law to use only the finest materials for their work and perfect exemplars from which to make their copy (see page 154). But no such regulations had ever been pressed upon the Christian churches, and by Cassiodorus' day there were endless variations and versions of Latin Bible texts in circulation, including several different versions of Jerome's great Vulgate. The gathering together of all the Bible's texts between a single set of covers to make one book – a *pandect*, a single Christian Bible – had not yet been done.

The purification of the Latin Bible, basically of Jerome's text, was one of the tasks that Cassiodorus and his southern monks took upon themselves. Their aim was the production of fine, clear text gathered into a single book. For the most part, the Vivarium scriptorium busied itself with correcting errors of spelling, of punctuation and grammar. Many of the biblical names, for instance, had different forms in the different versions of the text – Moyses rather than Moses or Ambacum for Habakkuk the Prophet. The use of different terms in the various translations had also created many inconsistencies. At Vivarium, all the careful procedures of classical learning were employed to make a standard Bible text. All spellings were regulated, and the Bible's Latin grammer too – even Jerome's inconsistencies were ironed-out. The monks also checked the texts themselves, consulting a Greek original and the works of early Christian writers when the wording of a line or phrase was in doubt: if two or three of these ancient sources agreed and together contradicted the contemporary versions, the ancient reading was substituted in the revised text. The Bible was then divided into chapters, each with a new title, and each of these chapters was divided into verses with every phrase and sentence broken down further by special spacings and punctuation, following a system that Jerome himself had sometimes used.

At Vivarium, Cassiodorus and his monks produced what may be called the standard Jerome Vulgate, and though many other versions continued to be used in the monasteries and churches of the West for centuries, it was essentially Cassiodorus' text that has become the European Latin Bible. And it is fascinating to see, in the centuries following Cassiodorus' day, this careful version of Jerome's Vulgate epitomized by the legendary one-volume Bible known as the *Codex Grandior* travelling slowly throughout the West, a major element in the spread of scholarship during the Dark Ages. Not only would this *Codex Grandior* become the West's Latin Bible, but also a vital model of consistency that embodied a literary scholarship surpassing all other Latin books; a store of fine scholarship that was almost as important to the West as the very words that the *Codex Grandior* enshrined.

Those who would still deny that a dark age ever descended upon the Western Empire after the days of Cassiodorus and Theodoric do not appreciate what had been lost. Never a haven of Christian piety, usually cruel and faceless, the ancient Empire had, nonetheless, supported hundreds of years of leisured scholarship of which the residue, fragmented and garbled texts, would form the greater part of the wisdom of the West for almost a thousand years. Even in Cassiodorus' time, most men had already retreated into farming and fighting. Now learning and books were to be found only in isolated monasteries, often on the very edges of the old Empire: Christianity had passed right through the ancient Roman world.

Northumbria and Ireland

That the world's oldest surviving one-volumed Latin Bible, made about AD 700 in Northumberland, is now housed in Michelangelo's Medicean Library at Florence is a tale of exquisite improbabilities, a tale largely told in the beautiful writings of Bede, the Northumbrian monk in whose monastery and in whose lifetime this great book was made. In its day, Bede tells us, this massive *Codex* was but one of three similar works written in Bede's scriptorium at the monastery of Jarrow. This volume was taken to Rome 'as a present for the Pope' by the monastery's elderly abbot who was intent upon seeing the City of the Apostles once more before he died. This abbot, Ceolfrith, had been as a father to Bede; together the young priest and the child had sung the services alone when the other monks were struck down with plague. Between them they had seen their monastery prosper over thirty years and more. Bede describes the abbot's final leave-taking from Jarrow with a sorrowful simplicity: 'on the morning of 5 June – which was a Thursday – as soon as Mass had been sung in the church of the Blessed Mother of God, the ever-Virgin Mary, and also in the church of the Blessed Peter at which those present had made their communion, he at once prepared to depart.'

The party of travellers with the great book and the monks who had come to take their leave of them, all made their way down to the banks of the River Wear. 'They arrived at the shore; once again he gave them all the kiss of peace amidst their tears. They fell to their knees and, after he had offered prayer, he and his companions boarded the boat. The deacons of the church embarked with them, carrying lighted candles and a golden cross. After crossing the river, he venerated the cross, mounted his horse and rode off, leaving behind him in his monasteries brethren to the number of around six hundred.'

After riding down through Saxon England, Ceolfrith and his party crossed to France, and there he was struck down with sickness. 'He had got as far as Langres about the third hour of the day and his soul took flight to the Lord at the tenth hour of that same day. The following day he was buried with all dignity in the church of the Three Brother Martyrs amidst the tears and lamentation not only of the eighty or more English men who made up his company but also of the local inhabitants who were deeply affected at the thought of so worthy an old man being disappointed of his wish. It was hard for anyone to restrain his tears at the sight of some of Ceolfrith's party starting out to continue their journey without their father, while others revoked their intention of going to Rome, preferring to turn back for home to report the news of his burial: and the rest, in their undying love for him, remained to keep watch by his tomb in the midst of a people whose language they could not understand . . .'

While Ceolfrith's body lay in France performing prodigious miracles, his huge Bible continued on its pilgrimage to Rome, finally finishing its journey as a papal donation to one of the numerous abbeys that stood at the foot of Mount Amiata, that high round hill at the centre of south Tuscany. From here in the eighteenth century it was taken to the Laurentian Library at Florence, part of the rich harvest of the Medici dukes. A hundred years later, two bibliophiles made the imaginative leap that re-connected Bede's history of Ceolfrith's pilgrimage with the Florentine Bible, now known as the *Codex Amiatinus*; coming to their conclusion by deciphering part of a much-altered dedication page at the beginning of the book in which Ceolfrith's name had been changed for that of an Italian bishop.

Yet more remarkable is that this ancient northern book contains the Vulgate text of Cassiodorus' *Codex Grandior* which must have been taken to Northumberland in the decades before Ceolfrith's last pilgrimage. Bede himself must have handled one of the volumes made in the Vivarium scriptorium. The Jarrow Bible, the *Codex Amiatinus*, is a direct link between the dying classical Mediterranean culture and the cold Christian northlands. And so respected was the text of Ceolfrith's *Codex* that when in the sixteenth century the popes ordered the final reformation of the Vulgate Bible to provide a perfect exemplar for the printing presses, the *Codex Amiatinus* was the text most widely used —

FACTUM EST AUTEM CUM
TURBAE INRUERENT INEUM
UTAUDIRENT UERBUM DI
ETIPSE STABAT SECUS STAGNU
GENESARETH
ETUIDIT DUAS NAUESSTANTES.
SECUSSTAGNUM
PISCATORES AUTEM DISCENDE
RANT ETLAUABANT RETIA
ASCENDENS AUTEM INUNAM
NAUEM QUAEERAT
SIMONIS
ROGAUIT AUTEM ATERRA
REDUCERE PUSILLUM

this ancient text, written out in a dark and tiny room by English scribes in their curious local script.

Jarrow monastery had been founded in the years of Bede's childhood by Abbot Benedict Biscop, a Northumbrian nobleman. He had trained in the monastic order of St Benedict, at the famous island abbey of Lérins in the south of France, around the year 665. Biscop brought stonemasons and glassmakers from France to build his monastery and, in regular trips to Rome, brought back many ecclesiastical treasures to decorate his churches and educate his monks. The Italian paintings that he brought to Jarrow were the first religious paintings to be seen in England; he also brought the choir master of St Peter's, Rome to instruct the monks in the ritual and singing of their services. Of all these wonders in a dark age, only the *Codex Amiatinus* along with some church walls have survived. But happily, in its vast text of some two thousand pages, the *Codex Amiatinus* holds copies of some of the original illustrations of Cassiodorus' Bible: the signs of the Four Evangelists that head their respective Gospels and, as an appropriate frontispiece to such a work, a splendid picture of the Old Testament scribe Ezra in his library (see Plate 31).

This drawing of a white-haired old man with the Law upon his head and the breast-plate of the High Priest of Israel upon his chest is also a picture of Cassiodorus himself working in his monastery at Vivarium. This Ezra sits upon a late Roman chair, writing on his knees propped by a footstool in the classical manner. He writes, too, with a quill pen stripped of its feather, taken from a crow or a similar bird and sharpened to a fine point with the triangular Roman razor that lies by his side. Sensibly, he has placed his inkwell upon the floor; on the table above sits a little palette of the type on which Roman scribes prepared their colours and the black ink, a remarkably permanent medium based on holly or oak gall. The compasses and stylus that lie by Cassiodorus upon the floor were used to gently scratch in the writing lines and borders on the vellum sheets. And when they made a mistake in the text, the ink was erased by rubbing the vellum with a piece of pumice – a technique that left enough traces of the original ink to allow modern scholars to read the original text with the aid of ultraviolet light.

Evidence that this Ezra is none other than Cassiodorus himself is to be found in the drawings of the books that are scattered through the picture. Cassiodorus tells us that he prepared three separate editions of the Bible; firstly, a nine-volumed edition of an old pre-Jerome Latin text which he used as a working copy; secondly, a large one-volumed Bible, which he called his *Codex Grandior* – this was the Bible that Bede says he saw and used at Jarrow; and thirdly, another one-volumed Bible, smaller in size, which held his first corrected text of Jerome's Vulgate. In the picture the artist has carefully drawn all these volumes lying around the scribe; the nine-volumed Bible lies in the bookcase shaped exactly like the one in the mosaic in the Tomb of Galla Placidia at Ravenna; the *Codex Grandior* is the one in which the scribe is writing, and the smaller Bible, the Vulgate, lies open upon the floor.

This, then, is a very remarkable picture, a document that stands between two very different worlds. And as if to emphasize the fact, the English artist has drawn out this ancient southern scene in a curiously half-understood way. The shadows in the picture, a copy of the angular perspective so beloved of late classical artists, have been misinterpreted. The scribe's robes, though faithfully recorded in their outline, are randomly coloured in patches of bright red, the better to brighten the thin northern light. The decoration drawn upon the bookcase is altered; animals that in the original represent two stags drinking at the Fountain of Life here are drawn like two old oxen, while the peacocks of paradise have been transformed into northern pheasants.

Here, you can quickly sense the knife-edge on which the West was poised, the edge between darkness and learning, between reason and unreason. Northern abbots rich enough to travel frequently to Rome to buy treasures for their churches conducted services in times of plague sung by just a single choirboy and a priest. Fifty years after Bede's time, the Norsemen came down upon England killing monk and peasant alike, destroying even the draughty damp monasteries. How fragile, then, was this link between Cassiodorus, living pleasantly on his southern estates, and this later learning of the monks of

Jarrow when odd volumes travelled across Europe in lonely and tenuous communication from one literate person to another. And the making of these books required tremendous expenditure, a king's ransom in such poor times. *Codex Amiatinus* required several thousand hours of work, the labour of seven scribes – one of whom, perhaps, was Bede himself – and it consumed the skins of some five hundred animals. No wonder that people revered these great old books even when they could not understand their words. In 1909 fragments of the other two Bibles, the sisters of *Codex Amiatinus*, were discovered by a vicar in a Newcastle junk shop. They had been bound into the account books of a local estate, preserved there by chance for more than a thousand years.

In Bede's day there was another, older monastery some fifty miles up the coast from Jarrow on the little island of Lindisfarne. This community, however, had not received its training, as Bede's had done, direct from Roman scholarship and the Benedictine rule, but from the older Irish tradition of monasticism, a relic of the Christianity which Roman missionaries had taken to the north centuries before, and which had been preserved after the Empire abandoned the British Isles to their own devices. Eastern monasticism, which had so fascinated Jerome, had also found ready expression inside the Irish tradition of family farming and the monks had soon found their own distinctive forms of living quite independent of the western rule of St Benedict. In the late seventh century, these two traditions met in Northumberland at Jarrow and Lindisfarne and after eyeing each other somewhat warily, embraced as Christian brothers.

So Bede, raised in the Roman tradition, wrote histories of the Irish saints and of their monasteries. And the Irish monks in their turn took up the reformed Vulgate of Cassiodorus as an exemplar for their Gospels. The oldest Irish manuscript, the so-called *Cathach of Columcille*, said to have been written by St Columba himself and certainly the oldest surviving book in northern Europe, is taken from part of a psalter written out in Jerome's Vulgate. With their long traditions of travelling and preaching, the Irish missionaries took their texts, decorated with the wild colours and extravagant designs of the northern tradition, down through mainland Europe. And some of the monasteries that the Irishmen founded still preserve the bright old books in their libraries. So the text of Cassiodorus' Vulgate went to Germany, Austria and Switzerland, even back to Italy itself, carried by these gentle Irish monks. Their biographers tell us that they sailed across the seas on tombstones and held communion upon the backs of friendly whales, they believed that birds were little fallen angels whose very clothes held the perfume of paradise and in their simplicity, hung their washing up to dry on rainbows. These men and their scribes made some of the world's most beautiful books: Columba's Psalm book, the Book of Durrow, the Book of Kells, Macregol's Gospels and the Gospel Book of Lindisfarne.

Curiously enough, this marvellous tradition of illumination seems to have begun not in Ireland at all but in Northumbrian Lindisfarne, the work of Englishmen drawing upon Anglo-Saxon traditions. For the Lindisfarne Gospel is the oldest of these wonderful books. Laid out on its splendid pages is another part of the same tradition of design that Theodoric's Syrian masons cut so carefully under the eaves of his stone tomb at Ravenna – the so-called 'animal style' of Central Asia, brought to England first by the Saxons and again in a second wave by the Vikings. In the Lindisfarne Gospels (see Plate 33), this lively art is laid out with care, measured with compass and stylus onto the pages with such delicate, obsessive other-worldliness that in medieval times people thought it was drawn by angels.

The Lindisfarne Gospels were made at the same time as the *Codex Amiatinus*, by the scribe Eadfrith in honour of St Cuthbert, a northern saint who had died a few years earlier. The great book had been covered – 'made firm on the outside' – by one Ethilwald, while Billfrith, a hermit jeweller, had decorated the bindings with gold, silver and precious stones. Two hundred and fifty years later, a certain Aldred, who describes himself as 'an unworthy and most miserable priest', wrote an Anglo-Saxon paraphrase in the Northumbrian dialect between the lines of Eadfrith's text and this is the oldest surviving Bible text in English. Beyond all these words, however, it is the Gospels' decorated pages that hold interest; they lie like fine carpets at the beginning of each of the Gospels, often decorating and elaborating a single letter, making it resonant with repeated detail. Such pattern is not the product of clear southern minds, of Cassiodorus' Mediterranean that gave Northumbria the matter-of-fact rendering of scribe Ezra at his desk. These are the mystical meditations of a northern solitary, a little faint perhaps, from fasting and the love of God, a man who was able to take a few pennyworth of powdered colour and ink and

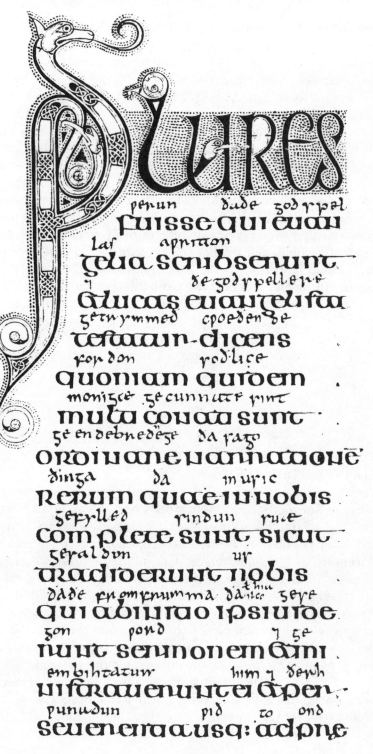

make jewels with it. At Lindisfarne in the summer months the sun flashes on the cold bright waters in patterns like those of the great Gospel Books; they harvested fine fish and oysters and took rabbits and hares in the fields. All this life they have left us in their great books.

An ancient tale tells us that the body of St Cuthbert, along with the Gospels that Eadfrith wrote in his honour, were taken away from England in a boat by monks anxious to protect their most precious treasures from the Vikings. And so angry was Cuthbert at leaving his native shores that he made a great storm, and the book was washed into the sea, to the great sadness of the monks who saw their error and put back into harbour again. That same night Cuthbert appeared to one of them in a dream, telling him to go down to the shore where he would find the ancient book. And the next day the monk found the Gospels dry and unharmed on the sand at low tide. In those days books were kept in large boxes and it could well be that the Lindisfarne Gospels were once sent floating on the cold North Sea as the waterstains along the edges of the pages would suggest. In medieval times, the Gospels were called 'The Book of St Cuthbert which fell into the Sea'; everything about the book seemed to be miraculous.

Constantinople: The Divine Wisdom
As the West quietly sank into its dark age, the Eastern Empire went brightly upon its way. In Constantinople classical texts both pagan and Christian were widely read. The abstractions of the Greek theologians were avidly debated by a fiery and literate population, as interested in theology as in the relative merits of the charioteers of the hippodrome. Constantine's successors had greatly enlarged the city, building huge new land walls marking the greatest of all Roman fortresses that served to keep the enemies of the Empire at bay for a thousand years. Close to the southern end of the walls, where they met the Sea of Marmora, was a grand triumphal archway that had once stood in the fields outside the city and now formed a part of the new land fortifications. Part-sheathed in gold plate, it was known throughout the East and West as the Golden Gate. For a thousand years a succession of Byzantine emperors and armies rode through this gate, sometimes in triumphant procession, sometimes in flight from their perennial enemies – the Persians, the Bulgars, the Russians, the Goths, the Arabs and the Crusaders from the West. In the sixteenth century,

the thousand-year-old gate was finally bricked up and ringed with towers by the workmen of Sultan Mehmet, the Turkish conqueror of Constantinople who made around the ancient arch a castle in which he stored his treasure and occasionally imprisoned ambassadors.

Between these walls and the eastern sea, shaped like a great V on seven impressive hills, Constantine's classical Christian city played out this millennium of Christian history surrounded sometimes by a large protecting empire, sometimes by the enemy at the gate. And through it all, the fabled imperial city, 'the eye of all cities' as it was known, kept something of the air of a small town, though its emperors and empresses claimed near-divinity. But even in their splendour, they were also familiar individuals to the people of the town. In a way then, this city was a classical ghetto, and like most ghettos it held a solid, stratified and highly conservative society within it. And there was good reason for this satisfaction and superb self-confidence. Was not their city Constantine's own? Had not its patriarchs been among the first men to set Christianity on an imperial course? Had not God himself delivered up the final, crowning glory of classical literature, the New Testament in Greek, the city's very own tongue? Throughout the dark age of the West, Constantinople's scholars studied and copied all the ancient texts and even, on occasion, decorated them with suitably classical illuminations. In this city, the classical past was still part of the present, there was no destruction, no breakdown of the ancient world. Right up until the city's fall, its enemies were called by the classical names of the lands from which they had come, just as Constantinople's second name 'Byzantium', the Greek name of the small town that Constantine had made into Constantinople, was also used. Splendid oratory, the Roman games, the practice of fine art and subtle court diplomacy continued apace. When in the tenth century a German ambassador came to Byzantium and said that he found the city eccentric, its people badly mannered, strangely dressed and smelling curiously of exotic food, its emperor a 'monstrosity of a man, a dwarf, fat-headed and with snake's eyes', we read the words of a barbarian reporting on an ancient world he did not understand. As for the Byzantines, they were in no doubt that they alone held the mantle of civilization. After all, that disgruntled ambassador had come to Constantinople on an unsuccessful mission to ask for the hand of one of the emperor's daughters for a northern king.

In the sixth century, at about the same time that the city's new walls were being built, a series of Bible books was prepared in Constantinople. Their pages, stained with the imperial purple, held a carefully corrected version of the original Greek texts, and these texts are the ones that the Eastern church uses to this day. Today their rare pages are also the oldest-known decorated Bible texts, pre-dating the Northumbrian and Irish books by more than a century. Interestingly, their pictures not only illustrate the Bible's stories but also offer interpretations of several awkward points; early examples of the use of biblical images to explain and underline political dogma. Jesus, for example, had clearly been the victim of the imperial Roman machine, and the imperial church had always been at pains to reconcile this unfortunate example of imperial authority – which had ordered the death of Jesus – with the general bene-ficence of imperial culture and administration.

Confronting the problem head on, the Bible illustrators chose to show Pilate surrounded by all the apparatus of a contemporary sixth-century Byzantine provincial governor – pen, ink and book upon the court table in front of him, his advisers at his side and the icons of the emperor and his family hanging behind him. Jesus stands before them; the imperial officials regard him with care and curiosity. The next picture shows the unfortunate result of the interview; a group of Jews cry for Jesus' blood; Pilate, suitably exasperated with his unruly subjects of whom as a good governor he must take notice, tells the imperial scribe to make a proper record; Christ is held for execution, Barabbas is unchained. This careful distinction of temporal and spiritual power was as close to the heart of the Byzantine emperors as it had been to that of Constantine.

Another of these purple Bibles, called the *Codex Rossano* after the Italian town where it found its home, also shows strong traces of its classical heritage. A most splendid St Mark, one of fifteen illustrations in the *Codex*, sits in a high-backed chair scratching out 'The beginning of the Gospel of Jesus Christ the Son of God'. But he is writing not upon a contemporary *codex* but an archaic scroll, and standing beside the saintly author is a woman in a blue dress directing the movements of his pen. She is the poet's muse of ancient classical tradition, named Sophia or Wisdom; and like Boethius' Lady of Philosophy, she had guided classical artists and poets at their work. St Mark, in this illustration, writes his Gospel in a thousand-year old tradition. Yet the drawing also looks forward: the simple forms of the architectural frame in which Mark sits and the apostle's elegant pose show an artist firmly of his own time. The hard flat forms of the Muse's costume show, too, the beginnings of the Byzan-tine tendency toward abstraction and formalization that developed further as the centuries passed. Small volumes like this *Rossano Codex* were carried from town to town and from country to country, and in their travels they had tremendous influence upon all the arts of Christendom; for these small pictures were used as models of design by fresco painters and mosaic artists. Many of the standard poses and compositions of the most famous Bible pictures can be traced back to these small scenes drawn in these ancient Bibles.

On the one hand, Constantinople saw itself as the heir to the classical tradition, on the other, its character as constantly changing and developing. Imagine that the city's slow rolling outline had been planned as a truly classical city; then, on the very ending of the V, on the spit of land that runs into the sea, ancient Greek architects would surely have built a temple or a fortress, just as Constantine had built a palace and a church on this same ground. But Greek temples dominated their surrounding landscapes, announcing the presence of classical man with clean-cut buildings. But by Justinian's day Christian monks and nuns had long shunned the outward appearances of prosperity and power and had turned toward an inner life, so even the imperial buildings of Byzantium turned in upon themselves and shunned the splendid façades of ancient Greece and Rome. Justinian replaced an earlier church on Constantine's acropolis with a huge, low, slow-rising building that told not of exterior domination, but of the power, the majesty of the great church within, the theatre for the imperial rituals that were the centre of the Eastern church's public life (see Plates 24 and 29). And so powerful was the architectural impact of this church that its form dominated Byzantine architecture from that time onward. Justinian dedicated the vast building to the Divine Wisdom, *Haghia Sophia*, the lady that guides the Apostle's hand on the *Rossano Codex* and the ancient muse that eastern Christianity had transformed into a personification of the inspiration of Christ.

It is said that when Justinian first walked under the dome of his massive new church, in his awe he looked up and cried 'Solomon, I have surpassed you'. This most mighty emperor had measured himself against the Bible's heroes: the hero who was the Bible's wisest king had been surpassed in the Church of the Divine Wisdom. The Psalm says that, 'The beginning of wisdom is fear of the Lord and by that fear you will prosper' (Psalm 111ff.). Now as God ruled in Heaven, so by the grace of God did Justinian rule on earth: fear of Justinian, obedience to his commandments was the beginning of wisdom and earthly prosperity. As Justinian entered his church in procession with his bishops and clergy carrying the bread and the wine bowl of communion, the jewelled Bibles and the great gold crosses, the hymn *Cherubikon* – 'the image of the cherubim' – was sung by the choir. 'The King of the Universe is come,' they announced, 'accompanied by choirs of angels'. And the courtiers in all their jewels and silks would have looked much like that too.

As the setting for this extraordinary liturgy, Justinian's two architects, Anthemius of Tralles and Isidore of Miletus, made one of the world's finest buildings, as gentle and humane and as gaunt as God; part of a new visual language of Christianity for which Anthemius and Isidore defined the spaces and surfaces that, in the following centuries, would be enhanced by Bible scenes. Here in Justinian's church the only Bible pictures were the four Cherubim of Genesis drawn in mosaic upon the quarter vaults under the huge dome. As in

Galla Placidia's tiny mausoleum, it is the *spirit* of the New Testament that guides and dominates the new building. The main entrance, the imperial doorway at the west end, sets the tone for the entire church. Placed above it, almost invisible to the eye, is a bronze relief of the heavenly dove and an open codex that shows the words of the Gospel of John (10:9), where Jesus, disputing with the Pharisees in the classical manner, says that *He* is the door; if anyone enters he shall be saved. The church beyond the door is an image of paradise, and a beautiful, quite tiny, band of ivy cut into the massive copper door frame quietly underlines the text. For this is the ivy that decorated Jonah's bower which, the Eastern theologians all agreed, was a prophetic image of the Christian paradise. In this spirit, then, in an illusive, abstract way, Justinian's great church is filled with the Bible. Just as the cross of Jesus gave scale and unity to the Christian universe, so the golden mosaics of the domes and vaults of Haghia Sophia once had crosses drawn inside them to give the building its scale and unity.

Inside the imperial door the great liturgical theatre that unfolds all around you seems almost to fulfill the doorway's claim – and Solomon is surpassed in a vision of earthly paradise. But the massive architecture has a human scale; it is gently rounded, relaxed, almost appears soft to the touch. Unlike a Greek or Roman building where if you would change the size of one of its parts, all its others must be changed proportionally, if you enlarged Haghia Sophia most of its architecture, the little arches, the domes, the tiny decorations could stay the same size. The building is fitted to humankind. Heaven, here, is in the details, as well as in the central dome. This is still one of the largest in the world and made and re-made by men who built with prayer as much as plumb lines, working in an ancient tradition, making the cold old forms of classicism come alive under their fingers. Held in the building's centre under the dome is a space that seems as large as God. The supporting walls, which in Roman buildings would have been a dour mass of brick engineering, are perforated by rows and rows of columns that seem to disappear into an infinite darkness. And every surface that remains is clad in shimmering sheets of stone or with an infinity of golden *tesserae*. And all this is lit by a light that seems to come from high up in the building's centre, held in a trembling balance under the huge slow dome.

This is the Byzantine understanding of God and his Bible, a model of the biblical universe. The congregation is held inside an architecture built around the vast space at the building's centre. The building is not only a model of heaven and its order, but also, by implication – Justinian's throne stood on the floor close by the building's centre – of imperial earthly unity as well. In the West, the Dark Ages left Rome without an emperor and with bishops with a power they never attained in the Eastern Church, which stayed close to its emperor. That air of meditative holiness that is still under the domes of eastern churches, the mystery at their centre, is not only the mystery of deity, it also holds an earthly vacuum; one that was filled by the figure of the Emperor of Byzantium.

In the Image of the Bible: The Emperor of Byzantium

In the 530s one of Justinian's armies was slowly fighting its way up the Italian peninsula just as the Allies in the Second World War would do some 1400 years later. For the Italians, already impoverished by continual wars, it was an uncertain time. A story goes that a worried pig farmer decided to test the results of the conflict with a wargame that consisted of matching three bands of pigs against each other, which he called the Goths, the Greeks and the Romans. 'Of the first,' we are told, 'almost all were found to be dead; of the second, almost all were alive; of the third, half had died and the rest had lost their bristles'. As Gibbon remarks, the pig war was 'no unsuitable emblem of the event'. The Byzantines fought a long and bloody campaign; at Ravenna, Cassiodorus retired from the court and founded his monastery at Vivarium, while the Gothic lords left the city to the invaders. So the Greeks finally conquered all of Italy, and Justinian himself arrived at Ravenna in 540 to dedicate a new court church at the palace there; the church of San Vitale. And it remains today the best place in the world to experience the reality of Byzantium. For here, all in mosaic, along with a plethora of Bible scenes, are the emperor and his court in all their finery. At Ravenna Justinian wanted his presence to be firmly stamped upon his newly conquered province. The mosaic portraits are powerful and immediate; certainly among the greatest of all work in this most intractable of mediums (see Plates 26 and 28). Whitefaced, somewhat impatient, Justinian leads the imperial entry into church. In front of him to the left stands his church; a bishop and two priests; behind him his administration; with Justinian, the unholy trinity that ran the Empire. Opposite this panel, across the apse, is another of the same size, filled with women decked in jewels and silks set amid glittering golden treasures. Here is the lovely, lively Theodora, Justinian's empress, her personable portrait inevitably recalling that most scurrilous account of her in Procopius' *Secret History*.

These two panels show all the arrogance, the superb peculiarity of the Eastern court; and here, too, is that unique eastern relationship between God and emperor, carefully described and justified in a magnificent collection of pictures; pictures that hold meanings quite separate from the Bible stories they describe. For here the Bible and its characters are used as little blocks of sacred truth assembled together to make a statement about the role of the Eastern emperor on earth. And in all this, the church of San Vitale at Ravenna would have a profound effect upon the West, its rulers, their churches and their art.

That earlier ruler of Ravenna, Theodoric the Ostrogoth, had been an Arian Christian, believing that Christ on earth had been but the human son of God in Heaven – a heresey vigorously condemned by the Eastern emperors who held that Christ was not a separate being at all but a co-existent third of the Trinity of Father, Son and Holy Ghost. Such arguments may seem purely theological, but they also hold in them expressions of political and cultural differences too; Arianism, for example, implies that other men, apart from Jesus, could also have a heavenly father. Imperial orthodoxy, however, insisted that the only divine power on earth was invested in the imperial office, which was a mirror of heaven, a notion clearly expressed in the magnificence of the court and the omnipotence of the emperor. To strengthen this earthly hierarchy, Christ had long since been dispatched to heaven, so avoiding all possible ambiguities. No one might claim divinity or special kinship with God; the emperor rested alone on his earthly throne.

Constantine had been buried as the thirteenth apostle, his sarcophagus surrounded with the cenotaphs of the other twelve. His successors, however, could not quite support such architectural pretensions and the great Emperor's porphyry sarcophagus had been removed to a mausoleum standing beside his huge church in Constantinople. By Justinian's time the boundaries of earth and heaven had been more precisely drawn and in great part the mosaics of San Vitale are a pictorial statement of this position, a manifesto set up in the heart of a recently reclaimed heretical province. The Bible stories so clearly and beautifully illustrated upon the walls of San Vitale were never intended to educate the illiterate or merely to celebrate the prophets and the saints that they

PLATE 30 (Opposite): Codex Argenteus; *a page of the beautiful incomplete manuscript, that preserves the largest known fragments of the texts of Ulphilas' Gothic Bible. A fifth–sixth century manuscript probably made in Italy,* Codex Argenteus *has gold and silver lettering on purple stained vellum. This page is from the gospel of Mark (4:21–28). University Library of Uppsala, Sweden.*
PLATE 31 (Overleaf): Codex Amiatinus. *The opening illustration shows Cassiodorus as a scribe working in his study on* Codex Grandior. *The Roman senator is dressed as Ezra the Prophet; he has a phylactery upon his forehead and wears the breastplate of the High Priest of Israel. Made in Bede's scriptorium at Jarrow in Northumbria around* AD 695. *Laurentian Library, Florence.*

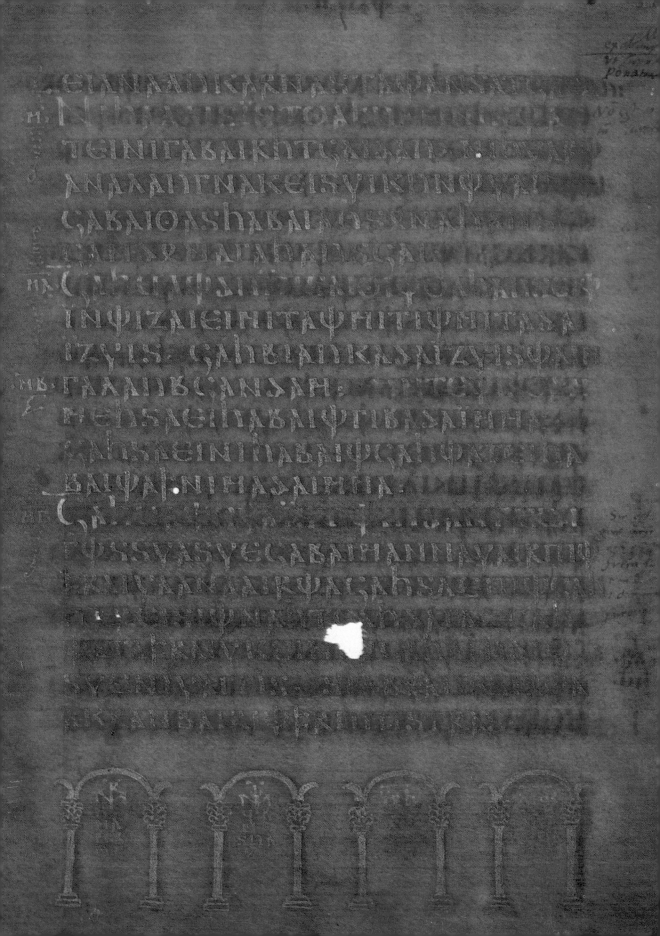

DE LITTERA

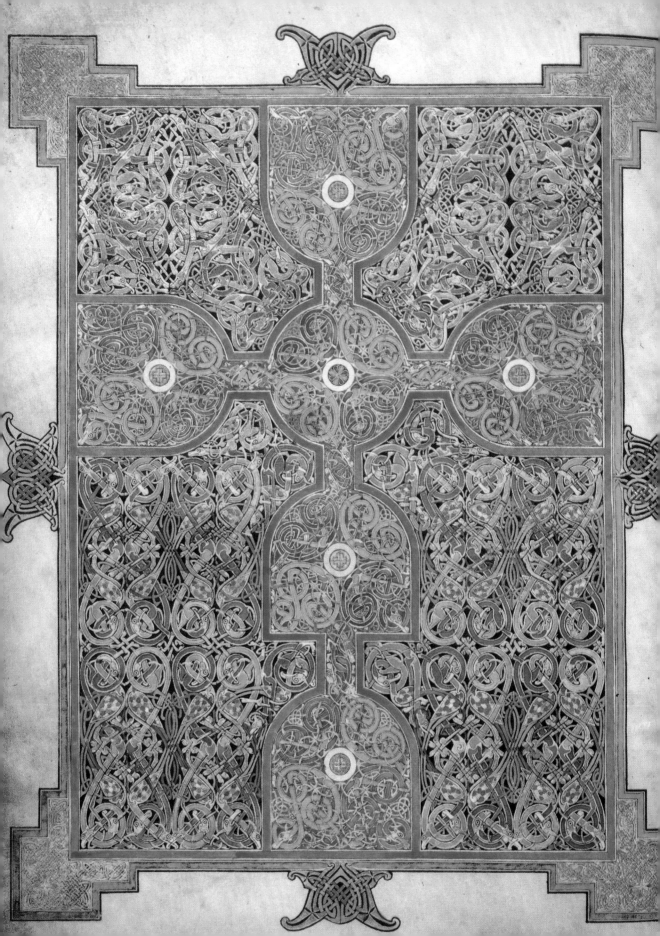

portray. But neither are such churches only places of propaganda; they are theatres for the rituals of the faith where gods and men might meet. In San Vitale, Justinian's artists and architects have used a combination of liturgy and Bible images to push home their central message. Of all Byzantine church rites, the Mass was the most powerful, the most central, and at Ravenna the portraits of Justinian and Theodora and their courtiers show them walking to that celebration, carrying the equipment used in the Eastern church ritual.

Watch how they move: the Emperor follows his clergy into the church; Bishop Maximian holds the jewel-encrusted cross that will be elevated at the height of the ceremony; one of his priests carries the censor that will perfume both the church and the congregation; another carries the great Bible from which passages are read during the service. The clergy all wear ecclesiastical robes – the simple courtly robes of the time of Diocletian and Constantine that have remained the clerical dress down to this day. And behind the men in another panel and doubtless heading for the *gynaceum*, the women's gallery on the first floor, is the Empress Theodora leading her ladies. With the subtlest of movements, through the patterns of the dresses and Theodora's gestures, the clever artist leads the eye from right to left across the scene to where a courtier holds open an embroidered curtain by a fountain – a rarity at Ravenna where wine was said to be cheaper than water. The little jet, splashing seductively, aids the group's movement out of the scene; in a second all their fine richness will have passed.

All these decorations, illuminated by that dim marbled light that the young Oscar Wilde described as 'Gothic twilight', were concentrated upon the altar table which, standing in the centre of the apse, was the focus of the Mass. Two rooms on either side served the function of a vestry. Here, in a complex ritual, the Host was prepared, priests were enrobed, the special leavened bread was cut into the prescribed sections, the wine warmed to the temperature of blood. Then, after the first part of the service was finished, psalms and responses sung, a sermon perhaps delivered, the main bronze doors of the church were shut and the solemn rite of the Great Entry began. The Host was taken in procession from one of the side rooms and paraded through the church – perhaps at San

PLATE 32 (Previous page): Priscian's Latin Grammar, *a copy made by Irish scribes about* AD *850. The* codex *preserves some of the most vivid of the marginalia that tell us so much about the lives of the ancient Irish scribes. Priscian's grammar,* Institutio De Arte Grammatica, *compiled in Constantinople in the sixth century, was widely used in the monasteries – a basic tool of education in the Dark Ages. Library of the monastery at St Gallen, Switzerland.*

PLATE 33 (Opposite): The Lindisfarne Gospels, *written and decorated by Eadfrith the Scribe between 696 and 698. He made this page, one of the so-called 'carpet' pages, to face the beginning of the Gospel of Matthew. Eadfrith, who later became the Bishop of Lindisfarne, was working in the scriptorium of his monastery at the same time as* Codex Amiatinus *was being made in nearby Jarrow. British Museum.*

Vitale making a circuit of the ambulatory that runs right around the nave. This is the procession in which Justinian and Theodora are portrayed in the mosaics. At Haghia Sophia the magnificence of the Great Entry was considered to be one of the world's greatest spectacles; the living complement of the building that still stands. Here at Ravenna, the same gorgeous procession passed through the little church carrying that most 'holy and memorable mystery of the Host', and as they made their way to the altar the hymn *Cherubikon* was sung: 'Let us now lay aside worldly cares, that we may receive the King of the Universe, who comes escorted by unseen armies of angels'. At the centre of this courtly congregation stood Justinian surrounded by the signs of imperial majesty; the service had come to its climax.

In these orthodox churches, the act of communion took on a different meaning to the communion of the Arian heretics. For an Arian who believed that Jesus was but a man, it would follow that the Mass, the celebration of Christ's earthly sacrifice, was a continuous ritual, a communion that had started with the Last Supper at Jerusalem and on Jesus' command was to continue through the generations. The orthodox, however, those who saw Jesus as existing eternally with God, saw Christ's sacrifice as an event outside of time, something eternal. If this was so, then theologians could expect to find examples of this holy sacrifice and of the Mass that is its celebration, in the history of the world before Jesus' lifetime, especially in the stories of the Old Testament; and of course this would *prove* that the orthodox belief was sanctified by the Sacred Book itself.

As the procession of the Great Entry made its way to the altar of San Vitale it passed through two archways facing each other at either end of the altar, whose lunettes were decorated with mosaic representations of precisely those Old Testament events – those 'pre-echoes' properly called prefigurations – that foreshadowed Jesus' earthly sacrifice and the office of the Mass. Above one of these archways is a mosaic showing the three angels who had come to tell Abraham that his wife would bear him a child (see Plate 27). They are seen eating the bread and wine that the Patriarch offers them in the Book of Genesis – a prefiguration of the Mass. Another scene in the same archway shows God restraining Abraham who is preparing to sacrifice his son Isaac. Isaac carries the wood for *his* sacrifice up to the summit of Mount Moriah at Jerusalem, just as Christ carries the wood of *his* sacrifice to nearby Calvary. Standing beside Abraham, patiently awaiting his fate, is the ram who will be substituted by God for Isaac.

On the opposite archway at the other end of the altar is a picture of Abel. He is standing beside a simple hut, raising up his hands and offering a sacrifice of a lamb to God (see Plate 25). In the same scene, in mirror image to Abel and his hut, Melchizedek the King of Jerusalem stands in front of his palace, and he offers up a chalice of wine to God though in the single verse in Genesis that mentions this shadowy ruler (Genesis 14:18), he offers his bread and wine to Abraham. On the walls above are more pictures of the biblical Prophets writing the Bible books in which, for the orthodox, the imperial church is validated. And above everything, at the very centre of the high glimmering vault, is the single symbol of the Lamb of God holding a cross, that image from the Book of Revelations of Jesus' sacrifice and offering, through which all these Old Testament prophecies are finally pulled into single focus. A prayer written centuries before Justinian's artists ever worked at Ravenna identifies the Christian unity of these same Old Testament stories: 'Accept the offering of your servant Abel and the sacrifices of our father Abraham and that which the High Priest Melchizedek sacrificed to thee.' In San Vitale the bread and wine of Melchizedek's hospitality to Abraham are drawn as if they were the bread and wine of the Host. These marvellous mosaics become a beautiful complement, an illumination of the central ritual mystery. When the priest's hands that held the wine-filled chalice soared upwards to announce the moment of Communion, they were held inside the golden vaults like a relic in a golden shrine. And all the subtle arts of the mosaic workers illuminate that gesture too; the priest and Abel and Abraham and King Melchizedek make the same gesture.

From the centre of the high vault, with its single image of the Lamb of God, downward through the elaborate mosaics, everything now seems clear. Only the figure of Melchizedek, that slightest of all Genesis' heroes, requires some explanation; why is this insignificant personage so insistently proclaimed in these imperial arts, and why is he, of all the prophets and sages in these scenes, the only figure to wear a halo around his head? Because the theologians agreed that Melchizedek's charity to Abraham was not only a prefiguration of the office of communion but also that his role as the king of Jerusalem prefigured the divine right of emperors like Justinian. As Melchizedek was the king of Jerusalem, so the emperor of Constantinople was the king of the new Jerusalem, the Empire. So in San Vitale, the Emperor and his Empress Theodora both wear haloes in their portraits, along with Melchizedek their predecessor. Though never spelled out in so many words the implications are crystal clear. As the imperial priest elevated the Host, as Jesus came down into the church, so the emperors, Melchizedek and the prophets were all joined together in the timelessness of eternity.

In Justinian's time the mysteries of the Holy Trinity and the Eucharist served as ecclesiastical justifications for the divine right of emperors to rule on earth. Theologians grappled with the implications of this for centuries – but most Christian kings and emperors instinctively insisted upon this orthodoxy as an expression of the divine order and some of them would die for their beliefs. So the men who made the fine mosaics at Ravenna were not merely telling edifying tales to illiterate congregations, nor were they merely memorializing the Bible's ancient heroes. They were validating the emperor's rule with precise biblical parallels, as a modern scientist builds new theories with previously known facts. In this, the Bible is used in precisely the same way as modern politicians use historical analogies to justify their actions and beliefs. And in Justinian's time the Bible was considered as infallible as the 'lessons of history' are today.

Charlemagne and Alcuin

In 801 as the Emperor Charlemagne returned to Germany after his Roman coronation, he passed through the old imperial city of Ravenna and took from its ruins quantities of fine marbles and some antique columns. His northern court was threadbare, his huge empire ignorant and illiterate; Charlemagne, a magpie, was collecting bright and glittering things to decorate his notions of a new Imperium. Inside San Vitale, Justinian's building and mosaics had spoken to Charlemagne as one emperor to another, and he took the old imperial imagery for himself, ordering his architects to measure up the church and later, to reproduce its architecture at his palace at Aachen, the capital of his Empire. The age of Charlemagne was a strange and special blend of style and aspiration. And from it all came the seed of a new European prosperity.

Of Charlemagne himself, opinions differ greatly. Some see the man as another Napoleon or as 'the founder of modern Europe'; others as a shadowy figure ruling a poverty-stricken and barbarous kingdom who was later inflated by Gothic legend into the first saintly monarch of Western Christendom. But it is certain that the real Charlemagne founded many monasteries in which, for the first time in centuries, learning and literacy were cherished; he founded many scriptoria, too, where the word of God was carefully copied out and decorated. These were the nurseries of medieval Europe. In these monasteries Latin, the language of the law as well as of God, was taught to the children of his illiterate nobles; this, it has been said, is the beginning of modern Western education. Perhaps Charlemagne's greatest gift to the future, however, was his longevity; a rule of nearly fifty years – from 771 to 814 – which gave a rare stability in a raw and brutal age, and time for his government, for his laws and administration to make a mark. And at the heart of this revival stood the Bible, the seat of wisdom and the word of God.

That his forbears were successful in their wars and had left their children large kingdoms, was fortunate for Charlemagne; that his brother had died while on his way to fight a ruinous war with him was another piece of good luck, both for Charlemagne and the poor kingdom that he ruled. After that, there had been no one left for the bellicose monarch to fight but pagan Saxons, the Moors and some Italian princes at the edges of his Empire. Through the years, Charlemagne added province after province to his kingdom until even the Pope of Rome saw that his security now lay in the hands of this pious northerner and had crowned him, much to the anger of the Byzantines, as the Emperor of the West; a Holy Roman Emperor. That Charlemagne himself had realized that this was all a unique conjunction of events may be seen in his will, where his huge kingdom is divided once more between his children in the time-honoured way of his people. This was no political vision of permanent European union; nonetheless, the fifty-year Imperium set Europe onto its future course.

How the warrior-emperor saw his own role in all this is less than clear. Of the two best ancient biographies of him, one, written by a contemporary, is pedestrian; the other, full of life and character, was written much later when Charlemagne was already halfway into legend. But both of them tell us that the king was a plain man who hunted and fought all his life, that he was a pious churchgoer, that he employed good scholars and scribes and that he opened a court school in Aachen and subsidized the production of fine Bibles. Perhaps the most potent vision of how the Emperor himself saw his reign is in his chapel at Aachen, based upon the memories and measurements of San Vitale; for here he presents himself as a successor of the ancient Roman emperors. Yet he did not understand them – neither their arts nor their architecture and certainly not their civilization. Nonetheless, he tried to build a northern Ravenna and a northern Rome, and made in the process a bright collage of styles, scholarship and materials; a new style for Europe and its Bible. His Aachen court continued after the great king's death, and it was one of Charlemagne's descendants who ordered a golden pulpit to be placed at the right side of the altar, to be used only for public readings of the Word of God from the new Bibles of the court scriptorium. Set in the pulpit's golden panels are elements that made this new northern art: bone pictures from Egypt of pagan gods, Dionysius, Isis, Pan, even the goddess of ancient Alexandria, fitted down the sides of the central panels as if in submission to the great barbarian cross at the centre. And the big bright stones of this cross – agate, rock crystal, chalcedon – are really Roman tableware set upside down and used uncomprehendingly simply as splendid shining objects. On the bottom of the central bowl set in the cross was fixed a famous antique cameo of the imperial Roman eagle and this became the symbol of the Holy Roman Empire. The new style had not been caught in the forms of clever architecture and exquisite mosaic, but in the brooding splendours of gold and stone.

On the pulpit's rim was set a large lectern for the Carolingian Bibles covered in ivory, silver and gold. In Charlemagne's time, these glittering books were the spearhead of civilization, the most valuable products of the West, the silicon chips of the Dark Ages. The Emperor was hungry for learning. 'Why,' demanded Charlemagne, when he was first told of the genius of St Augustine and St Jerome, 'cannot I have twelve such ministers?' And his patient minister, the Yorkshireman Alcuin, replied that the Most High himself had had but these two and would the Emperor then have twelve? Between the rugged enthusiasm of Charlemagne and the phlegmatic learning of his chief scholar, the major achievements of the time were accomplished. Throughout his huge kingdom, comprising most of modern Germany, France, the better part of Italy and central Europe, the Low Countries and northern Spain, people lived on farms and in little towns. Stone buildings were not common, metal tools and weapons were a rarity, bandits and raiders, Vikings and Saxons were commonplace. A few dozen monasteries and churches alone supported learning. Very few people were literate – Charlemagne himself never learned to write – and there were not enough books in Western Christendom to fill a modern village library. In most churches, the words of God and Christian hymns were spoken and sung with more sincerity than understanding. All this Charlemagne wanted to change. He determined to civilize his kingdom so that God and good rule might both shine through it.

> We, Charles, by the grace of God, King of the Franks and Lombards and Patrician of the Romans, to Abbot Baugulf and all your congregation . . . Letters have often been sent to us in these last years from certain monasteries, in which was set out what the brothers living there were striving to do for us in their holy and pious prayers. And we found that in most of these writings their sentiments were sound but their speech uncouth. Inwardly their pious devotions gave them a message of truth, but because of their neglect of learning, their unskilled tongues could not express it without fault. And so it came about that we began to fear that their lack of knowledge of writings might be matched by a more serious lack of knowledge of holy scripture . . .

It was the Bible itself, the kernel of the faith and central to the understanding of all things in this world, that formed the spearhead of Charlemagne's drive for literacy. But there were many different Latin Bible texts in Charlemagne's Empire – French, Spanish and Gothic versions, some of which included spurious and garbled passages with many other changes and additions. A new standardized edition of the Latin Bible – Cassiodorus' version of Jerome's Vulgate – was central to Charlemagne's ambition to revive piety and learning in his Empire. This task was given to Alcuin to supervise, using the very sparse resources of learned men and scribes who lived in Charlemagne's domain.

Omnis qui credit quoniam ihs est xps ex do natus est et omnis
qui diligit eum qui genuit diligit et eum qui natus est ex do
In hoc cognouimus quoniam diligimus natos di cum dm dili
gamus et mandata eius faciamus. Haec est enim caritas
di ut mandata eius custodiamus. et mandata eius
grauia non sunt quoniam omne quod natum est ex do uincit
mundum et haec est uictoria quae uincit mundum fides
nra quis est qui uincit mundum nisi qui credit quoniam ihs est
filius di. hic est qui uenit per aquam et sanguinem ihs
xps non in aqua solum sed in aqua et sanguine. et sps
est qui testificatur quoniam xps est ueritas. quoniam tres sunt
qui testimonium dant sps aqua et sanguis et tres unum sunt.

In the north of Europe, the Irish monks in particular had maintained a live tradition of scholarship. French and English monks studied in their remote monasteries – Alcuin, it was said, had spent time at Clonmacnois in the centre of Ireland before returning to his native York to supervise the abbey school. In such Irish monasteries Greek was taught – in western Europe it was said that only the Irish knew the language – and Latin was composed into new mellifluous poetry. And it was these monasteries that had bred a wanderlust into the Irish scholars. By Charlemagne's day, Irishmen with an Egyptological bent had already measured the pyramids – 'the granaries of St Joseph' they called them – and they found them to be 400 paces from corner to corner. And they also searched for the ruts of Pharaoh's chariot wheels cut during the pursuit of the Israelites. In the written account of their journey, part of a pilgrimage to the Holy Land, the learned monks cite more than thirty classical authors. So when two Irish monks appeared at a French market offering wisdom for sale (having deemed it unlikely that anyone would value their scholarship if it were offered for nothing), they were quickly taken off to Charlemagne's court. From there they were sent to Italian monasteries where, a little later on, the first universities of western Europe were founded. Drunk as much on words as on the hospitable monastery wines, these Irish scholars went right through Charlemagne's Empire preaching the love of God and spreading their precious wisdom as they went.

One of Charlemagne's most magnificent foundations was the Monastery of St Gall in modern Switzerland which, to this day, has in its library beautiful Irish manuscripts made by some of these travelling scholars. The monastery itself was named after an earlier Irish missionary, who had lived a century before 'like a bear' in a cave close by. The library of St Gall has also preserved a fine plan of Charlemagne's monastery with its sties and stables, its sheepfolds and fowl houses, threshing floors and market gardens all carefully laid out and recorded in the inventories that Charlemagne's civil service made of these imperial holdings, noting everything down to the last chicken and egg. As well as this farm neatly laid out in a great rectangle around the central church, the monastery of St Gall had a hostel and a kitchen for its guests, schools and accommodation for the abbot and his monks, a doctor's clinic, an infirmary and a cemetery. Such settlements formed the high culture of Europe in the reign of Charlemagne.

And near the abbey church of St Gall, in a small building of its own situated behind the high altar, stood the scriptorium and the library, the little rooms where the works of civilization were copied out and stored. 'We are from Inch-Madoc, Cairbre and I', wrote one Irish scribe in the margins of his copy text at St Gall. Others ruminated at greater length:

> I and Pangur Ban my cat,
> 'Tis a like task we are at:
> Hunting mice is his delight,
> Hunting words I set all night.
>
> 'Gainst the wall he sets his eye,
> Full and fierce and sharp and sly;
> 'Gainst the wall of knowledge I
> All my little wisdom try.
>
> So in peace our task we ply,
> Pangur Ban, my cat, and I;
> In our arts we find our bliss,
> I have mine and he has his.

In the margins of a copy of a single Roman grammar brought from Ireland (see Plate 32) are whole conversations: comments and observations upon the weather, on wine, and even on the beauty of the day, and all as lively as the monk's chatter in the scriptorium must have been – 'To go to Rome, much labour, little profit'; 'Wondrous is the robin there singing to us and our cat has escaped!'; 'Alas, my chest, O Holy Virgin'; and 'A curse on thee O pen'.

So the scribes spread learning and humour throughout a dismal Europe. And the beautiful individual handwriting of the Irish scribes helped to mould the character of a distinctively Carolingian script which, mixed with an Italian style, produced the forms on which both modern printed type and handwriting style are based.

Finally, a single small verse gives good reason why travelling had become 'a second nature to the Irish race'. The Danish longboats had begun to sail the north seas, sacking the surrounding lands, shaking the very bones of the saints from their monastery shrines:

> Bitter and wild is the wind tonight,
> Tossing the tresses of the sea to white,
> On such a night as this I feel at ease;
> Fierce Norsemen only course the quiet seas.

It was, however, not to the travelling Irishmen that Charlemagne gave the major literary task of the age, the revision of the Latin Bible text and the establishment of a school and scriptorium at the imperial court at Aachen. Alcuin, said to have been taught by Bede, was brought from his abbey school at York especially for this purpose. And he stayed at Aachen for some ten years, attending to the revision of the Bible and writing, in the process, new prologues for all its books. He oversaw the work not only of the court scriptorium but also of the school where the nobles' children were educated. Out of the Carolingian Bibles went the so-called 'Johanine Comma', where a phrase – 'The Father, the Word and the Holy Ghost, and these three are one' – had been pushed into a sentence of the First Epistle of John (5:7) to introduce the notion of the Trinity into the Bible text. Out, too, went all the different garbled versions of the Vulgate until the Bible, now called Alcuin's Vulgate, was left: a cleaned and re-purified copy of Jerome's Vulgate, replete with Alcuin's up-to-date commentaries. Alcuin's scholarship at Aachen, reinforced by English texts sent from his old library of York, reflected the purity of Cassiodorus' southern Italian text, which had been used in the making not only of Northumbrian bibles like the *Codex Amiatinus* but also of a Latin bible sent from Rome to Canterbury a hundred years before, as part of the Pope's missionary activities to England. And this Carolingian text was transmitted, via the medieval University of Paris, directly to the studios where the first bibles were printed in the 1460s.

Although Alcuin's Vulgate was another step along the road to the modern Latin text, it was not in this field of textual study but in the physical production of Bible books that Alcuin's work was vital for the West. Some of the finest bibles ever made were produced in Charlemagne's scriptoria under Alcuin's aegis; bibles written in beautiful script with fine illuminations and covers of precious metals, gems and ivories; decorations like those that covered the churches' most revered reliquaries now adorned the written word. And such work raised the status of books and learning among a largely illiterate and indifferent aristocracy. Not only was the Bible copied in the monasteries of Tours and Fulda, Reims and Etternach, Orléans, Corbie and St Gall, but also all the surviving texts of classical literature. The greater part, some eighty-five per cent it has been estimated, of our oldest copies of classical literature are those made by Carolingian scribes, all of them written out in that characteristic firm round hand in gall-black ink on creamy vellum.

A lively illumination, a frontispiece of a Bible presented by Alcuin's successor Abbot Vivian of Tours to Charles the Bald, one of Charlemagne's grandsons, shows the courtly presentation of one of these wonderful books, the richest, most valued product of the day. That any book achieved such status was due to Alcuin's labour and Charlemagne's patronage. And it was not only the Bible that benefitted; even the meters of the rhythms of the Roman legions' marching songs, meters that Kipling would employ again for his Indian army poetry, were preserved in Charlemagne's scriptoria.

Alcuin had a deep love of antiquity and a determination to preserve it. His letters to abbots and kings often talk, among his sermons on the Christian life, of making presents of writing materials, pigments and inks, and of encouraging the monks at their work. When on 8 June 793 Lindisfarne was sacked and burned by raiding Vikings, he wrote long letters both to Ethered the Northumbrian king and to Bishop Higbald and his congregation on the island; to the

former he talked of God's earthly judgments upon sin and the visitation of misfortunes, and exhorted him with all love and respect to lead a pure and good
life; to Lindisfarne's bishop, he sent sympathy and promised to encourage his
Emperor Charlemagne to help restore their loss; 'either the youths who have
been led into captivity by the pagans or any other of your needs,' and he also
exhorted the monks to get back to their work at the abbey; 'it is God's wish to
try you', he says, and reminds them that even mighty Rome had recovered, 'by
the pity of God,' from the invasions of barbarians. The sacking was but one
of many. Life along the northern coastlines remained uncertain for hundreds of
years and brought the precarious age of Irish monasticism to an end.

After ten years' work at the Aachen court, Alcuin retired to the monastery of
St Martin at Tours. There he oversaw the work of another scriptorium, while
remaining in correspondence with the Emperor whom he addressed in his
letters as 'David'. At Tours, he told his David, he fed his monks with 'the
honey of the sacred scriptures, . . . inebriated them with the old wine of ancient
learning'. Alcuin always remembered with affection his home town of York
and its great library – with several hundred books it was considered to be
enormous – but he never regretted his move to the Continent and Charlemagne's Empire. 'The beer,' he wrote to a French colleague while he was on a
visit to England, 'burns in my stomach; send some good wine to me.' That he
and his monks drank the wine of the grape as well as the wine of wisdom – the
joyful liquid accounting for about a quarter of the monastic diet – helped to
keep something else of civilization alive too. Alcuin died in 804, ten years
before Charlemagne, and was buried at Tours. He had composed his own
epitaph, a three-verse apostrophe that tells of the futility of earthly delight,
ending with two small lines:

> Alcuin was my name: learning I loved.
> O thou that readest this, pray for my soul.

Beneath that, his monks have added: 'Here lieth the Lord Abbot Alcuin of
blessed memory, who died in peace on the nineteenth of May'. Above all,
perhaps, he was the man who added the yeast to Europe which would rise and
make the brioche of Gothic civilization.

> A steady stream of wisdom springs
> from my well-coloured neat fair hand;
> on the page it pours its draught
> of ink of the green-skinned holly.

In Charlemagne's age war went abroad and became adventure. His Empire was
placid, slowly building its prosperity. It was remembered by Gothic civilization

as the first great age of Christian kingship. Three hundred years after his death Charlemagne was canonized. In the fourteenth century, fragments of the skull of this sainted emperor were taken from his tomb and built into a golden reliquary, a great mask no less gilded than Tutankhamun's. Here, in the flamboyant high Gothic style, is the image of a perfect monarch: the straight face set against rolling waves of hair and beard; the symmetric fringe above it, crowned by classical gemstones and a Gothic cross. And the figure of Charlemagne is dressed in the eagle-adorned cape of the Holy Roman Emperor – the title which the Pope had awarded him on Christmas Day in the year 800.

In the court-chapel at Aachen that Charlemagne had copied from Ravenna, he set up a marble seat in the gallery of the first floor, from where he could sit and watch the daily service in the church below. After his death the chair became the throne on which all the Holy Roman Emperors were crowned, and chapels were set up around the gallery for each of the imperial provinces. Six steps were placed beneath the throne because Solomon had sat on such a podium. Medieval pilgrims used to bend down to pass through a lucky space in the masonry under the throne, in hope of a lifetime's good fortune. Mass is still celebrated at a small altar behind the throne. Charlemagne's biographers report that he spent hour upon hour here, watching the services, carefully observing the order of the liturgy and later correcting mistakes and rewarding special pieties. Day after day, month after month, year after year, the great king sat upon his throne in the gallery over the heads of his congregation, halfway between the earth and the mysteries of heaven, certainly above the twinkling stars of lamps that filled the space of the marble octagon. Up there, the Emperor sat among beautiful bronze screens, incorrectly made in imitation of antiquity, upon his marble throne whose design was taken from the chairs of the old Italian bishops. And what did it really matter if the enthusiastic Frank had set up his throne in what had been at Ravenna the *gynaceum*, the women's gallery; and did it matter if the formalities of Roman and Byzantine arts and ceremonial were here misinterpreted and misplaced? For this was now the seat of Western Christendom; and Europe was girded about with a true faith based on a true Bible. When the Emperor rode into battle, his troops carried a lance containing one of the nails of the Cross; and two tiny fragments of the Cross, held in a little polished gem of gold and crystal, swung about the Emperor's neck.

In the Image of the Bible: the Kingdoms of the West

Charlemagne's faith was held inside a fortress of a chapel at Aachen; in the Gothic cathedrals that followed, Carolingian solidity was replaced by a tent of stone. After Aachen, heavy and turned in upon itself, the Gothic cathedrals seem light, tense and filled with aspiration; their buttresses swing up to hold high thin walls. The inside promises a miracle; and as the great passion of the people who made the cathedral was to make order the airy stonework becomes an analysis of stress and strain. But these upward-flying stones do not function in a modern sense; they do not hold up a bridge or support a billboard; they have no other end than in their being. This is a dance before God. The buildings' dizzy aspirations show them to be the product of a new society; they bubble with the skills and virtuosity, with all the precocious power of the newly rich.

In great part, it had been the Church itself that changed old Europe. The monasteries nursed and nurtured Charlemagne's poor Empire. Under the monks' directions new lands were opened up, forests cleared and drainage channels cut. New harnesses had greatly increased the efficiency of draught animals; water mills, the major source of mechanical power, grew in number and effectiveness; sheep-breeding had strengthened and enlarged the different breeds – this meant that by the end of the first millennium, Bible parchments had greatly increased in size. In Charlemagne's day, Europe's population stood at less than thirty million. Four hundred years later, in the age of the great cathedrals, it had almost trebled. And in that same period, some three thousand European cities had been founded and the old ones greatly increased in size and prosperity. Twelfth-century Paris held nearly a quarter of a million people. A new *bourgeoisie* had come into being, and eagerly assisting in their progress, the Church encouraged their industries and the formation of their trade-guilds under saintly patrons. New commercial fairs held on Holy Days sent merchants travelling through Europe once again, buying and selling their goods.

Some of the bishops also opened schools which became the universities of Europe, and these were usually built beside their churches and cathedrals. Twelfth-century Chartres was a famous centre of learning, its cathedral school staffed by scholars who had studied with Arabs and Jews in Spain and Africa and who could read Greek. For the first time since Charlemagne's day classical literature was read in the West, and now, too, the mathematical propositions of Euclid were again studied. The movements of the stars were observed and recorded. Meteorologists tell us that from the time of Charlemagne to the thirteenth century, Europe slowly warmed up; lizard-like, the population popped its nose out of the cracks of Charlemagne's rough masonry to stretch and sniff and look at the sun.

In their day, buildings like Chartres cathedral were seen as the sum and celebration of this brave new world and, for a while, the new drive, the

[277]

sensibilities, the growing intellect of Europe was held in their stones. So the architecture of these cathedrals not only shows us the aspirations of the architects, but the whole world of this new culture. In this world, the single central factor, its common truth, was the Bible: Charlemagne's Bible, Alcuin's Vulgate, with his prologues still standing at the head of every book. The Bible was the rulebook, the text which justified and explained the world. Today, science has a shorter list of absolutes; the speed of light, the interior vibrations of certain crystals and a few more. The Gothic world had every statement and every word of the Bible. This gave literate people, especially the teachers and students at new schools like that at Chartres, two main problems; firstly, how to interpret holy words – throughout the Middle Ages and beyond people were both burned and sanctified for their variations of opinion – and secondly, how could the brilliantly intelligent writings of the pagan classical world, that were coming into the light once more, be integrated with the Bible. How, for example, could Plato's astute assertions about the physical world be subsumed into the biblical account of Creation in the Book of Genesis? Nobody denied that he lived in the world that the God of the Bible had made; but now, however, people were beginning to require a more detailed explanation of the world than that which the Bible gave them. 'You poor fools,' protested a scholar when told that such understanding did not really matter because God could do anything, 'God can make a cow out of a tree, but has he ever done so? Therefore show some *reason* why a thing is so, or cease to hold that it *is* so!' For people like that, looking for the order of the universal system, looking for something beyond the 'tumult of the senses', it was the pagan classical writers who promised detailed answers.

By the thirteenth century, building upon a century of scholarship and disputation, Thomas Aquinas had produced the great body of writings, culminating in the *Summa Theologica* that has remained a basis of Roman Catholic theology until this day. Thomas' thought was shaped by the writings of Aristotle – the basic distinction in his writings between reason and faith is, in some measure, the difference between pagan and Christian writings which he welded together triumphantly into a single system of thought. What he made was virtually a machine that created proofs for faith – an intellectual scaffolding for Christendom. But the greatest expression of his time, that which moved whole nations and embodied Thomas' own age in a way that no amount of medieval theology ever had, was still the great cathedrals, where God and reason were held in balance high among the spires and buttresses.

Sometimes, though not very often, these great churches fell down, even upon their congregations as they prayed. Such accidents remind us that medieval architects were genuinely daring; intent on going beyond what others had done before them. (It was widely believed that these building disasters, like all misfortunes, were caused by the devil and his accomplices; human fallibility allowed Satan to loosen the scaffolding ropes and cause the craftsmen on them to fall to the ground, as he maliciously shook the timbers.) It was the God-given learning of previous ages which had produced the wealth and knowledge that now allowed these huge building enterprises. 'We are dwarfs mounted upon the shoulders of giants, so that we can perceive much more than they, not because our vision is clearer, nor because we are taller but because we are lifted higher thanks to their gigantic height,' affirmed Bernard of Chartres, who taught classical philosophy in that city during the first years of the twelfth century. And just as the devil loosened the ropes, so these wise men pulled them tighter and showed the craftsmen how to make their work safer and stronger. They made the scaffolding for this new society and many of them and their fore-runners, biblical and pagan alike, are grouped around the cathedral doorways, portraits cut in stone, footnotes of the new age. At Chartres the giants of the past are all lined up: St Jerome with his Bible stands next to an ancient pope who writes commentaries upon the sacred writings, aided by a dove of divine wisdom that sits upon his shoulder. On the façade there is a calendar of the farming year, and the Zodiac from ancient Babylon, the sun and moon, and figures of Virtue and Philosophy, the latter dressed just as Boethius had des-cribed her. And alongside them all stand the people of the Bible, the prophets and the saints – the forerunners through whom God sanctioned the order in this brave new world.

The combination of classical scholarship and biblical figures dominated even the building of these great cathedrals. Classical authors, for example, identified the number seven as the harmonious number of the universe: there were seven planets, seven zodiacal signs, seven notes in a harmonic scale and so on. So Christians detected seven virtues and seven sins inside man, and seven ages for his life as well. And the Book of Genesis gives Jehovah's sanction to this mystic numeration; the world was made in seven days, and in the cathedrals seven services each day praised his name. Theologians pointed out that this number seven was also three plus four, or the Holy Trinity plus the Four Evangelists – the soul and body of the faith united. And they pointed out further that if you multiplied the three facets of the soul by the four elements of the universe – and here Christian theology was joined to Aristotle's theories – the product twelve was the number of the Apostles and their universal Church. Numbers ran through the theology and architecture of the Gothic world as do repeating shapes in a kaleidoscope. And they found their proof in the Bible's word.

Such arguments were far from fanciful, for it was on these sacred numbers, geometric harmonies, that the great Gothic churches were all built. A triangle with sides that are proportionally three, four and five makes a right-angle triangle: with compasses and string and just such simple systems you make a geometry as subtle as a great cathedral, just as God had measured out creation with his compasses. In this, these buildings were models of the Gothic universe.

The representation of ancient heroes, of biblical figures and their stories in these buildings was not a mere impulse to tell simple people ancient stories nor even to educate their moral sense; just as peasants did not require church pictures of the agricultural life to tell them when to prune their trees or cut their corn. All the Gothic world, God's own creation, was gathered into these vast cathedrals and no one man could properly expect to understand it all. These extraordinary buildings were a celebration of the new society, built according to the sacred rules of God's universe, as they were discerned in the Bible. Gothic architects also saw this same abstract order all around them in the natural world. Beautiful faces were perceived as conforming to the same divine geometry; artists drew their figures over geometric grids of lines. In their natural elegance, plants and animals, too, seem to conform to these sacred harmonies. Everything in the world was seen to have its roots, its significance in the Bible's order, and the world was seen to be beautiful – for the first time in many centuries.

At Aachen Charlemagne's chapel is entered between two doors of Roman bronze, their handles held in the mouths of fearsome lions. When you enter Chartres cathedral, the rows of sculptured kings look down upon you and they smile as you pass. Here is a new delight in living. When a French king of the time was asked by a cleric whether he would sooner suffer the stain of sin or the mark of leprosy, he unhesitatingly chose sin; 'rather thirty sins than leprosy,' he exclaimed. The world had changed. European aspirations had expanded beyond the confines of a dark guarded cell in which to suffer, to write and pray and wait for salvation and the raiding Vikings. The world was a bright and open place, full of passion, love and profit; there was a growing lust for gold, flower-fine gemstones, good wine and the joys of life. If avarice and sloth were the sins that most agitated the Dark Ages, then, it has been remarked, lust was the most formidable enemy of the medieval period. The world had been warmed by this promising spring and there was a quickening of the blood. Peter Abelard, the greatest theologian of the twelfth century, was castrated by an irate guardian after the seduction of one of his pupils. Some twenty years later, in 1139, the Lateran Council decreed that no churchman was free to marry and those who had found their marriages declared invalid. And at this time the cult of the Holy Family was fast growing into another sacred Trinity. Mary the Virgin Mother was now celebrated in poems, in words more usually reserved for the objects of more earthly passions. There was a growing expression of human warmth, celebrated by a great host of people from Francis of Assisi to François Villon.

Stand back from the east front of Chartres cathedral, which is dedicated to the cult of the Virgin Mary, and the story of the age appears before you. Part of it stands, as does all Europe, upon Carolingian foundations. Indeed, it was Charlemagne's grandson who presented this church with the holy relic which gave the town its celebrity and this grew along with the Virgin's cult – a robe which, it was said, Mary had worn at the moment of her Assumption into heaven. Burned down and then re-built, the cathedral that held this evidence of heaven had grown on the hill of Chartres like an oak. Above the Carolingian foundations are echoes of more ancient architectures: the three great doors with the largest at the centre, like a Roman triumphal arch above which God sits triumphant, surrounded by the Four Evangelists. And there is still the suggestion behind this façade that the church follows the plan of a Roman basilica, with two side aisles and a wide central nave, like the churches of Constantine. There is, however, a quite unclassical passion in Gothic architecture for building upwards; an ecstatic rush toward God, a single-minded impulse just as all earthly ecstasies hold in them a single overwhelming sensation. Between the massive semi-circular arches of the Chartres Romanesque towers and the flamboyant pinnacles and arches at the top of the northern spire that search the sky like the tendrils of a vine was a period of 400 years. The coming together of these parts into a single masterpiece is a tribute to the humility of generations of architects who, wishing neither to dominate nor exclude each other despite their own individuality, made diversity into a harmonious whole. The secret is that every element of this façade is held in a net of numbers, of proportions, of simple geometric harmonies that radiated from a handful of fixed points. Inside this unity, each separate stone has been made separately by its masons, measured out and cut in their small yards, then hoisted up the wooden scaffolds and cemented with lime plaster, each one into its own appointed position. Just as each line of the Bible has its own meaning, yet is also part of the unity of the entire book, so in the great cathedrals each individual stone is subservient to the main enterprise.

In their enthusiasm for the construction of these two great towers in the twelfth and thirteenth centuries, thousands of people came from the country around Chartres, nobles and peasants alike fitting the halters of the draught oxen to their own shoulders and dragging the masons' wagons that carried the building stones from the barges on the river up the hill to the cathedral. It was later said that these strange devotions were accompanied by an intense silence, broken only by an occasional pious exclamation as the thousands of penitents moved under their loads. Quoting the Book of Ezekiel, the bishop said that God himself was in the slow-moving wheels of the stone carts. Ezekiel in a vision had seen the throne of God itself that was moved by the four zodiacal signs of Taurus, Leo, Scorpio and Aquarius, which Christians had later adopted as the signs for the Four Evangelists – Scorpio being anciently represented on occasion by an eagle. That this marvellous vision of an exiled prophet on a river bank in ancient Iraq had foretold the coming of the Four Evangelists and also, the bishop said, the manufacture of two huge towers in France was yet further example of the mystical powers of their universal book, the Holy Bible.

I saw a storm wind coming from the north, a vast cloud with flashes of fire and brilliant light about it; and within was a radiance like brass, glowing in the heart of the flames. In the fire was the semblance of four living creatures in human form. Each had four faces and each four wings; their legs were straight, and their hooves were like the hooves of a calf, glittering like a disc of bronze.

As I looked at the living creatures, I saw wheels on the ground, one beside each of the four. The wheels sparkled like topaz, and they were all alike: in form and working they were like a wheel inside a wheel, and when they moved in any of the four directions they never swerved in their course. All four had hubs and each hub had a projection which had the power of sight, and the rims of the wheels were full of eyes all round. When the living creatures moved, the wheels moved beside them; when the creatures rose from the ground, the wheels rose; they moved in whatever direction the spirit would go; . . . the spirit of the creature was in the wheels.

Above the heads of the living creatures was, as it were, a vault glittering like a sheet of ice, awe-inspiring, stretched over their heads above them. Under the vault their wings were spread straight out, touching one another, while one pair covered the body of each. I heard, too, the noise of their wings; when they moved it was like the noise of a great torrent or of a cloud-burst, like the noise of a crowd or of an armed camp; when they halted their wings dropped. A sound was heard above the vault over their heads, as they halted with drooping wings. Above the vault over their heads there appeared as it were, a sapphire in the shape of a throne, and high above all, upon the throne, a form in human likeness. I saw what might have been brass glowing like fire in a furnace from the waist upwards; and from the waist downwards I saw what looked like fire with encircling radiance. Like a rainbow in the clouds on a rainy day was the sight of that encircling radiance; it was like the appearance of the glory of the Lord. (Ezekiel 1:4ff. NEB)

And all this too, the architects and artists, the glassblowers, the glaziers and painters, the sculptors and the stonemasons made in the medieval cathedrals – dazzling visions of another world and a fertile mystery. Like the sculptures around the cathedral doors, the stained-glass windows, those vast carpets of glass – those western Mantras – hold the whole world of the Middle Ages in them: Gothic people and the Bible's characters all mixed together. Once the architect's designs for the building had been realized, the stained-glass crafts-men designed their panels in the church, fitting their patron's ideas into the general scheme. And these small scenes, these individual masterpieces of story-telling, are not here to teach the unlettered Bible stories or theology, but to place all the people of Christendom inside the new world order created in the medieval schools.

So alongside Moses, Jacob, David and other biblical figures, medieval butchers proudly slaughter oxen, bakers make their bread, water carriers sit in poses echoing those of classical river gods, pouring the glistening liquid from their pots in rhythm with the actions of the Bible heroes nearby. All the guilds of medieval Europe, all the local nobles and notables and the kings of Christen-dom are celebrated in the stained-glass windows, paid for by gifts of money. Indeed, most of these cathedrals were built by subscriptions; the clergy would put a large part of their church's income into the building work while preachers fanned out all over Europe to collect money. Miracles often attended these fund-raising efforts; heaven and earth seemed to come together to make the great churches. Sometimes the Virgin would appear to prospective donors. Quite often the efforts of ordinary people donating labour and materials to the churches instead of gold were illuminated by miraculous lanterns and heavenly visions. Kings gave windows to the cathedrals, French monarchs donating pictures of their patron St Denis, while Spanish kings preferred St James, a knight of their court who had fought the Moors. Labourers donated windows with subjects such as Adam, the first man who had dug the earth. Coopers might donate windows of Noah the carpenter and the man who had first planted the vine. Basket-makers might donate a window of St Anthony, the Egyptian hermit who had plied their humble trade. Christian knights gave windows picturing saints who had died in battles or windows of the Apostles who had carried swords. In an age where everybody belonged to something – when even lepers and bandits had their brotherhoods, though no stained-glass windows – almost everybody in Gothic society found reflection in these great cathedrals. And no doubt the lepers and the bandits, too, stood beside the cathedral doors. In this way a masterpiece of stone and glass became a model of the universe, reflecting and dignifying the society that made it, in images from its most sacred book.

As the travelling merchants rode toward these Gothic cities, as the peasants stopped at their work in the fields and looked to their church, they all saw advertised in its exciting silhouette the power of Christendom and, by implication, the intricacy of the great book that held its order. On feast days that came, perhaps, four times a year, the people of these fine new Gothic towns gathered to walk through their streets in long processions, passing through the open doorways of the cathedral, arriving together inside this model of the Church of God. Every element in society from the court to the guilds, from the merchants to the peasants, was there, moving toward their church.

But perhaps there was another deeper urge in this soaring architecture – the urge to leave such careful social stratification, such a well-ordered, conforming society. More heretics and scholars were burned in the Middle Ages than were ever killed in Carolingian times. For at this time the Inquisition came into its own, and torture, largely unused as an instrument of government since Roman days, was reintroduced. These then are the passionate buildings of the new age. They were not built in the image of a medieval fairyland or on the sufferings of serfs, but by the better part of a society on the cusp of change. They represent one of those rare moments in human culture of absolute sureness, the brief fresh time before passion becomes routine. It was an age when God was felt to be close to the earth, and the Bible held the visions of society.

Tuesday 29 May 1453

A ruined wall, blackened stones and a gaudy row of brothels now mark the place where the last emperor of Byzantium fell fighting the Turkish armies that streamed into Constantinople on the morning of 29 May 1453. For centuries, Gothic West and Byzantine East had run side by side; the West slowly transforming with riches, plague and scholarship and evolving beyond all imagination, the East slowly turning into a beauteous plundered museum filled with the relics of classical and early Christian culture. From the eleventh century waves of Western armies – the Crusaders – had gone to fight in the lands around the eastern Mediterranean, in Palestine and Syria, capturing Jerusalem from Arab armies and setting up a series of castled kingdoms from the edge of Anatolia down to the Egyptian border. In 1204 the Fourth Crusade plundered Constantinople, and most of its holy relics and treasures were taken away to decorate the cathedrals of the West. Byzantium was never the same again. The old Empire was shattered, the city itself sometimes appeared to be little more than a vassal of the Turkish sultans who controlled the better part of Asia Minor.

The last emperors of Byzantium travelled frequently to the West, to Paris, Rome and London, begging assistance against the Muslims. And several times the two churches, East and West, met in council and finally, after a thousand years of schism joined together again at Florence in 1439. But this last-hope alliance was rejected by the people of Constantinople, a city whose soldiers were now afraid to mount cannon on the great old walls for fear they would be shaken down with the vibration of the blasts. Now, too, poverty ate away inside the city. The last Byzantine emperor was crowned in a court in southern Greece in 1449; in the deciding battles most of his generals were Italians from Genoa. When Sultan Mehmet, the Turkish Conqueror, finally rode triumphantly through the burning streets on Tuesday 29 May 1453, the old walls were half-down and he found most of Byzantium's fabled places stripped and lying in ruins.

The Turkish army stormed the land walls at their centre, pounding them for weeks on end with a battery of European-designed cannon. Once inside, the triumph was immediate; in a few hours they had streamed down the ancient streets past Constantine's statue on its column and on to the hippodrome, by the Church of Haghia Sophia. On the evening before, the great jewelled Bibles of Byzantium were carried in procession to the high altar, the Great Entry and the Imperial Mass were conducted for the last time. The Emperor, a young and brave man, the eleventh Constantine, had taken communion with his generals, then left the church to spend the night in preparation for the attack next day. Four days later on the Friday morning, Sultan Mehmet's muezzins had cried the call to prayer from the roof of Haghia Sophia, 'There is but one God, and Mohammed is his Prophet,' and the Conqueror's brow brushed the old marble floor in ardent devotion. Justinian's great bronze doors briefly barred the inevitable plunder, but the Janissaries easily forced them and quickly poured into the church. There they faced what seemed to be the better part of the city's people crowded onto every floor and landing. Then the women and children, the old senators and scholars, the courtiers and servants from the nearby palace were all pulled from the protection of the Virgin, who still looks down from the golden apse, above the spot where once the altar stood. With the nuns and priests all these people were roped into lines, slaves and masters together, and taken off into captivity. All together, the Turks took 60,000 people from Byzantium.

Phranzes the historian, a friend of the last Emperor who later wrote an account of the siege and its ending, was himself enslaved, along with his wife and two children. Four months later, he purchased his freedom and travelled to the Ottoman capital city of Edirne to ransom his wife from Sultan Mehmet's *Mir Bashi*, the Master of Horse. In this he was successful, but his two children he never saw again; his young son, he tells us, was killed in the imperial bedchamber; his daughter incarcerated in a harem. At first Sultan Mehmet was inclined to be lenient with the Byzantine nobles, but after a few months the old hippodrome was opened and used as an execution ground and thousands were put to death. It was said that when the Sultan had first entered Haghia Sophia he pushed his thumb into a porphyry column and, with a flick of the wrist, had spun the old church around to face Mecca. In his triumph, the Sultan saw that this building had been made to honour God and Mehmet let it stand intact, ordering looters to stop their destruction. When he first entered the church he directed his masons to obscure only the most obvious signs and symbols of Christianity. So the Church of the Divine Wisdom became the Mosque of the Divine Wisdom and the supreme masterpiece of Justinian's Greek architects became the architectural yardstick of gentlemen with far cooler dispositions. Through the succeeding centuries Istanbul's Ottoman architects built their mosques in competition with the great old dome.

The Emperor's body, Phranzes says, was found by the wall's first breach in a heap of corpses, identified by the imperial eagles embroidered in jet and seed pearls onto his red socks. Legend says that he was taken for burial to a little church, now the Mosque of Gul Jami. Muslims of that neighbourhood hold that a tomb in their mosque, reputedly Constantine XI's, is really that of a Muslim saint, Baba Gul or Father Rose. On the day that the city fell, the church had been celebrating the birthday of its saint, Theodosia, and had decorated her doors, as tradition demanded, with red roses. Whatever the truth, the classical world had ended and the West was embarrassed. In Burgundy the court composer, Guillaume Dufay wrote a fine lament for Constantinople, the tenors quietly singing the words of Jeremiah (Lamentations 1:2): '*Omnes amici eius spreverunt eam*: all her friends have dealt treacherously with her . . .'

The Italian mercenaries had sailed out of Constantinople the day the city fell, taking their fatally wounded commander with them and leaving the ancient city to its new rulers. All the city libraries were plundered. One hundred and twenty thousand manuscripts, it is said, completely disappeared; ten old books could be bought for a single coin: 'That same ignominious price,' says Gibbon, 'too high perhaps for a shelf of theology, included the whole works of Aristotle and Homer, the noblest productions of the science and literature of ancient Greece.' But some remained behind and many of these were later collected by the Greek nobles who survived and indeed prospered under the Ottomans; they sent the volumes off to the monastic libraries at Mount Athos in northern Greece. Even in the twentieth century, a perfect copy of a lost work of Archimedes was found in Istanbul still shelved and entombed in some Byzantine ruins. The exodus of Byzantine scholars to the West had begun with the city's poverty and had long preceded the arrival of the Turks. By 1400 Greek monks from southern Italy were teaching literary Florentines how to read their ancient language. Later, when the last Byzantine emperors came to Europe seeking help, many scholars and priests in their entourages stayed behind. Indeed, the visit of John VIII to Florence in 1438 with Cardinal Bessarion is sometimes taken to be the starting point of the Italian Renaissance.

In the same year that Constantinople fell, as the Turks were streaming through the ancient city, a German goldsmith, Johann Gutenberg was casting cold letter type and printing the first book. Inevitably, the book was a Latin Bible, Jerome's Vulgate, the first bible, as Gutenberg puts it, to be made 'without help of reed, stylus or pen, but with the marvellous concord, proportion and harmony of punches and types'; all this he tells us, with 'the aid of the All-Highest, who often reveals to the humble what he hides from the wise'.

Though this was a more modest event than the cataclysm in the Eastern Empire, nonetheless these craftsmen in their workshops at Mainz on the Rhine started a machine that, in half a century, changed the world. After Gutenberg, the Bible would be made in hundreds of editions, many of them inexpensive, and printed in a dozen different languages. And this would subvert and change forever the old religious order of the West. As it had ever been, the Bible was still at the front of Christendom, at once its guide and mirror; now it would become a medium of political struggle and social change.

Chapter Seven
PARADISE LOST

Introduction: 'Style is the Man'

A few years ago, an Italian news programme reported the theft of one of Titian's minor paintings from a small church in the Veneto. It struck me as sad that the thieves had provided yet another good reason why such paintings are collected from their proper places to be displayed in high security museums with a dozen other refugees, a row of catalogued antiquities. Suddenly the camera showed a group of elderly women standing beside the empty church, crying and embracing each other. 'She was our Virgin,' one of them shouted indignantly at the camera, 'she has seen our family baptisms and funerals for hundreds of years. She was *our* Virgin.' This was a world where the abstract beauty of a Titian, so admired in museums, still served to clothe a sacred image, making it easier to approach and giving that village Virgin its individual identity.

Just as the modern secular world has separated abstract beauty from its images, so the Bible has lost the golden covers that it wore for a thousand years and changed into paperback: the Bible has become a book. And piety cannot replace the golden covers once again, as some Victorians would try to do; that was a work of reaction and imitation and was not born in simplicity and innocence. The terrible threat of this loss of innocence had hung over Europe for several centuries and people fought and died around the issue. The new vision had begun to grow inside Europe in the late Middle Ages. Indeed, the Bible's slide from sacred to profane may be said to have been started, though inadvertently, by that most gentle Tuscan scholar, the poet Petrarch. For Petrarch popularized the awareness and the love of style, a fascination with form, with the abstract beauty of words and of nature. In many ways, this was the birth of modern man.

Francesco Petrarch grew up in Provence, amid the splendid entourage of the exiled popes. When he was sixteen, his father, Ser Petracco, determined that his son should follow him into the law and he sent him off to study at the University of Bologna. There, Francesco quickly developed a dislike of the occupation which he later called the 'sale of justice' and rather than spending his time 'merchandizing the mind' he collected classical texts. So incensed was Ser Petracco when he visited his son that he built a bonfire for the young man's books and only desisted when Francesco burst into tears at the thought of 'such sweetness and sonority of word' going up in smoke. This was the birth of a new attitude to words and writing.

Italia scriptis vivit celeberrimus omni
Qui nunc Euganeo colle Petrarcha Jacet.

On his father's death, Petrarch returned to Avignon and joined the 'Babylonian captivity' of the papal court. And there, he tells us, he fell in love, wrote ardent poetry, cultivated courtly fashion and changed his name from the gutteral Petracco to the sonorous Petrarca (of which Petrarch is an anglicization). Young Petrarch saw the style and form of things as their *essence*: 'the style is the man,' he writes, 'something singular and of our own.' And this became a large part of the manner of the Renaissance, where style and flair were everything; the arts a matter of aesthetic exploration.

Throughout his life, Petrarch spent a great deal of time searching for ancient texts, many of which were lying forgotten in the libraries of ancient monasteries. A few other people were also looking; the first copy of the poems of Catullus, it was said, was found twisted and stained, serving as a bung in a Mantuan wine barrel. At Liège and later at Verona, Petrarch himself rediscovered the writings of the Roman Cicero and at the same time in Florence his great friend Boccaccio, the celebrated author of the *Decameron*, was paying a southern Italian to read Homer out aloud to him in Greek so that he might 'hear the music of its words'. Boccaccio lodged the man in his own house, employing him to translate Homer's *Iliad* into Italian for the first time. These people were providing the coming Renaissance with well-springs of thought and imagery.

Petrarch loved the countryside; he chose to live in remote farmhouses and spent much time walking in Provence and northern Italy. But this was by no means a retreat from the world, and such was the fame of his own poetry that in 1349 the Senate of Rome invited him to leave his farmhouse and visit the ancient city where, in imitation of an antique ceremony, he was crowned with laurels as the Poet Laureate. In his finest works Petrarch combined his knowledge of classical verse with his own love of nature and, especially, his love for a married woman of Avignon, whom in his verses he calls Laura, after the poet's antique laurel: Petrarch was in love with fame and women. His poetry is a process of self-analysis. In its intimacy, you feel that he speaks to you as one person to another, one of the first writers since antiquity to do so. These ancient writers he treated as friends. He wrote literary letters to Cicero and Homer, and in his writing they appear as individual people. His precious books, forming one of the first private libraries in Gothic Europe, he saw as brothers, each one sitting in its appointed place upon their shelves. When a heavy volume fell upon his foot he wonders, in stylish verse, how he had annoyed his ancient friend.

It is not surprising that Petrarch's celebrated ascent of Mount Ventoux, just north of Avignon, was conceived by him as a thoroughly literary affair, planned after reading an account of another mountain climb in classical times. And when he came down the mountain Petrarch rushed back in the moonlight to his lodgings and there immediately wrote an account of his experience. For this unusual adventure, he tells us, none of his friends was a suitable companion, so his younger brother was called upon to help indulge the poet's whim. They set off together from Avignon, travelling some twenty miles to an inn at Malaucène where they stayed the night, and next morning 'with only two servants' they set off up the mountain.

The sun rose as they climbed through the trees on the lower slopes and picked their way through the loose rocks, the sweet herbs and bright flowers on the mountainside. But it was hard work. Petrarch consoled himself with the lines of another poet, 'remorseless labour conquers all'. Then they came across a shepherd grazing his sheep, who was puzzled as to why they were climbing the mountain at all. He told them that once in the 'ardour of youth', he had climbed to the top but he got nothing for his trouble except fatigue, scratches, torn clothes and a feeling of repentance. There was nothing there. Still, the shepherd kept an eye on Petrarch and his party as they climbed, shouting directions to lead them to the best paths. For him, as for everybody of his age, life was dangerous enough without issuing such invitations to disaster. The great mountain, the shepherd said, was a useless thing, suited only for grazing sheep. But in his mind Petrarch was climbing on another mountain. He had seen that the ancient writings had contained a real world. He had read of an ancient Greek climbing a mountain in Thessaly and claiming that he had seen two seas from its summit. Petrarch had wondered if such a thing was possible, if his ancient friend was right, and now he tried the experiment for himself, just as some of Petrarch's contemporaries were dissecting corpses to verify the writings of the ancient doctors: a century later, at the height of the Renaissance, Leonardo da Vinci was still dissecting corpses but then to make his *own* investigations. At that same time, too, the dissection of the Holy Bible had begun; for the Bible had become just another book upon a shelf, whose style and manner might be liked or disliked and whose statements could be questioned, even tested, as Petrarch had done in his experiment on the mountain.

When he arrived at the bleak summit of Mount Ventoux, Petrarch found a 'little level place, where we could, at last, rest our weary bodies'. Emulating the Greek, he looked at the horizon searching for his beloved Italy, which, like Laura, he largely preferred to worship from afar. And then his thoughts turned to a book in his pocket, a volume of St Augustine's autobiographical *Confessions*, given to him by a friar at Avignon: 'I opened the little volume,' he says 'small in size but infinitely sweet, with the intention of reading whatever came into my hands ... Now, I happened by chance to open it at the tenth book. My brother stood attentively waiting to hear what St Augustine would say from my lips. As God is my witness, the first words my eyes fell upon were, "And men go about admiring the high mountains and the mighty waves of the sea and the sweep of the stars, but they themselves they abandon".' At Avignon, Petrarch had been undergoing some deliciously poetic torments about his love for Laura and the fires of hell that his lust seemed to promise. The reading from St Augustine, Petrarch tells us, brought him a flash of revelation, a happening that repeated an event that St Augustine had described in his *Confessions*.

Petrarch's climb up Mount Ventoux had been a literary outing. His imagination and energy had filled the old books of his library and their words had carried him off on a journey that almost no one else of his time would have understood. It was a sign of the beginning of a new awareness in the West. At that moment Petrarch, looking down from his literary mountain, was a different man from the Gothic farmer in the hills below; he was like an anthropologist looking at an Amazonian tribe. Petrarch's detachment from the 'real world' below has since become a part of common experience – part of the loneliness of modern man. In the centuries after Petrarch's death, this new vision would make a revolution for Christendom and its Bible.

The Black Death came to Europe in Petrarch's lifetime, killing not only his beloved Laura and half his own family but half the population of France as well. In Italy the disaster caused such a discontinuity in society that when it died down people thought of the time before as a separate age, a Middle Age set between classical antiquity and their own time. Europe took a century to recover. Then trade and commerce expanded as never before and merchants became princes. The new wealth engendered a confidence not seen since Petrarch's day. The new age was a rebirth, a Renaissance. And in all this sparkling optimisim, the little crack that Petrarch's detachment had made in Christendom was all but forgotten. Now Petrarch was seen as one of the cornerstones on which the new Renaissance scholarship was founded. For Petrarch's admiration for the classical writers, his warm awareness of their personalities, had led him to study his copies of the ancient texts with especial care. He was after the truth of their life and times, and this he found as much in the manners of their writing as its contents. Petrarch had learned to distinguish different writers by their style; he worried about the authenticity and the accuracy of many of the surviving texts. He and his followers spent a great deal of time reconstructing the exact words of ancient texts from many different versions. In such scholarly circles, medieval scholastics like Peter Abelard and Thomas Aquinas were regarded with no little scorn as being hopelessly uncritical of their sources and frequently inaccurate in their interpretations. They had used but a handful of ancient texts to support and augment Christian teaching. Insisting on a more critical scholarship, Petrarch had fathered a new kind of learning.

Florence became a centre of this new scholarship where it was fostered at the courts of the Medici dukes. Here there grew up a great love of classical literature and of the life that the old texts often described; a noble democratic spirit, a love of life and good manners. Merchant princes like the Medici sent their agents out into the old monasteries of Europe, many of them founded in the days of Charlemagne, searching for more ancient literature and for Carolingian copies that had lain unread for centuries. In many ways these fifteenth-century scholars were romantics trying to rediscover an ancient literary world, reviving visions of the ancient people whose lively thoughts and writing and art so delighted them. Many people of the Medici court now lived out this vision of an antique literary world in their own lives.

As Petrarch had understood, this work of literary resurrection greatly depended upon a firm grasp of the Latin language. At Rome Lorenzo Valla, an especially pugnacious scholar and a secretary of the pope, devoted the best part of his life to a systematic understanding of the ancient language – this, ironically, at the very time that Latin, in its final forms, was disappearing as a living, popular tongue, transforming into the Italian dialects that persisted until the nineteenth century. Just at the time when the words of Jerome's great Vulgate Bible were lost to the Roman population, Valla and a few other scholars were turning Latin into a fixed, and therefore highly self-conscious, literary language. Valla developed a great sensitivity to antique Latin styles which led him to detect many forgeries and incorrect attributions. He pointed out that the popular and long-accepted correspondence between St Paul and Seneca was an obvious fake and performed similar services for other spurious Christian texts. In 1440 Valla recognized that the celebrated document known as the *Donation of Constantine*, an edict in which the first Christian emperor granted the Roman popes control over Christendom and the Church, was, in fact, a forgery. In 1448 in the *Adnotationes*, he compared Jerome's New Testament Vulgate text with a Greek original, and he made long lists of Jerome's errors in translation. It was the first time that the Bible's sacred words had been treated in this way since the days of Jerome himself. As with most of his work, Valla confined himself to observations upon language and not upon theology or science. But many of his contemporaries took a different view. 'Valla finds fault with Aristotle's physics,' wrote a friend with amusement. 'He finds Boethius' Latin barbaric, destroys religion, professes heretical ideas, scorns the Bible.'

Fifty years later Valla might have been burned as a heretic, but in that last era of innocence before the Protestant Reformation and the spread of printing, Valla's employer, the pope, regarded his often acerbic scholarly judgments with equanimity, as the grist of the courtly discussions that for Valla and his fellow scholars were almost a profession and certainly a way of life. Valla's ideas had no effect upon the course of religion in his own lifetime. Yet he inadvertently lit a slow fuse; sixty-five years later, when printers were established throughout central Europe, the chance discovery in a Belgian abbey of the manuscript of *Adnotationes* and its publication in 1516, proved to be the inspiration for a new generation of scholars, intent upon the re-examination of the Bible which they were preparing to translate into contemporary European languages. So Petrarch's kindly but critical attitudes to scholarship entered the mainstreams of Bible scholarship just at the height of the Protestant Reformation.

In Valla's day, of course, the most powerful and most public means of expression in Italy had passed away from the scholars and writers to the fine artists. Just as the fame of the Renaissance scholars had largely died with their conversations, so their written work is overshadowed by the sheer bulk of beautiful paintings, sculptures and architecture of their contemporaries. And these works also testify to the revival of classical style and taste in Italy. Just as Valla and his fellow scholars made their own individual versions of the classical world, so the fine artists did not make a real renaissance – a re-birth – of ancient art but a brave new world; and for almost a century most of them celebrated this beautiful vision of a new world with great skill and cleverness.

But the uncanny sensitivity of individual genius detected the worm in the apple. Michelangelo clearly felt the slow-opening crack in Christendom; even as he decorated the courts of the new popes and merchant princes, he felt something of the real loneliness that this bright new world of style, this new perspective, this detachment would bring with it. Michelangelo sensed that the shift from medieval manners to Renaissance high self-consciousness would lead to the de-valuation, the de-sanctification of Christendom, and with it the divine order of society, of kings, popes and even of the Holy Bible itself. As a young man, one story goes, Michelangelo watched a Gothic sculptor at work high up on the roof of Milan cathedral, and he asked him why he was taking such care with his work when no one would see it from the ground. God and all his angels would see it, his fellow sculptor replied; and here is the difference between the two ages. With his clear contemporary eye and his vast talents whose influence was so destructive to the older forms of reality and sacredness, Michelangelo gave powerful visual expression to the dark currents moving within the courts of Europe.

Men of the Renaissance had eaten from the Tree of Knowledge and Michelangelo, sensing the break-up of the divine order of society, offered his own tremendous remedies for the fall from grace. Re-making the biblical world with the powerful landscape of his new classicism, he made his great heroes and prophets the models of the men for this new world. Even as a young man he had made a great statue of David, a modern David with Tuscan limbs and a classic torso, and the synthesis had gained him celebrity and work. Altogether an agreeable enterprise. Twenty years on, however, with some of his best works destroyed and several major projects blocked for lack of money, he took a different view of his society, of those banker-princes and warrior-popes who sometimes fancied to be immortalized by him in the grandest antique manner. As Michelangelo's family might well have observed, many of these men who so hotly disputed the merits of ancient prose and the latest art were of neither ancient nor medieval nobility. Michelangelo's father, a poverty-stricken nobleman, was proud to claim that he had never descended to trade or banking in his life and regarded his son's chosen career, which had seemed to him to consist of manual labour, with distaste.

Michelangelo's massive designs of tragic and heroic Europeans have lived until today, right through the vapid poses of the eighteenth century to the grotesque musculations of the stars of contemporary cinema. But these heroic prototypes were not the products of Michelangelo's old age. The last sculpture on which he worked before he died in 1564 is thinly Gothic (see Plate 38); the great muscular forms of an earlier version cut down to the bone in an old man's act of piety. Increasingly in middle age he had taken to architecture, making a new world for the frail new men who would inhabit this lonely new Christendom. In his hands classical architecture became more expressive than it had ever been.

'Architectural members,' he said, 'should follow the same rule as the members of the human body.' The great man set about designing buildings for a society he saw as being in decay, despite its contemporary splendours. Obviously not many of his contemporaries would have agreed, yet his deep pessimism affected his judgment in all things. Sardonically, he described the beautiful Renaissance plans of the new St Peter's, bequeathed to him by an earlier papal architect, as being for a church filled with 'gloomy lurking holes above and below, in which all sorts of knavery could be accomplished . . . the hiding of banished persons, the coining of false money, the rape of nuns and other misdemeanours'. This is hardly the language of the Renaissance, nor a part of the vision of the brilliant architects who had re-made Italy's greatest churches in the language of classicism. Michelangelo took this design, at once balanced, humane, a product of the High Renaissance, and he transformed it with simple massive columns and a vast dome – a colossal distortion of the same humanity which, he had once said, all good architecture must possess. Yet this was a dome under which his church could embrace and protect, could support and warm a colder Christendom.

Martin Luther

Carlyle once remarked that the three greatest elements of Western society were gunpowder, printing and the Protestant religion. The trio is closely interwoven; printing and Protestantism grew up together with gunpowder in close attendance. Protestants thought that every person in their new, reformed church should *know* the contents of the Bible. That book alone held God's revealed truth and the salvation of mankind. Translated into European languages, printed bibles were sold throughout the Protestant north. Not only did this change the place and function of the Bible but sometimes its very words.

As Michelangelo worked in Rome and Florence, a veritable revolution was in progress north of the Alps. By the 1520s printing presses were pumping out hundreds of thousands of books and pamphlets; the writings of the Renaissance scholars and editions of the new-found classical texts were appearing in the universities and in the houses of an emerging middle class. There was an unparalleled explosion of learning and information. And at the same time, northern princes who had always been reluctant to concede their authority to either the pope or the Holy Roman Emperor had found a most eloquent voice in Martin Luther, a monk teaching at the University of Wittenberg in Saxony. In 1521 inside the dark Gothic church of St Mary's that still stands over Wittenberg's town square the first Protestant communion was celebrated, without the vestments of the cathedral mass, without the prayer of consecration, without the elevation of the Host and with the entire congregation taking the bread and wine. The following day, 26 December, the priest announced from the pulpit that he would marry a nun from a local convent. In 1529 it was rumoured that printed New Testaments, in Martin Luther's translation, had been in the pockets of the unpaid German mercenaries of the imperial army that had so brutally sacked Rome – the city that the northern reformers had named, after Babylon, the 'Scarlet Whore'.

By this time the Reformation of the northern church was supported by an ever-increasing number of princes, from Switzerland to the North Sea, in a direct and unambiguous challenge to the old order of Christendom both temporal and spiritual. But so diverse in attitudes and opinions were the reformers that their only common bond was their antagonism to the papacy, to its doctrine and power. Yet the response to this was slow and diffused, both from the Roman popes and from the Holy Roman Emperors, Charlemagne's successors and sovereigns of that shifting, ramshackle collection of European states stretching from Spain to Poland. Luther had spelled out the basis of his attack upon the Roman church when placed on trial for his life before the Emperor at Worms. He would stand, he said, by his writings, 'until I am convicted by the testimony of Scripture or plain reason'. The teachings and traditions of the church held no authority for him: only the Bible and his northern common sense were valid. At the end of his speech the imperial Spanish guard shouted for him to be burned, yet the German princes had protected him. To suppress this 'festering disease' an imperial decree was issued ordering that 'no one shall feed or nourish him . . . that you shall take him prisoner . . . that the words of Luther [and no doubt, Luther himself, if it was possible] are to be burned and by this means and others, utterly destroyed'. Protected by the German princes, Luther did not go up in the smoke of heresy but died of old age and was buried with due honour in Wittenberg, leaving behind him the church that still bears his name, and a translation of the Bible as powerful as Jerome's Vulgate and, perhaps, yet more influential. In the high street of this quiet dark town, you can see the apparatus of the man's career laid out in the buildings – all the workshops and houses of his day are still there; the offices of propaganda, of finance and of military organization that all revolutions require.

Gothic Saxon builders were still working upon Wittenberg's four-square town hall as Michelangelo's craftsmen were building his Renaissance architecture at Florence, and the town hall's gables are all measured out in the new style, like postcards sent from the sunny south. Wittenberg's town hall stands for a new wealth in the north, in the city's guilds, in a new middle class. Like the south, northern Europe had also recovered from the terrible plagues of the previous centuries and, by the sixteenth century, industry and trade had made it richer than it had ever been before. Duke Frederick the Wise, the ruler of Saxony and a powerful and often dissenting voice in imperial councils, had given Wittenberg a fine new university with celebrated teachers, first-class printers, good artists and a string of booksellers. And, of course, the monk Luther.

Like most successful ideas, the central, sustaining insight of German Protestantism was born in a single mind. Young Luther, a promising university student, had become a monk as a result of a vow made in holy terror when a lightning flash had thrown him, in an echo of St Paul, down to the ground. After studying at Erfurt Monastery, Luther was sent in 1508 to the brand new

University of Wittenberg, to lecture there upon the Ethics of Aristotle, a traditional adjunct to theology in medieval education. Luther was thoroughly versed in traditional theology but neither Aristotle nor Thomas Aquinas could supply him with the key to a balanced life. He was haunted by the inevitability of sin and damnation, despite the Church's teaching that mankind could escape from hell-fire by repentance and penance. Luther later recalled that he had 'hated this God who punished sinners, if not with silent blasphemies at least with huge murmurings. I was indignant against God. As if it were not enough that miserable sinners, eternally ruined by original sin, should be crushed ... through the Law of the Ten Commandments ... And so I raged with a savaged and confounded conscience ...'

Luther turned to the Bible. As a student, he had imbibed enough of the critical attitudes of Renaissance learning to question if the Church's traditional interpretation of the Holy Word was correct: whether, for example, the Latin word that signified grace – the grace of God through which mankind was redeemed from hell – had been correctly understood. In a flash, as he read the first chapter of St Paul's Epistle to the Romans, he saw a different meaning. Instead of the usual interpretation that this grace was the *active* grace of God – a grace that operated at the day of judgment when the souls that would be saved were separated from the damned – Luther saw that the passage might refer to a *passive* grace, a grace by which God granted everybody the possibility of salvation by allowing everyone the potential of belief. If this was what Paul had really meant, then it was man's own faith that redeemed him from eternal damnation, and if that were so – and Luther soon found innumerable passages in the Bible and in the writings of the early Fathers to support his reading – then man's salvation was not made by acts of penance and repentance, nor through the intercession of saints and martyrs or the prayers of the church, but by belief, by faith alone. As a contemporary remarked, 'Luther has attacked both the Pope's authority and the monk's dinners.' And for this revelation, Luther needed nothing more than his own reading of the Bible.

In the Epistle to the Romans, Paul writes of his eagerness to preach the Gospel in Rome (Romans 1:16–17 NEB): 'For I am not ashamed of the Gospel. It is the saving power of God for everyone who has faith ... here is revealed God's way of righting wrong, a way that starts from faith and ends in faith; as Scripture says, he shall gain life who is justified through faith'. At this Luther tells us, 'I felt myself straightaway born afresh and to have entered through the open gates into paradise itself.' The Gospels, the word of God, were the first and only authority. For true salvation the Church must return to the Bible's teachings and the writings of the early Fathers. Though throughout the centuries many monks had had identical thoughts, reticence was never Luther's way. The truth had been revealed to him and it had taken a terrible load from his spirit; this could be the salvation of mankind. In the contemporary German climate of dissatisfaction with Rome and with the emperor, there were also practical political applications for Luther's insight.

In Rome itself, at precisely the same time, the popes were rebuilding the ancient church of St Peter's – the same church which at a later date Michelangelo would transform with his huge columns and beautiful high dome. From the beginning the vast project was financed in the traditional manner, by raising money throughout Christendom just as the medieval bishops had done for their cathedrals. Now, however, the generosity of the faithful was further encouraged by the sale of indulgences, an act of penitence by which money given to the church was rewarded with a 'letter of pardon' which, coupled with genuine inward repentance, granted a remission from the temporal penalties of sin which traditionally ran from formal prayers to excommunication.

This system had first found favour hundreds of years before Luther's day, when indulgences were not purchased but earned by all those who had joined the crusading armies in the East. By Luther's time the system had degenerated to the point where, by giving a few coins to specialized indulgence sellers, they would assure you that you had ransomed the soul of a dead relative from purgatory. To pay for St Peter's, the pope had granted the sale of all the indulgences in Saxony to the Archbishop of Mainz, a man who had bought his office from the Church with a loan obtained from some south-German money lenders. The deal was that half the money from the sale of indulgences would go to Rome for the building of St Peter's and half would go to the Archbishop's bankers to pay his debt. Though Luther never knew of this shameful shareout, the preposterous claims of the indulgence salesmen, who were taking considerable sums from the ordinary people of Wittenberg, were quite enough to anger him. For Luther now had a new understanding of St Paul's scripture. He *knew* that God's grace was not to be bought with money, but had been given freely through the gift of faith. But Luther was still a medieval monk, however fluent and numerous his protests were, and in the medieval manner of debating, he made a list of statements, ninety-five of them in all, which detailed his objections to the sale of indulgences. These he wrote out in the form of a thesis and he posted them, it is said, in the usual way that announcements were made at Wittenberg University, on the wooden door of the castle church.

The door to which in 1517 Martin Luther is said to have nailed his list of objections has long gone – blown to smithereens by the shells and gunpowder of an eighteenth-century Prussian army. Luther's statements, however, are still as clear and angry as the day they were written:

> . . . 27. It is mere human talk to preach that the soul flies out [of purgatory] as soon as the money clicks in the collection box.
> 28. It is certainly possible that when the money clinks in the collection box both greed and avarice can increase . . .
> 32. All those who believe themselves certain of their own salvation because of the Letters of Pardon will be eternally damned, together with their teachers.
> 92. Away, then, with these prophets who say to Christ's people, 'Peace, peace,' when there is no peace.
> 95. And let them thus be more confident of entering heaven through many tribulations rather than through a false assurance of peace.

Though the thesis would hardly seem sufficient to set all Germany on fire, the reaction to Luther's ninety-five objections was immediate and quite phenomenal. Unexpectedly, it struck a strong chord in Germany and soon it was published and circulated by Frederick and several other German princes, who for many years had been moving into a close federation and struggling for greater freedom from both their temporal and spiritual overlords, the Holy Roman Emperor and the pope. Quickly printed and widely circulated, Luther's denunciation of this most obvious corruption enjoyed a great celebrity.

For centuries the traditional northern impatience with their rulers and the Roman Church had found expression in the words of such reformers, men who had occasionally established small free communities, living in equality and sometimes promiscuity, with a faith derived from the Bible and the writings of the early Fathers of the Church. Now Luther asserted the equality of all men before God: 'between laymen and priests, princes and bishops, or as they call it, between spiritual and temporal persons, the only real difference is one of office and function and not of estate.' Such sentiments, of course, are inherently political; indeed Luther is now recognized inside the German Democratic Republic as a prophet of that modern state. In his own time, however, Luther soon saw that if both he and his plans for church reform were not to go up in smoke, he had to come to terms with the ambitious German princes who alone would help secure his vision of a free and German church. One of his first published writings, following the '95 Theses', was a pamphlet addressed 'To the Christian nobility of the German Nation'. Writing in his native German rather than in scholarly Latin, Luther appealed to the imperial princes and to the Emperor himself to establish a reformed church in their kingdoms. They ruled, he argued, by the divine right of all legitimate monarchs and were therefore obliged to establish a just church inside their kingdoms. This 'divine right' was the spiritual sanction of all medieval rulers, part of the sacred order of Christendom, and was underpinned by the powerful myth surrounding Charlemagne. Though popes and princes might fight each other, they would certainly join forces against those who denied the innate sacredness of their authority. This Luther never did. Later in his life, the wretched German peasants who had not profited from the rising wealth inside the cities revolted and were backed by many ministers of the new church. Luther at first sympathized with them; but as the revolt turned into open war he issued a polemical pamphlet 'Against the Robbing, Murdering Hordes of Peasants', and appealed to the princes to annihilate them, a feat which they speedily accomplished. 'I always said,' Luther wrote, 'that if the peasants won, the devil would win.' Luther stood for the old sacred order in society.

The reaction of the Roman popes to this northern unrest was first negligent then clumsy. Luther was excommunicated and driven beyond the influence of the church. The reaction of the Holy Roman Emperor was similarly confused.

The young Spaniard, Charles V, had aroused little enthusiasm in the breasts of the reforming German princes. When in 1529 an imperial council called for a re-imposition of papal authority throughout Christendom, they countered the edict by an indignant declaration, a *protestia* – the word 'protestant' was born – and shortly afterwards the Emperor was forced to cede many of his temporal rights to a powerful German Federation. From that year onwards, all imperial decrees concerning Germany were written in German. Through it all Luther was living under threat of being burned as a heretic. At first, the princes had protected him surreptitiously; then as their union grew stronger, he was openly espoused. Luther's tremendous eloquence and personal fame had washed right through Germany, helping to weld the ambitious states together in a common bond.

Wittenberg was such a small town that Luther had only to walk a few hundred yards down its high street from his monastery to the court church, a stocky figure in a brown monk's habit, carrying his hammer, nails and his thesis. As in Oxford and Cambridge, all the resources of a medieval university were set along this single cobbled road. At Wittenberg there was everything needed to propagate Luther's new religion, and as more and more pamphlets and books issued from Wittenberg's presses, Luther persuaded a master printer, Hans Lufft to come to the university and establish a printing shop. For half a century Lufft continued to print accurate and quickly made works that were published by three booksellers in the city. Some 200,000 bibles in numerous editions were printed upon Lufft's presses and sold at a price equivalent to a carpenter's weekly wage. And Lufft did not just produce simple spartan work; his elegant bibles, with columns of text and a rectangular woodcut at the heading of each book in the style of the Swiss printing shops, became a standard design for Protestant bibles in every tongue.

Some of these bibles also held superb woodcuts, the work of the studios of Lucas Cranach, a native of Wittenberg and one of the finest artists in Germany. Cranach had helped to publish Luther's first Bible even before Lufft's arrival in the town. Throughout his life Cranach drew and painted his friend Luther with that splendidly intense manner of the best northern artists; Luther as a young monk, as university lecturer, as a great religious reformer and finally Luther on his death bed. And he painted Luther's wife too – he had married an ex-nun, he said, to 'spite the devil' – and he loved her and his many children. And all of these pictures Cranach painted with the same glowing sensuousness that filled his celebrated nudes, those Reformation pin-ups as popular today as in Cranach's own time. His portraits of Luther and his circle participating in the Last Supper or standing on the hill of Calvary are the icons of the new church and they show something of the personal power, the magnetic attraction of Luther himself. And something of that power is also felt in a vivid account of a contemporary conversation that took place by the fireside of an inn at Jena in Thuringia. One traveller admitted to the assembled party that he did not know if Luther was a saint or a devil, but he added, he 'wouldn't miss giving ten guilders if I might make my confession to him . . . for I think he knows about quieting souls'. Luther had intuitively struck a cord in the German soul.

A major drawback in basing a spiritual revolution such as Luther called for upon the unquestioned revelation of a single human being is that the example permits spiritual egalitarianism. The validity of similarly powerful and possibly quite contradictory revelations of the other members of the congregation cannot be excluded. Luther's passionate and inspired texts, his insight into the spiritual needs of his country, had all to be carefully organized into a coherent doctrine that could then be claimed as a genuine and universally accepted revelation. This feat was accomplished by Philip Melanchthon, a scholar who like Luther had come to Wittenberg to teach, and who stood by Luther throughout his whole career, aiding and advising him. His huge tome, *Loci communes* of 1521 laid out arguments which showed that Luther's revelation held a truth valid for all men, on which a new spiritual order could be founded. Luther regarded the book as fundamental to the Reformation and he thought his friend a genius. But he was also frequently exasperated with this mild-mannered man; 'your nature as always,' Luther once told him, 'is too gentle'; yet they formed a powerful combination. In 1529 Luther led a delegation of German reformers to a delicate meeting with their Swiss counterparts. It was quickly realized that Luther and the Swiss reformer Zwingli were 'both of them, hot tempered and vehement' and they were paired off with each other's assistants. Zwingli faced Melanchthon whom he found 'uncommonly slippery'. Unlike Luther, Melanchthon was a diplomat. Melanchthon it was who presented the Lutheran confessions of faith to the Imperial Council of 1530, while Luther himself, labelled as a heretic, fretted away his time in a castle nearby. In many ways, Philip Melanchthon was the founder of modern-day Lutheranism; he was also the man who in 1521 had encouraged Luther to start his translation of the Bible, a basic requirement for their new Church.

Luther began his translation in another castle-refuge shortly after his dramatic encounter with the Imperial Diet. As he finished his work upon each Bible book, Luther sent it to his friend 'Philip' at Wittenberg, and Melanchthon provided the exile with a learned commentary. But the work is undeniably Luther's. The magnificent lively text is in a German so vigorous that it fathered the birth of that tongue as a literary language and forged a vital element of a common German identity. Lufft's books were cheap enough for the large and literate German middle class to buy in quantity, and all Luther's writings, from his earliest pamphlet manifestos to the Bible books and commentaries, were very widely read. The conversation of the travellers at that Jena inn in 1540 shows just how deep his influence ran. Two merchants came in from the cold after a hard ride and ate at a common table where a single man, apparently a nobleman, sat close to the fire, reading a book printed in Hebrew. Fifty years before such an esoteric sight would have aroused a deep suspicion; now it was greeted not with amazement but with keen interest. 'I'd have my little finger cut off if only I could learn that language,' said one of the travellers to the man. 'You can master it,' he answered, 'if you stick to it; I do a bit each day'. This was Luther travelling for safety in disguise. Later that same evening the three men were joined by more travellers and after taking off their wet cloaks and setting them by the fire, one of them, from Switzerland, was seen to be carrying a new and unbound book with him. Luther, still incognito, asked him what it was. 'Why, it is Doctor Luther's exposition of certain Gospels and Epistles, just printed and newly published,' came the reply. 'Haven't you seen it yet?' And Luther replied that he had not, but he would be getting a copy soon, which was

der herr ist eyn reych
Denn das __ ist des herren
und er ist eyn herr unter den heyden

__ essen und beten an alle __ auff erden __ __
__ fur yhm alle die yn dem staub ligen
und der __ seyne sele mehr __ leben lest

yhn seme wirt yhm dienen
den herren wirt man verkundigen zu kinds kind
Sie werden komen und seyne gerechtigkeyt predigen
dem volck das geboren ist, das ers thut

Xiij
Eyn psalm Davids

er herr ist meyn hirtt
myr wirt nichts mangeln

Er lest mich weyden __ __ __
und __ mich __ __ __ __ erbeytet

Er __ wider meyn sele

er furet mich auff rechten __ __ __ __ __ __
Und ob ich schon wandert ym finstern tal, furcht ich keyn ungluck
denn du bist bey myr

Deyn stab und stecken trosten mich
Du bereytest __ eynen tisch __ __ meyne __
du machest meyn heubt __ mit ole, __ __ __ __
Gutte und barmhertzigkeyt werden myr nach __
leben lang
und werde __ ym haus des herren __ __

Xiiij
Eyn psalm Davids

__ __ ist des herren und was drynnen ist
der erdboden und was drynnen wonet

true as he was travelling back to Wittenberg. They had a good meal and Luther paid for all their food. And then they went their different ways.

Though the Swiss traveller had bought Luther's commentaries, it was the Bible translation that attracted the greatest attention. 'This is not the Bible; it is a piece of outright heresy which seeks to blaspheme against God and the Pope,' said the critics; and others wrote that 'Luther has warped the original to suit his own doctrine'. In return, Luther, who worked steadily throughout his life on improving his translation, gave his critics as sharp and as short a shrift as had Jerome in Bethlehem.

I have constantly tried, in translating, to produce a pure and clear German, and it has often happened that for two or three or four weeks we have sought for a single word, and sometimes have not found it even then. In working at the book of Job, Master Philip and I could sometimes scarcely finish three lines in four days. Now that it is translated and complete, anyone can read and criticize it, and one now runs his eyes over three or four pages and does not stumble once. But he is not aware of the humps and lumps out of the way so that one could slide over it so finely. It is good ploughing when the field is cleaned up; but rooting out the woods and the stumps and getting the field ready – that is work that nobody wants . . .

Here, in Romans 3, I know right well that the word *solum* was not in the Greek or Latin text and had no need of the Papists to teach me that. It is a fact that these four letters *s-o-l-a* are not there, and at these letters the asses-heads stare, like a cow at a new door. At the same time they do not see that the *sense* of them is there and that the word belongs there if the translation is to be clear and strong. I wanted to speak German, not Latin or Greek . . .

We must not, like these asses, ask the Latin letters how we are to speak German; but we must ask the mother in the home, the children on the street, the common man in the marketplace about this, and look them in the mouth to see how they speak, and afterwards to our translating . . .

. . . I translated the New Testament to the best of my ability and according to my conscience . . . No one is forbidden to do a better piece of work . . . It is my Testament and my translation, and it shall continue to be mine. I will not suffer the Papists to be the judges . . . I know very well, and they know even less than the miller's beast, how much knowledge, work and reason and understanding is required in a good translator; but they have never tried it . . .

Please give these asses no other and no further answer to their blathering about the word *sola* than simply this: "Luther will have it so, and he is a doctor above all the doctors of the whole Papacy" . . .

Following in Cranach's footsteps, the printer Wolfgang Stuber published an edition of etchings, a very popular medium in those days, showing Luther working at his Bible translation. Stuber's print is a copy, a mirror image of Dürer's famous etching of St Jerome; like Jerome, Luther is working at *his* translation sitting in the front room of a southern German house. Both Jerome and Luther are drawn with cardinal's hats and rosaries, but only Jerome has a crucifix standing on his desk; Stuber has erased the one that stood on Luther's. Nonetheless Stuber's comparison is an apt one. Both Luther and Jerome had a lovely passionate style of writing filled with candour and clarity. Both of them loved invective and the play of words, and both of them believed that they *knew* the true meaning of the sacred words. And their sure grasp and inspiration has given their translation the fire of the ancient original.

While Luther made his Bible and the Wittenberg reformers set up their churches in calmness and prosperity, the reformers of other lands and cities were harried, hunted and burned. As the potential of this movement dawned upon them, Catholic kings and princes also saw that printing itself, the mass medium of Protestantism, was the reformer's most potent weapon. Along with the reformers themselves printers were also executed; one in Paris being burned on a pyre of his own books. The crime was heresy, the punishment automatic: burning for men, burial alive for women – and there were many women working in the printing and book trade. By 1540 laws aimed at booksellers and printers had been framed in many countries. In England the Company of Stationers was formed specifically to police the new industry on behalf of the Catholic goverment of Queen Mary. In the imperial cities on the continent printing shops were permitted only in approved sites – and the master printers were made liable under law for the contents of the books they made.

Despite these restrictions, Bible translations in all European languages continued throughout the sixteenth century, and most of these, printed in Protestant towns, strongly reflected the teachings of the Protestant churches. In England, religious reformation was mixed, as it was in Germany, with rising nationalism and also, during the reign of Henry VIII, with the divorce of an ailing monarch seeking an heir to the throne. And through it all there were burnings and executions.

William Tyndale, a university scholar from Gloucestershire, made the first Protestant translation of the Bible into English, a radical book filled with contentious footnotes and commentaries and with many biblical words changed in translation to suit the Protestant congregation. So the word that was traditionally understood as church became, in Tyndale's translation, congregation; priests became elders; penance became repentance; charity became love. Such levelling Protestantism was hardly likely to endear Tyndale to King Henry VIII or his archbishops, even though the king had displaced the pope as head of the Reformed Church. Protestant monarchs were uncertain of the place of the divine right of kings in the new church and it would take generations of kings and conferences to achieve a fresh balance of king and God. Many Protestants had delightedly recognized the vulnerability of the rulers of the Reformed states, stripped as they were of the spiritual sanction of

Rome. A visitor to the printers engaged in 1524 upon producing Tyndale's New Testament at Cologne describes how the workmen laughed among themselves at the 'revolution' they were making for export to England. Whether the tale is true or merely propaganda, it clearly shows that the protagonists understood the nature of the game. Denounced to the city authorities, both Tyndale and his editors fled with some 30,000 printed sheets up the river Rhine to the city of Worms, to finish the printing in the workshops of Gutenberg's foreman, who had overseen the production of the first book to be printed in Europe some seventy years beforehand. Tyndale's translation was the first version of the Bible to be printed in English and was so thoroughly hunted down and burned that only one partial copy has survived.

During the time he worked at Worms, William Tyndale travelled 400 miles east to Wittenberg and there, it seems, he met Luther, the man whose writings had so influenced his vision of the new church. Tyndale's translation of St Paul's Epistle to the Romans was based upon Luther's revolutionary interpretation of that key text. And the translations of both Luther and Tyndale share the same magnificence of prose. In Saxony both men were safe. At Wittenberg the only thing burned in the Reformation was a papal bull of excommunication – Luther had taken the great vellum scroll with all its seals out of the monastery where he was living with his family and burned it in the fields. But poor Tyndale, after ten years of exile, acrimony and imprisonment, was himself caught and burned at the stake – as a concession to his celebrity he was strangled first.

After he left England as a young scholar intent upon translating the Bible, Tyndale never returned to his home country again. Exile strengthened Tyndale's appreciation of his mother-tongue, though his increased closeness to Luther's thought alienated him from the English Reformers, and when he was in prison near Brussels, under sentence of death, none of them moved to petition for his reprieve. Yet still today, the greater part of the traditional English Bible, the great King James' Bible, the so-called Authorised Version, is Tyndale's work:

> Considre the lylies of the felde, how they growe. They labour not nether spynne. And yet for all that I saye unto you, that even Salomon in all his royalte was not arayed lyke unto one of these. Wherefore if god so clothe the grasse, which is to daye in the felde, and to morowe shal be caste into the fournace: shall he not muche more do the same unto you, o ye of lytle fayth?

> *Authorised Version*
> Consider the lilies of the field, how they grow; they toil not, neither do they spin: And yet I say unto you, That even Solomon in all his glory was not arrayed like one of these. Wherefore, if God so clothe the grass of the field, which to day is, and to morrow is cast into the oven, shall he not much more clothe you, O ye of little faith?
> (Matthew 6:28–31)

Betrayed into the hands of a Catholic prince, Tyndale spent his last year imprisoned in the grim fortress of Vilvorde on a river marsh, his only requests while he was there were for a better shirt to keep out the cold and a Hebrew dictionary so that he could work upon his translation of the Old Testament. His famous last prayer was that God should open the eyes of the King of England. The year was 1536 and Tyndale was about forty-five years old.

WILLIAM TINDALL

Luther died in his bed ten years later, just before the destruction that visited Wittenberg in the course of the German wars. Though it is true that he had been used by the German princes to serve their own ends, it is also true that the princes were sincere reformers in their own right, and several of them would die for the new Church. Today, it is difficult to appreciate what courage it had taken to begin this process of reform, what strength of mind for both princes and reformers to abandon, for all its faults, the vast spiritual shelter of the Church of Rome. For in many of their attitudes Luther and his princes were thoroughly medieval. They well knew of the menace of hellfire and the correct order of kings, prelates and commoners in Christendom. And even though the sale of indulgences was obviously corrupt in Luther's day, the power they held, like the power in the holy relics, seemed deep and wide. In Luther's letter that tells about the death of his life-long protector, Duke Frederick, you catch a glimpse of his new Church in its real setting: 'My Gracious Lord departed this life in the enjoyment of his full reason, taking the sacraments in both kinds and without supreme unction. We buried him without masses or vigils but yet in a fine noble manner ... The signs of his death were a rainbow which Philip Melanchthon and I saw one night last winter over Locau, and a child born here at Wittenberg without a head, and another with feet turned round.'

The beautiful late-Gothic doorway that decorates the entrance of the Augustinian monastery that became Luther's family home was given to him by his wife to mark his fifty-seventh birthday. Luther was a large, rather scruffy, red-faced man. His wife once complained that he had patched his trousers with a piece of material cut from his son's trousers: 'The hole was so large,' replied Luther indignantly, 'that I *had* to have a large patch for it. Trousers seldom fit me well, so I have to make them last long ... think what an eyesore it is to see a man with trousers like a pigeon and a coat so short that one can see his back between it and his trousers.' You may imagine them both in the little garden by his doorway, the great bluff man and his small slim wife that Cranach painted so well: A man who loved the world, its birds and plants, and its music and fine paintings too. A man whose personality still affects our modern world and is, therefore, part of us still.

'even that I burned': The English Bible

'I had no man to counterfet, nether was holpe with englysshe of eny that interpreted the same, or soche lyke thinge in the Scripture before tyme.' So Tyndale assures his readers in the introduction to his Bible.

Though I spake with the tonges of men and aungels, and have no love, I am even as sounding brasse: or as a tynklyne cymball. And though I coulde prophesy, and understande al secretes and all knowledge: yea if I had all fayth, so that I could move mountayns out of their places, and yet had no love, I were nothynge. And though I bestow all my goodes (to fede the poore) and though I give my body even that I burned and yet have no love, it profetheth me nothynge.

Tyndale's translation of St Paul's Epistle to the Corinthians (1, 13:1–3) remained largely untouched in the King James' Bible of 1611, and the rhythms, the style and the tone of all later English Bibles were influenced by his work. Listened to and read out aloud by English-speaking people for hundreds of years, the literature of millions of people, the English Bible has had more influence upon the English language than any other book. So splendid are its words that many have taken them to be the unmediated word of God. Yet the process by which the great old book was manufactured was convoluted indeed. And not the least remarkable fact about the King James' Bible is that it was the product of several separate committees. In the Translator's Preface, Dr Miles Smith, one of the editors of the Bible, says that they had 'aimed to walk in the ways of simplicity and integrity as before the Lord'. But this did not mean that they would produce pedantic nor dull prose, 'For is the Kingdome of God become words or syllables? . . . to savour more of curiositie than wisdome, that rather it would breed scorn in the Atheist than bring prophite to the godly Reader'. The translation, at once tactful, robust and imaginative, was a literary marvel in which even the most abstruse and obscure passages ring out firmly in the best manner of the age.

The King James' Bible has sometimes been compared to an English cathedral, a harmonious agglomeration of bits and pieces that make a splendid unity.

Between Tyndale's lonely translation and that of King James's committees were generations of suffering and scholarship; and to all this the committees gave due deference and dignity. 'Translation,' says Dr Smith, 'is that that openeth the window, to let in the light; that breaketh the shell, that we may eat the kernel; that putteth aside the curtain that we may looke into the most Holy Place'. But whether vulgar men should be allowed to peer at that most Holy Place, and what would happen to their kings should this revolution occur, is the greatest part of the story of faith and suffering in the English Reformation.

And the story of the King James' Bible is, in microcosm, the story of the Reformation. For though Tyndale's translation of the Bible may seem today to be close to King James's text, in its own time there were many things about it to raise the ire of priests and kings and so to send him to the stake. There are, for example, Tyndale's Lutheran re-interpretations of certain words; he also wrote lengthy introductions and footnotes filled with observations about the vanities of the world and its social order, those little texts which Tyndale called his 'profitable annotations against all the hard places'. In Tyndale's day, too, the question as to whether or not the Bible should be translated was not yet resolved. Most of the English Reformers were unwilling to depart from the traditional order of Roman Christendom. Highly apprehensive of the German Reformation, leading English Reformers sermonized the spectators, as the public hangmen burned Luther's translations, together with 'Philip Melanchthon's naughty writings', at St Paul's Cross in London in 1521. In the same year, King Henry VIII himself had written a tract against Luther for which an apprehensive pope had promptly awarded him the title *Fidei Defensor*, which in the abbreviated form F·D· still remains as an ironic memorial to Tudor piety on British coinage to this day. At the same time laws governing the printing of books and pamphlets in England were framed which limited production to London, Oxford and Cambridge. (This importation of the Essex-London accent into the two University towns seems to be the root of that distinctive university accent.) Severe penalties were threatened for secret printers; each printer was allowed only one apprentice at a time and the numbers of presses were carefully controlled. There were also more immediate restraints on the Reformers' scholarship. In the early years of Henry VIII's reign, English printing was of such poor quality that books such as the Bible which required a high level of accuracy were printed abroad. Further laws were made concerning the importation and smuggling of books such as the Bible of Luther, and that of Tyndale with its unapproved footnotes and introductions.

> That it shall be lawful . . . in any ports or other suspected places, to open and view all packs, dryfats [wooden cases], maunds [wicker baskets] and other things wherein books or paper shall be contained, brought into this realm, and make search in all work-houses, shops, warehouses and other places of printers, booksellers, and such as bring books into the realm to be sold . . . and to seize and carry . . .

A small and powerful group of English Reformers who were close to the king had attacked the writings and translations of the continental Protestants from the first. In London Sir Thomas More publicly disputed with Tyndale on the Continent in a pamphlet war; John Fisher, Bishop of Rochester, Chancellor of Cambridge University and its first Professor of Divinity, had denounced Luther's books as they were burned. And both Fisher and More had joined to answer Luther's scathing response to King Henry's pamphlet – 'The growling lion who calls himself the King of England', as Luther called him. 'The ignorance his book displays,' Luther remarked in a letter to a friend, 'is not to be wondered at in a royal author, but the bitterness and lies are gigantic . . . I shall embitter him more'. And indeed he did, with studied insults that did little to promote harmony among the reforming churchmen. Prime examples of his barbs, and those of Tyndale, were aimed at the immorality of King Henry's proposed divorce from Catherine of Aragon. When Henry had both More and Fisher executed during his flight from Rome into marriage with Anne Boleyn, the English Reformers were completely isolated from Luther and his 'poor beggars, the Wittenberg theologians' and were left with no middle ground; their choice lay between the uncertainties of Henry's loyalist Protestantism or the Swiss Puritanism of Calvin who made very little concession to the traditional prerogatives of monarchy. Though neither More nor Fisher left the Roman Church, both of them had wanted a Bible translated into English. 'I have never yet heard,' wrote More, 'why it were not convenient to have the Bible translated into the English tongue.'

Though highly conservative in the visual arts, where Renaissance style is represented by a few Italian importations and some squat plaster decorations set into Tudor brickwork, English intellectuals had taken happily enough to the new literature from Italy. In 1497 the Oxford professor John Colet had already lectured upon St Paul's Epistles, not in the moralizing or mystical manners of the medieval scholastics, but in a manner designed to re-discover the man Paul himself. Colet, who had been inspired to work upon St Paul after reading Petrarch's essay upon Cicero, in his turn impressed the peripatetic Dutch scholar Desiderius Erasmus, then a young man on his first trip to England. Erasmus became firm friends with the English scholars, living for some time with More and his family at their house in Chelsea, and lecturing at Fisher's invitation on St Jerome at Cambridge where he was appointed the University's first lecturer in the Greek language.

Just a few years later Erasmus found the copy of *Adnotationes*, Valla's scholarly appraisal of Jerome's Vulgate Bible, in a Belgian monastery; the book inspired his life's work of issuing accurate printed editions of ancient Christian texts like the works of Irenaeus and Jerome. For this arduous task which had never been undertaken before, Erasmus required an accurate and efficient printer, and it is no surprise to find that by 1515 he had left England for good

and was living at Basel, in the house of one of Europe's finest printers, Johannes Froben known as Frobenius. In 1526 Frobenius printed and published Erasmus' *Novum Instrumentum*, the first New Testament to be published in

Greek, accompanied by a new Latin translation. This was destined to be one of the Reformation's most important texts. Though prepared quickly and from Greek manuscripts so inaccurate that, on occasion, the standard Latin of Jerome's Vulgate reflected the ancient Greek original more closely, Erasmus' *Novum Instrumentum* remained for centuries a standard source book for New Testament translators. Two years after its publication, Luther's German New Testament appeared, translated straight from Erasmus' Greek; three years after that came Tyndale's English New Testament, also taken from the *Novum Instrumentum*. And contemporary Dutch, French and Italian Reformers also used Erasmus' text as their starting point.

Frobenius' editions of the *Novum Instrumentum* also exercised great influence upon the design of Protestant Bibles. Its two-column lay-out, with Erasmus' Greek text to the left, the Latin to the right, was copied by Luther's printer Hans Lufft at Wittenberg, and soon became a standard Protestant design. Frobenius was the first Bible printer to use a classical Roman typeface designed by Venetian typographers, instead of the older German 'black letter' face which was derived from Gothic script. He also used a wide variety of woodblock decorations based on the calligraphic patterns and flourishes found on handwritten Italian Renaissance manuscripts, and these also were widely copied in Germany and beyond. And here for the first time, the beginning of each book of the Bible was given a new page and specially designed title. Even the dull red ink which Frobenius used on his title pages became a standard colour for biblical decorations and page divisions for hundreds of years.

ΚΑΤΑ ΛΟΥΚΑΝ

SECVNDVM LVCAM 141

οἱ μαθηταὶ αὐτοῦ λέγοντες, τίς εἴη ἡ παραβολὴ αὕτη. ὁ δὲ εἶπεν. ὑμῖν δέδοται γνῶναι τὰ μυσήρια ϙ βασιλείας τῷ θεοῦ, τοῖς δὲ λοιποῖς ἐν παραβολαῖς, ἵνα βλέποντες μὴ βλέπωσιν, καὶ ἀκούοντες μὴ συνιῶσιν. ἔσιν δὲ αὕτη ἡ παραβολή. ὁ σπόρος ἐστὶν ὁ λόγος τῷ θεοῦ. οἱ δὲ παρὰ τὴν ὁδὸν εἰσιν, οἱ ἀκούοντες, εἶτα ἔρχεται ὁ διάβολος, καὶ αἴρει τὸν λόγον ἀπὸ ϙ καρδίας αὐτῶν, ἵνα μὴ πιστεύσαντες σωθῶσιν. οἱ δὲ ἐπὶ ϙ πέτρας, οἳ ὅταν ἀκούσωσιν μετὰ χαρᾶς δέχονται τὸν λόγον, καὶ οὗτοι ῥίζαν οὐκ ἔχουσιν, οἳ πρὸς καιρὸν πιστεύουσιν, καὶ ἐν καιρῷ πειρασμοῦ ἀφίσανται. τὸ δὲ εἰς τὰς ἀκάνθας πεσόν, οὗτοί εἰσιν οἱ ἀκούοντες, καὶ ὑπὸ μεριμνῶ

discipuli eius, dicētes, q̃ esset hæc para/ bola. At ipse dixit. Vobis datum est nosse mysteria regni dei, cæteris autem in parabolis, ut uidentes non uideant, & audientes nō intelligant. Est autem hæc parabola. Semen est uerbum dei. Qui autem secus uiam, hi sunt qui au/ diunt, deinde uenit diabolus, & tollit uerbum de corde eorum, ne credentes salui fiant. Nam qui supra petram, qui cum audierint, cum gaudio suscipiunt uerbum. Et hi radices nō habent, qui ad tempus credunt, & in tempore ten- tationis recedunt. Quod autem in spi/ nas cecidit, hi sunt qui audierunt, & a

Many of Erasmus' own writings, books and essays upon doctrine and theology, were soon proscribed by the Roman Church but, like his friends More and Fisher, the mild-mannered man never broke with Rome. The rudeness – he once remarked that the Protestants of Basel did not raise their hats as they left their church – and the blunt passion of the Reformers offended him as much as the corruption and superstition inside the Roman Church. The letters of St Paul, Erasmus once remarked, are even more sacred than his bones, and he dedicated his life to making the ancient words live again inside the offices of the church.

In England More and Fisher and King Henry himself all shared a common sense of apprehension at the thought of unlocking the huge power of God's written word. In practice access to the Bible was carefully controlled. Tyndale, after all, had been burned at the stake after a year of imprisonment, without any of the English authorities saying a word in his defence. Ten years later Sir Thomas More, his old opponent, was still proposing that bishops alone should decide who should be allowed to read the Bible; one man, he suggested, might be permitted to read some of the Gospels according to his individual disposition and intellect, but not all four of them; and others, 'busybodies', should be forbidden the 'meddling with any part at all' – arguments that are strangely reminiscent of the present debates surrounding the use of nuclear fuel. More, of course, reflected traditional Catholic attitudes which had long held that Bible reading should be confined to the informed and intelligent; it was highly undesirable to allow the word of God to run riot through an uninformed populace.

It was Anne Boleyn, with 'eyes which are black and beautiful, and take such great effect', Henry's second, short-lived Queen, who persuaded the King to order on 5 September 1538 that every church in his realm should have a Bible translated into English. Henry had already commanded that the Psalms and the services should be translated and read in the mother tongue. Now a picture of the king as the head of the new English Church appeared in the frontispiece of a great new Bible. He was shown handing down copies of the tome to his chief cleric, Archbishop Cranmer and his chief minister, Thomas Cromwell, both of whom worked to set this Bible in the churches, and who both later died at the order of the Crown. Further down the page the English populace are shown crying 'Vivat Rex' and 'God sayve the Kynge!' Henry's Bible, known as the Great Bible, or Cranmer's Bible, was largely Tyndale's translation, partly completed by his assistant Miles Coverdale, and edited by Tyndale's close friend John Rogers. That the translation was Tyndale's was disguised by presenting the work under a pseudonym, that of Thomas Matthew. This 'Thomas Matthew' was probably an invention by Rogers, Matthew being traditionally the first evangelist to have written a Gospel. The pseudonym was perhaps invented at the insistence of Thomas Cromwell, to avoid the embarrassment of the Crown if it were seen to give its *imprimatur* to the work of a

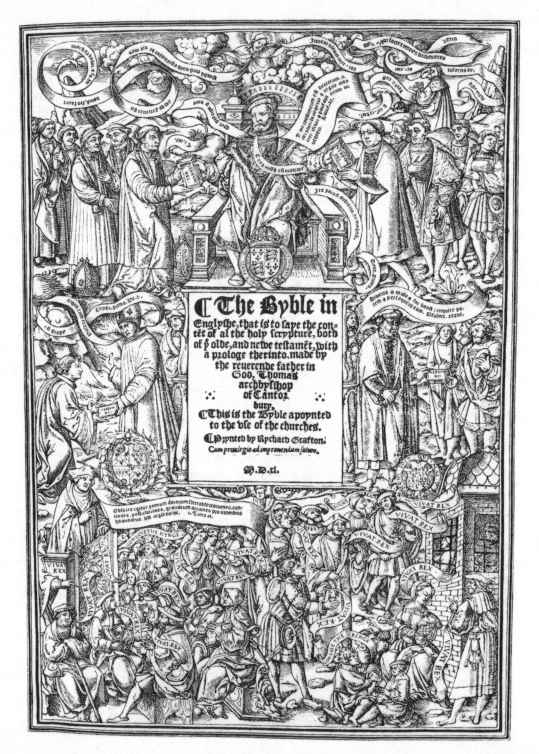

man executed just two years previously. At all events this Great Bible of King Henry is the primary version of the English Bible.

Popular interest in the Bible and its contents had been slowly growing in England for a long time. When the Great Bible appeared in the churches, crowds thronged around the lectern on which the book was displayed; 'diverse willful and unlearned persons inconsiderately and indiscreetly' read passages aloud even during the sermon of the Bishop of London in Old St Paul's, who reported that he was forced into vocal competition with eight Bible readers standing down the length of the old church. The Great Bible was also sold privately; 'diverse poor men in the town of Chelmsford,' we are told, 'bought the New Testament of Jesus Christ, and on Sundays did sit reading it at the lower end of the church'. So Tyndale's dream that 'if God spares my life, ere many years, I will cause a boy that driveth the plough shall know more scripture than thou dost' had begun to come true. Henry's proclamation had brought the English Bible into England.

Despite his seizure of church property and renunciation of papal authority Henry VIII still saw himself as a devout Catholic and had little inclination to reform either the doctrine or the worship in his English churches. Just as Justinian appears in the mosaics at Ravenna standing between his leaders temporal and spiritual, an earthly trinity, so Henry appears in the centre of an unholy trinity in the frontispiece of his Great Bible, in affirmation of the traditional seat of Christian royalty. But by seceding from papal authority, Henry had inevitably raised the whole question of the validity of the divine right of kings, with which the pope's authority had traditionally invested Christian monarchs. Luther's studied disrespect for the English throne must have served to reinforce Henry's deepest fears about the continental Protestants. Henceforth English Protestant kings found their own salvation in their own church.

No such worries, of course, afflicted Henry's Roman Catholic daughter Mary, 'Bloody Mary', once she ascended the throne in 1553. The aged Archbishop Cranmer, the first architect of the Church of England, was sent to the stake, along with several hundred other Reformers, all commemorated from Calvinist Geneva by the Puritan John Foxe in his *Book of Martyrs* which after the Bible itself soon became the most widely read book in England. Most hardline Reformers like Foxe were driven abroad during Mary's reign, many leading scholars and divines travelling to Basel or Geneva, both of which by the 1550s had severe Calvinist governments. Working at first under John Knox, the Scots Reformer, then under his successors and using funds provided by other refugees, a group of Englishmen produced a new English Bible, the so-called Geneva Bible. Not only was this a fine modern work of scholarship, but it was also a pretty little book decorated in the latest fashions of printing. That it shared some of its woodblocks with a contemporary French Bible also printed

THE
NEWE TESTAMENT OF
OVR LORD IESVS
CHRIST.

∴

Conferred diligently vvith the Greke, and best approued
translacions in diuers languages.

*This is the message vvhiche vve haue heard of him, and declare vnto
you, that God is the light, and in him is no darkenes.*
IOHN. I. VER. f.

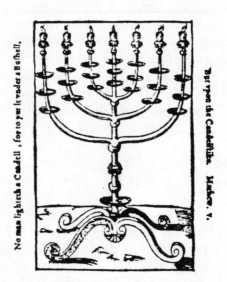

If vve vvalke in the light as he is in the light, vve haue felovvship one
vvith another, and the blood of Iesus Christ clenseth vs from
all sinne.   Iohn. I.   Vers. 7.

PRINTED AT GENEVA.

M. D. LXI.

at Geneva shows how close these exiled Protestant communities were at Geneva, that 'store of heavenly learning and judgement', overseen first by Calvin and later by Theodore Beza. Beza, Calvin's learned successor, was in the 1550s already engaged upon the first edition of his Latin translation of the New Testament, working directly from a Greek original. The Geneva Bible gave later Bibles some of their most familiar phrases: the 'childish things' that Paul would have us put away in his Epistle to the Corinthians and the visions in that same book seen 'through a glass darkly'; and the Old Testament enemies that are smote 'hip and thigh'.

While its editors remained in Geneva to put the finished Bible through the press, their fellow exiles were hurrying back to England on Queen Mary's death. Elizabeth I, Mary's successor, granted a London printer the right to publish the Geneva Bible in England, and it went through about 140 editions, remaining popular long after the appearance of the King James' Bible, due perhaps to the small and convenient size of the English edition. The Geneva Bible was used in English schools and households for centuries; it was, for example, the Bible that Shakespeare knew as a boy – its phrases find their way into the mouths of Shylock and Prince Hal. But it was never appointed to be read in churches: church authorities generally disliked its cast of fundamental Protestantism and Queen Elizabeth herself always opposed the Puritans who embraced it at the time. In Scotland, however, the strongly Calvinist sentiments of its annotations were immensely popular. In the Civil War of the mid-seventeenth century the famous Bible pamphlets that Oliver Cromwell issued to the soldiers of his Model Army consisted mainly of extracts from the Geneva text. 'The Souldiers Pocket Bible: Containing the most (if not all) those places contained in Holy Scripture, which doe shew the qualifications of his inner man, that is a fit Souldier to fight the Lords Battels, both before the fight, in the fight, and after the fight'. The soldiers of Cromwell's Model Army carried this biblical approval with them through their English wars and on into Roman Catholic Ireland.

It was the Roman Catholics who had to flee for their lives in Queen Elizabeth's reign, a fate compounded by a papal decree that excommunicated the Protestant queen, England's first, and enjoined her Catholic subjects to rise up against her government. Jesuit missionaries to England were hung, drawn and quartered at Tyburn as traitors: 'And the reason is that his body, lands, goods, prosperity, etc., should be torn, pulled asunder, and destroyed, that intended to tear and destroy the majesty of government. And all these several punishments are found for treason in Holy Scripture'. The exiled Roman Catholics established a seminary at Douai in Belgium and from there William, Cardinal Allen, ran a church in exile, supported the Spanish Armada sent against Queen Elizabeth and sent priests into England to minister to Roman Catholics. Allen's 'traitorous seminarie' as it was called, produced an English Bible to counter the

Protestants who now had 'every passage at their fingers' ends'. This, the so-called Douai Bible, was not made with an eye upon the Protestant version, nor was it based on Erasmus' Greek text, nor upon the numerous printed Hebrew Bibles, but upon Jerome's Latin Vulgate, which since the previous century had been confirmed by Papal Council as an authentic Bible text. The translators' adherence to this Latin source led them to invent a whole glossary of new English words built on Jerome's Latin originals, and some of the fabrications have passed into the English language: words like victim, allegory, acquisition and adulterate. The contribution of the Douai Bible to the King James' Bible was considerable, but this was due more perhaps to the zealous and often erudite attacks upon it by English Protestants, some of which achieved a greater circulation than the early editions of the Douai Bible itself.

In Elizabeth's reign a new Bible called the Bishop's Bible was issued under the auspices of Archbishop Parker – 'The holie Bible conteynyng the olde Testament and the newe'. This was a revision of the Great Bible shorn of its commentaries and footnotes. Stressing the role of the sovereign in the reformed church, the Lutheran-style woodblocks of the Bishop's Bible were not only decorated with the usual biblical characters but with portraits of Elizabeth's ministers, her favourite the Earl of Leicester, and her chief minister Lord Burghley. Elizabeth herself appears on the frontispiece clutching the orb and sceptre. It was in Elizabeth's reign that Protestantism took root in England. The Reformed faith was encouraged and popularized by the re-issue of the martyred Cranmer's *Book of Common Prayer*, which he had written in the reign of Henry VIII to simplify and shorten the medieval Latin services. The prayer book was revised and re-issued with the heading 'Primo Elizabethae' which it still bears today.

Even as King James journeyed south to take the English throne upon the death of Queen Elizabeth in 1603, he was met by a party of reforming Puritans intent upon putting their complaints about an excessive 'burden of human rites and ceremonies' in the English church to the new king. No nimble monarch like Elizabeth, the Scot was sustained by his belief in his divine right as king and a heavy wit. And he well knew the mettle of the Puritans. In a Scottish council a Genevan cleric, whom he had reminded of his divine right, told him to his face that he was naught but 'God's silly vassal' like the rest of humanity. James had taken the comment to heart; he understood that the levelling of the offices of the church which the Puritans now demanded would lead inexorably to a levelling out of King James as well. 'No bishops; no King,' he had trenchantly observed, and drew a line of reform that stopped well before the steps leading to his throne. But now, riding to the throne of England James wanted to accommodate his new subjects whom he considered to be more civilized than his fellow Scots. So he convened a clerical conference as the Puritans had petitioned at Hampton Court Palace. There, throughout January 1604 James argued doggedly with his bishops and the Puritans. At the end James gave nothing away, the only lasting effect of the proceedings being an edict to produce another revision of the Bible. This resulted from a petition of the Puritan John Reynolds, an Oxford don who observed of English Bibles that 'those which were allowed in the reignes of Henrie the eight, and Edward the sixt, were corrupt and not aunswerable to the truth of the Originall'. Reynold's petition led to the revised Bible of 1611, the King James' Bible that has served the English church for centuries.

It has been estimated – the records of the government of the period were destroyed in a fire at Westminster – that the work of Bible revision cost some £3500; each translator received between £50 and £60, the revising editors about thirty shillings a week. And these sums were paid, not by King James's impecunious exchequer but by the Company of Stationers, the watchdog of the book trade which had sold monopolies to print the Bishop's Bible in the previous reign. The work of revision – the King James' Bible was never considered to be a new or original work – was split into six committees working at three centres in Westminster, Cambridge and Oxford, and so echoed the old royal licence for printing bibles, a unique Tudor monopoly that continues to this day. Most of the celebrated scholars of the time served upon these committees; a small sample of their names – Lively, Andrews, Harrison, Smith, Brett, Fairclough – shows the quintessential Englishness of these 'learned men to the number of four and fifty'. Each of the six groups worked upon an appropriate section of the Bible text. Hebrew professors revised the Old Testament, Greek scholars the New, and each was allowed to consult any other scholar 'for his judgement'. After the preliminary work, two men from each committee joined another committee that reviewed the entire Bible. Finally two editors, the Bishop of Winchester who wrote the chapter headings, and Dr Smith, who wrote the 'Translator's preface', saw the finished book to press.

As the king had specified at Hampton Court, the revisers based their work upon the Bishop's Bible using the texts of five other translations – 'Tindoll's' was now included by name – 'when they agree better with the text'. All the familiar biblical names and popular passages were to be kept 'as they were vulgarly used', similarly all the chapters and verse divisions which had grown up in the sixteenth century were to be retained. King James himself expressly forbade any prefaces or marginal notes other than explanations of Greek or Hebrew words, 'having found in them that which are annexed to the Geneva translation, notes partial, untrue, seditious, and savouring too much of dangerous and traitorous conceits. As, for example, Exod. 1:19 where the marginal note alloweth for *disobedience to kings*'. The king had also noticed many errors of translation in the earlier Bibles and 'the worste of all, his majestie thought the Geneva to bee'.

Avoiding the ire of the king and the passions of the Puritans, the revisers maintained a true spirit of compromise and took every advantage of all the translations. Whenever possible they used old renderings, so that Tyndale's English, already rather archaic in James's day, was retained. It has been estimated that about ninety per cent of the King James' Bible is taken directly from Tyndale's translation, yet there are also some powerful additions – the occasional Latinisms of the Douai Bible; the scholarly niceties of the Geneva text and, above all, a new and grander prose used for the passages that describe the Bible's kings and courtiers and the presence of God. These passages, often rather simply translated by Tyndale, were now rendered in a vein that echoed the manner of contemporary literature: the plays and poems of Shakespeare and his fellows. This rich and slow-moving pomp added now to the fast clear narrative of Tyndale's prose produced one of the finest works in the English language. Ultimately, of course, the final English text was dependent upon the qualities of the original ancient texts; and as it has often been observed the Hebrew of the Old Testament found a remarkable equivalence in Tudor prose. But that these committees and two boards of revision should have so successfully incorporated such diverse elements in a single book shows something of a spirit of compromise that had grown up in England after the years of burnings and executions. The King James' Bible, however, was an exception. His reign has been described as a prelude to disaster – the execution of James's son King Charles I on a Whitehall scaffold in January 1649. Whatever the long-term political causes, Charles died for refusing to dismantle the established English church and for refusing to deny the divine right of kings. 'Know you,' Charles shouted from the scaffold, 'a subject and a sovereign are clean different things.' After his execution handkerchiefs dipped in royal blood were claimed to have worked miracles just as a living king's touch was believed to heal the sick.

With his last steps to the scaffold, King Charles passed under the great palace ceiling painted by Peter Paul Rubens, a regal apotheosis, then out through a window of the Banqueting House that Inigo Jones had built for him, its white stones announcing the arrival of pure Renaissance style at the heart of gabled, Gothic England. Though Charles upheld the divine sanction of his office even with his life, to artists and intellectuals like Rubens and Inigo Jones, the king was a man playing a role. For them kingship was a glorious property to be fêted and decorated in a variety of different styles, and yet they still moved in circles of royalists and courtiers who were prepared to fight and die for the ancient order of Christendom. The poet Milton, an ardent Puritan and Oliver Cromwell's Latin secretary, directly denied the old order of Christendom: 'It is lawful,' wrote Milton, 'and hath been held so through all ages, for anyone who had the power to call to account a tyrant or wicked king, and after due conviction to depose him and put him to death.' And he cited classical texts to back his argument. As Petrarch had done before, all these people had seen that their lives held a choice, that life was not lived in a sealed universe of a monoculture but inside a style with manners and attitudes which you could choose yourself. The unquestioning acceptance of Christendom's integrity and sacredness, the world in which the Bible was honoured as a sacred *container* of the word of God, had been shattered as surely as the integrity of a tribal society is shattered by the appearance of foreigners. All Christendom could see that there was now a choice: its innocence had gone.

Carnifex Maiestatis Regis Angliæ

As King Charles's head was held up to the public gaze, it is said that a 'great groan' went through the crowd. It was the end of social innocence perhaps, just as Inigo Jones's building behind the scaffold was signalling the end of London's architectural innocence. Michelangelo's premonitions had held that same despairing groan. Charles's son when re-instated as King of England never asserted the divine right of the kings of Christendom for which his father had died. 'Kings,' observed a respected jurist of the time over dinner, 'are things men have made for their own sakes, for quietness sake . . .' And so, too, the sacred Bible also died. Though it was cherished by all of England's warring parties, Protestant, Papist and Puritan alike, the great book lost its innate sanctity; it could be approached and opened. And now its style would be dissected along with its geography and history and all its worldly details and all stuck on the pins of experts. The King James' Bible was the last English edition of the book that held the full power and clarity of that ancient, sacred world.

A New Heaven and a New Earth
Rome had recognized the challenge of the northern Reformers and their churches long before the death of Luther, but its response had been slow and piecemeal. In 1537 Pope Paul III summoned a Universal Council of the Church to discuss and define church doctrine and discipline and after several false starts a Council finally convened in December 1545. At first it was just a small and predominantly Italian gathering of senior clerics who met in the small alpine town of Trento. Over a period of almost twenty years, sometimes in large assemblies and sometimes in small rooms, the most ancient customs and dogmas of the church were examined and systematized, voted upon, written down and isued in a magisterial succession of decrees. And this marks the beginnings of the modern Roman Catholic church. At the same time, the role and content of the Bible in this renewed church were specified and defined.

The northern Reformers had claimed the Bible was itself the sole source of Christian doctrine on earth and that all men should have access to its words. At the beginning of its work on 8 April 1546, the Council of Trent decreed that the Bible was the word of God, but that its correct interpretation was dependent upon the traditions of the Church; and these were defined as the wisdom of the church – the doctrine, creeds and interpretations that had been passed on from the Church's earliest days. This, then, directly opposed Protestant doctrine; with such specific repudiations, the Council of Trent carefully defined the differences between Protestantism and the Roman Church. And the break was made clear to all. But differences also emerged at Trento between conservatives and moderate humanists inside the Roman Catholic church itself. It was only after long debate that members agreed that not all modern language Bible translations which were already widely used in churches but which a Spanish bishop called the 'mothers of heresy', should be banned outright. They were not, however, allowed the same status as the Latin Vulgate Bible, which by recourse to the earlier-established rule of the sanctity of church tradition, was now counted as an authentic Bible text. This decision was not as conservative or traditionalist as it might first appear. In the sixteenth century very few of the ancient Bible texts that we have today were known to exist, and those that were known had not been subjected to skilful scholarly analysis. Jerome's great Vulgate text was as accurate – sometimes more accurate – as many of the known Greek and Hebrew manuscripts.

The Council still had to consider what precisely were the Bible's authentic contents; for although in the previous century the Council of Florence had fixed the list of the Bible's books, it had not stated exactly which versions of these books were considered to be authoritative. For even the Vulgate text existed in many different variations – there were well over a hundred printed editions in Italy alone. Not until 1528, less than ten years before the convening of the Council of Trent, had the first scholarly edition of the Vulgate been printed with a careful critical apparatus and this by the Protestant printer-scholar Stephanus of Paris. The decrees of the earlier church councils, along with many ancient Bible texts, were called for and sent from Rome to Trento where many of them were subsequently mislaid and lost, never to be seen again. Some of the variant passages of the Vulgate Gospels were discussed; that famous phrase 'the Johannine Comma' which it was observed did not appear in the oldest manuscripts; the various versions of the ending of the Gospel of Mark; the story in John's Gospel that tells of the woman taken in adultery (8:1–11). As to the Apocrypha, the Old Testament books that the early Christian churches had accepted as sacred but the rabbis of the period of the destruction of Jerusalem had rejected, most were accepted into the Vulgate as sacred texts and only three, the two Books of Esdras and the Prayer of Manasses, were excluded outright. This decision was at variance not only with the opinion of Jerome, but also with the Protestant churches which regarded these Apocryphal books as 'usefull and good', as Luther put it, if not the Word of God. At the ending of the Council session dealing with the Vulgate, it was also decided that further detailed debates about Bible matters should be resolved by papal commissions which would also issue reformed, authentic texts of Greek, Hebrew and the Latin Vulgate Bibles. Later in the sixteenth century,

popes Sixtus V and Clement VIII oversaw the production of a Greek and Latin text, using a wide variety of ancient manuscripts that included the noble fourth-century *Codex Vaticanus*, one of the oldest surviving Bibles, and that venerable English offspring of Cassiodorus' Italian monastery, the *Codex Amiatinus*. Fortified by a papal bull of 1592, these texts remained the authorized Roman Catholic Bible text until the twentieth century, despite the fact that scholars had soon seen that this so-called Clementine Bible departed from the ancient manuscript in a myriad details. The nineteenth-century explosion of scholar-ship and the discovery of a host of previously unknown ancient manuscripts finally pressed the need for a new revision of Jerome's text. In 1904 Pope Pius X established the International Committee for the Revision of the Vulgate, which, in a Roman Benedictine monastery named appropriately enough after St Jerome, continues its work down to this day.

PLATE 34 (Opposite): Paolo Veronese (1520–88) A detail from 'The Feast in the House of Levi' (1573, originally called 'The Last Supper') Galleria dell'Accademia, Venice.
PLATE 35 (Overleaf left): Horace Vernet (1789–1863) A detail from 'Judah and Tamar' (1853) The Wallace Collection, London.
PLATE 36 (Overleaf centre): W. Holman Hunt (1827–1910) A detail from 'The Finding of the Saviour in the Temple' (1860) Birmingham Museum and Art Gallery.
PLATE 37 (Overleaf right): Charlton Heston as Moses in The Ten Commandments (1956). Directed by Cecil B. de Mille (1881–1959) with costumes by Edith Head.

Nearly ninety years after the Council of Trent had decreed that the correct interpretation of the Bible's words depended upon the traditional interpretations of the Church, the Florentine scientist Galileo Galilei was brought to his knees by those same words. In the Church of Santa Maria Sopra Minerva at Rome, precisely for challenging the traditional biblical cosmology, the old man was made to swear an oath that he did not hold, nor would he spread, heretical opinion, and that he would submit to the punishment of isolation from human society and the daily repetition of penitential Psalms for what he had already written. In a splendid church filled with Renaissance art, amid the remains of some of Christendom's most celebrated saints, the Church had inadvertently created a hero, a scientific martyr, and at the same time appeared to set itself against the march of progress. This was one of the ancient Bible's first skirmishes with Renaissance science – with experts who had thought a great deal about a very small part of the universe described in the Book of Genesis.

It was Galileo's particular misfortune to investigate the heavens themselves. Though he had merely observed the ticking of the cosmic clock and had never attempted to approach the throne of the clockmaker, for many contemporary churchmen God was in the sky and they regarded scientists, who gazed at the stars through the telescopes that this same Galileo had recently invented, as impious men. For such people religion itself furnished a way of understanding the universe and its order. The sun and the stars, the constitution of the earth, the hierarchy of men and animals and plants not only held physical reality but also the moral order of Christendom; a mirror of the order of heaven so beautifully and precisely described in the Bible; a single entity that held both heaven and the estate of men. The burning of heretics who questioned this biblical order simply gave them a taste of the bigger fires of hell that would inevitably come to them, and also protected the rest of mankind from the earthly chaos that such people clearly promised.

How innocent these Renaissance scientists seem as they tried to bring this tremendous universe down to size, like plumbers measuring the pipes in a nuclear power plant. Hauled-up for the crime of wrecking the cosmos, they protested that God was the proper mystery and not his creation, and that *they* were interested only in what their eyes and brains might see and comprehend. But that was hardly good enough for the Church which, for the most part, did not understand them.

The issue that exercised Galileo and his accusers revolved around several Bible passages that seemed to imply, just as the words 'sunrise' and 'sunset' do, that the sun moved through the sky and that the earth itself was stationary, fixed. Although the Bible texts offered no concise description of the operations

PLATE 38 (Opposite): Michelangelo (1475–1564) The Rondanini Pietà (from 1552), on which Michelangelo continued to work up to his death. Museo del Castello Sforzesco, Milan.

of the solar system, traditional Church teaching based on Aristotle and several vague biblical allusions, held that the earth stood at the centre of the universe as a king is surrounded by his court, and God by his angels.

Following the theories of the Polish astronomer Nicholas Copernicus, however, Galileo had long held that the sun stood still and the earth moved around it, thus changing an age-old social and hierarchical metaphor for a mechanical theory. The pope had approved Copernicus' theory when it had first appeared in 1531 and the conundrum of where the true centre of the universe lay was much discussed in both scientific and religious circles, two aspects of society that were still not greatly divided. The most powerful participants of this debate, churchmen like the scholarly Cardinal Bellarmine, a Tuscan as was Galileo, held that the matter had not yet been resolved because Copernicus' theory had not been proven, and that if at some later date it should be proven, then the words of the Bible, which themselves could not be wrong, would require a new interpretation. At the same time Bellarmine had also suggested that the Bible, though the sacred word of God, had been written down in a form suitable for the understanding of 'less advanced' people than those of the sixteenth century, an argument that would reappear in following centuries as apparent contradictions between science and the Bible continued to multiply.

As a young university professor, Bellarmine had lectured upon the cosmos and its workings with great success. Later he had been a powerful voice on the commission that oversaw and published the Clementine Vulgate. He stood, therefore, in the mainstream of both science and Roman Catholic theology; and it was this knowledge and sensitivity that had led him to the belief that the traditional interpretations of the Bible should be accepted until science had proved them wrong. Anything else, he asserted, was an unnecessary sacrilege. When, some twenty years before Galileo's humiliation, debate first grew up over the new teaching of cosmic theory and Copernicus' writings had been put upon the church's Index of Forbidden Books, Bellarmine had offered the famous scientist advice and encouragement; indeed, Galileo was personally assured by the pope himself of his high standing inside the church and had even been encouraged to continue his researches. Twenty years later however, the church had changed. A young friend, visiting the elderly Galileo shortly before his last disastrous trip to Rome, advised the old man to sprinkle his speeches before his inquisitors with 'salutary phrases of submission to the Holy Mother church'. The church now demanded submission in its thrust against the northern Reformers; the Counter-Reformation had begun. By the 1630s all of those who attended the Council of Trent and who framed its resolutions had died. Cardinal Bellarmine was also dead. But Galileo, the old and eminent scholar lived on, still a robust and sarcastic debater in the best tradition of Renaissance scholarship. And now he sought, with the aid of somewhat unconvincing novel proofs, to have Copernicus' works removed from the

Church's Index of Forbidden Books, for he saw the listing as an affront not only to science but also to the Church itself of which he was a pious member. In 1632 he published his *Dialogue Concerning the Two Chief World Systems* which attacked geocentric theory and argued for Copernicus' vision of the solar system. Denounced to the Florentine Dominicans, he was called to Rome, questioned under threat of torture and judged by his inquisitors in three days. The old man was run through a mindless system of repression that forced him to his knees, in frightened penitence, in a Roman church.

At this point, the Church might appear simply as the unthinking guardian of Christendom's ancient integrity, and this would seem to be a terrifying example of its shift away from the spirit of the Renaissance. But in fact the inquisitors let Galileo return to his house near Pisa, and the old man was not prevented from continuing his work. Galileo's trial, the public humiliation of the most famous scientist in Europe, had been precipitated not by the Church authorities at all, but by another professor, a reactionary scientific colleague who taught in Florence and was a man intent upon protecting his position, a far smaller universe than that which held the interest of the Church of Rome. In this sense, Galileo's trial represents a part of Europe's fall from innocence into modernity, an instinctive reaction of many different people, churchmen and scientists alike, who saw the heavens as set in the enduring order of the universal hierarchy of Christendom. For them the universe was unmoving, solid, enduring. Galileo, however, had seen a new world, a world both dynamic and mobile, a system of balanced forces in which God did not sit atop a static universal pyramid but found majestic expression in the interaction of a cosmos that he had invented and set in motion. Galileo had not discovered or defended a new scientific fact – the Copernican system was never proven in his lifetime – but a new conception of God and his universe. And Galileo himself had truly understood the heart of the matter. In the flyleaf of his own copy of the little book that had precipitated his trial, he wrote these prophetic words:

> Take care, Theologians, that in wishing to make matters of faith of the propositions attendant on the motion and stillness of the sun and earth, in time you probably risk the danger of condemning for heresy those who assert that the earth stands firm and the sun moves; in time, I say, when sensately and necessarily it will be demonstrated that the earth moves and the sun stands still.

Galileo had tried to save his church from error.

The ancient church of Santa Maria Sopra Minerva had been the stage of Galileo's punishment because it stood beside the Dominican convent used by the Jesuit priests who as the masters of scientific teaching in Rome were Galileo's judges. Beside the Dominican convent they had raised a sombre Jesuit College where they taught the sciences, still mostly in the tradition of medieval scholarship in which Aristotles' theories of the universe were exquisitely matched with biblical statement and the arguments of Thomas Aquinas. Some of the cleverest men of the day taught in this college, many of them Roman Catholic refugees from the religious wars in northern Europe. Here, in the years immediately after Galileo's trial, the German Jesuit Athanasius Kircher taught mathematics and organized one of the first museums of natural science in the world. Kircher had been a child prodigy and he grew, perhaps, into the last Renaissance man. Like Galileo, Kircher was interested in everything around him; but whereas Galileo had sought to see with an unrestrained vision, to look for as yet unperceived symmetries, Kircher spent his life running about over-turning every stone, every library, every landscape, in search of secrets – secrets once known to ancient men; secrets that would describe the mystic order in the static universe of Galileo's judges. In his time Kircher invented clever machines to ventilate mines; he made statues that with the aid of hidden trumpets appeared to talk; he invented magic lanterns that projected images of light upon a wall; and, in his own fashion, he deciphered Egyptian hieroglyphs, the root, he thought, of all earthly wisdom. In most beautiful steel engravings he reconstructed the Tower of Babel and Noah's Ark; he explored musical scales, observed sunspots and made a sundial based upon the heraldry of the Holy Roman Emperors. He speculated upon ancient irrigation, the situation of Babylon, and the gods of China. He was, in short, a Jesuit Leonardo.

Kircher's account of Noah and his Ark is a masterpiece of fabrication, a fitting together of medieval cast of mind and Renaissance pragmatism. He calculated precisely the date of the Flood and the amount and duration of the rain that had fallen and he showed its effects upon antique humanity. He also designed a completely rational Ark. All the animals of the world were given their places, all divided and subdivided into different categories and all housed in their appropriate lodgings. The snakes, which Kircher asserted God wanted to preserve as a memento of the Fall of Man and to assist in the cycles of growth and decay, were consigned to the bilges; the larger animals filled the bottom storey underneath a deck filled with supplies for the voyage ahead. Humans and birds occupied the upper layers, so that Noah's biblical dove and raven would easily come to hand. Kircher worked out everything as carefully as did Galileo, but in a universe that is static and unmoving. Kircher's impressive books, his incredible energies and extraordinary research represent the ending of an ancient world, just as Galileo's trial had heralded the beginnings of another.

Neither was Roman Catholic scholarship alone in its adherence to such traditionally biblical interpretations of the universe. Most Protestants were set in the same mould; Charles I, after all, had died for the divine integrity of kings and a Protestant church. And at the same time that Galileo and Kircher were working, a Calvinist scholar, Bishop Ussher of Armagh with a truly Renais-sance combination of enthusiasm, industry and biblical scholarship calculated the dates which, until quite recently, appeared in the margins of many King James' Bibles – those annotations that informed you that God had created the heavens and the earth in 4004 BC, that Noah's Ark had floated upon the Flood 1659 years later and that Solomon had sung his Song in 1074 BC. As Ussher well knew, there is no single chronology in the Bible that connects the Old Testament with the New. His trick was to effect a connection and this the ingenious bishop had accomplished with some degree of precision. For medieval tradition asserted that there had been exactly 4000 years between the Creation and the Coming of Christ upon earth, and this was also substantiated by many more ancient texts. Melanchthon, Luther's amanuensis, had argued in elaboration of these old beliefs that the history of the world would last 8000 years in four equal spans of time; the first 2000 years would be of flames; the second merely inanimate; the third, under the rule of kings; the last, with the Kingdom of Christ. Christian tradition maintained that Jesus had been born at the point where BC became AD; but Ussher knew from Josephus the historian that Herod had died in the twenty-third year of the Emperor Augustus' reign, that is, by Christian reckoning, 4 BC. So it was obvious then that Creation had taken place four years earlier in these bi-millennial cycles, that is in 4004 BC. By similar processes of deduction, Ussher further calculated that the Creation had actually occurred on Sunday 23 October precisely at twelve o'clock. Chaos had been created, suitably enough, on the previous Saturday night. But these Protestant assertions were soon rebuffed by the brilliant French Jesuit theologian Petavius whose calculation showed that the Creation had actually taken place on Monday 26 October, twenty-one years later than Ussher's date. Neither Ussher nor Petavius, however, had taken into account the Old Testament assertion that the sun had stood still in the heavens upon several occasions, timeless cosmic events with which even Galileo had to wrestle in his descriptions of a dynamic Copernican universe.

In science, Protestant and Catholic could share the same research and this, to many people, was a further sign of its godlessness, just as Galileo's contacts with northern scientists had been another area of disapproval with his church authorities. For the majority, however, north or south, very little had changed. In England and the Low Countries, for example, Cardinal Bellarmine, who as a university lecturer at Louvain had brought a savage inquisition to Flanders, was regarded as a friend of the devil. For several centuries, witch bottles of cold grey-blue saltglazes were often decorated with the Cardinal's bearded face. Shaped like a human bladder and called Bellarmines, such pots were filled with urine and pubic hair and red hot nails were sent sizzling into them in order to injure those suspected of making evil spells. In 1679 a student of Edinburgh University was hung for his assertion that, among other things, Ezra and not Moses had written the first five books of the Bible. In Spain the burning of heretics continued into the mid-eighteenth century.

Within such diversities of attitude and opinion, Isaac Newton began his mathematical exploration of Copernicus' solar system, carefully asserting at the beginning that God made this terrestrial scheme and that his calculations would merely describe this divine order in scientific terms. Newton, the great mathematician, spent years working upon calculations which, like Ussher's, dealt with the mystical numbers of the Bible, especially the ancient mysteries in the Book of Revelations. But slowly the educated laity also began to read the Bible critically, checking its statements against their own experience and questioning some of its ancient morality. In 1792 Tom Paine, the English revolutionary, scandalized the public and caused the prosecution of his publisher with his book *The Age of Reason*, a collection of essays that revolved around such ethical criticisms of biblical characters. It seemed strange, Paine observed, that the Almighty would leave infinity and 'come to die in our world because they say one man and a woman ate an apple'. Such parochial judgments of the Bible had already led to something of a scandal in a previous generation when a university don had garrulously asserted that if Jesus had bewitched and destroyed a flock of sheep in Cambridgeshire as the Bible asserts he destroyed the Gadarene Swine, the laws of England would have made him swing for it. The issue of these massacred swine – the destruction of individual property – continued to exercise middle-class English morality. In the nineteenth century Gladstone, the retired prime minister and Thomas Huxley, the agnostic scientist publicly debated the same issue.

By Huxley's day, however, an avalanche of theory and data was threatening to bury all the traditional interpretations of the Bible and its world. There was considerable proof that the earth's rocks and fossils were far older than Ussher's date for the Creation. Neither was the explanation of one pious geologist that the Almighty had installed fossils in the earth's rocks to test man's faith thought to be particularly convincing. Biologists, too, had developed theories about the mechanisms of change in plants and animals which were quite independent of the notion of God's creation of a perfect world, all at once. By the 1840s, in Huxley's youth, the biblical description of creation was one of the last bastions of that unchanging, unmoving universe that Galileo had so bravely attacked. But it was a bastion heavily defended by the clergy and public sentiment. The siege between attackers who viewed creation as a scientific phenomenon and defenders who saw it as a theological abstraction was well and truly joined. In 1859 the first edition of Darwin's *The Origin of Species* provided a first-class battleground. 'My first reaction,' said Huxley who took it upon himself to publicly defend Darwin, 'was of annoyance that I had not already thought of it myself.' It was the fact that Darwin's thesis was in itself so academically elegant, so simple, which provided the followers of his evolutionary theories with the impulse that simply swept aside the issue of the challenge to traditional biblical interpretation in a great rush of enthusiasm.

But the churches and many churchgoers well understood that Darwin's thesis had substituted a system of chance for God's order of creation, and this for many was the negation of moral values. Two prime ministers and a large body of clergy attacked the theory of evolution. Darwin, usually rather a retiring man, claimed to be bemused; he had never intended, he said innocently, to raise ethical matters adding privately, and rather less innocently, that 'Moses can take care of himself'. In public debate, however, it was Thomas Huxley who best defended Darwin and his theories. In 1860 he faced Bishop Wilberforce, son of the famous abolitionist and private adviser to the Prince Regent, in the celebrated public debate of the British Association at the Oxford Museum. Previously the press had amused itself with graphic speculations about the relationship of Darwin's profile to his 'monkey ancestors'. As the debate was beginning, Wilberforce unwisely asked Huxley a similar question about his grandparents, an enquiry which allowed Huxley to seize with great effect upon the popular image of the clergy as a bastion of ignorance and conservatism. According to popular legend, as Wilberforce uttered his fateful question Huxley turned to his neighbour, clapped his thigh and said, 'The Lord has delivered him into my hand.' By popular acclaim Huxley won the debate but his biblical exclamation (Judges 12:3) points to the vital power of the words of the Bible which, to this day, hold enough force in their images to inspire scientific visions of a fiery apocalypse.

Huxley had taken up the cause of evolution not only as a biologist, but also as an advocate of agnosticism, a term which he himself had invented; an agnostic, a not-knower, someone who thought that it was impossible to know whether God existed or not. The debate was still conducted around the images of church and Bible – Huxley himself using the patterns of biblical and liturgical language in his speeches and writings. When serving as an adviser to the London School Boards he acknowledged that he could see no real alternative to biblical instruction for the moral preservation of society. Like many agnostics and atheists of his day, he read the Bible regularly and adapted some of the forms of Christian ritual for the events of family life. Yet Huxley was also filled with a deep anger. He hated the mental brake that traditional church attitudes had placed upon the progress of the sciences. 'I should like to get my heel into their mouths and scr-r-r-unch it around,' he once said to a friend who had protested that Huxley's public pronouncements about the clergy were overly ferocious. But the battle that he fought was not primarily concerned with the words of the Bible but with the intellectual status and credibility of the church. 'I remember,' Huxley had continued, 'when Lyell and Murchison [two eminent geologists] were not considered fit to lick the boots of a curate.' Though Huxley may have been concerned about the status of scientists inside English society, inadvertently but largely due to the popular advocacy of Darwin and Huxley, the Bible's ancient role as the guidebook to the physical universe had ended. And now, unwittingly, the scientists themselves now took on much of the clergy's traditional role in society. Cardinal Bellarmine, the Roman Jesuits, Bishop Wilberforce and the 11,000 clergymen who in 1864 signed a declaration saying that the whole of the Bible was the word of God and that sinners will be punished everlastingly, were all defending the ancient order of government and the natural world, which by faith and common acceptance had sustained Christendom since its beginnings. Bellarmine's and Kircher's science had retreated into alchemy, where truth was uncovered, like the Holy Grail, in distant secret places. In their innocence Galileo and Darwin and the new experts had created a godless universe and turned Christendom's great book into a puzzle. Darwin might declare that Moses could take care of himself but, as the subtle Bellarmine had known, those biblical characters needed constant attendance if they and their ancient order were to survive.

And they did not survive. In the climate of nineteenth-century capitalism, it was asserted that Darwinian evolution, not the Bible, now provided 'basic truths' about humanity, though this had not been either Darwin's or Huxley's remotest intention. But now mankind's societies and behaviour might be studied as if they were animals. No wonder, then, that churchmen had talked of the publication of Darwin's theories as a 'Second Fall'; the ethical parables of Adam and Eve had been replaced by an often brutal vision of self-justifying materialism. In its role as the guidebook to the Western world, the Bible slowly died during the nineteenth century and all there was left to do was to perform the autopsy.

Explorations and Autopsies

Appropriately enough, the Bible's dissection was begun by a royal surgeon, Jean Astruc, the physician of King Louis XV in the gloomy court of that king's old age. In 1753 Astruc published a little book (anonymously and at a safe distance from Versailles), stating that Genesis had been compiled by Moses from two older and quite separate narratives. Astruc had arrived at this conclusion after dividing the narrative of the Book of Genesis into two separate columns; one holding the passages in which God was called *Elohim* and the other in which he was called *Jehovah*. To his great surprise Astruc had immediately seen that his simple mechanical division of the text had produced not two dislocated fragments of narrative as you might expect, but two independently coherent narratives. Astruc's theory that Genesis was a conflation of these two separate sources also accounted for some of the obvious anomalies in the Genesis text: the two contradictory accounts of Creation in the first and second chapters; the contradictory ages of Sarah, Abraham's wife; the discrepancies in the descriptions of the Flood and of the number of animals in the Ark. Two stories have been joined together, asserted Astruc, but the repetition and discrepancies that resulted had all been piously preserved. Once Dr Astruc had isolated the two narrative strands, they were clear for all to see.

It is difficult today to appreciate the effect of such revelations upon the people of Christendom. In Oxford during the 1830s a young girl sitting reading Ovid in her garden had suddenly seen a strong similarity between two of Ovid's characters and Samson and Delilah. 'What difference is there,' she then wondered to herself, 'between the love of the sons of God for the daughters of men [Genesis 6:4] and those of the gods of Greece for the girls of Athens?' She fainted dead away at her presumption and grew up to become a celebrated agnostic novelist.

Throughout the nineteenth century, as the debates about science and the Bible were fought out, the technique of textural analysis spawned by Dr Astruc grew into a full-blown academic discipline; and this largely at German universities where scholarship was not overseen by religious authorities as it was in most other European countries. At the same time German academia was undergoing a veritable philosophical explosion. The shape of history and the nature of divinity itself, as one cynic recently observed, had come into human consciousness in the mind of Herr Doktor Professor Hegel. In truth, many of the techniques and disciplines of modern academic research were in the process of formation. In the study of the humanities a revolution was taking place. Western history was divided up into its modern components – Gothic, Renaissance, Baroque and all the rest. Definitions, connections and interconnections were sought for and established. The apparatus of modern academia was being invented and naturally those insights and methods had immediate impact upon the study of the Bible. Textural analysis was allied to studies of historical and cultural material. By the 1880s, perhaps the decade when this technique was at its height, Professor Julius Wellhausen had distinguished not two but four separate strands in the Book of Genesis and by analysis of their individual characters had attempted to set their authors in time and place. One strand might be said to mirror the attitude of a specific group inside biblical Israelite society, another to be particularly skilled at narrative or preoccupied with descriptions of ancient songs or religious ritual. As well as Astruc's two narratives — now called 'J' and 'E' (Jehovah and Elohim) — crowds of ghostly authors with names like 'The Priestly Narrator' and the 'Deutero-Isaiah' had now appeared. The New Testament was also subjected to similar analysis. Several independent texts were isolated inside the Four Gospels and each one was categorized in terms of its contemporary ethnic and religious attitudes. A very substantial industry of biblical scholarship had grown up. Some of the ghostly authors, for example, might be seen to reflect the myths and rituals of other ancient religions; the Four Gospels might be treated as narratives woven around a body of traditional church material made many centuries after Jesus' death. Speculations commonplace in other areas of ancient history entered into the studies of the learned and energetic German Bible scholars. There were entire millennia, whole civilizations, to be played with. The Bible became a stepping-stone into a wide academic arena.

Outside Germany many scholars and churchmen observed this new scholarship with interest and enthusiasm. But many others, Protestant and Roman Catholic alike, treated it with about the same enthusiasm with which the inquisition in Rome had regarded Galileo. An elderly Bishop of Ely, reflecting on the education of many clergymen of his generation, wished all the 'Jarmin Poison' to the bottom of the 'Jarmin Ocean'. Enthusiasm and fury over the new Bible discipline were immense and ran apace with the debate that surrounded the Bible and the natural sciences. Heroic debates were conducted with all the considerable skill, pomposity and innocence of the age. Many churchmen still asserted that the Bible was 'none other than the voice of Him that sitteth upon the throne' while others now doubted if the Bible alone could support the faith without the sanction and tradition of the church — just as the Council of Trent had asserted centuries before. Yet the British public was largely uninformed about the detail of the German scholarship. It was said that in the mid-nineteenth century only two people at Oxford could read the German language; that, at least, allowed some measure of insulation from the 'Jarmin Poison'. Then in 1881 a series of articles upon the Old Testament which dealt with Wellhausen's researches in some detail appeared in the ninth edition of the *Encyclopaedia Britannica*. The author, an eminent Scottish professor William Robertson Smith, was put on trial in Edinburgh for libel — in reality, of course, for heresy.

Smith made a distinguished defence. He maintained that the Bible was the word of God, but that the word was held inside a record made by many men over a considerable period of time, and that, as with all of man's enterprises, errors and imperfections were inevitable, and therefore careful analysis of the text was not only desirable but essential. Smith won his battle but lost the war when he was deprived of his university chair at Aberdeen. He spent the last years of his life as a fellow of Christ's College, Cambridge, where among other things he greatly influenced the young James Frazer, encouraging him to start the immense labours in comparative religion that led him to write *The Golden Bough*. Though Frazer, like the young woman reading Ovid on the lawn, saw many obvious parallels between myths and Bible stories, he wisely left such contentious comparisons to others.

By the turn of the nineteenth century, however, there were some practical objections to many of the more imaginative assertions of the schools of textural Bible scholarship. Discoveries of ancient manuscripts in excavations in Egypt, for example, had already put paid to the well-supported theories that the Gospels had been written as late as the third and fourth centuries: Gospel texts very much older than that were now being dug out of the ground (see page 184). And once textural analysis had been shown to have produced some distorted conclusions, the entire premise of the work based upon Astruc's observations was also brought into question by more conservative scholars. Indeed, a fundamental objection to this whole method of analysis is that to this day not one scrap of ancient text has ever been found to prove the existence of the theoretical strands of different texts so beloved of modern scholarship. However, the broad conclusion remained that there clearly were separate strands running through many of the Bible's books. But this method of biblical analysis which had become ever more subtle and intricate had also become somewhat sterile and its reasoning somewhat circular. Yet allied with the assault of Huxley and the evolutionists, the damage to traditional attitudes to the Bible had been immense. For the Bible was no longer regarded as the clear voice of God; now, to make matters worse, one of the very disciplines that had helped to do the damage itself seemed fallible. Public confusion was compounded.

One scholarly reaction to this impasse was for the next generation of scholars to concentrate upon different areas of analysis. One, for example, isolated the 'essential morality' of the Bible from the 'myths' – the unprovable historical assertions of the Bible's stories. In the process Jesus became a 'Christ Myth'. In their heyday, before the learned speculations of text criticism had prompted this drift into the rich pastures of theology, this grand debate about the Bible's text had, in the common eye, merely served to increase the growing confusion that was ever more surrounding the Bible. Many conservative clergymen considered that the scholars had tried to take the Bible away from ordinary people; 'have we to await a communication from Tubingen, or a telegram from Oxford, before we can read the Bible,' an irate evangelist asked rhetorically. From 1909 onwards a series of pamphlets by eminent evangelists entitled 'On Fundamentals' insisted upon a return to the basis of the Protestant faith – for doctrine derived solely from Holy Scripture. And this was the origin of the term 'fundamentalism'. Faith that had been held in innocence could now be held only in the knowledge that there were alternative explanations. That the Bible was the unadulterated word of God was now but one opinion among many. Now you could choose what you would believe: the Bible was turned inside-out.

But not all these nineteenth-century scientific observations upon the Bible were destructive of traditional belief. As the debates upon evolution and the Bible's authorship rumbled around Europe, archaeologists were beginning to dig up the remains of the real biblical world, the belongings and sometimes even the written memorials of the Bible's own people. New and often exotic life was breathed into the Bible's words; the ancient East was re-discovered. In the 1850s the celebrated Black Obelisk was brought from Nimrud to the British Museum (see Plate 11). With its lively relief of Jehu of Judah bowing down before an Assyrian king, it gave the West its first contemporary picture of a biblical character; the first glance, too, of how Israel had been viewed by her ancient neighbours. Evidence, too, was coming to light that corroborated the accuracy of much of the Bible's detail. In the last few years of the nineteenth century, for example, the explorations of Sir William Ramsey in Ottoman Turkey established that far from being a mere geographical fantasy as much of the German text analysis had suggested, the journeys of Paul as they are recorded in the Book of Acts, actually reflected the conditions in Asia Minor and Greece in the mid-first century, in the historical period of Paul's lifetime. The pretty maps of St Paul's voyages that illustrate so many older Bibles, with their spaghetti lines of blue, red and green, originally celebrated this splendid archaeological vindication of St Luke's Book of Acts.

Public awareness of the potential of the biblical history that was still buried in the Near East was greatly heightened in 1872 when a young deputy keeper at the British Museum, one George Smith, read an account to the Society of Biblical Archaeology of his translation of a cuneiform text from Nineveh. The text was nothing less than a hitherto-unknown Babylonian version of the story of the Flood and the Ark; Gladstone adjourned Parliament so that its members could hear Smith speak. That such stories could be found outside the pages of the Bible, in the ruins of the ancient East, was novel. Great popular interest was aroused and the *Daily Telegraph* awarded Smith £1000 to go to mighty Nineveh himself and search for further pieces of the same clay tablet, which had been sent in fragments to the British Museum some twenty years earlier. Optimistically, Smith undertook the unlikely expedition and to his 'great surprise and gratification' found the missing pieces during the first week of his excavation at the top of the dusty mound. At first glance this story of the Babylonian Flood seemed to support those scholars who had suggested that the Bible was partly a huge receptacle of ancient myths, and that the Christian faith required careful excavation to lift it from the pages of the Bible. But other discoveries had appeared to uphold the Bible accounts of ancient political history. Shortly before Smith's first lecture on the Flood, the French consul at Jerusalem published the text of a long inscription inscribed upon a big black stone, now called the Moabite Stone after the biblical kingdom of Moab. The inscription, which dated to about 845 BC, described a rebellion of the people of Moab against their Israelite overlord, King Omri (see page 98). It was a direct confirmation, indeed a much more complete account, of the events recorded in 2 Kings 3:4–5; and this was also the first specific mention of Israel to be found in a contemporary inscription. A few years later another stela, from Egyptian Thebes, again recorded the name of Israel (see page 72ff.) and this pushed back the written record of that small state to the first centuries of the second millennium, considered by many to be close to the historical date of the Exodus. At last the biblical kingdom of Israel was scientifically proved to have had existence.

Long before that, however, in the 1840s ancient Israel had found its cartographer – the American Baptist minister and Bible scholar Professor Edward Robinson of Connecticut. Robinson's austere Protestantism viewed most church traditions with disbelief, only scientific method was good enough for him. In a series of volumes Robinson laid out the geography of ancient Israel, Jerusalem to Jaffa, from Dan to Beersheba, on the soil of the Near East.

Robinson had seen that many of the Bible's place names still survived among the modern population of Palestine, often in the villagers' words that they habitually used in preference to the other names which had been imposed by the Romans and later rulers. This had been Robinson's key to ancient Israel; he had ridden the length and breadth of the land, studying its geology and geography, its rainfall, its winds and sandstorms. Robinson re-traced the biblical journeys; he walked over the ground where Samson had fought in the hills of the Wadi el Surar – the Bible's Vale of Sorek. He explored Bethlehem, called Beit Lahm; and Nazareth, Nasivah; he rowed around Galilee and the Dead Sea tracing the biblical journeys of Jesus. At the same time that academic arguments raged in Western universities about the possibility of Jericho's ancient walls having fallen in an earthquake, Robinson had first identified the ancient site in Palestine now celebrated as the oldest city in the world (see page 64ff.). 'The mounds above the fountain [a spring],' he wrote, 'are covered with substructures of unhewn stone ... Here then are traces of enough ancient foundations ... this is the site of ancient Jericho.' Excavations began there twenty years after Robinson's book had identified the site at Tell es-Sultan. It is true to say that most of the modern archaeological excavations in Israel are made at sites identified and described by this careful Baptist from Connecticut.

With all of this, the Bible's words seemed to be moving out of literary and sacred history back into the realities of the ancient world. Even in the 1880s when, baited by Huxley, Gladstone embarked upon a public debate about Jesus and the Gadarene Swine and the ethics of killing off other people's pigs, the arguments on both sides revolved around the social and religious differences between Hellenism and the ancient Jewish culture. But despite the rationalism of modern biblical archaeology, there are essential differences between these biblical researchers and other archaeologists working in the ancient East. For ancient Israel was never the centre of a civilization with an individual material culture. Its highly ephemeral remains would not have attracted the attention of scholars for one moment unless they were concerned to match their discoveries with the words of the Bible. So until quite recently when the study of ancient trading and migration patterns assumed increasing importance, archaeologists working in the Holy Land were primarily concerned in joining the Bible to scientific history. And it is certainly true that a broad picture of the ancient history of the region has now been painstakingly established. Ancient Israel is still unique, however, in that a large part of its history is still based upon a book – the Bible. And nowadays, as archaeological data becomes more and more refined, many of the concordances that had seemed to link Bible history and archaeology have been proved to be mistaken. That rush of grand discoveries in the nineteenth century has not continued, despite intensive excavations. Once again the ancient book seems to spin in a blur of confusion. And this, perhaps, is how it should be, for the profound relationship of history, faith and literature, the works of man's mind, are surely too complex for the disciplines of science to define.

Exodus II

Amid all the biblical confusions of the nineteenth century, one clear image of the Bible and its world has continued to this day; and this is the popular representation of the Bible in paintings and films. So strong is this singular vision of the Bible world that there are few who have completely escaped its thrall. And this vision also has its history, its creators and its reformers; and their story stretches from pre-Raphaelite London to twentieth-century Hollywood, where the word Exodus is as likely to refer to a Paul Newman film as to Moses' biblical adventure. And the Bible still has such prestige that even the most celebrated actors are happy to play harlots and spear-carriers in star-studded Bible epics.

The link between nineteenth-century painting and Hollywood's biblical movies is easily seen in the great set-pieces of directors like Cecil B. de Mille and is documented in detail in the huge art folios of reproductions brought from New York and Europe which were used by Hollywood's costume and set designers, and, until recently, were still to be found in the libraries of the great film studios. Hollywood found its images of the ancient East in the visions of the European artists and photographers who visited that region during the nineteenth century. The inadvertent inventors of this popular European vision, not only of a Technicolor Bible world but also of the 'East' itself, were a gallant band of French artists who had sailed to Egypt with Napoleon in the last years of the eighteenth century, a dramatic campaign of revolutionary tourism that also inspired a rash of pictures of this stirring eastern adventure. Napoleon himself saw the campaign in a suitably epic glow. 'Gentlemen, five thousand years of history look down upon you!' he had shouted to his soldiers before they virtually exterminated the Mamluk army at the Battle of the Pyramids. And other set pieces followed: 'The Battle of Bethlehem' and 'The Seige of Acre', all memorialized in the following years on vast canvases of smoky battles in desiccated palm-strewn landscapes drawn in the style of Claude, with the Mamluk cavalry falling before French sabres in the poses and compositions of

Poussin and David. For the 'East' in such pictures, the artists relied upon their memories, museums and the folios of Napoleon's artists and scientists, huge tomes laid out the land of Egypt with an engineer's precision and a touch of late rococo.

As a result of this first major contact, Napoleon's eastern playground was viewed by Europeans as a never-never land where the sun shone as golden as eighteenth-century varnish – later came Technicolor – and the deepest day-dreams could be bought and held. Many of the rules that governed and repressed so much of nineteenth-century Europe did not seem to exist in the Muslim East. Most nineteenth-century travellers saw only the things which seemed different from their own world. They did not notice the mass of constraint and custom that imposed upon the inhabitants of Cairo and Jerusa-lem in precisely the same way that similar restrictions governed the people of Kensington and Kansas. Here was a world, the West thought, where a pasha might have a thousand wives just like Solomon; yet when Gérard de Nerval inquired of one Cairene gentleman how he managed in the crush he was astonished to be met with an outburst: 'God alive! Is there a woman in the world, even an infidel, who would consent to share her husband's honourable couch with another? Is that how they have become in Europe?'

Opium and slaves, Damascus silks and dusky courtesans, damascened swords and public executions, djinns and demons, a visible excess of wealth and beggary, summoned up powerful dreams in the European middle class, and this all flowed into the popular imagery of the ancient East and the Bible's literary worlds. The dusty poverty of Arab villages and the exotic savagery of the cities had convinced most Westerners that this was a world which had never changed; they saw a sort of 'noble savage' of city life where the 'instincts of human nature' had ruled from the beginning of time. It was an instant ancient East and one that is still with us, though nineteenth-century Araby has long gone. So comforting a vision was this that, despite the dangers, the boredom and the dirt, the Middle East quickly became a tourist magnet. In the 1840s, at the same time that Robinson was leaving Connecticut for Palestine, Parisian artists like Émile Vernet were travelling in the Middle East – he took the first photographs on the continent of Africa in Alexandria in 1839 – and buying props for their Bible paintings, making beautiful pictures with vivid, cool south Mediterranean light and viewing the people as so many Abrahams and Sarahs. In Vernet's time, too, fine art also had to serve the needs met today by monthly magazines. Vernet's 'Judah and Tamar' (see Plate 35), painted for the Parisian salons, shows a Circassian slave from an Ottoman harem, one of Europe's most potent Eastern images, revealing a white thigh and a tip-tilted breast to a desert sheikh. Tamar is reminiscent of Ingres' beautiful portraits of French *bourgeois* wives; Judah's robe is painted with the craftsmanship and care that Ingres lavished upon the dresses of those fine ladies. The scene describes Genesis 38.

After her brief marriage to Er and Onan, the widowed Tamar, seen in the disguise of a temple prostitute, seduces her father-in-law Judah. In Vernet's painting, detail is enlivened by anthropology rather than archaeology; the seal that Judah gives his daughter-in-law is set into a modern ring, he holds a string of Ottoman beads, he carries a nomad's camel goad, wears an Algerian *abiya* and the leer of a Parisian banker visiting a *demi-mondaine*. Vernet's skilful mixture of accuracy and fantasy remains a staple ingredient of Bible epics to this day.

Vernet's pictorial daydream, 'When Judah saw her, he thought she was a prostitute although she had veiled her face. He turned to her where she sat by the roadside and said "Let me lie with you",' uses a Bible passage for an essay in sensuous textures. But artists such as the Pre-Raphaelite William Holman Hunt, as stern as Calvin, were also going to the Holy Land. Hunt saw immorality in the brown *sfumato* of high Victorianism, and the pure light of God in the sunlight of the Holy Land.

Holman Hunt's 'Scapegoat' was painted on a sunblasted shore by the side of the Dead Sea during his first season in the Middle East, in the winter of 1853–4. In many ways this goat is a suitable image of the Bible in the nineteenth century, after the debates of Huxley and the scissors of German scholarship have left it naked, its stories stuck, like this goat, halfway between reality and myth. Popular images of Jesus made him into a human being operating in a political environment; his miracles and Resurrection were re-interpreted in scientific or anthropological ways. And ancient ways of thought, even those of the Bible writers, were largely ignored. By the 1860s Cardinal Newman had already protested that the Bible stories were used only as a series of moral parables. Bible study consisted of extracting the kernel of Christian morality from the 'oriental fog' in which Jesus walked. Prophetically Hunt has painted a goat, slightly sanitized but genuinely zoological, standing in the syrupy water of the Dead Sea. Under Hunt's rational scrutiny, the animal is hardly drawn as the sacrificial scapegoat upon whose bony back the Jews of Jerusalem symbolically loaded the sins of the world, to be carried out of the gates of the Holy City. Hunt gives us a fantasy made with a sort of salesman's pseudo-accuracy; the form is simple, the colour super-real, the symbolism literal and literary.

Hunt went on to paint a life-long series of religious pictures based upon biblical themes that look, today, like episodes from Bible films; that antique Arab movie world where Jesus looks like Lawrence of Arabia, and the Jews and Romans are remarkably similar to the figures that Hunt and his contemporaries invented. In Hunt's Bible painting of 'The Finding of the Saviour in the Temple' (see Plate 36), little Jesus, a spoilt suburban child lost in the Orient, wears a Damascus silk confection, like the garment that Hunt habitually wore in his own studio, one of several hot-houses of orientalism in London's Kensington and Notting Hill. But in all this, it is well to remember what Hunt and his contemporaries were opposed to – the dark grandiloquence of baroque and post-baroque Roman Catholic church art, those vast celebrations of technical skill. And to discover something of that world, with the aid of the minutes of the Venetian inquisition we can eavesdrop upon the proceedings against Veronese, the great baroque master painter.

> '*In this supper [i.e. the Last Supper] which you have made for the Church of ss Giovanni e Paulo; what is the significance of the man whose nose is bleeding?*'
> 'I intended to represent a servant whose nose was bleeding because of some accident . . . They are placed here so that they might be of some service, because it seemed to be fitting, according to what I have been told, that the master of the house, who was great and rich, should have such servants . . .'
> '*And that man dressed as a buffoon, for what purpose did you paint him on that canvas?*'
> 'For ornament, as is customary.'
> '*Who are those people at the table of our Lord?*'
> 'The Twelve Apostles.'
> '*What is St Peter, the first one, doing?*'
> 'Carving the lamb in order to pass it to the other end of the table . . .'
> '*. . . tell us what the next one to him is doing?*'
> 'He has a toothpick and cleans his teeth.'
> '*Does it seem fitting at the Last Supper of the Lord to paint buffoons, drunkards, Germans, dwarfs and similar vulgarities?*'
> 'No, Milords . . .'

And so the inquisition continues its course until Veronese apologizes, saying that he had not intended to offend their lordships, and the lordships accept that the painting's name and not its figures should be changed or 'improved' as they term it. So the Last Supper became 'The Feast in the House of Levi' (see Plate 34). Yet Veronese had simply seen Jesus' life as an immediate and completely contemporary thing, co-existent with his own. So fervent was Veronese's vision of the Last Supper that he had brought a life so brisk to it as to offend the masters of good order! By Hunt's time, however, some three hundred years later, 'science' and the camera had begun their rule of 'visual objectivity'; and faith was now self-conscious, a thing hard won.

A literary expression of the new piety of the nineteenth century is *The Life of Jesus* by Ernest Renan, a French professor who mixed archaeology, Araby and faith every bit as prettily as Holman Hunt. His book is a sort of speculative biography of Jesus tricked out 'with all the latest scientific facts'. We are given a Jesus with the destiny of a nineteenth-century poet. Renan's description of the Infant Jesus resembles Holman Hunt's portrait in 'The Finding of the Saviour in the Temple'. 'His amiable character,' writes Renan, 'accompanied doubtless by one of those lovely faces which sometimes appear in the Jewish race, threw around him a fascination from which no one in the midst of those kindly and simple populations could escape.' The age of Hunt and Renan was also the age in which nationality and history were re-invented, an age of fake Druids, of medieval masonry in high street halls, of Parsifal and Good Queen Bess. Artists like Hunt and Vernet re-invented the Bible world. And the ancient Jewish race was also re-invented. All the fascination and fear once felt by the neighbours of the Jews in medieval Europe were dressed up in Middle Eastern gowns by Vernet and Hunt and their colleagues. The 'Wandering Jew', that thirteenth-century legend of a man condemned to live until the Second Coming because he had struck Christ on his way to Calvary, was revived in plays and novels. The notion of an unchanging race of Jews was born, and this, fifty years ago, greatly helped to bring modern Jewry almost to an end. Strong echoes of nineteenth-century costume painting were often seen in Nazi parades – this is not so much an indictment of honest painters like Vernet and Hunt but an indication of the power of the imagery that they created. They and their successors have worked in subtle ways. A great part of the twentieth-century's most powerful clichés of race and religion flourished and was sanctioned by this nineteeenth-century portrait of the Bible world.

A Book of Revelations

By the 1880s fast printing machinery and cheap paper were enabling Protestants to sell a complete bible, with all its million words, for a penny piece. And it was, by far, the West's favourite book. A revision of the King James' Bible published in 1885 sold a million copies on the first day; a Chicago newspaper gave the revised New Testament away printed in the form of a news-sheet. The Bible has been translated into over a thousand languages, printed in hundreds of millions of copies; its ancient images, its moralities, its rituals and its stories have been sent round the world. Oxford University Press, one of three English publishers entitled, by Tudor law, to produce and sell the Holy Scriptures, presently issues a seventy-page catalogue of different bibles; from yapp-bound miniatures in grey suede suitable for bridesmaids, to giant-sized lectern editions bound in morocco that weigh fifteen pounds and are printed in large type for church readings; the Bible is still the world's bestselling book.

The immediate effect of this explosion of Bibles was a proliferation of churches in the world of non-conformist Protestantism, many of them inspired directly by its written words: precisely that fragmentation of faith which the Council of Trent and the Inquisition, with their insistence upon the importance of traditional interpretations of the Bible, were so concerned to prevent. Nowadays biblical prose and imagery is widely used outside the church. It bolsters political rhetoric; it is re-interpreted in hundreds of diverse ways to back a plethora of crackpot theories – everything from notions of extra-terrestrial visitations to the profitable re-discovery of medieval myths that trace a dynasty of French kings back to Jesus Christ! Yet these usages have popular force, because they tag on to the familiar world of the Bible, of Adam and Eve and Moses, Isaiah and Jesus, the Promised Land, the Cross and the Apocalypse. Perhaps most Westerners believe that history has the shape given it by the Bible, from the Creation to the Last Judgment, from Genesis to Apocalypse: from ecologists planning their own Edens to those who make bombs that can destroy the world, everybody still wants Paradise.

Underneath the Technicolor images of the cinema, there is this deeper Bible memory in the West: vague images of Eden and the Apocalypse. Dying in the South of France in 1930, D.H. Lawrence wrote a meditation upon the Bible and its images, in the tradition of the medieval mystics, and in Provence he thought again of his childhood in a Nottinghamshire mining village.

> . . . what a strange book it was that had inspired the colliers on the black Tuesday nights in Pentecost or Beauvale Chapel to such a queer sense of special authority and of religious cheek. Strange marvellous black nights of the North Midlands, with the gaslight still hissing in the chapel, and the roaring of the strong-voiced colliers. Popular religion; a religion of self glorification and power, for ever! and of darkness . . . And the capital letters of the name: MYSTERY, BABYLON THE GREAT, THE MOTHER OF HARLOTS AND ABOMINATIONS OF THE EARTH thrill the old colliers today as they thrilled the Scotch Puritan peasants and the more ferocious of the early Christians . . .

Like Lawrence, his colliers had taken the Bible's images deep into their minds. If, above everything, language is the mark of man, the determining

factor that distinguishes him from other forms of life – the tool, too, by which the natural experiences that he shares with the beasts are modified into culture – then the Bible has supplied a vital part of the West's vocabulary. Lawrence's colliers responded immediately and instinctively to the ancient words emanating from the Middle East, precisely because they are part of a common culture handed down through the millennia. The blessings and faults of the Bible are still with us. Armageddon certainly is, with a new nuclear ring about it now. 'These spirits were devils with power to work miracles. They were sent out to muster all the kings of the world for the great day of battle of God the sovereign Lord . . . So they assembled the kings at the place called in Hebrew Armageddon. Then the seventh angel poured his bowl on the air; and out of the sanctuary came a loud voice from the throne, which said, "It is over!" And there followed flashes of lightning and peals of thunder, and a violent earthquake, like none before it in human history, so violent it was . . . the cities of the world fell in ruin'. (Revelation 16:14–19 NEB). And the kings of the earth shall witness this ending, the Book of Revelation tells us, at Armageddon/Har-Megiddo, that strange, soft hill sticking out of a low range which looks across the plain of Esdralon to Nazareth. Ancient Megiddo was once a prosperous fortified Canaanite city lying on the route from ancient Egypt up to Mesopotamia. And the kings of the world will all come here to fight at the end of time because, no doubt, they have fought there so many times before. Several Egyptian texts tell us of pharaohs fighting battles there in the fifteenth century BC. One of the Bible's most ancient texts, the Song of Deborah in the Book of Judges, celebrates an Israelite victory near Megiddo; Solomon re-fortified the town; King Josiah was killed in battle on the green plains below it. For St John, Megiddo and its plain was a suitable spot to end the Age of Kings. And St John's book is also the end of the Bible; a desolate vision built entirely from older biblical images, a sort of literary excavation to find, in the biblical words of the world's beginning, the story of its ending.

Just as each generation acquires its vocabulary from its parents' words so the Canaanites of Megiddo used yet more ancient stories about the gods to speculate upon the universe. Their view was of a cosmos that was made by the loves and hatreds of a single family of seven generations and this the Bible changed into the abstract universe of Jehovah made in seven days. And this has changed again into the universe of Copernicus and Galileo and so on, down until today. But still the Western design is tense with the conflicts of that most ancient family of gods. And the Bible, too, has provided the West with its active sense of historic destiny; provided in the struggle to attain it, that energy, that lack of satisfaction, which is a hallmark of our culture.

SELECT BIBLIOGRAPHY

There have probably been more books written on the Bible, and over a longer period of time, than on any other single subject. Even the recent literature still holds within it incredibly diverse attitudes and opinions, and not a little that is wrong or wildly out of date. This bibliography contains some basic reference books, both old and new, which can serve as a useful introduction to various aspects of the Bible and its history and which will also supply scholarly references to the literature of their own specialised areas. I have also included some of the works, often brief or obscure, whose information or ideas have directly influenced the story that I have told.

Akurgal, E. *Ancient Civilisations and Ruins of Turkey*. Istanbul, 1985

Albright, W.F. *The Archaeology of Palestine* (4th edn.). Harmondsworth, 1960

Amiran, R. *Ancient Pottery of the Holy Land*. Jerusalem, 1969

Annan, N. *Leslie Stephen: The Godless Victorian*. London (2nd edn.). 1984

Auden, W.H. *The English Auden: Poems, Essays and Dramatic Writings 1927–1939* London, 1977

St Augustine, *Confessions* (trans. R.S. Pine-Coffin). Harmondsworth, 1961

Avigad, N. *Discovering Jerusalem*. New York, 1980

Aviram, J. *et al.* (ed.). *Biblical Archaeology Today*. Jerusalem, 1985

Bagatti, B. *Un anello in Transgiordania*. Jerusalem, 1978

Barkay, G. *Ketef Hinnom: A Treasure facing Jerusalem*. Jerusalem, 1986

Barnett, R.D. *Ancient Ivories in the Middle East*. Qedem, 14. Jerusalem, 1982

Baur, J. 'Why the World was Created in 4004 BC. Archbishop Ussher and Biblical Chronology.' Bull. John Rylands Library 67. Manchester, 1983

Baynes, N.H. *Constantine the Great and the Christian Church* (2nd edn.). London, 1972

Bede. *A History of the English Church and People* (trans. L. Sherley-Price), Harmondsworth, 1968

Beeskow M. *et al. Martin Luther 1483 bis 1546 in der Staatlichen Lutherhalle*. Wittenberg, 1982

Beitak, M. *Tell el-Dab'a II*. Vienna, 1975

Bell, H.I. *Egypt from Alexander the Great to the Arab Conquest*. Oxford, 1948

Bianchi, U. (ed.). *Mysteria Mithrae*. Leiden, 1979

Biran, A. (ed.). *Temples and High Places in Biblical Times*. Jerusalem, 1981

Boethius. *The Consolation of Philosophy* (trans. V.E. Watts). Harmondsworth, 1969

Bovini, G. *Il Mausoleo di Teodorico*. Ravenna, 1977

Bowersock, G.W. *Julian the Apostate*. London, 1978

Breasted, J.H. *Ancient Records of Egypt*. Chicago, 1906–7

Brown, P. *Augustine of Hippo*, London, 1967; *The Making of Late Antiquity*, Cambridge, Mass, 1978; *The Cult of the Saints: Its Rise and Function in Latin Christianity*, Chicago, 1981; *Society and the Holy in Late Antiquity*, London, 1982

Bruce-Mitford, R.L.S. *The Art of the Codex Amiatinus*. Jarrow, 1967

Cambridge Ancient History (12 vols. and revisions). Cambridge, 1923–39 (rev. edns. 1970–)

Cambridge History of the Bible (3 vols). Cambridge 1963–70

Cambridge History of Judaism (vol. 1). Cambridge, 1984

Chadwick, H. *Early Christian Thought and the Classical Tradition*, Oxford, 1966; *The Early Church*. Harmondsworth, 1967

Chiera, E. *et al. Joint Expedition at Nuzi*. Harvard, 1927–39

Corbo, V. *The House of Saint Peter at Capharnaum*. Jerusalem, 1969; *Il Santo Sepolcro di Gerusalemme*, Jerusalem, 1981

Coüasnon, Ch. 'The Church of the Holy Sepulchre in Jerusalem'. Schweich Lectures 1972. London, 1972

Crossland, R.A. and A. Birchall (eds.). *Bronze Age Migrations in the Aegean*. New Jersey, 1974

Crowfoot, J.W. and G.M. Crowfoot. *Early Ivories from Sumaria*. London, 1938

Cruden, A. (ed. C.H. Irwin). *Complete Concordance to the Bible*. Cambridge, 1977

Dahmani, S. *Hippo Regius*. Algiers, 1973

Darlow, T.H. and H.F. Moule (rev. A.S. Herbert). *Historical Catalogue of Printed Editions of the English Bible*. London, 1968

Demus, O. *Byzantine Mosaic Decoration*. London, 1948

Dothan, T. *The Philistines and their Material Culture*. Jerusalem, 1982

Einhard and Notker the Stammerer (trans. L. Thorpe). Harmondsworth, 1969

Eissfeldt, O. *The Old Testament; An Introduction*. Oxford, 1965

Encyclopaedia Britannica (14th edn.). London, 1929

Encyclopaedia Judaica. Jerusalem, 1971–

Encyclopaedia of Religion and Ethics. London and Edinburgh, 1908–26

Encyclopedia of Archaeological Excavations in the Holy Land. Oxford, 1975–78

Eusebius *The History of the Church* (trans. G.A. Williamson). Harmondsworth 1963.

Finegan, J. *Encountering New Testament Manuscripts*. London, 1975

Focillon, H. *Art d'Occident, le moyen Age, roman et gothique*. Paris, 1938

Frankfurt, H. and H.A. Frankfurt *et al. Before Philosophy (The Intellectual Adventure of Ancient Man)*. Harmondsworth, 1949

Freedman, D.N. and D.F. Graf (eds.). *Palestine in Transition*. Sheffield, 1983

Freely, J. *Istanbul (Blue Guide)*. London, 1983

Frye, N. *The Great Code*. London, 1982

Garstang, J. and J.B.E. Garstang. *The Story of Jericho*. London, 1948

Gibbon, J. (ed. J.B. Bury) *The Decline and Fall of the Roman Empire*. London, 1896–1900

Golb, N. 'Who Hid the Dead Sea Scrolls?' Biblical Archaeologist 48. Philadelphia, 1985

Grabar, A. *Christian Iconography: A Study of its Origins*. London, 1969

Graves, R. *Greek Myths*. Harmondsworth, 1958

Graves, R. and R. Patai. *Hebrew Myths: The Book of Genesis*. New York, 1964

Grenfell, B.P., A.S. Hunt *et al. Fayûm Towns and their Papyri*. London, 1900

Gray, J. *The Legacy of Canaan*. Leiden, 1965

Halevi, B.A. *A Modern Guide to the Jewish Holy Places*. Jerusalem, 1982

Halsberge, G.H. *The Cult of Sol Invictus*. Leiden, 1972

Hastings, J. (ed.). *Dictionary of the Bible*. London and Edinburgh, 1898–1904

Heidel, A. *The Gilgamesh Epic and Old Testament Parallels*. Chicago, 1949

Hengel, M. *Judaism and Hellenism*, London, 1974; *Crucifixion*, Philadelphia, 1977; *Jews, Greeks and Barbarians*, London, 1980; *Between Jesus and Paul*, London, 1983

Herodotus. *The Histories* (trans. G. Rawlinson). London, 1858–60

Heyden, A.A.M. van der. *Atlas of the Classical World*. London, 1960

Hoade O.F.M.E. *Guide to the Holy Land*. Jerusalem, 1983

Holman Hunt, W. *Pre-Raphaelitism and the Pre-Raphaelite Brotherhood*. London, 1905

Holt, E.G. *A Documentary History of Art*. Princeton, 1958

SELECT BIBLIOGRAPHY

Huitzinger, J. *The Waning of the Middle Ages*. New York, 1949

Jacobson, T. *Treasures of Darkness*. Yale, 1976

James, M.R. *The Apocryphal New Testament*. Oxford, 1924

Jerome. *Select Letters* (trans. F.A. Wright). London and Yale, 1933

Jones, C. *et al.* (ed.). *The Study of Liturgy*. New York, 1978

Josephus. *The Complete Works* (trans. W. Whiston). Halifax, 1864

Jungman, J.A. *The Early Liturgy to the Time of Gregory the Great*. London, 1960

Justin, Martyr and Irenaeus. (trans. A. Cleveland Coxe) *The Ante-Nicene Fathers vol I*. Edinburgh, 1867

Juvenal. *Satires* (trans. J. Dryden). London, 1726

Kahle, P.E. 'The Cairo Genizeh'. Schweich Lectures 1941. (2nd edn.) London, 1960

Kelly, J.N.D. *Jerome, His Life, Writings, and Controversies*. London, 1975

Kenyon, F. *Our Bible and the Ancient Manuscripts* (5th edn.). London, 1958

Kenyon, K. *The Bible and Recent Archaeology*, London, 1978; *Archaeology in the Holy Land* (4th edn.), London, 1979

Kiblansky, R. *et al. Saturn and Melancholy*. London, 1964

Krautheimer, R. *Early Christian and Byzantine Architecture*. (3rd rev. edn.) London, 1981

Krautheimer, R. *et al. Corpus Basilicarum Christianum Romae*. Rome, 1962–

Lang, B. (ed.). *Anthropological Approaches to the Old Testament*. London, 1985

Lang, M. *Cure and Cult in Ancient Corinth*. Princeton, 1977

Lawrence, D.H. *Apocalypse*. London, 1931

Layard A.H. *Nineveh and its Remains* London, 1851

Leach, E. *Genesis as Myth and other Essays*. London, 1969

Leach, E. and D.A. Aycock. *Structuralist Interpretations of Biblical Myth*. Cambridge, 1983

Loewe, M. and C. Blacker (eds.). *Divination and Oracles*. London, 1981

Loud G. *The Megiddo Ivories* Chicago 1939

Lyon, H.R. and J. Percival. *The Reign of Charlemagne*. London, 1975

Maas, J. *Holman Hunt and the Light of the World*. London, 1984

Mâle, E. *Art religieux du XII siècle en France* (5th edn.). Paris, 1947

Marasovic, T. *Diocletian's Palace*. Belgrade, 1982

Marrou, H. *St Augustine*. London, 1957

Marx, K. and F. Engels. *The German Ideology*. Moscow, 1964

Meeks, W.A. and R.L. Wilkinson. *Jews and Christians in Antioch*. Missola, Montana, 1978

Meer, F. van der and C. Mohrmann. *Atlas of the Early Christian World*. London, 1959

Mendenhall, G.E. 'The Hebrew Conquest of Palestine'. Biblical Archaeologist 25. Philadelphia, 1962

Michael Psellus. *Chronographia*. (trans. E.R.A. Sewter) Harmondsworth, 1966

Milne, H.J.M. and T.C. Skeat. *The Codex Sinaiticus and the Codex Alexandrinus*, London, 1951; *Scribes and Correctors of the Codex Sinaiticus*, London, 1951

Murphy-O'Connor, J. *The Holy Land: An Archeological Guide from Earliest Times to 1700*. Oxford, 1980

Murray, G. *The Rise of the Greek Epic*. Oxford, 1907

Newman, S. *A Concordance to the Holy Scriptures*. (1672) repr. London, 1889

Nietzsche, F. *The AntiChrist*. (trans. R.J. Hollingdale) Harmondsworth, 1968

Nordenfalk, C. *Die Spätantiken Kanontafeln*. Gothenburg 1938

O'Neill, T. *The Irish Hand*. Portlaoise, 1984

l'Orange, H.P. *Art Forms and Civic Life in the Late Roman Empire*. Princeton, 1965

The Oriental Institute Epigraphic Survey. *Medinet Habu* (vols. i-viii), Chicago, 1930–69; *The Bubastite Portal*, Chicago, 1954

Otto, R. *The Idea of the Holy*. Oxford, 1923

Oxford Classical Dictionary (2nd edn.). Oxford, 1970

Oxford Dictionary of the Christian Church. Oxford, 1974

Paine, Tom. *The Age of Reason (1794–5)*. London, 1938

Panovsky, E. *Gothic Architecture and Scholasticism*. New York, 1951

Pauly-Wissowa, *Realencyclopadie der klassischen Altertumswissenschaft*. Stuttgart, 1893–1981

Petrarch. *Selections from the Canzoniere and other Works* (trans. M. Musa). Oxford, 1985

Petrie, W.M.F. *Tell el-Hesi*, London, 1881; *Seventy Years in Archaeology*, London, 1933

Pfeiffer, R. *History of Classical Scholarship from 1300 to 1850*. Oxford, 1976

Pollard, A.W. *The Holy Bible: An exact reprint of the Authorised Version 1611*. Oxford, 1911

Porter, R. and R. Moss (rev. J. Málek). *Topographical Bibliography of Ancient Egypt*. Oxford, 1927

Possidius. *Life of St Augustine* (trans. M.M. Muller). Washington, 1952

Pritchard, J.B. (ed.). *Ancient Near Eastern Texts relating to the Old Testament* (3rd edn.). Princeton, 1969

Proceedings of the Cracow Conference 1984. Vatican City, 1985

Renan, E. *Life of Jesus*. London, 1864

Roberts, C.H. *An unpublished fragment of the Fourth Gospel*. Manchester, 1935

Robinson, E. *Biblical Researches in Palestine*. London, 1841

Robinson, H.W. *The Bible in its Ancient and English Versions*. London, 1954

Robinson, J. (ed.). *The Nag Hammadi Library in English*. Leiden, 1977

Roud, R. (ed.). *Cinema. A Critical Dictionary*. London, 1980

Rudolf, K. *Gnosis*. Edinburgh, 1983

Runciman, S. *The Fall of Constantinople, 1453*. Cambridge, 1985

Rupp, E.G. and B. Drewery. *Martin Luther*. London, 1970

Ste Croix, G.E.M. de. *The Class Struggle in the Ancient World*. London, 1981

Sandars, N.K. (trans.). *Epic of Gilgamesh*. Harmondsworth, 1964

Sanders, E.P. *Paul, the Law, and the Jewish People*, London, 1983; *Jesus and Judaism*, London, 1985

Santillana, G. de. *The Crime of Galileo*. London, 1958

Sayce, A.H. *Reminiscences*. London, 1923

Schaeffer, F.C.A. *et al. Mission de Ras Shamra* (vols. 1–18). Paris, 1929–78

Schürer, E. *A History of the Jewish People in the Age of Jesus* (new rev. edn.) M. Black *et al.* Edinburgh, 1973–85

Segal, J.B. 'The Sabian Mysteries' in *Vanished Civilisations*, London, 1963; *Edessa 'The Blessed City'*, Oxford, 1970

Shiloh, Y. *Excavations at the City of David* (vol. 1). Qedem 19, Jerusalem 1984

Simpson, von O. *The Gothic Cathedral*, Princeton, 1962

Smith, G.A. *Historical Geography of the Holy Land* (25th edn.). London, 1931

Smith, M. *Palestinian Parties and Politics that shaped the Old Testament*, Columbia, 1971; *The Secret Gospel*, New York, 1973; 'The Difference between Israelite Culture and other Major Cultures of the Ancient Near East', Journ. N. East Soc. Columbia U. Columbia 1974; *Jesus the Magician*, London, 1978

Stager, L.E. 'Merenptah, Israel and the Sea Peoples'. Archaeological, Historical and Geographical Studies. Chicago, 1984

Stanley, A.P. *Sinai and Palestine*, London, 1856; *Lectures on the History of the Eastern Church*, London, 1861; *Sermons in the East*, London, 1863; *Christian Institutions*, London, 1881

Stevenson, J. (ed.) *A new Eusebius*, London, 1960; (ed.) *Creeds, Councils, and Controversies*, London, 1966

Stronach, D. *Pasargadae*. Oxford, 1978

Tanner, J.R. (ed.). *Tudor Constitutional Documents*. Cambridge, 1922

Theophilus. *On Divers Arts* (trans. J.G. Hawthorne and C.S. Smith). Chicago, 1903

Thomas, D.W. (ed.) *Archaeology and Old Testament Study*, London, 1967; (ed.) *Documents from Old Testament Times*, London and Edinburgh, 1958

Tischendorf, C. *Codex Sinaiticus*. (8th edn.) London, 1934

Tolnay, C. de. *The art and thought of Michelangelo*. New York, 1964

Vaux, R. de. *Ancient Israel* (2nd edn.), London, 1965; *Archaeology and the Dead Sea Scrolls*, Schweich Lectures 1959, London, 1972

Vallée, G. *A Study in Anti-Gnostic Polemics*. Waterloo, Ontario, 1981

Vatican Observatory Publications. *Galileo and the Council of Trent*. Vatican City, 1983

Vermes, G. *The Dead Sea Scrolls: Qumran in Perspective*, (2nd edn.) London, 1982; *Jesus the Jew*, London, 1983; *Jesus and the World of Judaism*, London, 1983; (ed. and trans.), *Dead Sea Scrolls*, Harmondsworth, 1968

Vitruvius. *The Ten Books on Architecture* (trans. M.H. Morgan). Harvard, 1914

Ward-Perkins, J.B. *Roman Imperial Architecture*. Harmondsworth, 1981

Webb J.F. (trans.) *The Age of Bede*. Harmondsworth, 1983

Weitzmann, K. *Late Antique and Early Christian Book Illumination*. London, 1977

Wilkinson, J. *Jerusalem Pilgrims*, Warminster, 1977; *Jerusalem as Jesus knew it*, London, 1978; (ed. and trans.) *Egeria's Travels to the Holy Land*, Warminster, 1981

Winter, P. *On the Trial of Jesus*. Berlin, 1961

Woolley, L. *Ur of the Chaldees*, London, 1929; *Alalakh*, London, 1955

Yadin, Y. *The Art of Warfare in Biblical Lands*, London, 1963; (ed.) *Jerusalem Revealed*, Jereusalem, 1975

Yurko, F. 'Merenptah's Palestinian Campaign'. Journal for the Study of Egyptian Antiquities, 8. Chicago, 1978

ACKNOWLEDGMENTS

Testament has been some nine years in the making. For a long time it was a Promised Land of a book; without the enthusiasm of my publisher Michael O'Mara, it would never have made it out of the desert. Above all, though, Elizabeth Romer, my wife, gave me the help and encouragement to bring *Testament* to its completion, just as she has done for all my work over the past twenty years.

I have had valuable and highly enjoyable conversations about the broader issues of Bible scholarship with Professors Peter Ackroyd, Henry Chadwick and Hans Goedicke, and I am especially grateful for their advice – even if I have not always followed it! Information about specific aspects of Bible history was also given to me by a great number of patient people, including: Amabile Audin, Dr Gabriel Barkay, Father Leonard Boyle O.P., Dr Said Dahmani, Dr Patricia Donlon, Dr Jozef Dorner, Rabbi Hugo Gryn, Alan F. Jesson, Bishop Guregh Kapikian, Akim Krekeler, Dr Michael Dayagi Mendels, Wajeeh Nuseiba, Dr Peter Parr, the Reverend John Sutton – to all of them, too, I am grateful.

The enthusiasm and friendly conversation of almost everyone who worked upon the 'Testament' television films was also especially valuable to me. Mischa Scorer, the series producer, enabled me to meet and talk with many of the people listed above; he also allowed me the facilities to travel to some of the places in the book which I had never visited before and for that I am especially indebted.

I should also like to thank Fiona Holman and Michael Foss who worked hard and long with a difficult manuscript.

I would like to thank the following for allowing me to quote passages:

Page 105 – 'September 1, 1939' by W.H. Auden. Reprinted by permission of Curtis Brown Ltd. from *The English Auden: Poems, Essays and Dramatic Writings 1927–1939*, London, 1977
Page 348 – from D.H. Lawrence *Apocalypse*. Reprinted by permission of Laurence Pollinger Ltd. and the Estate of Mrs Frieda Lawrence Ravagli.

Further acknowledgments

Page 37 – T. Jacobson *Treasures of Darkness*, Yale, 1976
Pages 99 and 102 – J.B. Pritchard (ed.) *Ancient Near Eastern Texts relating to the Old Testament* (3rd edn.), Princeton, 1969
Page 146 – G. Vermes (ed. and trans.) *Dead Sea Scrolls*, Harmondsworth, 1968
Page 225–6 – Eusebius *The History of the Church* (trans. G.A. Williamson) Harmondsworth, 1965

ACKNOWLEDGMENTS

Pages 237–43 – Jerome *Select Letters* (trans. F.A. Wright) London and Yale, 1933

Page 249 – Boethius, *The Consolation of Philosophy* (trans. V.E. Watts) Harmondsworth, 1969

Pages 251–52 – Bede *The Age of Bede*, Harmondsworth, 1983

Page 270 – H.R. Lyon and J. Percival *The Reign of Charlemagne* London, 1975

Page 272 – T. O'Neill *The Irish Hand*, Portlaoise, 1984

Page 292 – Petrarch *Selections from the Canzoniere and other Works* (trans. M. Musa), Oxford, 1985

Pages 298 and 311 – E.G. Rupp and B. Drewery *Martin Luther*, London, 1970

THE FILMING OF 'TESTAMENT'

Writing, like reading, is a solitary activity and the job of taking this silent world and projecting it onto a screen can be an unusually trying experience for an author. I am very grateful, therefore, that my friends and colleagues in the television industry made the transformation of 'Testament' such a delight. No one who has not seen this extraordinary twentieth-century cottage industry at work can appreciate the skill and expertise invested in a television series like 'Testament'. All through 1987 various film units re-travelled the routes of the Bible's ancient journeys, right through the Middle East and Europe. They were some of the most exciting filming trips I have ever made. No less enjoyable was the experience of working in the cutting rooms where this dazzling and daunting mass of film – over a thousand sound slates alone – was cut together into seven elegant programmes.

The two directors, especially, are responsible for the way that the films finally appear. Mischa Scorer of Antelope Films was also the series producer. He backed 'Testament' from our first discussions about the project in Tuscany in 1985, and even supplied the series title after our first choice was preempted by a radio programme! Ron Johnson, 'Testament's other director, came to the series at an awkward moment – it is only a slight exaggeration to say that we first met at Heathrow as we left on a filming trip to the Middle East: the 'Testament' films owe a great deal to his tact and style. But everybody in the list below has also made their own contribution.

Commissioning Editors, Channel Four
John Ranelagh and Robert Towler

Series Advisors
The Reverend Professor Peter Ackroyd and the
Reverend Professor Henry Chadwick

The Producer and Director of Films 1, 4, 5, 7
Mischa Scorer

The Director of Films 2, 3, 6
Ron Johnson

Cameramen
Barry Ackroyd, Mike Fox, Michael Miles, Graham Smith and Paul Sommers

THE FILMING OF 'TESTAMENT'

Camera Assistants
Mike Ely, Hugh Hood, Andy Horner, Tom Paterson, Robin Probyn and
Rob Southam

Sound Recordists
Fraser Barber, Michael Lax, Tony Meering and David Welch

Electricians
Gerard Birmingham, Jason Hunt, Jim McBride and Gary Willis

Editor-in-Chief
Charles Ware

Film Editors
Oliver Huddleston and Sheryl Sandler

Assistant Editors
Lisa Blundell, Annie Brown, Fred Hart, John Mackessy and
Monika Morawietz

Dubbing Mixer
Richard King

Production
Dee Edwards, June Ellwood, Diane Goldman, Yvonne Jones, Susan Kane,
Emma Laybourne and Melanie May

Location Fixers
Sevim Berker, Selim Abu Said, Diane Saccilotto and Elia Sides

I should also like to thank the many museum curators and archaeological site
staff in Europe and the Middle East who were so helpful and friendly during
the long hours of filming.

INDEX OF BIBLE
REFERENCES

GENERAL INDEX

GENERAL INDEX

ILLUSTRATION ACKNOWLEDGMENTS

All line drawings are by Elizabeth Romer unless listed in the credits below.

By permission of the Birmingham Museum and Art Gallery: between pp. 328 and 329 centre.
By permission of the British Library, London: opposite p. 265 (British Library, Cotton Ms. Nero D. IV, folio 26v.)
Reproduced by courtesy of the Trustees of the British Museum: opposite p. 89 below right
The Chester Beatty Library, Dublin: between pp. 184 and 185
Mary Evans Picture Library, London: pp. 20, 32, 34, 39, 45, 54, 62, 71, 106, 110, 129, 136, 181, 209, 223, 290, 301, 303, 306, 311, 315, 318, 325, 328, 336, 341, 347, 349
The Israel Museum, Jerusalem: opposite p. 89 below left
Kobal Collection, London: between pp. 328 and 329 right
Missione Archeologica Italiana in Siria. Università degli Studi di Roma 'La Sapienza'. Courtesy: Professor Paolo Matthiae: between pp. 40 and 41
John Romer: opposite p. 40, opposite p. 88, between pp. 88 and 89 above and below left, between pp. 88 and 89 above and below right, opposite p. 89 above, opposite p. 136, opposite p. 137, opposite p. 184, opposite p. 185, opposite p. 216, between pp. 216 and 217 above and below left, between pp. 216 and 217 below right, opposite p. 217, opposite p. 248, opposite p. 249
John Ross: opposite p. 41
SCALA, Florence: between pp. 216 and 217 above right, between pp. 248 and 249 above and below left, between pp. 248 and 249 above and below right, between pp. 264 and 265 left, opposite p. 328, opposite p. 329
Stifts-Bibliothek, St Gallen, Switzerland: between pp. 264 and 265 right
Copyright John C. Trever 1970, Claremont, California: between pp. 136 and 137
University Library of Uppsala, Sweden: opposite p. 264
Reproduced by permission of the Trustees of the Wallace Collection, London: between pp. 328 and 329 left